Critical Essays on
CHARLES W. CHESNUTT

CRITICAL ESSAYS
ON
AMERICAN LITERATURE

James Nagel, General Editor
University of Georgia, Athens

Critical Essays on
CHARLES W. CHESNUTT

edited by

JOSEPH R. MCELRATH JR.

G. K. Hall & Co.
New York

G. K. Hall & Co.
1633 Broadway
New York, NY 10019

Library of Congress Cataloging-in-Publication Data

Critical essays on Charles W. Chesnutt / edited by Joseph R. McElrath, Jr.
    p. cm. — (Critical essays on American literature)
  Includes bibliographical references and index.
  ISBN 0–7838–0055–X (alk. paper)
  1. Chesnutt, Charles Waddell, 1858–1932—Criticism and interpretation. 2. Afro-Americans in literature. I. McElrath, Joseph R. II. Series.
  PS1292.C6Z684   1999
  813'.4—dc21   99-34852
                                       CIP

10 9 8 7 6 5 4 3 2

To my son
Christopher M. McElrath

Contents

◆

General Editor's Note

◆

This series seeks to anthologize the most important criticism on a wide variety of topics and writers in American literature. Our readers will find in various volumes not only a generous selection of reprinted articles and reviews but original essays, bibliographies, manuscript selections, and other materials brought to public attention for the first time. This volume, *Critical Essays on Charles W. Chesnutt,* is the most comprehensive gathering of essays ever published on one of the most important African American writers of the period of American realism. It contains both a sizable gathering of early reviews and a broad selection of more modern scholarship. Among the authors of reprinted articles and reviews are Sterling Brown, Albert Bushnell Hart, William H. Ferris, SallyAnn H. Ferguson, William Gleason, and Lorne Fienberg. In addition to a substantial introduction by Joseph R. McElrath Jr., there are also three original essays commissioned specifically for publication in this volume, new studies by Charles L. Crow on the gothic in Chesnutt's fiction, Gary Scharnhorst on the neglected novel *The Colonel's Dream,* and Charles Duncan on the theme of the family in *The Wife of His Youth.* We are confident that this book will make a permanent and significant contribution to the study of American literature.

JAMES NAGEL
University of Georgia

Publisher's Note

◆

Producing a volume that contains both newly commissioned and reprinted material presents the publisher with the challenge of balancing the desire to achieve stylistic consistency with the need to preserve the integrity of works first published elsewhere. In the Critical Essays series, essays commissioned especially for a particular volume are edited to be consistent with G. K. Hall's house style; reprinted essays appear in the style in which they were first published, with only typographical errors corrected. Consequently, shifts in style from one essay to another are the result of our efforts to be faithful to each text as it was originally published.

Introduction

◆

JOSEPH R. McELRATH JR.

When Charles W. Chesnutt died at the age of 74 in 1932, more than a quarter century had passed since the publication of *The Colonel's Dream* (1905). During the years following the appearance of this third novel and the last of the six books published during his lifetime, it was patently and painfully clear that he had failed in the quest to which he had given himself in 1880. The dream of becoming a popular author—a gentleman who would make his living by the labor of words—he fervidly articulated in his journal that year. For more than two decades, he persevered in the faith that someday he would rise to the station of a Thackeray or Dickens. Moreover, this earnest Victorian wanted more than fame and fortune. He planned to accomplish a high and holy purpose with his writings, the exaltation of the racial group he hoped to represent brilliantly before a national readership that had too low an estimate of the African American's capabilities. He would follow in the footsteps of Christian social-reform novelists Harriet Beecher Stowe, George Washington Cable, and Albion W. Tourgée. Or more precisely, Chesnutt trusted that he could take up where they left off, passionately calling for justice and compassion in a new way. The world would know through him that African Americans no longer needed to rely on sympathetic whites but could as artfully plead their own case for full civil rights and the recognition of their kinship as brothers and sisters created in God's image.

1

In one sense, he did know success. In periodicals such as *Atlantic Monthly,* and then in his books, he showed the white readership of his time just how sophisticated a prose fiction writer and commentator on "the Negro Problem" he was, and by 1905, he did indeed succeed both Cable and Tourgée as the principal literary scourge of white racists. But Chesnutt never produced a best-seller, and neither his standing nor his earnings as an author approached those of Thackeray or Dickens. His crusade against Jim Crow fared poorly; worse, a quite different white-supremacist literary campaign conducted in the early 1900s instead resulted in huge royalties for novelist Thomas Dixon Jr. and in the reinforcement of white readers' attitudes of the kind Chesnutt had dedicated himself to mollifying. Further, Chesnutt's trial of literary work as a vocation proved by 1902 to be an especially costly one in two more personal respects.

Born to free African Americans in Ohio in 1858, Chesnutt demonstrated early in his life that he was precocious: in Cleveland, and then after his family moved to Fayetteville, North Carolina, following the Civil War, he enjoyed public education, and it was clear that he was a prodigy. Not only was he intellectually gifted, but as is manifest in the journal he kept from 1874 to 1882, his was a driven, achievement-oriented personality. He knew that knowledge is power, and by the turn of the century, his ego had long since become used to the gratifications attending success in many quarters where the fruits of rigorous self-cultivation were appreciated. As principal of the Normal Colored School in Fayetteville, North Carolina, he had become one of the preeminent black educators in the South when in his early twenties. Moving back to Cleveland in 1883, he employed his self-taught skills as a stenographer to initiate a more profitable career, beginning his own stenography practice near the downtown courthouses after he had read law under the direction of the retired judge for whom he worked in the offices of the Nickel Plate Railroad. In 1887 he scored highest among those with whom he sat for the Ohio Bar examination. Chesnutt did little by half measures, and by 1890 this workaholic's stenography business was flourishing. In October 1899, he was a distinguished member of Cleveland's black bourgeoisie and had even accumulated capital sufficient for him to retire from business at 41 years of age, so that he could devote all of his time to literary production. His first book had been published in March, and two others were scheduled to appear before the end of the year. He was not used to failure and certainly had no reason then to think that, in a few years, he would be disappointed so profoundly.

The second toll exacted by his discovery that he could not turn a literary avocation into a paying profession was not psychological but financial: from late 1899 through 1901, he used his savings to subsidize his literary activity with the expectation that within a short while, there would be a handsome return on his investment. How could it be otherwise? Publishers such as George H. Mifflin, editors such as Walter Hines Page, literary essayists such as William Dean Howells, and numerous reviewers encouraged Chesnutt to do that for which he was uniquely qualified: to develop the experience of the African American as a subject matter and to provide the perspective on it that white authors could not.[1] His books were widely reviewed, and even reviewers whose negative criticisms seemed to be motivated by their hostility to blacks, and particularly to an African American author from the North who found so much to criticize in the white southerner, gave him reason for confidence in himself as a writer with a reform purpose. Raising their hackles was interpretable as a measure of his success as a social critic working in the medium of prose fiction. Moreover, attention of any kind was attention, and that spelled visibility before book buyers. But the sales figures for his books were, to say the least, modest.

What neither Chesnutt nor his publishers and editors gauged correctly was just how weak the market demand for such fare would prove. Chesnutt's scrapbooks, in which he pasted articles about himself and the reviews and notices of his periodical publications and books, survive at the Fisk University Library, and they make it clear that he was far from overlooked by the press in the way that other African American authors of the time were. Those others published outside the mainstream book-publishing industry and enjoyed little visibility. From 1899 to 1901, on the other hand, Chesnutt was an author in the stable of one of the most prestigious American publishers, Houghton, Mifflin and Company, and he wrote as well for two other firms with high profiles: Small, Maynard and Company in 1899 and Doubleday, Page and Company in 1905. The publications of all three companies were regularly noted in the review columns of newspapers and magazines across the country. And so: with so much going for him; why did Chesnutt fail as a commercially viable author? Two theories suggest themselves for consideration.

First, although liberal-minded editors and publishers were personally interested in advancing the African American cause, it is difficult not to infer that most book buyers of the day were simply indifferent to stories about the plight of blacks or the point of view that Chesnutt, as an "insider," could provide. Very likely, the majority had had their fill of the subject matter he treated, since "the Negro Problem" had been focused on in nineteenth-century public discourse to such an extent that by the late 1890s it had become a tiresome topic. Indeed, impatience with the ever present "Negro Problem," which seemed never to advance toward a solution—despite measurable progress made by blacks on their own, the benefactions of white humanitarians, and the strong inducements to quiescence that were disfranchisement and lynching—may instead account for the success of the novels of Thomas Dixon Jr. He and his publisher, Doubleday, Page and Company, had no trouble finding readers interested in his depictions of the "White Problem" of dealing with blacks in the South. "How long, O Lord?" was the passionate query of those who sought to end slavery; in the post-Reconstruction period, it took on a different meaning, reflecting by 1900 the state of mind of whites

fatigued from repeatedly hearing pleas for sympathy for freedmen, their children, and grandchildren. Chesnutt believed that he was sounding a new note,
but it apparently fell on ears that could not, or would not, distinguish it from
the din generated by a half century's discussion of a problematic minority.

An alternative explanation that comes to mind is that negative reviews
turned away large numbers of short story and novel readers, but analysis of
the items pasted in Chesnutt's scrapbooks does not support such a hypothesis. Almost all of these clippings have been aptly summarized by Curtis W.
Ellison and E. W. Metcalf Jr. in *Charles W. Chesnutt: A Reference Guide,*[2] and as
will be seen in their annotations of early writings about Chesnutt, one cannot
conclude that his books were panned by the majority of reviewers, though
many of them offered little more than brief notices. Indeed, the pieces
reprinted in the "Reviews" section in this volume should be viewed as representative in only one sense. They do not reflect, quantitatively, actual ratios
between positive, negative, and neutral (or blandly descriptive) reviews and
notices. Rather, those selected for inclusion in this volume were chosen for the
sake of illustrating the variety of evaluations and the extremes that framed
typical reviewer discourse. Book buyers were not, generally speaking,
deflected from purchasing Chesnutt's works by the arbiters of taste who
wrote for periodicals. In fact, the majority of reviews of all his books were
inarguably positive.

The Conjure Woman (1899), it now appears, stood the best chance for
celebrity. This first collection of short stories is dominantly comical in tone;
its serious reflections on the predicament in which both ante- and postbellum
blacks found themselves are designed to elicit sympathy in a gentle manner
and become neither aggressively didactic nor bitter in tone. The hostility to
southern whites that became increasingly strident in Chesnutt's subsequent
volumes of fiction is not perceptible in his first.[3] Why it did not succeed as a
popular book whereas the roughly similar Uncle Remus tales made Joel
Chandler Harris a celebrity in the early 1880s may very well have had much
to do with Chesnutt's extensive use of southern rural dialect. By 1899 this
signature characteristic of the "local color" fiction vogue of the 1880s and
early 1890s was trying the patience of both readers and reviewers. But the
various reasons for the volume's lackluster performance in the marketplace
must remain matters for speculation, debate, and regret.

Whatever the exact causes, neither of Chesnutt's two 1899 collections of
short stories—*The Conjure Woman* and *The Wife of His Youth and Other Stories of
the Color Line*—was more profitable than his first novel, *The House behind the
Cedars* (1900); and over the years, that novel generated royalties almost as
meager as those for the brief biographical volume *Frederick Douglass* (1899).
The Marrow of Tradition (1901) was the make-or-break effort. Houghton, Mifflin had high expectations and invested heavily in advertisements for this
novel; Chesnutt was sure that it would be recognized as the modern equivalent of the antebellum best-seller *Uncle Tom's Cabin*. Both author and pub-

lisher were again disappointed, and when Chesnutt later approached Houghton, Mifflin with an early manuscript version of *The Colonel's Dream,* the firm's patience proved exhausted. By early 1902, it was clear that Chesnutt would have to return to stenography to make his living. With two daughters who had recently attended Smith College, a son who would graduate in 1905 from a no less expensive school, Harvard, and a wife who, like her husband, was long used to upper-middle-class amenities, he could not afford to continue his indulgence in the lifestyle of a man of letters. His last published novel, *The Colonel's Dream,* was written in hours stolen from business and conventional recreations. He would write other novels that never found a publisher during his life. By 1906, though, the eclipse of Chesnutt, a once-promising literary figure, had begun.

He now, of course, enjoys a much higher status than he did from 1899 to 1905. Neither *The Colonel's Dream* nor *Frederick Douglass* is available in paperback, but the two other novels and the pair of short story collections are. As significant are the recent appearances of *Collected Stories of Charles W. Chesnutt* (1992), *The Journals of Charles W. Chesnutt* (1993), *"To Be an Author": Letters of Charles W. Chesnutt, 1889–1905* (1997), *Charles W. Chesnutt; Essays and Speeches* (1999), and a novel that remained unpublished until 1997, *Mandy Oxendine.*[4] Given such obvious signs of burgeoning interest in Chesnutt's life and writing, what was unthinkable just a few decades ago—that virtually everything he wrote will eventually see print—is rapidly being realized. Although he is not yet widely viewed as a "major American literary figure" or even a "major African American author," he does loom large within the context of "minor figures"—at least the equal of Stowe and dwarfing Paul Laurence Dunbar, Bret Harte, the majority of the "Fireside Poets," and two of his late-nineteenth-century role models, Cable and Tourgée.

This change of fortune might have occurred much earlier had a powerful advocate refocused the nation's attention on one of the pioneers of the African American literary tradition and brought into high relief the tremendous achievement that was Chesnutt's when he, along with Paul Laurence Dunbar, effected integration of the de facto segregated American publishing industry. The long-term support of William Dean Howells, who lived until 1920, might have made a crucial difference. In 1900 and 1901, Howells used his considerable power as a giant in the literary world to boost Chesnutt, but that source of support was withdrawn when in late 1901 Chesnutt's assault on white racism in North Carolina, *The Marrow of Tradition,* alienated Howells.[5]

Through 1928 no champion commensurate with Howells appeared on the scene. That year, though, Chesnutt had cause to hope for at least a revival of the reputation he had enjoyed circa 1900: he was awarded the NAACP's Spingarn Medal, and Houghton, Mifflin reprinted *The Conjure Woman* for the first time in many years. But neither a black figure of high stature such as W. E. B. Du Bois nor a prominent white literary critic or historian seized the opportunity. An Edmund Wilson or a Granville Hicks might have turned the tide well before the 1960s. What was needed was a full-scale analysis of Chesnutt's place in history of the kind that Eric J. Sundquist offered in 1993 in *To Wake the Nations: Race in the Making of American Literature.*[6] But that was quite impossible. Although the Harlem Renaissance writers were receiving attention, race-based analyses of American literary history of the kind now being written were not then fashionable among liberal thinkers. Further, the study of the African American literary tradition per se was not a part of the liberal studies curriculum of the vast majority of American colleges and universities. A sociocultural upheaval and radical reorientation across humanities and social sciences schools in centers of higher learning would be required before Chesnutt received his due. Not only the popular media but university presses would have to reprioritize their concerns. Scholarly journals—save those at midcentury such as *Phylon* and the *CLA Journal,* which were already dedicated to the "black" subjects largely neglected by others—would have to refocus before Chesnutt and other early black litterateurs could be repositioned *within* the cultural mainstream.

This is not to say that Chesnutt was receiving no attention, but it was not until the late 1960s that he emerged from obscurity as the effects of the civil rights movement were being registered in the academy and, most important, in the textbooks from which college and university students derived their definition of significant American literature. An important step toward this end was taken in 1963 when *Black Voices,* edited by Abraham Chapman and including Chesnutt's 1904 short story "Baxter's Procrustes," was published in hardcover.[7] Dramatically more important was the next: this collection was made available in 1968 as a paperback and soon became ubiquitous on campuses across the country. Yet more influential was the 1968 reprinting of *The Wife of His Youth* by the University of Michigan Press, followed by its publication of *The Conjure Woman* and *The Marrow of Tradition* in 1969. In the same year, Arno Press also reprinted *Marrow,* Gregg Press brought *The Colonel's Dream* back into print, and Collier Books issued its paperback of *The House behind the Cedars.* Even Chesnutt's least noteworthy book, *Frederick Douglass,* was made available by Johnson Reprint in 1970. Ten years earlier, none could be purchased, except from dealers in rare books and from used book stores. The revival of his reputation that Chesnutt hoped to see in the late 1920s was at last occurring as courses in black American literature began to proliferate on American campuses and the academic publishers responded to that development.

That 1969 was the pivotal year will also be seen in another way. Chesnutt's art was then taken beyond the category of African American literature into the canon of American literature because of the inclusion of the satirical short story "A Matter of Principle" in an anthology for which there was a mass readership.[8] Used as a textbook for standard American literature survey courses conducted nationwide, the two-volume *American Literature: Tradition and Innovation* would introduce Chesnutt to thousands of readers each year.

Almost as important as this valorization of the author was the choice by editors Harrison T. Meserole, Walter Sutton, and Brom Weber of a story that
gave many students their first glimpse into the African American middle class
and an introduction to Chesnutt as a refreshingly candid author who pre-
dictably criticized white racism but expanded his critique to expose as well
the bigotry suffered by dark-skinned African-Americans *within* the black
community. Made available in a three-volume format as well in the same
year, and as four volumes in 1974, this anthology's various arrangements in
different chronological units ensured textbook adoptions by professors teaching both historical surveys and more specialized American literature courses
with narrower time frames. Competing anthologies published by other firms
followed suit; for example, the revised and expanded four-volume *American
Literature Survey* of 1975, edited by Milton R. Stern and Seymour L. Gross,
added the comical trickster tale "The Passing of Grandison" to its collection
of classic American literature.[9] Chesnutt thus became a standard fixture in
textbooks of the kind, and interest appears to have since waxed to fascination.
In 1990 *The Heath Anthology of American Literature* presented no fewer than
three short stories, and in 1998, the fifth edition of *The Norton Anthology of
American Literature* increased its representation from one to two.[10]

What may today prove surprising when students and younger scholars
turn to the "Essays and Articles" section of this volume is the brevity, tone,
and sometimes peculiar focus of the early-twentieth-century commentaries
on this now canonical author. What will not be apparent is the paucity of
articles and parts of books from which choices of representative reactions to
Chesnutt were possible; during the years in which Chesnutt was at his nadir,
the pickings prove extraordinarily limited. Perhaps dismaying, rather than
surprising, though, are the selections with which "Essays and Articles"
begins. By 1905, ethnologists and post-Darwinian theorists on race were
focusing on Chesnutt primarily for the purpose of gleaning the significance of
his racial makeup rather than measuring the quality of his thought and art.
They were interested in his heredity because the achievements that distinguished him from the mass of blacks lent support to the popular theory that
the "pure negro," as Albert Bushnell Hart termed the type in 1905, is
innately inferior in intellectual and other capabilities not only to whites but to
mulattoes such as Chesnutt. That is, Chesnutt—like Booker T. Washington
and W. E. B. Du Bois—is cited as an exception to the rule for African Americans because he is of "mixed" racial ancestry and, due to a beneficial infusion
of "white blood," does not truly reflect the limitations of monoracial individuals with African antecedents. What is most telling of Chesnutt's reputation is
that at this point, his name is known by Hart, Alfred Holt Stone, Ray Stannard Baker, and, presumably, their readers; but these commentators do not
appear at all cognizant of the substance of Chesnutt's writings.[11]

What one also finds published in these early years are the initial, brief his-
toriographic descriptions of Chesnutt's career and terse evaluations of his

major works—that is, sketches designed for a readership as unfamiliar with those writings as Hart, Stone, and Baker seem to have been. Benjamin Griffith Brawley's section on Chesnutt in the 1910 *Negro in Literature and Art* is not the earliest piece of this sort; while Chesnutt was still actively pursuing a literary career, articles focusing on him as the pioneer figure he was in the African American literary tradition abounded in periodicals. Brawley's encomium stands, however, as the first piece of its kind included in a book devoted to black artists. What is noteworthy, then, vis-à-vis Chesnutt's low visibility through and immediately beyond the time of his death in 1932 is the implication of Sterling Brown's section on him in *The Negro in American Fiction*.[12] As in Brawley's 1910 portrait, so in Brown's of 1937: little progress appears to have been made with regard to being able to assume the existence of a measurable readership of Chesnutt's works. One will note in the 1910 through 1930s sections of *Charles W. Chesnutt: A Reference Guide* that such is the commonplace situation in most books and articles describing black artists. Chesnutt is a figure treated passim—referred to briefly when the occasion warrants it—as illustrative of general points being made about the earlier phases of the African American literary tradition. As will be seen in "Essays and Articles," even black authors such as William H. Ferris and William Stanley Braithwaite, who had high opinions of Chesnutt, were parsimonious when focusing on him: Ferris does rank Chesnutt a "genius" in 1913; Braithwaite observes in 1924 that since 1904 the only "fiction by the Race of any importance" is a pair of novels, *The Colonel's Dream* and Du Bois's *The Quest of the Silver Fleece*.[13] But neither commentator can now be viewed as a contributor to a revival of interest in, and respect for, Chesnutt's achievement.

It is in this temporal and attitudinal context that one may again pose the question of why W. E. B. Du Bois, like Ferris and Braithwaite, did not do more. When the Spingarn Medal was given to Chesnutt in 1928, Du Bois asserted in *The Crisis* that the medal "has seldom, if ever, been more fittingly awarded," but afterward he did not make clear why he thought so. Before that, in 1924, he had lauded Chesnutt in *The Gift of Black Folk* as a "recognized novelist" who "gained his way unaided and by sheer merit"; two sentences, however, did not bespeak much enthusiasm. Twenty-one years earlier, in an article published in *Booklovers Magazine,* Du Bois seems to reveal what the long-term problem was: his dislike of, or minimal respect for, Chesnutt. Du Bois *had* to identify him as one of three black artists who had risen to "places of recognized importance." But Du Bois did so in a backhanded manner. True, he praised Chesnutt's most popular short story, first published in 1898 in the *Atlantic Monthly,* "The Wife of His Youth." Yet Du Bois's phrasing in 1903, less than two years after the appearance of *Marrow* and two years before *The Colonel's Dream* was published, suggested that Chesnutt was already a literary figure of the distant past: "Chesnutt wrote powerfully, but with great reserve and suggestiveness, touching a new realm in the borderland between the races and making the world listen with one short story."

Further, Du Bois's tone is at least mildly acerbic when he condescendingly relates that Chesnutt faces a "peculiar temptation" that Du Bois implies he himself did not. Aware from their correspondence that the disappointing sales of *Marrow* had driven Chesnutt back into his much more lucrative steno-graphic work, Du Bois was not at all sympathetic but chided him for being interested in "money making," asking the readership of *Booklovers Magazine*—subtitled *Advance Guard of the Race*—the loaded question: "Why leave some thousands of dollars a year for scribbling about black folk?" The obvious answer, that Chesnutt had abandoned his role, or duty, as one of the "advance guard of the race" for the sake of looking out for number one, was a severe indictment.[14]

It was instead the white John Chamberlain who, in 1930, provided the historical perspective on Chesnutt that his fellow black writer and competitor for primacy in belles lettres, Du Bois, would not. No, Chamberlain did not devote his article to Chesnutt. But "The Negro as Writer," published in a monthly with a much larger readership than that of *Booklovers,* began by giv-ing Chesnutt top billing: "Negro fiction in America properly commences with Charles Waddell Chesnutt. . . ."[15] Chamberlain admits the problems one might have with the by-then archaic style of Chesnutt's works, and he laments the "queer twists" occasionally rendering his plots unbelievable. These are not insuperable obstacles to admiration, though, when one consid-ers what lies behind them—the integrity of an artist who refused to veil the truth concerning life in his time: "Chesnutt blinks nothing." The award of the Spingarn Medal to Chesnutt two years earlier perhaps drew Chamberlain's attention; certainly the 1928 reprinting of the long out-of-print *Conjure Woman,* which he mentions, did so. But another development, in 1926, also seems to be related to Chamberlain's essay: the publication of Carl Van Vechten's *Nigger Heaven,* a novel set in Harlem in which the reader more than once encounters praise for Chesnutt, a writer who did not "blink." Therein a character who is an aspiring author, Byron Kasson, is Van Vechten's means of euphorically rating Chesnutt's achievement in a way that no one had since Howells in 1900. Byron, we are told,

> lifted *The Wife of His Youth* . . . and opened the pages for the hundredth time. How much he admired the cool deliberation of its style, the sense of form, but more than all the civilized mind of this man who had surveyed the problems of his race from an Olympian height and had turned them into living and artistic drama. Nothing seemed to have escaped his attention, from the lowly life of the worker on the Southern plantation to the snobbery of the near whites in the North.[16]

Reading this now, one would think that Chesnutt was a household name in literate America.

Surveying the history of commentary on Chesnutt in a 1968 issue of *American Literary Realism,* Dean H. Keller made it pathetically clear that such was still not the case in either American homes or the academy.[17] He observed that it was not until the 1930s that "serious criticism of a scholarly nature began to develop," first citing John Chamberlain's essay "The Negro as Writer" and then referring to two similarly focused studies of African American writers published in 1931 and 1939, Vernon Loggins's *The Negro Author* and J. Saunders Redding's *To Make a Poet Black*.[18] Neither of these books analyzes Chesnutt in a sustained way, but Loggins, while judging the novels inferior in aesthetic qualities, echoes Van Vechten and Chamberlain: the strength of Chesnutt's writings is to be seen in how the author, from a black point of view, provides insightful "social studies." Redding similarly views Chesnutt as the best black prose fiction writer before the 1920s and celebrates his ability in four of his fictional books to produce serious art unmarred by the propagandistic impulse that unfortunately dominated in and ruined *Marrow*. The last important advance of the 1930s that Keller identifies is Benjamin G. Brawley's *The Negro Genius* of 1937, but he perhaps overvalues it as the "most exhaustive analysis . . . up to this time" because he does not seem aware that Brawley had been reworking his 1910 *Negro in Literature and Art* through several editions and drew heavily on the Chesnutt section for his latest incarnation of essentially the same expression of appreciation.[19]

Turning to the 1940s and 1950s, Keller notes that Chesnutt was at last being acknowledged in standard biographical and historical reference works. James D. Hart selected Chesnutt in 1941 for inclusion in the *Oxford Companion to American Literature;* in the next year, Chesnutt appeared in Stanley J. Kunitz and Howard Haycraft's *Twentieth-Century Authors*. In 1948 he was given official sanction as an American author of note as he was inducted by Robert E. Spiller et al. into the *Literary History of the United States* (remaining therein in the revised edition of 1953, as noted by Keller). The forties and fifties saw more protracted treatments of Chesnutt than these, though. As the title chosen by Hugh M. Gloster indicates, Chesnutt's necessary presence in the history of American letters was simply taken for granted in *Negro Voices in American Fiction* in 1948; thus his five fictional books mandated description as exposés of social injustices originating in racist attitudes. (Gloster's contribution, however, was originally made several years earlier, since he here recycles the contents of the plot summary–heavy article "Charles W. Chesnutt: Pioneer in the Fiction of Negro Life," published in 1941.)[20] Then, in 1952, the first book devoted to her father was made available by Helen Chesnutt, *Charles Waddell Chesnutt: Pioneer of the Color Line*.[21] Particularly valuable because of its quotation of letters that no longer appear to exist and personal impressions that complement biographical fact made available by no one else, this biography stimulated new interest and served as the foundation upon which were based the initial book-length scholarly studies of Chesnutt published in the 1970s and 1980s. Indeed, the 1952 portrait is still a potential force for good in that it remains a source of biographical data not yet fully processed.

The curtain would not rise until the end of the next decade, but the stage was being set, and an important new development was finally occurring. Interpreters at last began to act as though writing about Chesnutt did not mandate a reintroduction of the man and the provision of yet another series of plot summaries. In 1945 Penelope Bullock anticipated this development. This risk taker was the exception to the rule in that she felt free in "The Mulatto in American Fiction" both to refer to Chesnutt as though he were a known quantity and to hazard the incomprehension of her readers by proceeding directly to commentary on the meaning and historical significance of *The House behind the Cedars,* without a plot summary. The next major advance in this direction, in 1953, will be seen in Russell Ames's testy but telling "Social Realism in Charles W. Chesnutt."[22] Inspired to right a wrong after reading Helen Chesnutt's detailed description of her father's achievements and the obstacles he faced as a reformist author, Ames chides the white intellectual establishment for virtually ignoring "the first distinguished American Negro writer" and for its "general neglect" of the African American literary tradition he represents. In this relatively brief essay-review, Ames exalts Chesnutt in another and equally important way, in this instance taking issue with both black and white literary critics whose modernist values precluded appreciation of the (by 1953) out-of-fashion period art produced by Chesnutt. That is, Ames appropriately associates this protest writer with the premodernism, social-realism literary tradition of the Progressive Era, lamenting the present-day dearth of morality-driven exposés for which the school had become famous and then notorious. Viewing modernist Faulkner as a "decadent" novelist whose ascendancy measures the decay of American writing since social realism came into disrepute, Ames ranks Chesnutt as the more significant author because his portrayal of life is less "garbled" linguistically and "far more inclusive, truthful, complex, interesting, and artistic."

In 1958 Robert A. Bone articulated the point of view that Ames had challenged. Bone could not echo such a high estimate of Chesnutt's abilities in *The Negro Novel in America.* He did observe that Chesnutt's short stories "raised the standards of Negro fiction to a new and higher plane" (and in 1975 he would, in *Down Home,* go farther by celebrating the *Conjure Woman* tales as the work of "a literary artist of the first rank").[23] But in 1958, when Bone turned to the novels, he described Chesnutt as an "overt propagandist, to the detriment of his art"—raising thus a question that Ames had already addressed but one that would not be answered emphatically in Chesnutt's favor until well over a decade later when being a "propagandist" for an oppressed minority would elicit praise rather than disapproval. Ames appears prescient in that, five years earlier, he not only treated Bone's objection but expressed a positive point of view on black "propagandist" art that is now current. Ames offers three telling observations on the bias in the 1950s against "purpose" literature. First, he notes with regret that authors such as Chesnutt are viewed negatively when they picture outrages suffered by blacks and allegedly lose all objectivity as they wax didactic in the face of constant affronts. For Ames, Chesnutt's reaction to the insufferable consequences of racism is instead admirable. Second, Ames detects a double standard: pro–African American art that is propagandistic is dubbed lamentably inartistic, yet white art that is anti-Semitic (Eliot's and Pound's poetry), pro–Ku Klux Klan *(Birth of a Nation),* or moralistic in the Victorian manner (he cites a British film adaptation of *David Copperfield)* somehow meets the criterion of objectivity held up by critics. Third, it is to some degree understandable that whites should not discern either the inflammatory causes of black protest or the appropriateness in prose fiction of overtly advocating remedies for persistent social problems. But exasperatingly, even fellow African Americans such as Alain Locke lament the "didactic emphasis" and "propagandistic motives" of pre-1920s black authors who did not write in the more objective manner of Richard Wright. In short, Ames sees nothing wrong, or inartistic, in Chesnutt's describing graphically the consequences of racism, commenting in a passionately humane way on the immorality of discrimination, and suggesting ethically sound solutions for the problems he has identified.

Ames, in consequence, is not only a touchstone in the history of progressive Chesnutt scholarship. He was a harbinger of change in critical values with regard to the once-assumed high merits of authorial objectivity and self-restraint in the face of social conditions that cry out for enlightened and compassionate responses. What modernist authors and practitioners of the New Criticism treasured but Ames did not—a post-Victorian narrative method that precludes moralistic intrusions by the author—has appealed less and less to subsequent generations interested in having access to the personal perspective of the spokesperson for a victimized minority group. Now available in the scholarly literature on Chesnutt is a large body of writing, the authors of which are not at all repulsed by Chesnutt's vital presence in his novels as both amazed narrator and outraged commentator. Rather, one finds that from the 1970s on, the vast majority shares Chesnutt's perspective and appreciates his reactions to the events and attitudes he pictures.

Other commentaries on Chesnutt published through the mid-1960s did not take one to the heart of the matter in so radical a fashion as Ames's essay-review did. But one very positive development should be noted: Chesnutt's versatility as an author was discovered by scholars with folk culture interests. Robert A. Smith, Donald M. Winkelman, and Sylvia Lyons Render enhanced Chesnutt's image by explaining how keen a student of southern folkways he was.[24] On the other hand, when his "southernness" was explored by Julian D. Mason Jr. in the *Mississippi Quarterly,* what was revealed in 1967 was just how much remained to be learned about Chesnutt's personality. Mason, that is, proposed the now impossible-to-countenance notion that the Ohioan who had once lived in North Carolina should be welcomed home and viewed henceforth as a southern author.[25] This has since become unthinkable in light of the published and unpublished correspondence and nonfiction prose revealing the deep-seated enmity toward the South of this man who was a Midwesterner by birth, choice, and temperament.

By 1962, the process of recovering primary data sources requisite for sound scholarship was initiated by Sylvia Lyons Render. She was the first to follow in Helen Chesnutt's footsteps, using the substantial collection of personal papers that Chesnutt bequeathed his daughter. Render's 1962 doctoral dissertation, "Eagle with Clipped Wings: Form and Feeling in the Fiction of Charles Waddell Chesnutt," is an interpretive study of his writings fully contextualized within a large body of unpublished papers made available by his daughter. Render's research would yield a biographical and critical study in the Twayne United States Authors series in 1980, and before that, in 1974, an edition of short stories not previously collected in book form, *The Short Fiction of Charles W. Chesnutt*.[26]

The early to mid-1960s, that is, were a prelude to the major events of 1968 to 1969—the reappearance of Chesnutt's major, long out-of-print fictional works and the first inclusion of one of his short stories in a successfully mass-marketed textbook. And those developments led, with little lag time, to the outpouring of interpretive articles and increase of attention given to Chesnutt in scholarly books that began in the 1970s. Spurring productivity was the signal given in 1971, when the imprimatur for the study of Chesnutt was conferred by the publication of Richard E. Baldwin's "The Art of *The Conjure Woman*" in *American Literature*.[27] *American Literature*, then the premier journal in the field of American literature, was a considerably more traditional and, politically, a radically more conservative quarterly publication than its modern namesake. One wrote on the lives and works of classic American authors—Irving, Melville, James, Norris, Hemingway, and so on—for *American Literature*, and admission to such august company for a heretofore marginal author signaled with finality that the occulting of Chesnutt had ceased. The tone of this article's first sentence provides an apt measure of the new status afforded Chesnutt: "In *The Conjure Woman* Charles Chesnutt analyzes with balance and subtlety the paradoxes and tensions of American racial life." In the following year, it was made doubly clear that things had changed: as distinguished a journal with a wider scope, *American Scholar*, devoted a "Reappraisals" section in its winter 1972–1973 issue to Chesnutt. Hiram Haydn, Walter Teller, and John Wideman paid tribute to, in Haydn's words, "an author who is only now being rediscovered," and Wideman echoed Richard E. Baldwin's characterization of *The Conjure Woman* when concluding his close reading of *The Marrow of Tradition*. Wideman did not embrace Bone's thesis concerning the debilitating propagandist dimensions of Chesnutt's novels but described *Marrow* as "subtle, complex and suggestive far beyond the [undiscerning] treatment traditionally accorded it."[28]

Almost 20 years after the biography by Helen Chesnutt appeared, that volume devoted to Chesnutt was finally joined by another, the first interpretive monograph. One of four works of the kind published by 1980, J. Noel

Heermance's *Charles W. Chesnutt: America's First Great Black Novelist*[29] is a bio-critical study taking the reader beyond the more detailed but wholly uncritical portrait of the ever congenial Victorian "papa" penned by his daughter. For example, Heermance's book focuses on the essential loneliness of, initially, a southern small-town intellectual who saw himself as standing apart from both the black and the white communities and, later, the self-contained individual Chesnutt remained throughout the rest of his life. But as the book's title blatantly indicates, the analysis of the writings within the context of Chesnutt's sociohistorical situation serves a purpose similar to Helen's and that of the other three authors of monographs who followed: champions were arising to compensate enthusiastically for decades-long neglect of their hero. And thus the equally hyperbolic title of the next book to appear: *An American Crusade: The Life of Charles Waddell Chesnutt* by Frances Richardson Keller.[30] Despite its spotty treatment of the life, occasional misdatings of events, and adulatory tone, this work complemented Heermance's portrayal by providing scholars with much previously unavailable data culled from the collections of Chesnutt papers at the Fisk University Library and the Western Reserve Historical Society Library. Moreover, Keller conducted interviews with contemporaries who knew Chesnutt and shared impressions of his personality quite different from daughter Helen's; and although Keller's inexperience as a literary critic is glaringly apparent, her research dealing with North Carolina census records resulted in an extraordinary contribution to our understanding of the autobiographical background to extramarital white male–black female relationships depicted in both *The House behind the Cedars* and *The Marrow of Tradition*.

A more sophisticated literary critic who made available in 1980 still more new biographical detail was Sylvia Lyons Render. Her *Charles W. Chesnutt* was limited in its scope by the standard format of the Twayne United States Authors series of bio-critical volumes, which are designed to provide introductions to literary figures rather than in-depth analyses suited for specialists. Yet it is one of the heftier Twayne volumes, for Render tested the limits of the series format by packing the book with close interpretations of the themes, characterizations, settings, and prose style of the fictional writings—giving particular attention to how Chesnutt imaged African Americans and used those characterizations in his campaign to modify the attitudes of his race-prejudiced readers. Keller's *American Crusade* had been the first book to make good use of the still largely overlooked nonfiction writings; Render's included illuminating references to many more, successfully employing them to clarify the points of view and argumentative intentions of Chesnutt in his novels and short stories.

Although Render's *Chesnutt* stands as the most comprehensive biographical and critical introduction to Chesnutt and his works, 1980 saw as well the publication of an exceptionally thorough volume that marked an end to the need for additional introductions of the kind produced by Render. William L. Andrews's densely detailed account, *The Literary Career of Charles W. Chesnutt,* is monumental not only as a testimony to the worth of Chesnutt but because of its breadth and depth as a study of how he conducted himself as an artful, reform-minded author. It closely examines the history of the avocation that, for a short while, became a career, providing apt interpretations of Chesnutt's intentions in critical readings of the literary works and related texts, as well as historically accurate analyses of Chesnutt's situation as a black author dealing with publishers, editors, and readers on the other side of the color line. Achieved on all counts are the goals Andrews enumerated in his preface:

> The book is intended to provide a unified, systematic, and thoroughgoing exam-
> ination and evaluation of the literary corpus of the first important Afro-American
> writer of fiction. The book is also designed to trace and assess Chesnutt's role in
> the evolution of late nineteenth- and early twentieth-century ethnic, regional,
> and social-problem literature in the United States. Within this historical context,
> Chesnutt is viewed as a major innovator in the Afro-American fiction tradition, a
> participant in the deromanticizing and socially analytic trend in post–Civil War
> southern literature, and a singular voice among other realists who treated the
> color line in American life.[31]

Achieved also by this discursive chronicle of the remarkable rise and unfortunate fall of Chesnutt as a litterateur and social critic is the realization of Russell Ames's 1953 call for a suitable approach to understanding and appreciating the predicament in which a black literary aspirant such as Chesnutt found himself and how, despite his failure as a professional author, he fashioned works in ways appropriate for an African American citizen sensitive to the injustices perpetrated against the minority of which he was a member. Although a full-scale scholarly biography meeting modern expectations remains to be written, Andrews's study approaches being one, and outside of the biography that will someday be written, no one need attempt another such description of Chesnutt's career.

With book-length works focusing on Chesnutt's life, career, and canon available by 1980, Ernestine Williams Pickens recognized that it was time for the production of more specialized monographs, and she acted accordingly. *Charles W. Chesnutt and the Progressive Movement*[32] situates her subject in the context of Progressive Era values and concerns, illustrating how Chesnutt reflected them in two of his novels, *Marrow* and *The Colonel's Dream.* Explained in detail in 1994 was how a black author fully expressed the Progressive sensibility traditionally associated with morally strenuous, civic-minded members of the white middle class—reminding them that they really ought to live up to the values they profess. An even more dramatic indication that a new phase of Chesnutt scholarship has been initiated is seen in Charles Duncan's recently published *The Absent Man: The Narrative Craft of Charles W. Chesnutt.*[33] That so specialized a monograph by a narratologist has appeared means that champions should no longer apply for employment; the need for them is no more.

What is most telling in Duncan's 1999 study is what it does not labor to explain because of what its author takes for granted as obvious to his readership. Much has been rendered lucid by critical analyses of Chesnutt's works, thanks to previous critics and especially those who have over the past quarter century duplicated one another's findings in their rush not to be left out of the late-twentieth-century discovery and reappraisal of the man and his canon. For example, the major, closely related points made by Chesnutt again and again in his short stories, novels, essays, and speeches are now easily summarized: all Americans should be viewed as participating in the same humanity that whites blithely assume is theirs but deny even to blacks whose personal qualities and attainments clearly bespeak equality with, and in some cases superiority to, the majority of whites; further, as U.S. citizens entitled to the civil rights specified in the Fourteenth and Fifteenth Amendments, African Americans should be neither disfranchised nor subjected to indignities by either Jim Crow laws or local customs; yet further, they should enjoy public education and equal economic opportunity; and last, the unregenerate South is tied to traditions antithetical to both humaneness and true civilization, to the degree that nothing short of federal intervention in its affairs can offer the hope of it someday joining the march of progress. The scholarship, that is, has advanced to the stage at which gross explanations are not needed, and Duncan's fine discriminations with regard to *how* Chesnutt's themes were articulated have become appropriate, even when the works examined are distinctly minor ones.

Clarification of Chesnutt's narrative techniques does not, however, promise an unqualified reaffirmation of Ames's 1953 conclusion regarding the premodernist clarity of the Chesnutt canon. Although Ames was correct in one respect, that Chesnutt is conventionally lucid when compared with modernist prose stylists describable as obscurantists, the close readings given his writings since the late 1960s have disclosed a radically more complex thinker, artist, and person than Ames perceived; and although there is consensus regarding what the major themes of the canon are, much has been and is likely to remain debatable because of intellectually engaging ambivalences and ambiguities encountered in Chesnutt's texts. That is, thematic implications not immediately apparent on first readings ineluctably surface, and one begins to suspect the presence of "mixed messages." In 1972, when David D. Britt analyzed John, the white narrator of *The Conjure Woman,* Britt celebrated what he saw as the previously unnoted sophistication of that volume's ostensibly simple stories: "The stories have . . . 'goophered' [their modern] readers in that more is going on in them than the critics have yet described."[34] Since then, critics have viewed the entire Chesnutt canon as similarly complex not only in terms of the artistry displayed but in regard to how it is symptomatic of the complicated and perhaps conflicted personality of its creator.

When attention is given to how Chesnutt addresses his dominantly white readership throughout his canon, one notes that he modulates his voice in sometimes puzzling ways, to the extent that it becomes appropriate to think of a Janus-like—even hydra-headed—Chesnutt, not as narrator but as narrators. For example, in the 1889 *Independent* essay "What Is a White Man?" and a short story originally published in the same periodical in the same year, "The Sheriff's Children," his tone is that of mordant invective directed at southern whites. In 1899, however, the persona projected was contradicted when "The Sheriff's Children" was included in *The Wife of His Youth* along with a radically different tale in which a decidedly jolly Chesnutt pictured a ne'er-do-well African American in the manner preferred by white supremacists. "Uncle Wellington's Wives" offers a comical portrait of a feckless hero worthy of the hand of Thomas Dixon Jr. or Thomas Nelson Page. Therein Chesnutt seems to be vying for honors with Booker T. Washington as a spinner of "coon stories" that will ingratiate him with whites. That he was deliberately doing so seems undeniably apparent, but on the other hand, Britt's point concerning the deceptive simplicity of Chesnutt's art comes to mind as one finds that critics have interpreted "Uncle Wellington's Wives" and Chesnutt's intentions in exactly opposite terms. For example, in 1994 Myles Raymond Hurd did not focus on the now shudder-inducing stereotyping of "Uncle" Wellington. The short story he read does not feature a clownish lout. Rather, it instead sympathetically portrays its African American hero, and Hurd divined as well an insightful and sensitive fictional commentary on the problems attending interracial marriages and the migration of southern blacks to the North.[35] That is, different "voices" are heard by different critics *within* one story as well as in discrete works. Indeed, two such clashing, seemingly irreconcilable "voices" may be heard even within the title of a short story in the case of "A Victim of Heredity, or Why the Darkey Loves Chicken." James R. Giles may at one time have been, as Britt puts it, "goophered" by Chesnutt, but by 1972 his readings of the too complex *Conjure Woman* led him to conclude that the key to understanding the contrary authorial intentions at work was simply to recognize and accept the paradox embodied in the collection. Giles proclaimed it a "schizophrenic book" intended to generate sympathy for the African American as, at the same time, it entertained by reproducing imagery and characterizations bringing to mind the most regrettable stereotypes current among white racists in 1899.[36]

In *The House behind the Cedars* one encounters a related interpretive challenge. The fair-skinned mulatto heroine is a victim of racism, and Chesnutt makes a pathetic appeal for recognition of the humanity she shares with whites; yet it may be perceived as ironic—and perhaps outrageous—that a major argument advanced in her behalf by the literary spokesman for African Americans is that she is, like her brother John, not black but, for all practical purposes, white and deserving of what is due the comeliest and most refined product of a finishing school for Southern belles. Chesnutt also pleads the case for those more obviously black, and yet manifest is the very dark Frank Fowler's inferiority to Rena and her brother John, both of whom are interpretable in 1900 as superior because of the degree of "white blood" that is theirs. Frank, displaying a doglike fidelity to Rena that results in more than one scene of self-debasement, reinforces the image of the docile, servile black; Rena's brother, on the other hand, models the mettle and can-do spirit traditionally assigned to the Anglo-Saxon gentleman.[37]

Another popular race theory of the turn of the century (with which Chesnutt was wholly familiar) may account for as challenging a reading experience when one turns to *The Marrow of Tradition* to encounter a mulatto hero and heroine who seem to have derived the same ennobling benefit from miscegenation. Again Chesnutt's intentions are debatable, and perhaps unclear because they were several in number. But among the possible motivations at work in the characterizations of Dr. Miller and his wife Janet may be a desire to champion the dignity and capabilities of mulattoes like Chesnutt himself, whom some race theorists of the eighteenth and nineteenth centuries viewed as not superior to blacks but inferior to both blacks and whites because mulattoes were prone to degeneracy resulting from "cross-breeding." If so, what is notable is that Chesnutt does not expend such energy on behalf of the African American characters unlike his hero and heroine. That is, when one looks beyond Dr. and Mrs. Miller, one finds less-than-attractive portraits of the African American. These characters, with two exceptions, appear debased in roughly the same way. As John M. Reilly explained in 1971, the negative measure of each is that he or she "is considered by the whites to be a 'good nigger,' which is to say that each accommodates himself to his lower caste position" in the way that lowly Frank does in *House*.[38] The exceptional African American inhabitant of Wellington is a nurse who is not at all docile, but—Chesnutt running the risk of giving affront to the subgroup to which he refers—she represents a new generation of African Americans with chips on their shoulders and so the group portrait is not enhanced by her inclusion. Thus, one wonders again, what is the "message" concerning such African Americans intended in this novel? More specifically, what was the obstacle to fashioning a dark-skinned Dr. Miller?

By far the greatest enigma of the novel, however, is created by the presence of the other exceptional character, Josh Green, who is literally black and yet invites at least tentative consideration as a heroic individual superior to fair-skinned Dr. Miller. Reilly, in fact, correctly identifies Green as "the only character" in the novel who "holds to principle without duplicity." Green, a Frank Fowler with a ramrod spine, will neither toady in the manner of the servile African Americans of the novel nor countenance the compromises that Dr. Miller, with his Bookerite go-slow orientation, accepts as necessary for amelioration of the long-term condition of African Americans. His militancy results in what many will today view as a saintly death, perhaps recalling John Brown's. Then again, his death changes little, if anything, in Wellington, and Dr. Miller may thus regain ascendancy in the reader's mind because he foresaw the ineffectuality of Green's radical, or rash, approach to problem solving. But the situation is yet more complicated. Chesnutt had to have known that though he is as morally resolute as the many abolitionist fire-eaters Chesnutt admired, Josh Green also resembles the "burly black brute" figure contemporary journalists pictured repeatedly as a menace to white society and particularly southern womanhood. Would Chesnutt have assumed that such a figure could have appeared at all heroic to a white readership in 1901? As Reilly argues, the novel ends inconclusively with regard to what Chesnutt's position is between the extremes of accommodation (Miller) and militancy (Green). Unresolved as well is the question of exactly what Chesnutt was implying about different varieties of African Americans he pictures.

Ricardo V. Burnette, responding to David D. Britt's analysis of *The Conjure Woman* and like essays and parts of books focusing on the problem of interpreting Chesnutt's complex manner of dealing with the subject of race, produced in 1987 an article that is paradigmatic with regard to what continues to transpire in the literature on this subject.[39] Britt, focusing on the description of Uncle Julius offered in "The Goophered Grapevine," had repeated the explanation of Julius's keen-wittedness given in that short story: it is biologically grounded in his racial makeup as a mulatto—as distinguished from what Albert Bushnell Hart termed the "pure Negro" and Chesnutt "the full-blooded." Chesnutt himself, however, was not charged by Britt with a pro-mulatto, antiblack bias. Not Chesnutt but the white character named John, who relates his encounters with Uncle Julius and transcribes the tales told by him, was identified as the one who thus reveals his a priori assumptions concerning the traits of different varieties of African Americans. Burnette, in response, admits that it is indeed John who articulates the point regarding the intellectually fortifying consequence of an infusion of "white blood," but he questions the legitimacy of Britt's exculpation of Chesnutt. Burnette believes that Donald Gibson was much closer to the truth in 1981: "Chesnutt has a good deal of sympathetic feeling for old Uncle Julius, the black retainer, but his close identification is with the primary narrator [John] and his wife, who are property owners, the landed gentry, the well-mannered aristocrats."[40] John's attitudes, Burnette goes on to observe, are the same as those that Helen Chesnutt, J. Noel Heermance, and Francis Richardson Keller assigned to Chesnutt himself. And thus Burnette comes to the sensitive, controversial issue in question:

> John's belief in the efficacy of "white" blood ... informs most of Chesnutt's "race" fiction. Characters who have "white" blood are usually "spirited" (that is, they have an aptitude for progress) and, perhaps, more tellingly, they are literate—as if an infusion of white blood brought with it special access to "correct" language and speech. These functions of blood were not, of course, unique to Chesnutt. They were so common in nineteenth-century fiction that one might almost take them as *merely* literary conventions. But the conventions themselves were based on popular assumption about the nature of heredity, and in Chesnutt we see only an instance of how pervasive such assumptions were.

That not only assumptions about racial determinants but class consciousness played a role in the demeaning distinctions made by the upper-middle-class Chesnutt through his white surrogate John is as well emphasized by Burnette—though it would be three years before Willard B. Gatewood's *Aristocrats of Color: The Black Elite, 1880–1920* provided the major stimulus for consideration of its shaping effect on the Chesnutt canon.[41]

One will note, then, that the tendency in literary criticism concerning Chesnutt's works dealing with race is away from the objective reading of the works as self-contained entities independent of their author's personality and toward the use of an autobiographical approach that promises the possibility of understanding the works' contradictory elements in terms of the conflicting impulses in, and inconsistent intentions of, the originator of those works.

One other related tendency in the criticism is worthy of special attention, in part because it involves an ironic reversal in reader response since the turn of the century. In Chesnutt's time, the severest criticisms of his writings chastised him for an antiwhite point of view.[42] Now there is virtually no discussion regarding unfairness in depictions of white southerners; rather, ire greets his "racist," tar-brush treatments of blacks. A case in point will be seen in an ad hominem critique that appeared in 1997 and—to observe a more spectacular irony—brings to mind Chesnutt's own angry diatribes against William Hannibal Thomas, the mulatto author of *The American Negro* (1900), a volume that described African Americans in the most negative terms. In his review entitled "A Defamer of His Race" and elsewhere, Chesnutt hotly denounced this volume as a "traitorous blow" by Thomas against his own race. Virtually the same charge was leveled by SallyAnn H. Ferguson, who lambasted Chesnutt when reviewing *The Journals of Charles W. Chesnutt*.[43] She excoriated him for his condescending attitudes toward dark-skinned African Americans in 1874 to 1882 and well beyond then in his later writings: "He mocked their looks and poverty, a behavior he never outgrew." She wholly agrees with Burnette concerning the degree to which Chesnutt identified with the landed white gentry. "Chesnutt dutifully attempted to meet the criteria for acceptance by . . . Eurocentric American culture, and to do so he embraced their racist standards." Thus this fair-skinned mulatto's "repulsion at dark skin color" and other African American "physical features" not his, which "led him to label as 'not pretty' . . . his darker-skinned wife Susan." Further, like "many of his fictional characters, Chesnutt was a master of masking his true feelings if some meaningful gain was on the horizon. How else could he have regarded the room of a black friend who put him up overnight as being simultaneously 'large and comfortable' as well as 'dirty,' with the drinking water spigot so close to the toilet that he could never drink from the former with relish . . . ?" That Chesnutt in 1900 advocated interracial marriage as the ultimate solution for "the Negro Problem"—his "formula . . . for ridding the country of the African-American racial group"—strikes Ferguson as simply a consequence of the mind-set clearly developed and recorded in his journals by 1882. Ferguson is not alone. Michael Flushe is more patient with Chesnutt, but in 1976 he too concluded that "Chesnutt accepted white as the norm and the ideal," and thus he as well accepted for himself "a stereotypical social role, that of the tragic mulatto."[44]

It will likely prove in the years ahead that Chesnutt, when visualized as standing within and speaking for the African American community, defies easy reduction to a wolf in sheep's clothing. June Socken, for example, pointed out nearly 30 years before Ferguson's essay appeared that Chesnutt "mocked the light-skinned" as well in satires such as "A Matter of Principle" and "The Wife of His Youth."[45] But when one adds to this the fact that he regularly mocked whites, comically in "The Passing of Grandison" and mirthlessly in *The Marrow of Tradition,* one may want to argue instead that his alleged condescension was not reserved for one particular group or subgroup. Indeed, in response to Ferguson, and following her line of reasoning for the sake of argument, one may instead pose the question of whether Chesnutt is not more properly termed a color-blind misanthrope or an idealist with extremely high expectations of others than a Negrophobe with a genocidal or "ethnic cleansing" agenda.

That Chesnutt will have emerged from obscurity, at the expense of so much scholarship, only to be weighed, found wanting, and treated as an embarrassment in the way that his distinguished contemporaries Paul Laurence Dunbar and Booker T. Washington have been does not appear to be in the cards. Given what Ferguson and others similarly anguished by Chesnutt's writings do not question—his acknowledged talent as an author—one speculates that instead, the constants in analyses of his life and works will be sensitivity to his complex historical situation and empathy for a conflicted man who could not identify fully with either the black or the white community as he participated in and reflected the viewpoints of both.

What also appears predictable about the future course of Chesnutt scholarship is limned by the three essays seeing publication for the first time in this volume, each of which demonstrates just how inappropriate it is for anyone to assume that the last word on anything that Chesnutt wrought has been said or that the full measure of the man has been taken. Each offers a remarkably positive and perhaps surprising insight into just how sophisticated an author Charles W. Chesnutt was and suggests the need for future interpreters not to approach his prose fictions casually but with both the respectful and cautious attitudes requisite for analyzing the complex art of Herman Melville or Nathaniel Hawthorne. That there is often more than first meets the eye is again emphatically made clear by Charles L. Crow's cogent explanation of Chesnutt's uses of gothic modes of representation. One might have thought in 1974 that Robert Hemenway had exhausted the subject in his near-monograph-length article entitled "Gothic Sociology,"[46] but Crow overturns Hemenway's conclusion regarding the inappropriateness of thinking of Chesnutt as a genuinely gothic author. He discloses in his description of Chesnutt's subtle and innovative appropriations of the conventions of that literary tradition a masterful hand at work. Charles Duncan, in his analysis of three stories in *The Wife of His Youth and Other Stories of the Color Line*, reveals again what Lorne Fienberg's 1990 article on that book did: that when one looks closely and begins to discern the thematic continuities in that collection, one must lament the comparative neglect it has suffered as attention has been lavished on *The Conjure Woman*.[47] Most neglected, though, is the work on which Gary Scharnhorst focuses, and he too gives one reason to pause and then reconsider how the Chesnutt canon has been viewed. If not the other two original essays, certainly his will prove a bolt from the blue to those who view *The Colonel's Dream* as Chesnutt's least successful effort. Scharnhorst's wholly unanticipated discovery is of a deftly ironic author who was capable of parody and satire while creating the serious-minded, no-nonsense work of anti-southern literary propaganda described by Heermance, Keller, Render, Andrews, and Pickens.

On reading Scharnhorst's historically informed, clearly reasoned, and fully verified interpretation of what once seemed the least significant, most "obvious" novel, one may conclude that it is actually Chesnutt's tour de force. And so one wonders, in light of Crow's, Duncan's, and Scharnhorst's contributions, what else have previous scholars overlooked when evaluating the man and his art?

Notes

1. Scholarly writing on Chesnutt is characterized by radical disagreements, even with regard to the most basic matters. See, for example, Cary D. Wintz's description of Chesnutt as a writer facing a "basically hostile environment" in "Race and Realism in the Fiction of Charles W. Chesnutt," *Ohio History* 81 (Spring 1972): 122–30. The extraordinary lengths to which Walter Hines Page went when mentoring Chesnutt, first at Houghton, Mifflin and then Doubleday, Page, are discussed by Joseph R. McElrath Jr. in "Collaborative Authorship: The Charles W. Chesnutt–Walter Hines Page Relationship," in *The Professions of Authorship: Essays in Honor of Matthew J. Bruccoli*, ed. Richard Layman and Joel Myerson (Columbia: University of South Carolina Press, 1996), 150–68. Howells, too, extended himself in a remarkably generous manner; see note 5.

2. Curtis W. Ellison and E. W. Metcalf Jr., *Charles W. Chesnutt: A Reference Guide* (Boston: Hall, 1977).

3. See Robert M. Farnesworth's cogent and succinct description of Chesnutt's turn to militancy after the publication of *The Conjure Woman* in "Charles Chesnutt and the Color Line," in *Minor American Novelists*, ed. Charles A. Hoyt (Carbondale: Southern Illinois University Press, 1971), 28–40.

4. *Collected Stories of Charles W. Chesnutt*, ed. William L. Andrews (New York: New American Library, 1992); *The Journals of Charles W. Chesnutt*, ed. Richard Brodhead (Durham, N.C.: Duke University Press, 1993); *"To Be an Author": Letters of Charles W. Chesnutt, 1889–1905*, ed. Joseph R. McElrath Jr. and Robert C. Leitz III (Princeton, N.J.: Princeton University Press, 1997); *Charles W. Chesnutt: Essays and Speeches*, ed. McElrath, Leitz, and Jesse S. Crisler (Stanford, Calif.: Stanford University Press, 1999); *Mandy Oxendine*, ed. Charles

Hackenberry (Urbana: University of Illinois Press, 1997). Noteworthy also is *The Conjure Woman and Other Conjure Tales*, ed. Richard Brodhead (Durham, N.C.: Duke University Press, 1993).

5. William L. Andrews analyzes the Howells-Chesnutt relationship in "William Dean Howells and Charles W. Chesnutt: Criticism and Race Fiction in the Age of Booker T. Washington," *American Literature* 48 (June 1976): 327–39. For a variant interpretation of this relationship shedding considerable light on Chesnutt's situation vis-à-vis the white readership of his time, see Joseph R. McElrath Jr., "Howells on Race: Charles W. Chesnutt Disappoints the Dean," *Nineteenth-Century Literature* 51 (March 1997): 474–99, reprinted in this volume.

6. Eric J. Sundquist, *To Wake the Nations: Race in the Making of American Literature* (Cambridge, Mass.: Harvard University Press, 1993), treats Chesnutt as a major American author and *The Marrow of Tradition* as a great American novel.

7. *Black Voices: An Anthology of Afro-American Literature*, ed. Abraham Chapman (New York: St. Martin's, 1963); published in paperback (New York: New American Library, 1968).

8. For a detailed description of Chesnutt's and other black writers' histories as American authors represented in mass-market anthologies, see Kenneth Kinnamon, "Three Black Writers and the Anthologized Canon," in *American Realism and the Canon*, ed. Tom Quirk and Gary Scharnhorst (Newark: University of Delaware Press, 1994), 143–53.

9. *American Literature: Tradition and Innovation*, vol. 2, ed. Harrison T. Meserole et al. (Boston: Heath, 1969); *American Literature Survey: Nation and Region, 1860–1900*, vol. 3, ed. Milton R. Stern and Seymour L. Gross (New York: Viking, 1975).

10. *The Heath Anthology of American Literature*, vol. 2, ed. Paul Lauter et al. (Lexington, Mass.: Heath, 1990); *The Norton Anthology of American Literature*, 5th ed., vol. 2, ed. Nina Baym et al. (New York: Norton, 1998).

11. Albert Bushnell Hart, "Conditions of the Southern Problem," *Independent* 58 (23 March 1905): 644–49, reprinted in part as "[Chesnutt as a Mulatto Figure]" in this volume; Alfred Holt Stone, *Studies in the American Race Problem* (New York: Doubleday, Page, 1908), 206, 428–31, reprinted as "[A 'Talented Tenth']" in this volume; Ray Stannard Baker, "The Mulatto: Problem of Race Mixture," in *Following the Color Line* (New York: Doubleday, Page, 1908), 173–74, reprinted in this volume; and Hart, *The Southern South* (New York: Appleton, 1910), 14–15, 325, reprinted as "[More Caucasian than African]" in this volume.

12. Benjamin Griffith Brawley, "Charles Waddell Chesnutt," in *The Negro in Literature and Art* (n.p., 1910), 21–28, reprinted in this volume; Sterling Brown, "Chesnutt," in *The Negro in American Fiction* (Washington, D.C.: Association in Negro Folk Education, 1937), 78–82, reprinted in this volume.

13. William H. Ferris, "The Negro's Contribution to Literature, Music, and Oratory," in *The African Abroad*, vol. 1 (New Haven, Conn.: Tuttle, Morehouse and Taylor, 1913), 255–56, 270–73, reprinted in this volume; William Stanley Braithwaite, "The Negro in Literature," *Crisis* 28 (September 1924): 204–10, reprinted in part in this volume.

14. W. E. B. Du Bois, "Postscript," *Crisis* 35 (August 1928): 276; *The Gift of Black Folk* (Boston: Stratford, 1924), 303, 306–7; "Possibilities of the Negro," *Booklovers Magazine* 2 (July 1903): 2–15.

15. John Chamberlain, "The Negro as Writer," *Bookman* 70 (February 1930): 603–11, reprinted in this volume.

16. Carl Van Vechten, *Nigger Heaven* (New York: Knopf, 1926), 176.

17. Dean H. Keller, "Charles Waddell Chesnutt (1858–1932)," *American Literary Realism* 3 (Summer 1968): 1–4.

18. Vernon Loggins, *The Negro Author in America: His Development to 1900* (New York: Columbia University Press, 1931); J. Saunders Redding, *To Make a Poet Black* (Chapel Hill: University of North Carolina Press, 1939).

19. Benjamin G. Brawley, *The Negro Genius: A New Appraisal of the Achievements of the American Negro in Literature and the Fine Arts* (New York: Dodd, Mead, 1937); as noted earlier,

the 1910 version of Brawley's appreciative section on Chesnutt in *The Negro in Literature in Art* is reprinted in this volume.

20. Hugh M. Gloster, *Negro Voices in American Fiction* (Chapel Hill: University of North Carolina Press, 1948); "Charles W. Chesnutt: Pioneer in the Fiction of Negro Life," *Phylon* 2 (First Quarter 1941): 57–66.

21. Helen Chesnutt, *Charles Waddell Chesnutt: Pioneer of the Color Line* (Chapel Hill: University of North Carolina Press, 1952).

22. Penelope Bullock, "The Mulatto in American Fiction," *Phylon* 6 (First Quarter 1945): 78–82; Russell Ames, "Social Realism in Charles W. Chesnutt," *Phylon* 14 (Second Quarter 1953): 199–206. Both of these precedent-setting articles are reprinted in this volume.

23. Robert A. Bone, *The Negro Novel in America* (New Haven, Conn.: Yale University Press, 1958); *Down Home: A History of Afro-American Short Fiction from Its Beginnings to the End of the Harlem Renaissance* (New York: Putnam's, 1975).

24. Robert A. Smith, "A Note on the Folktales of Charles Waddell Chesnutt," *CLA Journal* 5 (March 1962): 229–32; Donald M. Winkelman, "Three American Authors as Semi-folk Artists," *Journal of American Folklore* 78 (April–June 1965): 130–35; Sylvia Lyons Render, "Tar Heelia in Chesnutt," *CLA Journal* 9 (September 1965): 39–50; Render, "North Carolina Dialect, Chesnutt Style," *North Carolina Folklore* 15 (November 1967): 67–70. See as well Melvin Dixon, "The Teller as Folk Trickster in Chesnutt's *The Conjure Woman*," *CLA Journal* 18 (December 1974): 186–97; and Robert M. Hemenway, "The Functions of Folklore in Charles Chesnutt's *The Conjure Woman*," *Journal of the Folklore Institute* 13 (1976): 283–309.

25. Although he qualifies what is meant by "southern writer," Wayne Mixon supports Mason's characterization in "The Unfulfilled Dream: Charles W. Chesnutt and the New South Movement," *Southern Humanities Review* 10 (Bicentennial Issue [July] 1976): 23–33.

26. Sylvia Lyons Render, "Eagle with Clipped Wings: Form and Feeling in the Fiction of Charles Waddell Chesnutt" (Ph.D. diss., George Peabody College for Teachers, 1962); *The Short Fiction of Charles W. Chesnutt* (Washington, D.C.: Howard University Press, 1974); *Charles W. Chesnutt* (Boston: Twayne, 1980).

27. Richard E. Baldwin, "The Art of *The Conjure Woman*," *American Literature* 43 (November 1971): 385–98, reprinted in this volume.

28. *American Scholar* 42 (Winter 1972–1973): 122–34. Included in this section were Hiram Haydn, "Charles W. Chesnutt," 123–24; Walter Teller, "Charles W. Chesnutt's Conjuring and Color-Line Stories," 125–27; and John Wideman, "Charles W. Chesnutt: *The Marrow of Tradition*," 128–34.

29. J. Noel Heermance, *Charles W. Chesnutt: America's First Great Black Novelist* (Hamden, Conn.: Shoe String, 1974).

30. Frances Richardson Keller, *An American Crusade: The Life of Charles Waddell Chesnutt* (Provo, Utah: Brigham Young University Press, 1978).

31. William L. Andrews, *The Literary Career of Charles W. Chesnutt* (Baton Rouge: Louisiana State University Press, 1980), xi.

32. Ernestine Williams Pickens, *Charles W. Chesnutt and the Progressive Movement* (New York: Pace University Press, 1994).

33. Charles Duncan, *The Absent Man: The Narrative Craft of Charles W. Chesnutt* (Athens: Ohio University Press, 1999).

34. David D. Britt, "Chesnutt's Conjure Tales: What You See Is What You Get," *CLA Journal* 15 (March 1972): 269–83.

35. Myles Raymond Hurd, "Booker T., Blacks, and Brogues: Chesnutt's Sociohistorical Links to Realism in 'Uncle Wellington's Wives,' " *American Literary Realism* 26 (Winter 1994): 19–31.

36. James R. Giles, "Chesnutt's Primus and Annie: A Contemporary View of *The Conjure Woman*," *Markham Review* 3 (May 1972): 46–49.

37. Trudier Harris observes that "Frank seems heir to all the stereotyped notions of blacks that imagination can conceive" in "Chesnutt's Frank Fowler: A Failure of Purpose?" *CLA Journal* 22 (March 1979): 215–28. Even more critical of Chesnutt's performance in *House* is SallyAnn H. Ferguson, "Rena Walden: Chesnutt's Failed 'Future American,' " *Southern Literary Journal* 15 (Fall 1982): 74–82, reprinted in this volume.

38. John M. Reilly, "The Dilemma in Chesnutt's *The Marrow of Tradition*," *Phylon* 32 (First Quarter 1971): 31–38. P. Jay Delmar responds similarly to *Marrow* in "The Moral Dilemma in Charles W. Chesnutt's *The Marrow of Tradition*," *American Literary Realism* 14 (Autumn 1981): 269–72.

39. Ricardo V. Burnette, "Charles W. Chesnutt's *The Conjure Woman* Revisited," *CLA Journal* 30 (June 1987): 438–53.

40. Donald Gibson, *The Politics of Literary Expression: A Study in Major Black Writers* (Westport, Conn.: Greenwood, 1981), 129.

41. Willard B. Gatewood, *Aristocrats of Color: The Black Elite, 1880–1920* (Bloomington: Indiana University Press, 1990).

42. The harshest review—of *Marrow*—was "Literature," *Independent* 54 (March 1902): 582, reprinted in this volume. Almost as caustic was the defense of that racist tirade offered by the *Independent* literary editor Paul Elmer More; see *"To Be an Author": Letters of Charles W. Chesnutt*, 175 n. 5.

43. SallyAnn H. Ferguson, "Book Reviews," *Resources for American Literary Study* 23, no. 1 (1997): 133–35.

44. Michael Flushe, "On the Color Line: Charles Waddell Chesnutt," *North Carolina Historical Review* 54 (Spring 1976): 1–24.

45. June Socken, "Charles Waddell Chesnutt and the Solution of the Race Problem," *Negro American Literature Forum* 3 (Summer 1969): 52–56.

46. Robert Hemenway, "Gothic Sociology: Charles Chesnutt and the Gothic Mode," *Studies in the Literary Imagination* 7, no. 1 (1974): 101–19.

47. Lorne Fienberg, "Charles W. Chesnutt's *The Wife of His Youth:* The Unveiling of the Black Storyteller," *American Transcendental Quarterly* 4 (September 1990): 219–37, reprinted in this volume.

REVIEWS

◆

Chronicle and Comment

ANONYMOUS

. . . Mr. Charles W. Chesnutt, whose touching story, "The Wife of His Youth," published in the July *Atlantic* has, perhaps, caused more favourable comment than any other story of the month, is more than a promising new writer in a new field. Mr. Chesnutt has a firmer grasp than any preceding author has shown in handling the delicate relations between the white man and the negro from the point of view of the mingling of the races. Perhaps the most tragic situation in fiction that has ever been conceived in this country is that in which a mulatto finds himself with all the qualities of the white race in a position where he must suffer from the disadvantages of the coloured race. Mr. Chesnutt has for several years treated this subject in a capable and artistic manner, and has proved himself not only the most cultivated but also the most philosophical story writer that his race has as yet produced; for, strange to relate, he is himself a coloured man of very light complexion. Born in North Carolina, he made a career for himself in his native state as a teacher and a man of enterprise, and he won the high respect of the community by his integrity of character. He is also a scholar of no mean attainments. Seeking a wider field of usefulness he eventually went to Cleveland, Ohio, where for a number of years he has had his home and is known as a very successful lawyer.

Mr. Chesnutt has published more of his short stories through the *Atlantic Monthly* than in any other magazine, and this fact in itself speaks for the high literary quality of his work. We understand that he is now giving more of his time to literary work and that one of these days we may look for a novel from him in which his philosophical grasp, his imaginative power and literary skill may combine to give us an expression of the life of his people not yet realized by any writer either white or coloured in the States. Mr. Chesnutt is still a man in middle life, of a quiet, tranquil temperament, ambitious, industrious and successful. There is no reason why great things should not be expected of him. . . .

Reprinted from *Bookman* 7 (August 1898): 452.

Books of the Day

ANONYMOUS

It has been noted by those who minister to mental expectancy through perusal of publishers' announcements that a volume of stories would appear this spring from the pen of a writer whose name has become pleasantly familiar to *Atlantic* readers. The volume is now ready and a special interest attaches to its appearance. *The Conjure Woman* marks the arrival of a new force in the field of American letters—a force tempered to present in accurate yet picturesque literary form phases of a tragic period in our national life. Its best interpreters hitherto, however sympathetic, have been qualified to testify for one side only. But out of a blended inheritance and a fulness of knowledge Mr. Chesnutt can speak without uncertainty, without romantic gloss, without sentimentality, of times and customs whose sorrowful legacy abides, a debt yet unpaid to Nemesis and Astraea, a baffling element of perplexity in the complex of problems confronting the conscience of American civilization.

Mr. Chesnutt is a witness for the colored race, whose blood he shares in slight degree, from the standpoint of a man whose education, tastes, business associations, and close personal friendships associate him with the white race; moreover, he seems endowed with judgment of a poise so happy that he may be trusted to be fair to both.

As might be expected from the authority of [the *Atlantic* stories] "Po' Sandy," "The Wife of His Youth," and "Hot-Foot Hannibal," the present volume deals with characters and scenes drawn from life among the colored people before the civil war, a life whose intensity was smothered under an exterior of careless acceptance or passive endurance. It is a series of seven stories, linked by the fact that their narrator is each time the same person and that the power of the "conjure woman" is the dominant moral of each, set in a framework furnished by the incident of a Northern man's decision, when seeking beneficial change of climate for his wife's health, to establish himself in central North Carolina. The McAdoo plantation, five miles from the typical "county-seat and commercial emporium" of a Southern State, attracts his attention as being well adapted to grape culture, the business in which he intended to engage. In one of his visits, preliminary to purchase, he makes

Reprinted from *Boston Evening Transcript,* 22 March 1899, part 2, p. 10.

the acquaintance of old Julius, who, unable to break the habits of many years, had attached himself to the plantation where he had been born with a feeling which the author designates as predial, rather than proprietary. It is Julius who enlarges the knowledge of the Northern gentleman and his wife—the Annie whose verbal photograph is nowhere given, but whom we come to realize very clearly through the delicate touches by which we are taken into confidence on the femininity of her tastes and reasoning—with the information that people, places and things can be "goophered-conju'd, bewitch'," solemn proof of which is given in the stories which he at divers times and in sundry places relates to them, stories that form a collection unique in subject and unusual for mastery of knowing what not to say. . . .

The . . . stories with which from time to time Julius adorns his occupation as coachman for the Northern couple, or enlivens the quiet of Sundays and the tedium of rainy days in North Carolina, are more serious [than the comical "Goophered Grapevine" with which *The Conjure Woman* begins]. In fact, a distinctly tragic tone, deepening in intensity, may be heard all through the calm recital of the old negro, though at no time does he exclaim or protest against details in the system under which the greater part of his life had been spent. . . .

We shall hear from Mr. Chesnutt more fully, more clearly, in future work. We shall sometimes smile as we read, sometimes feel a white flame kindle within us, but as far as ardent rhetoric and exclamation points go, the author will not strive for effect. Holding the mastery over his subject and himself, he will, thanks to the saving sense of humor that bestows control over proportion and perspective, sin not against the law forbidding overmuch of either playfulness or pathos.

Literature

ANONYMOUS

The Conjure Woman, by Charles W. Chesnutt, is, as its title indicates, a book of plantation tales, all tinged more or less with voudou magic, slave superstitions, and old-time folk-lore. They are told in the dialect of the North Carolina negro, and the story-teller, who is called Julius, is in his way as impressive a character as the world-famed Uncle Remus. Shrewd, wily, picturesque, ingratiating, deprecatory in manner, rich in imaginative lore, and withal kindly and simple of heart, he is a distinct addition to American literature, and there is not a line out of place in the portrait of him.

The thread which binds the stories together is very slight. The writer, with his wife, is supposed to have settled in the South for the purpose of engaging in grape culture, and finds on the ruined plantation which he selects for his home this interesting human relic of ante-bellum times. While never obtrusive, Julius is often useful, proffering advice and suggestions as to the most profitable way of conducting the business, and sometimes cloaking a suggestion under the safe disguise of a ghost or "cunjur" story. The planter usually discovers sooner or later why that story was told, and sometimes suspects the intention of the old darky in the beginning; but it is noticeable that in five of the seven cases in which the story-telling method was brought into play Julius secured what he wanted, usually through the interposition of "Miss Annie," who appears to have been more impressed by the tales than her husband.

The book has a distinct atmosphere of its own, which is hard to describe, and would be difficult to reproduce effectively in a short quotation. Through it all runs a weird, quaint cloud of superstitious fancy—how much is real and how much feigned it is impossible to say; the effect is that of children who play at robbers or ghosts; they are half-frightened at the reality of their own imaginings, and to the younger ones it is all quite real. When Julius tells his story of the woman who "conjured" her husband into the shape of a big pine tree, that he might not have to go away from her; when he tells how the tree was, during her absence, cut down and sawed into boards, and describes the grief of the bereaved wife, it seems hardly possible that such vivid and glowing word-pictures could be coined by one who does not believe the story he

Reprinted from *Washington, D.C., Times,* 9 April 1899, 2.

tells; the pathos is real; the tenderness is genuine; the whole story is alive. But when, two or three days afterward, the master discovers that the schoolhouse which was built of wood sawed from that tree, and which, owing to his wife's protestations, he has not torn down for lumber, is coveted by Julius and his church society for a meeting-house, one doesn't know what to think. It seems probable, on the whole, that the old fellow made a cunning application of a story, well known to his childhood, which he may or may not have believed.

The titles of these tales are in themselves an indication of the fascination of the book. . . .—there is allurement in every one. A cunning mixture of pathos and humor is found in most of them, with pathos predominant, but "The Conjurer's Revenge" comes near being pure humor. It is the story of Primus, a negro, who was changed into a mule. No matter about the moral which Julius drew from the tale—it was useful to him. The doings of the mule on returning to the plantation which he had inhabited as a man were entertaining and mystifying to onlookers. He chewed up two rows of tobacco. He went on a spree with half a barrel of wine. But the most peculiar antics took place when he espied his former wife carrying on a flirtation with one Dan. . . .

[Catching Dan by the scruff of the neck and tossing him into a cotton patch] was not all that the mule did, and the picture of his head poking itself in at the cabin window one night and making threatening grimaces at Dan, is something to remember. Finally the conjurer "got religion" and on his dying bed turned Primus back into a man, but died before the job was quite finished, so that Primus always thereafter went about with one club foot. This is a fair example of the serio-comic grotesquerie of the tales.

"Mars' Jeems' Nightmare" is decidedly amusing, though there is a little too much obvious intention in it to make it a true folk-lore story. One can see between the lines a picture of life as it was on some plantations before the war. "Sis' Becky's Pickaninny" is a tender little story, with two or three charming pictures in it. "The Gray Wolf's Ha'nt" is perhaps the most like real primitive mythology. It has in it the old, old myth of the werewolf, one of the most blood-curdling and mysterious of traditions, and one which cannot fail under the most indifferent treatment, to be impressive. . . .

In Mr. Chesnutt's werewolf story a conjurer changes a woman into a black cat, and her husband into a wolf, telling the latter that to protect himself from a witch who is doing him injury he must kill the cat. . . . This story bears marks of being an original African folk-tale. Mr. Chesnutt has given it a touch of the pathos which is to be found in the lore of civilized lands, when he condemns the gray wolf to moan forever by the grave of his murdered wife; that part of the story does not belong to tribal life in a tropical forest. Perhaps he evolved this story out of his own brain, and perhaps it is only a transcription of something heard; he does not give a hint on this point.

"Hot-Foot Hannibal," the last of the stories, is a mixture of tragedy and comedy such as could occur only in the life with which it deals. The grotesque ailment of Hannibal and its pathetic consequences do not seem incongruous, because so skillfully interwoven. Laughter over the unfortunate house-boy with "light head and hot foot" hardly ceases before the tragedy of the denouement is developed, full of the eternal pathos of human life. Perhaps this close intermingling of laughter and melancholy is to become a leading characteristic of American literature. It may be found in much of our most popular poetry and fiction; but in nothing is it quite so obvious as in literature dealing with negro life. The tragic shadows in the life of the old-time slave, together with his happy-go-lucky disposition and inexhaustible drollery, make a picture which has appealed to almost every writer of American fiction at one time or another. When these sketches are written by white men they are apt to be either unrelieved tragedy or broad farce; witness "Bras-Coupé" and *Uncle Tom's Cabin,* on the one hand, and the work of Page, Edwards, and Harris on the other. Mr. Page's negro characters are never unhappy, apparently, except when the master's family is in trouble.

This particular delineation of plantation life has the endorsement of a South Carolina critic who says that Mr. Chesnutt is a close rival of "Uncle Remus" in the accuracy and finish of his work, and that his stories possess "a unique quality of mingled humor, pathos and mysticism about them which makes them singularly impressive." In short, this book is one more proof that the truest and most delightful pictures of the life of a race are always drawn by a member of that race. Mr. Chesnutt is a colored man, and that is one reason why his stories are so good. The other reason is that he knows how to make literature.

Reviews of Recent Fiction

ANONYMOUS

Uncle Remus tells the black man's fairy tales; Uncle Julius recites his creed, and it may be found in Mr. Charles W. Chesnutt's *The Conjure Woman*. Certain persons, by "wukking de roots" and by means of "mixtries," can transform men into trees, birds, quadrupeds, or even into men of another race, sometimes controlling their movements by direct efforts of the will, sometimes by means of insect or animal messengers, and the spell may endure even after the death of the conjuror. With the negro this is not a matter of faith, but of actual knowledge. The seven tales in Mr. Chesnutt's book are curious and interesting, and the shrewdness with which Uncle Julius relates each one at the moment when it will be most effective in his own interest suggests that the black man is no more above making his superstitions profitable as his white brother.

Reprinted from *New York Times Saturday Review* 48 (15 April 1899): 246.

About Books and Authors

ANNE PENDLETON

The author of this collection of stories writes very well and makes interesting matter of his tales of negro superstition, astuteness and wit. Nevertheless, to a Southern mind there is just the least suspicion of a false note in his delineations of negro character. There seems to be lacking that fullness of understanding which only those born and reared in dominance over this peculiar people can wholly possess. And while the pictures here given are of interest, and the blending of old-time superstitions of hoodoos and conjure folk with the child-like shrewdness of the darkey in his practical views of life are well-done and readable, yet the study seems to show evidence of a knowledge that is carefully garnered but not innate as that of the only perfectly satisfactory writers in this line has always been.

Reprinted from *Nashville (Tenn.) American,* 23 April 1899, part 3, p. 18.

The Reviewer's Table

NATHANIEL STEPHENSON

Few books could be more interesting in their matter than *The Conjure Woman,* by Charles W. Chesnutt. It is a collection of stories which relate to the superstitions of North Carolina negroes with regard to magic. . . .

All are curious. Some have the elements of supreme spectacular effect. Perhaps the most striking in the collection is the story called "Po' Sandy." This Sandy was married to a "conjure woman," who, in order to prevent his removal from the plantation, converted him into a tree. At night she would turn him back into a man. But one day she was sent away to nurse her master's daughter-in-law, and, while she was away, the tree was cut down. It was trimmed into a log and taken to the mill. Just as it was about to be sawed into boards, the conjure woman rushed into the mill and tried to throw herself before the saw. The workmen, supposing her out of her head, dragged her away, and before her eyes the tree was sawed up and ceased to exist. But the room which was made from those boards was always haunted.

A story with very right literary possibilities is "The Conjurer's Revenge." A conjure man turned another man into a mule. The wife of the bewitched man was then courted by another negro, and the mule objected. The new lover was sent out with the mule, one day, to plow. He met the woman and made love to her. Something caught him by the scruff of the neck and threw him over into the cotton-patch. The mule was very sly and did not let on, but presently he got another chance, and this time he used his hoofs. He kicked that rival into a brier patch on the other side.

These two will give a good idea of the quaintness of the stories which make up *The Conjure Woman.* A word, perhaps, is due to their literary form. The book is written with utmost simplicity, and would seem almost to contain a literal transcription of the talk of some actual old "Uncle Julius." It has the merit of what appears to be an absolute fidelity to nature, and, as a consequence, lacks that quality which converts bare fact into literature. In "Po'

Reprinted from the *Cincinnati Commercial Tribune,* 7 May 1899, 30.

Sandy," if Kipling had written it, the thrill of horror would have been over-powering; "The Conjurer's Revenge," had it been the work of Joel Chandler Harris, would have been one of the most humorous of humorous stories. But this is merely saying that Mr. Chesnutt, although he can put together an interesting volume, is not a master of writing.

Novel Notes

Florence A. H. Morgan

The seven stories in this volume are linked together by having one person relate them, "Ole Julius McAdoo, who 'uz bawn an' raise on dis yer same plantation," where all these marvellous things happened in bye-gone years. Uncle Julius is a venerable-looking coloured gentleman with a shrewd eye and a corresponding shrewdness of character which enables him to "point a moral and adorn a tale" wholly to his own liking or benefit. Of course, the Northern woman whom he eventually leads around to his way of thinking does not in the least believe in the efficacy of "de lef' hin'-foot er a grabe-ya'd rabbit, kilt by a cross-eyed nigger on a da'k night in de full er de moon," or in the "monst'us powe'ful goopher." It was never difficult to induce the old man to tell a story of the old slavery days, of which he seemed, indeed, to have an inexhaustible stock, some weirdly grotesque, some broadly amusing, some barely plausible, others palpable but entertaining inventions. Whether his own or not, it was impossible to tell, yet each one was evidently embellished to suit the exigencies of the occasion. But even the weirdest is not without an element of pathos—the tragedy, it might be, of the story itself; the sadness of life as seen by the fading light of an old man's memory. The keynote of the whole series is the blind superstition and duplicity of character fostered by the life of servility and cringing to the master. These stories stand out as an impartial picture of the life of the slave in the Southern States. Uncle Julius is a fine type of the old slave devoted to his master, never lacking in dignity and courage, but withal possessing an indifferent code of morals, the result, most likely, of his close association with the white man whose ethics were, to say the least, pliant. All the wrongs of the race are in these simple tales unfolded, but with never a complaint, a strict justice being displayed in the drawing of the good and bad master, the good and bad slave, each having a fair showing. Mr. Chesnutt does not strive for any dramatic effects, nor does he ever introduce any unnecessary harrowing situations; there is a surprising absence of false sentiment. Love, hate, jealousy and cruelty are dealt with in a thoroughly sane, good-natured, sensible manner. No hysterics, no posing, mar the simple recitals of Uncle Julius as he happens to talk to the Northern man

Reprinted from *Bookman* 9 (June 1899): 372–73.

and his wife who have come to North Carolina to recuperate the wife's health and incidentally improve and cultivate an old vineyard which had been bought greatly against old Julius's advice.

> " 'F I 'us in yo' place, I wouldn' buy dis vimya'd."
> "Why not?" I asked.
> "Well, I dunno whe'r you b'lieves in cunj'in' er not—some er de w'ite folks don't, er says dey don't—but de truf er de matter is dat dis yer old vimya'd is goophered."
> "Is what?" I asked, not grasping the meaning of this unfamiliar word.
> "Is goophered—conju'd, bewitch."

Old Julius's disinterestedness left something to be desired when it was discovered that he had occupied for years a cabin on the deserted ground and derived a respectable income from the neglected grapevines. His advice generally lay under suspicion.

Between the introduction of slavery into the South and the Civil War lies a picturesque period, something more dramatic and less than tragic, fraught with wonderful possibilities for just such a facile, discriminating pen as Mr. Chesnutt's. As we of this day look back over that shadowed bit of history, such a transaction as is set forth in "Sis' Becky's Pickaninny" seems absolutely incredible, and moves our hearts to an outspoken rebellion that such things could ever have been, and yet the author does justice to every one in the tale. The tragic episodes which befall poor Becky arise wholly from her carelessness in not providing herself with a rabbit's foot! In this story more than in any other of the group does Mr. Chesnutt place before his readers the two kinds of masters, and a strong wave of irrepressible compassion sweeps over us as we grasp the tragical undercurrent of those lives bowed down with ignominy and shame. Through the medium of "The Gray Wolf's Ha'nt" and "Po' Sandy" the author pictures the every-day, pathetic side of the negro's life, and forcibly brings out that peculiar mysticism which may be the black man's inheritance from the Orient; the beliefs and superstitions which have been transplanted along with the race. But across the darkest phase of the slave's life there flashes that quaint humour which saves even the most tragic scenes from too heavy a shadow of horror. So clever a master of literary skill, so keen a student of human nature is Mr. Chesnutt, that he never allows himself to drift into too great gloom, but plays with an artistic touch on our emotions and our sense of humour in an equal degree.

In *The Conjure Woman,* while there are several interesting studies of white people, the main interest, to the thoughtful reader, centres in the phase of slave life presented. We have viewed the plantation negro from every side but his own, which is here shown in a manner that furnishes evidence of its truthfulness. Few of this generation, even in the South, know anything from personal observation of the institution of slavery, except from the baneful effects that still survive it; but these stories are so perfectly consistent with human nature, that, aside from the supernatural element, which is palpably a vehicle for the deeper thought underlying, the stories prove themselves. *The Conjure Woman* is a collection of quaint tales, with an admirable Southern setting, replete with the humour and tragedy of slavery, so skillfully blended that often one does not know where the one begins and the other ends. The dialect in which the story-teller speaks is smooth and readable, evidently a means and not an end, and Mr. Chesnutt's English is remarkable for its literary style and quality.

Literature, Music, Art, and
Social and Personal Notes

ANONYMOUS

The Conjure Woman purports to be a story of Southern plantation life. Mr. Chesnutt is an Ohioan, and the book is written from his point of view. It has been favorably received; it was favorably advertised.

The Southern reader of such a romance naturally accepts it with comparative reservations. In a dialectic point of view, the same ground has been covered by "Unc Remus" of delightful memory, by "Mars Chan," and "Meh Lady," both perfect examples of negro speech and perfect expositions of negro character at its best and finest.

In so far as the effect of environment upon the relationship between slave and mother is concerned it would scarcely seem that Mr. Chesnutt could be a competent judge or critic, he never having lived South until the period of Reconstruction, and remaining there only for a short period of time in a section of whose institutions and abuses he speaks with such glibness, whose misfortunes he depicts in such a distorted and perverted light.

We well know the class who are eager to "rush in where angels fear to tread."

Mr. Chesnutt certainly does not belong to it, and yet he places himself in exactly the same light when he uses the talent which might instruct and delight elsewhere, in writing of matters about which he either knows nothing, or concerning which he has, to say the least, very unfortunate and unjust views and ideas. An Ohio pastoral or a Cleveland idyl we think would be much more in his line. He can safely leave the South and her institutions with their explanation and vindication to less biased and more familiar pens than his own, while he might do well in using some of his legal talent to redress the legislative wrongs and blots of the Reconstruction Period.

Reprinted from the *Richmond (Va.) Times,* 9 July 1899, 9.

Literature

ANONYMOUS

. . . On reading [*The Conjure Woman*] . . . it is more interesting and instructive if we put aside all questions regarding slavery, as once existing in the United States, and look upon the seven short tales united under this attractive title as a contribution to the folklore of the country.

Mr. Chesnutt, who shows an intimate knowledge of the superstitions, weaknesses, and character of the negro, gives us in a delightfully natural dialect a number of curious and whimsical stories, supposedly told to a man and his wife, who have recently moved to North Carolina, by an old negro Julius, who knows all the gossip of the county. The conjure woman appears in every story, and neither are her performances nor her capacities nor the belief in her powers exaggerated. "Aunt" Peggy appears in several of the tales, moving about mysteriously to "goopher"—i.e., bewitch or conjure or throw a spell upon—grape vines, animals or people. . . .

As "Aunt" Peggy was capable of making "goopher" mixtures, like powders, to put into people's food, of conjuring sweet potatoes and other things that would work charms of divination by means of roots and herbs and bottles containing various infallible decoctions, it is not to be wondered at that she was greatly feared and admired by the entire black-skinned community.

Of all the stories we prefer "The Goophered Grapevine," "Po' Sandy," "Mars Jeems' Nightmare" and "The Conjurer's Revenge"; for they exhibit more particularly the peculiar African imagination which is capricious, unique and fantastic without being, in any sense, poetic. Take, for example, the story of the club-footed nigger, who was once a mule, in the last-mentioned story. It is entirely African in its conception and treatment, especially in the conclusion where the dying conjurer invites the mule into his shanty, and, by means of his bottles, gourds and roots, turns the animal back into his natural state, but dies before he finishes his last hoof.

In no sense can these stories be compared to the Uncle Remus tales, for those marvellous creations belong to the beast lore of all nations, and the natural instincts of men are reflected in the "creeturs." This book, on the contrary, is very limited, and not, like Mr. Harris's work, artistic. It does, however, contribute something from a field as yet untilled.

Reprinted from *New York Commercial Advertiser,* 20 June 1899, 5.

The Rambler

Anonymous

It is less than a year since Mr. Charles W. Chesnutt of Cleveland, published, through Messrs. Houghton, Mifflin & Co., his volume of "Conjure Woman" stories. This book attracted wide attention, and promptly gave its writer a place in the front rank of those who have contributed to our knowledge of negro life and character. Before this Mr. Chesnutt had published, in the *Atlantic* and elsewhere, short stories of marked originality and power, dealing in one way and another with the negro race and its blendings with the white. A collection of these stories taking its name from one of the most memorable of them, "The Wife of His Youth," will be issued in the autumn by Mr. Chesnutt's first publishers. Still another work, upon which he is now engaged, is a life of Frederick A. Douglass for the series of "Beacon Biographies," published by Messrs. Small, Maynard & Co. Through his sympathies and acquirements there is probably no writer in the country more competent than Mr. Chesnutt to treat this picturesque subject, and the result of his undertaking can hardly fail to draw to itself many readers.

Reprinted from *Book Buyer* 19 (September 1899): 84–85.

Life of Frederick Douglass

O[RRA]. L[ANGHORNE].

Readers of the *Southern Workman* will remember Mr. Chesnutt's *Conjure Woman*, which was reviewed in our columns a few months ago. Another book by the same promising author, *The Wife of His Youth and Other Stories*, recently published by Houghton, Mifflin & Co., will be noticed in our February issue.

In the present little volume, which is one of the Beacon Biographies issued by Small, Maynard & Co., Mr. Chesnutt has done good service to the public in his history of Frederick Douglass. By permission of the publishers, the excellent portrait of this great leader of the Negro race, which is the frontispiece of the little volume, is reproduced as an illustration for the short sketch of Douglass by Hon. Archibald H. Grimké, printed on another page.

In this convenient little book the publishers certainly carry out their promise of furnishing "brief, readable, and authentic accounts of those Americans whose personalities have impressed themselves most deeply on the character and history of their country." In this telegraphic age, when life does not seem long enough for the work that must be done, a hundred people will read a book like one of the Beacon series, with one hundred and thirty-five pages, where only one would read a large volume of four or five hundred pages, no matter how thrilling the record might be.

Notwithstanding the limited space assigned him, Mr. Chesnutt has given us a full history of the leading events in the life of one of the most prominent figures in the long struggle for the emancipation of the Negroes in America. He tells of the birth and unhappy childhood on a Maryland plantation, of the little slave boy who was to make his mark among the great ones of his times. A rapid but graphic sketch is given of the earlier part of Douglass' career, when he tasted to the full the bitter sorrows of slavery—a dark picture only relieved by the glimpses of happy chances which enabled the slave boy to acquire the rudiments of an education in spite of hardships and obstacles. One can but think what wonderful progress the colored youth of the present day might make, if they would use the abundant opportunities given them, half as well as Douglass did his scant chances to acquire knowledge.

Reprinted from *Southern Workman and Hampton School Record* 29 (January 1900): 55–56.

45

In a chronology, well placed in the beginning of the handy little volume, the author gives the leading events of his hero's life, commencing with his birth as a slave in Talbot Co., Md., in 1817, and ending with his death at his handsome residence near Washington in 1895. Truly it is the record of a remarkable life, recalling in its wonderful vicissitudes the story of Joseph, the Hebrew slave boy in Egypt, who rose "to be second only to the king on his throne."

The life of Frederick Douglass is of interest to every American citizen. The leading events of his career were enacted in stirring times, and he affords an admirable example of a man born in the lowest station, rising by force of his great talents and indomitable will to rank among the prominent and successful men of his time. To the colored people of our country, the history of Frederick Douglass must be ever of inestimable value. The educated among them fully appreciate what he accomplished for the race, and it is but natural and excusable if they sometimes speak of him with even extravagant admiration. Douglass had the courage, the talent, the strong will, and wonderful common sense which fitted him to be a leader of his race in the struggle for freedom, but it is doubtful whether, now that slavery is a thing of the past, he could be as useful among his people as are Booker Washington and other men of a later day who can instruct the young Negroes in the use to be made of their opportunities as free men and citizens.

Mr. Chesnutt's story of Frederick Douglass should be a text-book in the hands of colored youth. A beautiful tribute is that given by his biographer to the character of this ex-slave, to whose youth was denied almost all of the elevating and ennobling influences usually deemed indispensable. What a lesson for those who read the record—what an example for his people! "A wholesome atmosphere always surrounded him. He never used tobacco or strong liquors. He was clean of speech and pure in life."

A New Author of Good Stories
of Southern Negro Life

ANONYMOUS

It is very rare to find a writer who touches the Southern negro without exaggeration. Joel Chandler Harris, Mrs. Burnett, Ruth McEnery Stuart, Thomas Nelson Page and James Lane Allen are the few exceptions. To these must be added Charles W. Chesnutt, a new Southern writer whose work easily outranks that of all the others except the creator of "Uncle Remus." Mr. Chesnutt's first book, *The Conjure Woman,* was a fine collection of tales of negro life, full of humor and pathos. His second book, *The Wife of His Youth and Other Stories,* is brought out by Houghton, Mifflin & Co. of Boston, and is sold at $1.50.

Most of the tales have already appeared in the magazines, but they are good enough to read several times. The title story relates the search of an old negro woman for the mulatto husband who ran away just before the war broke out to save himself from being sold. He had become rich and honored in a Northern city and on the eve of his marriage to a young and attractive widow, his old wife appears and tells her story. She does not know him, as he has changed his name, but at a party which he gave in the evening he tells the story of her twenty-five years' faithful search and asks the company whether this man should recognize the wife of his youth who had displayed such great fidelity to an old love. When they said yes, he steps to the door, leads in a little, old black woman and introduces her as his wife. The other stories are all good and each brings out some new trait of the negro race. "A Web of Circumstance" shows the ruin that followed an unjust charge against a negro blacksmith. It is told with great sympathy for the difficult position of the colored man in the South. Mr. Chesnutt gained his knowledge of Southern life from long residence in North Carolina. He spent his boyhood and youth in that State but finally moved to Cleveland, O., where he did court reporting and studied law. His first literary work was for the syndicates, but most of his stories have been printed in the *Atlantic Monthly.*

Reprinted from *San Francisco Chronicle,* 7 January 1900, Sunday supplement, 4.

The Book-Buyer's Guide

Anonymous

"The Wife of his Youth," and eight other stories of the color line, by Charles W. Chesnutt, [comprise] the second collection of stories by the author of *The Conjure Woman*. The underlying idea in this book is the negro problem—the tragedies accompanying the evolution of the negro toward that point where racial distinctions are not maintained. The stories bring home the solemn truth that no man lives to himself alone. Even though he rises socially and intellectually, he has responsibilities of family and race which he cannot shake off. In so far as he tries to free himself from them, in so far is he less of a man than before. There lies the irony of the situation. The subject matter of *The Wife of his Youth* marks a distinct advance over that of *The Conjure Woman,* in which the human interest in slight. We have had stories in negro dialect. We are ready to leave the objective for the subjective point of view; we want a consideration of the struggle which has already begun in the North. Therefore this book is timely. Mr. Chesnutt's descriptive passages show colloquialisms from which he will probably free himself.

Reprinted from *Critic* 36 (February 1900): 182.

Literature Section

ANONYMOUS

. . . In *The Wife of His Youth,* Mr. Charles W. Chesnutt tells a sad story of the conditions attending the colored people. The same note of sadness is struck in the other tales that compose the little volume which receives its title from the first story. Mr. Chesnutt is a colored man himself, living in Cleveland. This, and his other books, are among the most interpretive volumes recently issued regarding his race. As stories, the tales are of slight worth, but as suggestive interpretations of the character and condition of the colored people each page has peculiar value. . . .

Reprinted from *Advance* 39 (22 February 1900): 272.

Two New Novelists

[HAMILTON WRIGHT MABIE]

. . . Mr. Chesnutt finds his field in the life of the negro, and writes as one who knows that life at first hand, and who is able to comprehend and interpret it both on the side of humor and of tragedy, because he has to a certain extent shared its fortune. In *The Conjure Woman* he presented a series of studies in the old-time superstitions of the plantation negro; the darkest side of the life of slavery; reminiscences of barbaric religions brought from beyond the sea. Some of these stories are humorous; none of them lacks those quiet touches of humor which are so characteristic of the negro character; but they are also full of side-lights on the tragedy of slave life—a tragedy which is brought into more striking relief because it comes out, so to speak, incidentally and by the way. In his more recent volume, *The Wife of His Youth,* Mr. Chesnutt concerns himself largely with the negro of to-day under the new conditions under which he finds himself; and it is safe to say that no finer psychological study of the negro in his new life has been presented than that which is found in the story which gives its title to this volume—a story which, in keenness of perception, in restraint and balance, in true feeling and artistic construction, must take its place among the best short stories in American literature. The two volumes taken together constitute an important addition, not only to our literature, but to our knowledge of the negro race; exhibiting, as they do, the negro under two entirely different conditions. The tragedy of the slave is not the tragedy of the freeman; but the case of the latter is hardly less pathetic in many ways than the case of the former, and this pathos Mr. Chesnutt has brought out in several very effective short stories. The tragedy lies in the situation, and must remain there until the negro has reached a much higher stage of evolution. It is part of the artistic value of these stories that this revelation is made incidentally, and not with a didactic purpose. When the negro begins to speak for himself, as he is already doing through three or four men of distinct gift and insight, he is furnishing the best evidence of his ability to rise, and of the fact that he has already gone a considerable way on his journey toward higher self-development.

Reprinted from *Outlook* 64 (24 February 1900): 440–41.

It is in such work as that which Miss [Mary] Johnston [author of the novel *To Have and to Hold*] and Mr. Chesnutt have recently contributed to contemporary literature that the advancing movement of the American literary spirit has is to be discerned. For this work has its roots in reality; its chief concern is the portrayal of life; it deals at first hand with original materials; it gives us new aspects of American life; it is the expression of what is going on in the spirit of man on this continent.

Mr. Charles W. Chesnutt's Stories

William Dean Howells

The critical reader of the story called "The Wife Of His Youth," which appeared in these pages two years ago, must have noticed uncommon traits in what was altogether a remarkable piece of work. The first was the novelty of the material; for the writer dealt not only with people who were not white, but with people who were not black enough to contrast grotesquely with white people,—who in fact were of that near approach to the ordinary American in race and color which leaves, at the last degree, every one but the connoisseur in doubt whether they are Anglo-Saxon or Anglo-African. Quite as striking as this novelty of the material was the author's thorough mastery of it, and his unerring knowledge of the life he had chosen in its peculiar racial characteristics. But above all, the story was notable for the passionless handling of a phase of our common life which is tense with potential tragedy; for the attitude, almost ironical, in which the artist observes the play of contesting emotions in the drama under his eyes; and for his apparently reluctant, apparently helpless consent to let the spectator know his real feeling in the matter. Any one accustomed to study methods in fiction, to distinguish between good and bad art, to feel the joy which the delicate skill possible only from a love of truth can give, must have known a high pleasure in the quiet self-restraint of the performance; and such a reader would probably have decided that the social situation in the piece was studied wholly from the outside, by an observer with special opportunities for knowing it, who was, as it were, surprised into final sympathy.

Now, however, it is known that the author of this story is of negro blood,—diluted, indeed, in such measure that if he did not admit this descent few would imagine it, but still quite of that middle world which lies next, though wholly outside, our own. Since his first story appeared he has contributed several others to these pages, and he now makes a showing palpable to criticism in a volume called *The Wife of His Youth, and Other Stories of the Color Line;* a volume of Southern sketches called *The Conjure Woman;* and a short life of Frederick Douglass, in the Beacon Series of biographies. The last is a simple, solid, straight piece of work, not remarkable above many other

Reprinted from *Atlantic Monthly* 85 (May 1900): 699–701.

biographical studies by people entirely white, and yet important as the work of a man not entirely white treating of a great man of his inalienable race. But the volumes of fiction *are* remarkable above many, above most short stories by people entirely white, and would be worthy of unusual notice if they were not the work of a man not entirely white.

It is not from their racial interest that we could first wish to speak of them, though that must have been a very great and very just claim upon the critic. It is much more simply and directly, as works of art, that they make their appeal, and we must allow the force of this quite independently of the other interest. Yet it cannot always be allowed. There are times in each of the stories of the first volume when the simplicity lapses, and the effect is as of a weak and uninstructed touch. There are other times when the attitude, severely impartial and studiously aloof, accuses itself of a little pompousness. There are still other times when the literature is a little too ornate for beauty, and the diction is journalistic, reporteristic. But it is right to add that these are exceptional times, and that for far the greatest part Mr. Chesnutt seems to know quite as well what he wants to do in a given case as Maupassant, or Tourguénief, or Mr. James, or Miss Jewett, or Miss Wilkins, in other given cases, and has done it with an art of kindred quiet and force. He belongs, in other words, to the good school, the only school, all aberrations from nature being so much truancy and anarchy. He sees his people very clearly, very justly, and he shows them as he sees them, leaving the reader to divine the depth of his feeling for them. He touches all the stops, and with equal delicacy in stories of real tragedy and comedy and pathos, so that it would be hard to say which is the finest in such admirably rendered effects as "The Web of Circumstance," "The Bouquet," and "Uncle Wellington's Wives." In some others the comedy degenerates into satire, with a look in the reader's direction which the author's friend must deplore.

As these stories are of our own time and country, and as there is not a swashbuckler of the seventeenth century, or a sentimentalist of this, or a princess of an imaginary kingdom, in any of them, they will possibly not reach half a million readers in six months, but in twelve months possibly more readers will remember them than if they had reached the half million. They are new and fresh and strong, as life always is, and fable never is; and the stories of *The Conjure Woman* have a wild, indigenous poetry, the creation of sincere and original imagination, which is imparted with a tender humourness and a very artistic reticence. As far as his race is concerned, or his sixteenth part of a race, it does not greatly matter whether Mr. Chesnutt invented their motives, or found them, as he feigns, among his distant cousins of the Southern cabins. In either case, the wonder of their beauty is the same; and whatever is primitive and sylvan or campestral in the reader's heart is touched by the spells thrown on the simple black lives in these enchanting tales. Character, the most precious thing in fiction, is as faithfully portrayed against the poetic background as in the setting of the *Stories of the Color Line*.

Yet these stories, after all, are Mr. Chesnutt's most important work, whether we consider them merely as realistic fiction, apart from their author, or as studies of that middle world of which he is naturally and voluntarily a citizen. We had known the nethermost works of the grotesque and comical negro and the terrible and tragic negro through the white observer on the outside, and black character in its lyrical moods we had known from such an inside witness as Mr. Paul Dunbar; but it had remained for Mr. Chesnutt to acquaint us with those regions where the paler shades dwell as hopelessly, with relation to ourselves, as the blackest negro. He has not shown the dwellers there as very different from ourselves. They have within their own circles the same social ambitions and prejudices; they intrigue and truckle and crawl, and are snobs, like ourselves, both of the snobs that snub and the snobs that are snubbed. We may choose to think them droll in their parody of pure white society, but perhaps it would be wiser to recognize that they are like us because they are of our blood by more than a half, or three quarters, or nine tenths. It is not, in such cases, their negro blood that characterizes them; but it is their negro blood that excludes them, and that will imaginably fortify them and exalt them. Bound in that sad solidarity from which there is no hope of entrance into polite white society for them, they may create a civilization of their own, which need not lack the highest quality. They need not be ashamed of the race from which they have sprung, and whose exile they share; for in many of the arts it has already shown, during a single generation of freedom, gifts which slavery only apparently obscured. With Mr. Booker T. Washington the first American orator of our time, fresh upon the time of Frederick Douglass; with Mr. Dunbar among the truest of our poets; with Mr. Tanner, a black American, among the only three Americans from whom the French government ever bought a picture, Mr. Chesnutt may well be willing to own his color.

But that is his personal affair. Our own more universal interest in him arises from the more than promise he has given in a department of literature where Americans hold the foremost place. In this there is, happily, no color line; and if he has it in him to go forward on the way which he has traced for himself, to be true to life as he has known it, to deny himself the glories of the cheap success which awaits the charlatan in fiction, one of the places at the top is open to him. He has sounded a fresh note, boldly, not blatantly, and he has won the ear of the more intelligent public.

The Reviewer's Table

Nathaniel Stephenson

It seems almost as if we might as well give up, one time as well as another, the effort to make certain people understand that fiction is not "just telling things." So many well-meaning people persist in making themselves ridiculous by their futile attempts to make fact into fiction. If they would say, in substance, "Good friends, I have seen a few things which appeared to me curious; I thought some of the rest of you might be interested; with your permission, here they are"—if they would only do that, all were well. The fact that they will not do that is due, probably, to the epidemic of fiction-writing that has become among us a positive mania. . . .

This volume by Mr. Chesnutt is one more evidence of the fact. He is not in the least equipped to write fiction. To be sure, he has seen something—no more than any one else has seen who has kept open his eyes, but it must be remembered that most people keep their eyes shut—and he can write very fair English. If he would say what he has to say on the "color line" in straightforward unpretentious essays, every one would be interested in listening to him. But, alas! he is bitten with the mania to write fiction. He remembers a tale of a foolish, good-for-nothing old negro, a tale that could be told adequately as a passing illustration in a few pages, but, instead of telling it simply, and as he is capable of telling it, he torments it into a story of sixty-six pages. . . .

. . . It has not a redeeming quality! The author should blush to have written it, and the publishers to have published it. And the worst thing about it is that the one quality which might, at least, have mitigated the commonness and vulgarity of the story is entirely lacking. A great master of writing might, had he chosen to waste his powers on such a subject, have skillfully withdrawn Uncle Wellington to a distance; might have shown him to us through a haze of great illusion; might have so played upon our sense of pity, made so pathetically evident the baby-like creeping of the negro's intelligence, that the abomination of the story might have melted away into a haze of condoning sentimentalism. But of such art this story has not a trace. It is direct, realistic, matter of fact. Uncle Wellington never once feels a fine emo-

Reprinted from *Cincinnati (Ohio) Commercial Tribune,* 13 May 1900, 32.

tion, even in perverted form. He is merely common selfishness, dashed with cunning—an excellent specimen of Kipling's barbarian, "half devil and half child." The author is so little offended by this obnoxious compound that he makes no attempt to idealize or even equivocate.

This story of "Uncle Wellington's Wives" is, perhaps, the worst in the volume, but they are all on about the same level. They deal with matters which are either simply repulsive or strangely morbidly sad. . . . The few that are not of this sort are so spoiled by an unimaginative way of telling them that the charm [they might have yielded] is wholly lost. Taken altogether, this book has a slight claim to exist.

Two New Books by Charles W. Chesnutt

Anonymous

In his second volume of short stories, *The Wife of His Youth and Other Stories of the Color Line,* Mr. Charles W. Chesnutt strikes a deeper and a stronger note than in *The Conjure Woman.* The lighter and more amusing side of negro character was shown in the earlier volume. The darker and sterner features of negro life, and more particularly the perplexing problem involved when the color line is so faint as to be scarcely discernible but is always liable to discovery are presented in the collection of nine stories.

When "The Wife of His Youth" appeared in the *Atlantic Monthly* the writer of this notice called attention to it as one of the most noteworthy short stories of the time, and that opinion was corroborated by the judgment of the most competent critics all over the country. Re-reading the story has deepened the impression then formed. But the other tales in the volume are well worthy companionship with that striking sketch. The earnestness, the skillful management of the story to keep the reader in suspense, the dramatic denouement, the clear simplicity of style, are characteristic of all the nine stories, whether the scene is laid in the south or in "Groveland," or its pretty neighboring city of "Patesville," both of which places will be readily recognized under these slightly disguised names.

The Wife of His Youth has four illustrations by Clyde O. De Land, and can be strongly recommended as a holiday present that is certain to be appreciated. . . .

Another book by Mr. Charles W. Chesnutt is a volume in "The Beacon Biographies of Eminent Americans," in which Mr. Chesnutt tells the story of the life of *Frederick Douglass.* In introducing it the author says that the more he has studied the records of the life of Douglass the more it has appealed to his imagination and heart. Belonging to a later generation than this champion of his oppressed race he was only privileged to see the man and hear the orator after his life work was substantially completed, but often enough then to appreciate something of the strength and eloquence by which he impressed his contemporaries.

Reprinted from *Cleveland Plain Dealer,* 10 December 1899, part 2, p. 6.

Mr. Chesnutt, in noticing the fact that Douglass served two years as minister resident and consul general to the republic of Hayti, says he has heard him speak with enthusiasm of the substantial progress made by the Haytians in the arts of government and civilization, and with indignation of what he considered slanders against the island, due to ignorance or prejudice. When it was suggested to Douglass that the Haytians were given to revolution as a mode of expressing disapproval of their rulers, he replied that a four years' rebellion had been fought and two presidents assassinated in the United States during a comparatively peaceful political period in Hayti.

The little volume has a striking photogravure portrait of Frederick Douglass from one of the last photographs taken of him and the one most highly thought of by his family.

Our Literary Folks

Anonymous

The last of "The Beacon Biographies" is [*Frederick Douglass*] by Charles W. Chesnutt (Small, Maynard & Co., Boston). The publishers of these biographies seem to have made it a plan to select authorities in close sympathy with the subject to be treated, and in this view, Mr. Chesnutt is probably the happiest choice that could have been made of a biographer of Frederick Douglass. His recent volume of stories betrays a leaning to the doctrine of miscegenation, of which Douglass has been most conspicuous exemplar, and his general opinions concerning race relations coincide with those Douglass is known to have entertained.

John J. Ingalls said some years ago, in a speech in the Federal Senate that Fred Douglass derived his ability from his "white re-enforcement." This probably has been the accepted opinion, but Mr. Chesnutt takes the opposite and refreshing view that Douglass' intellectuality came from his mother—a negro field hand, whose complexion the author describes as "glossy black."

Frederick Douglass was unquestionably a man of great ability as an orator, and considering his lack of early education, he acquired a high degree of mental culture. He was an earnest and courageous character, and his private life was without blame. What further capacity he may have possessed outside of that of a public speaker had no test. He was not a writer, his field of activity was politics exclusively, and he filled no offices that required a high order of talent. The post of Minister to Hayti he resigned before his term of office expired. His biographer pictures him as having risen to eminence under great difficulties, but this view is questionable. The greater part of his youth was spent as a house boy with a well-to-do, refined, Christian family in the city of Baltimore, and unprejudiced people, who know the mild order of the slavery that existed under such conditions can readily understand that the manner of his bringing up was far more auspicious than that of many white statesmen who have struggled against adverse circumstances in early youth. Douglass, as a boy, had better opportunity and more wholesome environment for mental training than either Abraham Lincoln or Andrew Johnson, the men who composed the successful Republican presidential ticket of 1864. The fact that

Reprinted from *Nashville (Tenn.) Banner,* 9 December 1899, part 2, p. 14.

he was a slave did not alter this fact. His rise as an abolition orator was greatly facilitated by the fact that he was an ex-slave. As "a graduate from the school of slavery, with his diploma on his back," he was a trump card in the play.

In order to create sympathy for his subject, Mr. Chesnutt has gone out of his way to paint the horrors of slavery, and makes some statements that are hardly credible. The laws of Maryland, he alleges, allowed the master to kill a slave who resisted punishment. This statement is gratuitously interjected into the Douglass biography, and we doubt its truth.

Frederick Douglass was a conspicuous and active participant in the antislavery movement and after its consummation a picturesque and unique figure about the national capitol. His biography is an interesting contribution to the history of abolition times, and properly has a place among the lives of those who have figured prominently in American politics. We could not wish that his biography had been undertaken by an unfriendly hand, but it would be better if it were relieved of some of Mr. Chesnutt's prejudices, and could be better relished by the majority of American readers if it didn't unnecessarily display his abnormal predilections.

Biographies

ANONYMOUS

Frederick Douglass, by C. W. Chesnutt, is one of the "Beacon Biographies of Eminent Americans," of which M. A. De Wolfe Howe is the editor. The frontispiece is from a photogravure of Mr. Douglass taken shortly before his death. An editorial note states that it is the one most highly thought of by his family, by whose permission it is used.

Like all the other volumes of the series, *Frederick Douglass* is *multum in parvo.* The number of pages is 141. Within this brief compass Mr. Chesnutt has contrived to present the chief events in the life of the most distinguished of American negroes; and at the same time, to give to the fascinating story an appearance of completeness in detail. It is eulogistic, as it ought to be, as it must be, if truthful; but is at the same time discriminative.

This little book, which might easily be carried in one's coat pocket, is undoubtedly the best source from which, with little reading, one can gain a comprehensive and just knowledge of the subject of this biography.

Reprinted from *Boston Daily Advertiser,* 12 January 1900, 5.

Charles W. Chesnutt:
A New Delineation of Southern Life

W[ILLIAM]. W. H[UDSON].

The author of *The Wife of His Youth* and *The Conjure Woman,* whose short story, "A Victim of Heredity; or, Why the Darkey Loves Chicken," appears in this number of *Self Culture Magazine,* has lately sprung into prominence as one of the most, if not *the* most, original of American writers of fiction.

Mr. Chesnutt was born in Cleveland, O., June 20, 1858, of North Carolina parentage. His father served four years on the non-commissioned staff of the Northern army during the Civil War. The family returned to North Carolina after the war, where our author finished his course at school and became a teacher. He followed this profession for ten years and rose to the position of principal of the State Normal School. In 1883 he went to New York, doing work as a reporter on *The Mail and Express* for some months. He returned to Cleveland in the autumn of the same year and entered the office of the "Nickel Plate" Railroad. After a year and a half of railroad office work he began the reading of law in the solicitor's office of the same company, and was admitted to the bar in 1887. In the same year appeared his first story under the auspices of McClure's Syndicate. His reputation as an expert stenographer brought profitable employment in the Cleveland courts, though this interfered to some extent with the practice of law. Meantime, his growing literary aspirations drew him still farther from that profession.

His first story in the *Atlantic Monthly,* "The Goophered Grapevine," brought him immediate recognition, but his most distinct success was "The Wife of His Youth," published in August, 1898. The two stories are representative of the two distinct types of character and of the separate *motifs* which give to his two collections of short stories such well defined individuality and connected interest. Uncle Julius, whose tales entrance the reader of *The Conjure Woman,* is no way inferior to Uncle Remus as a *raconteur,* and the superstitions which give color to his tales are an interesting contribution to the folklore of the South. Mr. Chesnutt works an original field in this series, and works it with a skill not inferior to that of Joel Chandler Harris, Thomas Nelson Page, or James Lane Allen.

Reprinted from *Self Culture* 11 (July 1900): 409–11.

In *The Wife of His Youth* he touches the pathetic chord and portrays with rare dramatic ability the emotions of sensitive human beings under the ban and thraldom of caste. This is a subject on which Mr. Chesnutt feels very deeply. His sympathies are all with the race which suffers so grievously from Anglo-Saxon pride and prejudice both North and South, and he wields his pen as chivalrously in its behalf as ever knight of old wielded his sword.

Mr. Chesnutt has created a favorable impression in platform readings from his own works, and those who have enjoyed the rare pleasure of hearing him interpret his own dialect stories will appreciate the more keenly every new product of his pen. He is working very earnestly, and the readers of *Self Culture Magazine* are to have the opportunity of enjoying, besides the humorous dialect story which appears in the present number, his first serial-story, ["The House behind the Cedars"], a romantic novel of thrilling incidents, of great dramatic interest, of lofty humanitarian aims, and steeped withal in kindly humor, which springs as naturally from his generous spirit as melody springs from the throat of the nightingale.

The Bookman's Table

HUTCHINS HAPGOOD

Stonewall Jackson and *John Brown* are two little biographies which are very creditable to this usually excellent [Beacon Biography Series]. It is no light task to give an adequate impression of an eminent man in twenty thousand words. . . .

The other three books are to a greater or less extent examples of failure in biographical writing. *Sam Houston* is a poorly constructed book. The method is confused and rambling. . . . The faults of *Sam Houston,* however, are faults of workmanship rather than of taste and style. It is the taste and style of the other two books—*Stephen Decatur* and *Frederick Douglass*—which are most noticeable. Each of these books is full of superfluous matter, of unnecessary, voluminous comment and of an uncritical hero-worship. Mr. Brady in his *Stephen Decatur,* comments continually on the character of his hero, and in very much the same way in the different parts, does not, therefore, show the development of the man, ostensibly (as a matter of delicacy, as it were) glides over the faults and takes the obviously "patriotic" point of view, which is fitter for the poet than for the historian. His language is unchosen and conventional, and the commonplace quality of the sentiment sometimes approaches the naïve point. "Oh, the pity of it!" he abruptly writes after the description of Decatur's death, and ends with the following bit of false rhetoric: "High, brave, loyal and splendid, the great commodore stands before me, a glorious figure; and I salute him, 'The Bayard of the Sea.' " *Frederick Douglass* has all the faults of *Stephen Decatur* and others in addition. It has the sentimental vice of trying to make more of Douglass because of his race than as a man he deserved; and the frequent eulogies take so much space that we are justly indignant at not getting more information. He begins by devoting a valuable page to the very questionable statement that "if it be no small task for a man of the most favoured antecedents . . . to rise above mediocrity, . . . it is surely a more remarkable achievement for a man of the humblest origin . . . to win high honours and rewards, . . . to be deemed worthy of enrolment among his country's great men." On the contrary, it seems to me, that at a time when so many able abolitionists were eager to see the good in any black man and give

Reprinted from *Bookman* 12 (November 1900): 297–98.

him all possible help and make the most of his qualities, the possibility of distinction was much greater than under ordinary circumstances; and then, too, Douglass, with his really good abilities, shone more brightly in comparison with the degraded blacks than if he had been white and consequently forced into higher competition.

Talk about Books

A. E. H.

Within two years three books have appeared from the pen of Mr. Charles W. Chesnutt; the first, a volume of sketches in which folk-lore fancies of an eastern people play weirdly against the somber background of bondage in a western land; the second, a collection of short stories in which certain social and moral interests of human nature are treated in relation to a more or less clearly drawn color-line; the third, a novel which shows how human spirits may strive and human hearts may suffer while a great national problem waits for solution. Mr. Chesnutt has gone from strength to strength in these three books, so that we may with confidence expect still more forceful presentation of characters and conditions belonging to his chosen field. The commendation called forth by the earlier volumes will be bestowed with even stronger emphasis on *The House Behind the Cedars*. In the effective portrayal of both main and minor characters and in the management of the apparently slight, really dramatic, incidents by which the tragedy of the story is worked out, mastery of the story-teller's art is clearly shown. The interest of the story centers about John Warwick, the man who has mastered fate, and his sister Rena, the woman who is conquered by fate. Both were born free, apparently white, but under hopeless ban if it is indeed true that a slight admixture of African blood blends with the Caucasian in their veins. The white lover, George Tryon, is the well-born, active young man, sure of his honor in love as in business until his inherited standards and ideals are put to the supreme test. Mr. Chesnutt neither moralizes nor interrogates, but his story speaks to the deeper feelings of his readers.

Reprinted from *Chautauquan* 32 (December 1900): 334.

The Book-Buyer's Guide

Anonymous

The first seven chapters of Charles W. Chesnutt's third book and first novel are disappointing. In the eighth chapter the problem is stated—the ethnological impossibility of intermarriage between the whites and the blacks. The action from this point on is engrossing. Some of the chapters are uncoordinated, but the English is gratifyingly smooth enough almost to hide this defect. Mr. Chesnutt begs the question at the end, but he presents it with a vividness which leaves a logical conclusion in the mind of the reader.

Reprinted from *Critic* 37 (December 1900): 571.

New Books and Periodicals

The House Behind the Cedars is Mr. Chesnutt's second volume, in both of which he deals with a grave racial problem that has yet to be solved by the American people. He is one of the three most distinguished products of his race, having been justly classed with Booker T. Washington and Paul Laurence Dunbar. While Mr. Washington has chosen the educational field and urges his modern ideas in both periodicals and on the platform, Mr. Chesnutt follows in the footsteps of Mrs. Stowe and bases his arguments for the better recognition of his people in the form of romance. So far he has confined himself to appeals for that great portion of humanity which is neither black nor white. Mr. Chesnutt's . . . *The Wife of His Youth* was recognized as the foremost book of its kind by no less an authority than William Dean Howells. Mr. Howells commended the author and his work as promising a future for the colored race. While the author's co-workers in this field have confined their efforts to raising up a distinct colored civilization, Mr. Chesnutt appeals for the recognition of the half-whites by the whites themselves as belonging to their race. He singles out those persons known as octoroons, who bear no visible trace of colored ancestry, and pleads for their social recognition in a very fair manner. This particular phase of the racial question forms the groundwork and mission of *The House Behind the Cedars*.

Rena Walden, the heroine, is a beautiful young octoroon who by an interesting succession of events is taken from her old environment and placed in one of refinement and wealth, where she passes for a white woman. The inevitable happens. She loves and is loved by a scion of an aristocratic Southern family. They become engaged, but before the wedding he learns of her doubly unfortunate birth. The sin of it he can forgive, but not the racial taint in her blood.

Against the girl's deliberate deception the author says nothing. Her brother has gone to a distant town, passed for a white man, made a place for himself, and married a woman of position who never knew of his birth. When Rena came to him for advice as to whether she should confess her secret to

Reprinted from *Chicago Banker* 6 (December 1900): 385–86.

Tryon he told her: "What poor soul is it that has not some secret chamber sacred to itself where one can file away the things others have no right to know, as well as things that one himself would fain forget?"

Such a complication of affairs could only have an unhappy ending, and Mr. Chesnutt works it out well. From the first the story is well constructed and the style and characterization are fresh and original.

An Unfortunate Heroine

ANONYMOUS

If the man with the "high-bred features" who wrote a signature on the register of the hotel at Patesville, N.C., had not assumed the name of Warwick, then most of the troubles the author of *The House Behind the Cedars* describes would not have occurred. The so-called "Warwick" was John Walden, and through his veins ran negro blood. The romance Mr. Charles W. Chesnutt has written is a singularly distressing one. The theme treated is the not uncommon one of a handsome girl, John Walden's sister, who, on account of her negro origin, suffers all kinds of misfortunes. Mr. Chesnutt presents in an interesting way the claims of our colored brethren, and the injustice done them. The question of social inequity is always a difficult one. The beautiful and well-bred Rena always seems to be out of place. George Tryon, the white man, falls in love with her; then by accident learns of her negro origin and breaks with her. Then comes the mulatto Jeff Wain. Mr. Chesnutt has no liking for the man who is neither black nor white. There is no one faithful to poor Rena save Frank Fowler, the negro cooper. He finds Rena by the wayside, ill, bereft of her senses, and he cares for her during her last moments. True is it that: "There are depths of fidelity and devotion in the negro heart that have never been fathomed or fully appreciated." Mr. Chesnutt's two centres, around which the story revolves, are not far enough apart. In the episodes of action the personages are always stumbling over one another. Rena runs away from Tryon, and then falls right into his arms. When the man tries to evade the woman they come once more across each other.

Reprinted from *New York Times Saturday Review of Books and Art* 30 (15 December 1900): 931.

Recent Fiction

ANONYMOUS

The tragedy of *The House Behind the Cedars* is one for which the strongest literary presentation would fail to excite unquestioning sympathetic horror. A great many persons of kind and generous sentiment believe that a white man breaking his engagement to marry a woman who has left him to discover by accident that she has a strain of negro blood, is morally and rationally justified and without dishonor. Such an opinion does not necessarily shield itself behind law or custom, but may be rooted in natural antipathies and a belief that, for the happiness of the individuals and the good of society, such an engagement is better broken than kept. Within the limitations imposed by this point of view, the chief situation of Mr. Chesnutt's novel makes a strong appeal to emotion. While he leaves no doubt about his own judgement or feeling, he does not exaggerate iniquities or hurl recriminations. He probably has but faint hope of upsetting social beliefs, and indeed the catastrophe suggests that such tragedies as the sacrifice of Rena Walden seem to him inevitable, therefore all the more pitiful. As in his shorter stories of his own people, Mr. Chesnutt shows here frank recognition of racial differences, yet, seeing both black and white through a fine literary temperament, is not concerned to set one against the other either for praise or disparagement. He has an easy, educated way of telling a tale; and a special interest in the "negro question" is not at all necessary for enjoying his work, or for deriving an aesthetic pleasure from his sincerity, simplicity, and restrained expression of deep feeling.

Reprinted from *Nation* 72 (28 February 1901): 182.

A New Element in Fiction

Elisabeth L. Cary

Among the works of fiction published within recent years are four or five that appeal to our imagination, not so much through their intrinsic merit, though that is by no means negligible, as through the circumstance of their authorship. They are novels and stories written by two men with more or less negro blood in their veins, each of whom knows the negro race with an accuracy and insight not to be attained by an outsider, and each of whom has recorded his knowledge with the discriminating art so necessary to the complex process known as telling the truth.

One of these writers, Mr. Charles W. Chesnutt, has drawn his material chiefly from the interesting class composed of men and women whose light color, education, and predilections separate them widely from the majority of their fellow negroes and involve them in a dreary and apparently interminable tragedy attending the development of that unfortunate race along the lines of civilization. His novel, *The House Behind the Cedars,* is based upon this tragical element in the life of a young colored girl whose brother has made a place for himself in the very heart of the hostile South by the simple expedient of passing himself off as a white man in a town where he is not known. She becomes engaged to a man who is white in truth, and ignorant of her antecedents, and the climax is reached in his discovery of them. Mr. Chesnutt has a keen, a subtle, and at the same time a curiously impartial appreciation of the insidious forces fighting for mastery in this battle between old and new conditions. A remarkable poise of mind saves him from exaggerating the painful aspect of the unequal combat, and even prevents him, perhaps, from laying sufficient stress upon its poignant and pitiful interest. His reticence is so extreme as to give at times an effect of bareness and plainness ill adapted to win the sympathy of the casual reader. His direct statements of the most appalling circumstances and relations pelt like hailstones upon the resisting surface of the imagination, apparently without making their impression. It is only when we come upon some passage in which discretion is laid aside and comment and criticism freely ventured upon, that we perceive how desirable has been this withholding of the pen from superfluous sentiment.

Reprinted from *Book Buyer* 23 (August 1901): 26–28.

We instinctively resent the weakening of the somber picture of which the details are drawn with relentless realism, by even a single line of inadequate expression, and it cannot be denied that in these infrequent passages Mr. Chesnutt's power of expression plays him false and leaves the weak points in his equipment as a writer open to his enemies.

"If there be a dainty reader of this tale who scorns a lie and who writes the story of his life upon his sleeve for all the world to read," he says in *The House Behind the Cedars*, "let him uncurl his scornful lip and come down from the pedestal of superior morality to which assured position and wide opportunity have lifted him, and put himself in the place of Rena and her brother, upon whom God had lavished his best gifts and from whom society would have withheld all that made these gifts valuable." In this justifiable emotion we get the disconcerting glimpse of oratorical gesture, the suggestion of flourish to be expected in the work of an untrained writer, but not from the author of "The Wife of His Youth." It is in this story, the opening one of a collection for which it provides the title, that Mr. Chesnutt reveals his unusual qualities in all their dignity. The narrative in barest outline is sufficiently poignant. The leading character is a man belonging to a little society of colored people organized in a Northern city and doing everything possible to establish a high standard of education, morals and manners among themselves with the idea of the ultimate absorption of their class by the white race. At an important moment in his career when he is about to marry the woman of his choice, he is confronted by a problem the difficulty of which can be but partially discerned by readers to whom it is a theoretical problem only. The wife of his youth, married to him when in slavery (the bond a legal one only if they choose to make it so after the war), and separated from him by the familiar course of events upon a Southern plantation, reappears seeking her husband. He is comparatively young, and she is old, he is light and she is black, he has become a man of cultivation, she is ignorant. He has almost forgotten her existence, she has been looking for him for nearly a quarter of a century, he by the grace of the intervening years is absolutely safe from recognition unless he shall choose to reveal himself. Shall he acknowledge her or shall he not? is the question Mr. Chesnutt puts and answers. Nothing could be finer than the way in which he answers it, or more moving, when we consider the typical nature of the situation. Nothing could exceed the tenderness with which the old and faithful figure of the wife is brought before us, the soft dialect reproduced with indescribable art and charm. It is interesting to observe also that in this masterpiece of his accomplishment, as in much of his other work, we get the recurring note of comedy, suggesting that the farcical side of life is never wholly concealed from the writer's mental vision. At the most unexpected moments this capricious humor darts out at us, not always potent to amuse us, but always spontaneous and simple like the playfulness of a child. During the old wife's narrative, when she is describing her husband to himself she suddenly lightens the strain of the intense pathos by her frank recognition of his defects: "Perhaps he has outgrown you," the husband remarks to the woman who is still unconscious of his identity, "and climbed up in the world where he wouldn't care to have you find him."

"Indeed, such," she replies, "Sam ain' dat kin'er man. He wus good ter me, Sam wuz, but he wusn' much good ter nobody e'se, fer he wuz one er de trifl'es' han's on de plantation. I spec's ter haf ter supp't 'im w'en I fin' 'im, fer he nebber would work 'less'n he had ter. But den he wus free an' he didn' git no pay fer his work, an' I don' blame 'im much. Mebbe he's done better sence he run erway, but I ain' 'spectin' much."

Closely allied to this purely humorous tendency is an inclination toward a more ironical banter, the subject of it always the idiosyncrasies of the negro race. We see their delight in posing, their easy irresponsibility in matters of veracity, their pompous snobbishness, their swift alternations of gayety and gloom, their thousand and one indications of imperfect development, as clearly as we see their gentleness and kindness, their luxuriant imagination, their amazing possibilities. In a word, we have in Mr. Chesnutt's three books (the third being another collection of short stories called *The Conjure Woman,* and embodying the superstitions and eccentricities of the old-fashioned Southern negro) an ethnological study of extreme importance, such as only a peculiar union of two races and two historic periods could have made possible. Like Janus, the author turns his face toward the future and toward the past, his vision embracing a drama that is over and never to be revived, and a still more mysterious drama that is hardly yet begun.

When we turn from this work, marked by many excellences and also by an indefinable atmosphere of psychological truth in which minor defects are easily lost, to Mr. Paul Dunbar's three books entitled severally, *Folks from Dixie, The Uncalled,* and *The Love of Landry,* we have an entirely different manifestation of a not wholly dissimilar gift. *Folks from Dixie* consists of distinct and brilliant little sketches of the various negro types of the South, most of them extremely amusing, a few of them pathetic, all of them cheerfully impersonal, as if written from the standpoint of an interested but not deeply sympathetic observer, with an eye for all picturesque accidents and an intuitive knowledge of the temperaments he has to portray. Of the imagination and profound sentiment pervading Mr. Chesnutt's writing, making itself most felt where least stress is laid upon it, there is barely a hint. In one tale only, "The Ordeal at Mt. Hope," do we get really below the surface and decipher what the author is thinking about the life which he so faithfully depicts. The story is an account of the efforts of a young negro preacher coming from the North, where he has been educated, to meet the needs of his people at the South, concerning whom he is ignorant. Industrial education is the text from which he gains his inspiration and by which he raises the parish of Mt. Hope from its degradation.

Mr. Dunbar's other books of prose are novels in which the negro race plays no part. They have neither conspicuous merits nor conspicuous defects.

Like Mr. Chesnutt's novels, both are free from any elaboration or complexity of plot, following a single thread of interest from the beginning to the end. Mr. Chesnutt and Mr. Dunbar have, indeed, despite their unlikeness, what we may call a marked family resemblance in this extreme simplicity, and in a certain homeliness of metaphor relieved at times by the quaintness of phraseology characteristic of the race that gives them their great distinction among writers. We feel that much of what they have written could not have been written in just the same way by anyone less than kin to the people whose individuality they bring before us with such remarkable truth. They have added to our complex literature an element entirely new and greatly to be prized. How that element will develop in the hands of future generations is a question that awakens what Mr. James designates as our "moral curiosity."

Charles W. Chesnutt

John Livingston Wright

Of all the tragic and pitiful situations that this queer world can envelop, perhaps the most sorrowful is that of the person who aspires to a condition that he knows he can never reach. Indeed, is it not a blessed fact that most mortals are not beset by absorbing ambitions; are not bitten and stung by the desperate longing for a sphere of life beyond that in which Nature has started them; but can feel reasonably content if they get about so much food, about so much sleep, so much pleasure as is enjoyed by the class out of which they have sprung?

. . . And in the field of pathos and tragedy what volumes are yet to be written of the mental sufferings undergone by those whose mixture of blood makes them almost outcasts! Many and many are the beings who cover with all the carefulness and artfulness possible the fact that they have a touch of negro blood! They wouldn't have the truth known for worlds. Then, here are the thousands who are generally known as of hybrid blood. They are too "light" to be classed as black. Yet, not "light" enough to be accepted as "white." They go through life practically without kith or kin. They feel that they are accounted as not in harmony with the negro race. And the white race will not have them. What shall they do? Whither shall they go?

It is of this hybrid race, the "light-black" or the "black-light," its mental anguish, its pitiful life, its heart-rending experiences, that a subtle and powerful pen has come to treat. Charles W. Chesnutt has a field as a writer that is singularly his own and he is showing himself a master. His work is marked by feeling, understanding, grace and polish. As Mr. Chesnutt himself says of his work, "it lies along the line where the two races come together."

Chesnutt is practically the pioneer in his especial vocation. We have had much writing upon the lighter, the rollicking, not to say, coarser, phase of negro character.

But there is a phase that is too pitifully serious. It is found in the superstitions, in the negro view of religion, in those strange recesses where the black man seeks to commune with what he regards as the Fateful, Omnipotent, Awful, All-Powerful. Here he is most abjectly in earnest. He is groping for

Reprinted from *Colored American Magazine* 4 (December 1901): 153–56.

light. His superstitions, his prayers, his spiritual longings are not altogether comical, ridiculous, nor absurd, as so many writers have apparently thought.

It is the mission of Chesnutt to delineate this deeper and, as was once held, unbelievable, phase of negro character, the spiritual and ambitious element of his nature, and with such analysis and fidelity has he written that today. Charles W. Chesnutt undoubtedly holds the honor of being the Foremost Colored Novelist.

Of his book of nine short stories, entitled *The Wife of His Youth* (1899), a critic gave the following synopsis:

"To Mr. Chesnutt may be given credit of the first publication of a subtle psychology of the negro's spiritual nature, the first actual revelation of those secret depths of the dusky soul which no white writer might hope to approach through his own intuition."

It is but a few years ago that certain short stories began to appear in the *Atlantic Monthly*. No one in the literary world knew aught of the new comer who signed himself "Charles W. Chesnutt," but it was recognized that here was a writer of peculiar power. He was dealing with the weird superstitions, the ominous incantations, and the strange religious system that prevailed among the Southern negro before the Civil War. Much of this life has absolutely disappeared, and these stories were written with such unmistakable knowledge of the subject, with such skill and subtlety that they were conceded to be more than passing "short stories." They were bits of psychological history. Finally, under the title of *The Conjure Woman,* seven of these short stories were put into a book (1899) and Charles W. Chesnutt was fairly before the literary public. Of this first volume of the new author, an able reviewer wrote as follows:

> Unlike many books with negro characters, *The Conjure Woman* was not written expressly to display the author's knowledge of dialect. Nor is this series of sketches an attempt to portray modern negro life. The seven stories are told in dialect—for in what other tongue could Uncle Julius have spoken? Incidentally, too, they disclose the negro of to-day, his ways of living, and his ethical views. But all this is secondary to Mr. Chesnutt's chief aim, which is to make vivid some of the superstitions current in slavery times. Uncle Julius himself only half believes the wonderful tales that he tells. A smile lurks at the corners of his mouth as he narrates them to the Northern purchaser of the run-down North Carolina plantation on which he had been a slave "befo de wah."
>
> The humor of Julius is unconscious. There is no horseplay, nothing to raise a laugh. The humor really lies in his application. Pathos is the other strong element of these sketches, that pathos which is inseparable from a true mirroring of the daily life of the slaves. This comes out strongly in "Sis Becky's Pickanniny" and "The Gray Wolf's Ha'nt."

The writer kept sending his short stories to the *Atlantic,* the *Century, Independent, Outlook* and other standard publications, since the best magazines were eager for him now, and presently nine more short stories composed Chesnutt's second book, *The Wife of His Youth.* The foremost critics were still favorable to him for the volume was characterized as:

> Remarkable for its literary skill and distinction, its dramatic quality, its tactful treatment of a delicate race problem, and above all, for its genuine human feeling.
> Mr. Chesnutt has not only an exceptional knowledge of the negro character and environment, but he has also marvelous subtlety and wisdom in the treatment of their difficulties.

. . . Last year, Mr. Chesnutt published his first novel. It bears the picturesque and charming caption, *The House Behind the Cedars,* and has had excellent fortune. The volume is a satisfactory realization of the literary advance the public was to expect from his *Conjure Woman* and *The Wife of His Youth.* This novel is an effort to present in vivid colors the tragedy that invariably accompanies the "taint" of negro blood when he or she who bears it seeks to exchange "black" society for "white."

The events of the narrative arise in the South soon after the war for the Union, and the principal characters who participate in them are octoroons—a brother who had, in a community where he passed as a "white" man, married into a white family, and a sister whom the brother introduces into his new social sphere. The sister, transplanted from a "black" world into a "white" one (though she exhibited no trace of negro blood other than a wavy quality in her beautiful hair), becomes the object of a white man's devotion. Here is a mine needing—to spring it with terribly explosive effect—only an exposé of the real "color" of the girl and her brother. This is what happens, and the romantic and sociological interest of the novel attaches thenceforth to the consequences of a "white" man's honorable love for a "colored" woman—for only a tragedy could such a love have been, or even now be, in the South.

Some months ago, Mr. Chesnutt came to the Eastern cities to give a series of platform readings from his own writings. The reception accorded him was thoroughly cordial. He was greeted by excellent audiences, and his modest and charming manner merely enhanced the interesting impression to the hundreds who had read his stories.

Now in the prime of his intellectual powers, Charles W. Chesnutt is undoubtedly destined to reach a prominent position in American literature.

There Is No Frigate like a Book

GEORGE HAMLIN FITCH

No writer of the day has been able to bring out more strongly the peculiar conditions of the colored people in the Southern States and the efforts that are being made in their behalf than Charles W. Chesnutt. Himself of negro blood, the author appears to write with a sure hand. In several novels, notably in *The Wife of His Youth* and *The House Behind the Cedars,* he has drawn strong pictures of the harsh legacy left by slavery and of the struggle between the two races that so often ends in tragedy. In his latest book, *The Marrow of Tradition,* published by Houghton, Mifflin & Co., of Boston, Mr. Chesnutt has done his best work. In it he has drawn several characters of unusual interest, and he has painted a graphic picture of social conditions in a Southern city. Major Carteret is a good type of the generous, prejudiced Southern gentleman, who, as editor of his town newspaper, is finally held responsible for the fierce race riot that stains its streets with blood. The story turns on the contrasted fortunes of the Major's wife and of her colored half-sister. Mrs. Carteret hated the colored girl who resembled her so closely that many people mistook one for the other, and this hatred was not softened when the girl married a rich young negro surgeon and helped to found a hospital and school for negro children in her own town. The bitterness of race prejudice is seen in many incidents that serve to define very sharply the gulf that has been widening between the whites and the blacks. Very skillfully the author sketches that fine loyalty to the old master and mistress which was one of the best features of the institution of slavery, but along with it he shows the rank injustice that so often embittered the lives of the innocent children of black mothers and white fathers. The fortunes of the two sisters, who look on each other as enemies, are followed very closely. In the bloody race riot which breaks out in the town the colored sister's child is shot, and the story ends with the white sister begging the woman she has scorned to allow her husband to give medical aid to her own child, who is in danger of death from croup. The story is full of side lights upon Southern life. Several of the characters are full of humor and serve to relieve the gloom of the tragic episodes. The book is the strongest story of the South that has been written in years,

Reprinted from *San Francisco Chronicle,* 17 November 1901, Sunday supplement, 4.

and in its stern unveiling of the sins of slavery it reminds one of *Uncle Tom's Cabin*. In reading it one feels that the author has known something of the miseries of the servile race which he has pictured so movingly. And with this knowledge comes the wonder that with such experience he is so free from bitterness and prejudice.

Talk about Books

A. E. H.

The previous work of Mr. Charles W. Chesnutt, has offered a twofold interest to the reader,—the present pleasure of an unusual story well told and the implied promise of something better yet to come. His new book, *The Marrow of Tradition,* is a triumphant fulfillment of the promise given between the lines of earlier writing, a surprise even to those whose expectation was high for the sweep of power with which an indictment is brought, story-fashion, against the code of manners, morals, ethics, even against the every-day logic of simple justice, as practised by certain American citizens, proud of their culture and refinement against other American citizens, neighbors and sometimes kinsmen. The life of a Carolina town as expressed on political and social questions is pictured as in a mirror. The play of elemental feeling among the various characters grouped according to their connection with the life of the little Theodore Felix Carteret shows sympathetic understanding of the universal human heart and a master's skill in lifelike expression of that heart's instinctive feeling. The fearless portrayal of the unreasoning passion with which mob violence wreaks its blind fury makes the book a valuable contribution to the social studies on our latter-day civilization. If it shall avail to give the advocates of "white supremacy," which being interpreted means setting at naught constitutional enactment and the administration of justice, a glimpse of themselves as others see them, it will have rendered honorable and welcome service in a time of desperate need.

Reprinted from *Chautauquan* 34 (December 1901): 327–28.

A Psychological Counter-current
in Recent Fiction

WILLIAM DEAN HOWELLS

. . . I wish that I could at all time praise as much the literature of an author who speaks for another colored race, not so far from us as the Japanese [pictured by Onoto Watana in *A Japanese Nightingale*] but of as much claim upon our conscience, if not our interest. Mr. Chesnutt, it seems to me, has lost literary quality in acquiring literary quantity, and though his book, *The Marrow of Tradition,* is of the same strong material as his earlier books, it is less simple throughout, and therefore less excellent in manner. At his worst, he is no worse than the higher average of the ordinary novelist, but he ought always to be very much better, for he began better, and he is of that race which has, first of all, to get rid of the cakewalk, if he will not suffer from a smile far more blighting than any frown. He is fighting a battle, and it is not for him to pick up the cheap graces and poses of the jouster. He does, indeed, cast them all from him when he gets down to his work, and in the dramatic climaxes and closes of his story he shortens his weapons and deals his blows so absolutely without flourish that I have nothing but admiration for him. *The Marrow of Tradition,* like everything else he has written, has to do with the relations of the blacks and whites, and in that republic of letters where all men are free and equal he stands up for his own people with a courage which has more justice than mercy in it. The book is, in fact, bitter, bitter. There is no reason in history why it should not be so, if wrong is to be repaid with hate, and yet it would be better if it was not so bitter. I am not saying that he is so inartistic as to play the advocate; whatever his minor foibles may be, he is an artist whom his stepbrother Americans may well be proud of; but while he recognizes pretty well all the facts in the case, he is too clearly of a judgment that is made up. One cannot blame him for that; what would one be one's self? If the tables could once be turned, and it could be that it was the black race which violently and lastingly triumphed in the bloody revolution at Wilmington, North Carolina, a few years ago, what would not we excuse to the white man who made the atrocity the argument of his fiction?

Reprinted from *North American Review* 173 (December 1901): 872–88.

Mr. Chesnutt goes far back of the historic event in his novel, and shows us the sources of the cataclysm which swept away a legal government and perpetuated an insurrection, but he does not paint the blacks all good, or the whites all bad. He paints them as slavery made them on both sides, and if in the very end he gives the moral victory to the blacks—if he suffers the daughter of the black wife to have pity on her father's daughter by his white wife, and while her own child lies dead from a shot fired in the revolt, gives her husband's skill to save the life of her sister's child—it cannot be said that either his aesthetics or ethics are false. Those who would question either must allow, at least, that the negroes have had the greater practice in forgiveness, and that there are many probabilities to favor his interpretation of the fact. No one who reads the book can deny that the case is presented with great power, or fail to recognize in the writer a portent of the sort of negro equality against which no series of hangings and burnings will finally prevail. . . .

News in the World of Books

Katherine Glover

In at least one respect, [*The Marrow of Tradition*] is one of the most remarkable [novels] that has ever reached the writer of these lines. It is a book that is worthy of being called remarkable because it is on a line that is totally at variance with those on which all that come from this section have been writing. True it has its heroes and its heroines, its exciting scenes and its dramatic interest and the author's style, as have all other books, but above all is the general plan of the story itself, which is different.

If the author was endeavoring to have his book read because of its uniqueness of plot he will doubtless succeed with some, but this will not be a compliment to him nor to his ability. If he has attempted to arouse the emotions of his readers he has succeeded so far as any southerner who is unfortunate enough to run across the book is concerned.

Chesnutt should print his picture with his book in order to allow his readers to know whether he is a white man or a negro. This is said with all seriousness. After reading the work it is impossible to tell. The preponderance of evidence suggests that he is a negro. It really makes a difference, because it is possible to understand how an educated, ambitious and disgruntled negro could have written the book, but it is not possible to understand how a white man of sound mind in his sober senses could have been guilty of the book upon which Chesnutt places his name.

If a negro wrote the book his work may in these days be overlooked; if a white man wrote the book it should be calmly but promptly dismissed with contempt. Report has it that Chesnutt lives in North Carolina. If that be true it is hardly probable that his neighbors are proud of him.

The scene of the book is laid in Wilmington, N.C., which is called "Wellington" in the story, and the plot revolves around the Wilmington riot at the time that the whites of North Carolina made their determined and successful effort to wrest the state from negro rule, into which it had been given by the thoughtlessness of the populists in aiding the republicans of the state in the election of a fusion ticket.

The story tells how the white people plot against, oppress and persecute the negroes. Every white man in the book is made to be a villain, and the

Reprinted from *Atlanta Journal,* 14 December 1901, sec. 2, p. 4.

white women are made to be designing creatures without a semblance of honesty or any other virtue that is esteemed in the south. All the white characters in the story, both men and women, spend their time in figuring out problems that will aid them in persecuting the negroes. Wills are hidden to keep negroes from obtaining property, white men marry negro women and the latter are kept from receiving social or legal recognition. The laws of both the courts and the church are ignored in this downtrodding of negroes. The climax of the story is the murder of an old white woman by her nephew for the purpose of obtaining money. He purposely leaves evidence behind him that will point to the guilt of a negro servant of his grandfather. The negro narrowly escapes being lynched. This latter is natural. What story of this kind is complete without a lynching? The white characters all come from fine old families, and are in society.

And then the negroes of the book! They are all depicted as absolutely honest and upright. There is no such thing as a negro villain in Chesnutt's book. They are either meek and lowly, accepting the persecutions of the whites without a word, or they are depicted as elegant ladies and gentlemen. These negroes the author holds to be superior to the white persons of his book, and they treat the attempted persecutions of the whites with contempt.

In the end all the white characters are made to grovel in the dust before the negroes, and one of the white women does in fact prostrate herself before a negro physician, hugs his knees in her sorrow and begs him to forgive her for her treatment of him and his wife, which he does after much persuasion and pleading. Finally the white woman goes into the house of the negro and puts her arms around the negro wife of the physician, greeting her familiarly as "sister."

The whole story is ridiculous, it is not unusually well written and it is easy to predict oblivion for it. The American people are too sensible to waste their time upon such silly rot.

Novel Notes

F. M. H.

Whatever faults Mr. Chesnutt may have, insincerity is not one of them. He is intensely in earnest in everything that he writes. Four novels are now to his credit, in each one of which he pours out his feelings on the subject of racial conditions in one form or another. The question of what to do with the negro is the dominating theme with Mr. Chesnutt. He loves the race which is in part his own, and he idealises it whenever he can. There is much to criticise in *The Marrow of Tradition,* but somehow the pathos of it all makes one a little blind to its faults. . . .

Almost all the white personages of the book have very black souls. They destroy wills, thereby depriving the blacks of their rights. They hamper them in their progress. They do not give them any chance at all. The book is undoubtedly an exaggeration, as *Uncle Tom's Cabin* was an exaggeration. But in spite of this, and deep down beneath style and construction and climax, one recognises the under-lying strength of a man who thinks. It is the cry of one human soul against the great injustice which he feels is being done his race.

Reprinted from *Bookman,* 14 (January 1902): 533.

Literature

ANONYMOUS

[*The Marrow of Tradition* is a] novel written apparently by a man with a racial grievance, and for the purpose of exposing conditions rather than to gratify any literary instinct in the author. All the traditional virtues of the negroes are contrasted with all the reputed vices of Southern whites with the lively distinctions of a mulatto imagination. And the result is vigorous and vindictive to a remarkable degree. Mr. Chestnut will do well to remember that in order to make his enemy appear thoroughly despicable, he should be treated with a show of fairness instead of a malignant hatred, which always excites sympathy. He tips the scales of justice too far in favor of his own indignant emotions. But these, however justified by the fact of his own experience, are never safe foundations to build a romance upon. They are too rash, too personal. And art at least is no respecter of persons. There is no color line in its eternal fairness.

Reprinted from *Independent* 54 (March 1902): 582.

More Fiction

ANONYMOUS

The medium of fiction is used by the author of *The Marrow of Tradition* to make a statement of existing relations between negroes and whites in several of the Southern States. Plot, characters, and situations are all conceived with this object in view. The combination of fiction and fact is not perfect, but it is closer and smoother than in most of the current purpose novels. The characterization of both races is excellent, and to many of the scenes the author has given a genuine dramatic touch, the touch that thrills and convinces. In statement of conditions and in criticism Mr. Chesnutt is calm, acute, and just—surprisingly so when he discusses lynch law and disfranchisement by the "grandfather clause" and other ingenious methods. The tone of his argument throughout is admirable, and the expression often eloquent. While his novel is inferior to his short stories in form and method, it shows more vigorously than they do the capacity for cool observation and reflection.

Reprinted from *Nation* 74 (20 March 1902): 232.

Note and Comment

T. THOMAS FORTUNE

Charles W. Chesnutt will probably have a higher and more permanent place in prose writing than Dunbar will have in poetic writing, mainly because the former writes in a higher atmosphere of American thought and action than Dunbar. All of Mr. Chesnutt's conceptions are high, and his work has the polish and the finish which usually characterize high ideals. His education and environments were different from those of Dunbar, as well as his ancestry. Dunbar thinks and writes as an American black man, for the most part, and there is always present in his work the melancholy note and the tropical profusion which are a part of the African nature, as far as I understand it, while Mr. Chesnutt thinks and writes more as an American, from the broad stand point of country rather than of race. In *The Marrow of Tradition,* for instance, it would not be easy to tell that Mr. Chesnutt is an Afro-American by any bias disclosed in his work, while a white man could not have written Dunbar's *Sport of the Gods,* simply because he could not feel and think in the language of that book. Mr. Chesnutt shows in his literary work that he takes very lofty ground, without limitations of race, which is not always true of Southern writers of the present school. The broad, humane note so often struck by Mr. Chesnutt is present [as] much in the work of Joel Chandler Harris and Frank L. Stanton, and appeals to the [human] race rather than to a race group.

Reprinted from *New York Age,* 20 July 1905, 6.

Literary Notes

ANONYMOUS

An interesting contribution to the literature of the race problem will be Charles W. Chesnutt's novel, *The Colonel's Dream,* which Doubleday, Page & Co. will bring out September 7. Mr. Chesnutt tells here the story of a man born in the South who has made a fortune in New York and returns to his old home to live. He speedily finds himself involved in an ever-complicating set of circumstances, owing to the conflict of his feeling for the negroes with that of the community, and this culminates in one final dastardly outrage that convinces him he cannot live in the South. The book is singularly temperate in its dealing with these complex questions, but it presents the negro's side with all the force of quiet reality.

Reprinted from the *Cleveland (Ohio) World-News,* 17 August 1905, 6.

Books of the Week

ANONYMOUS

It has not been an infrequent occurrence in the history of American fiction that a writer of excellent short stories fails lamentably when he attempts to write a novel. Mr. Chesnutt a few years ago printed a volume of short stories which deserve to rank very high in their own class of literature. The present book, however, is loosely constructed and is often prolix and dull. [*The Colonel's Dream*] deals with some of the recent problems of the race question in the South, and has references to the peonage system. Some of the characters are fairly well drawn, and occasionally the dialogue is clever and interesting; but, taken all in all, the book is not as successful as one could wish, and certainly is distinctly inferior to the author's earlier work, as seen in the two volumes called *The Conjure Woman* and *The Wife of his Youth*.

Reprinted from *Outlook* 81 (30 September 1905): 278.

A Shattered Arcadia

ANONYMOUS

Rather thinly disguised as a novel, [*The Colonel's Dream*] sets forth conditions in certain Southern States which affect the black man and his chances, as the author, a negro, sees them. The part of the South selected is that in which the system of contract convict labor exists and is subject to more or less administrative abuse. The author finds the abuse due to the descendants of the overseer class, who have gained wealth by hook or crook, rather than to the descendants of the old slave owners. The trouble with the latter is that in spite of a kindly feeling toward the negro they are too supine to interfere.

The story tells of an ex-Confederate officer who came to New York as soon as the war was over and there grew rich and lost touch absolutely with his native State and village. Ill-health takes him South after twenty years. . . . He sets about getting justice for a worthless negro who has offended the local low-born money lender and magnate, and so gets cordially hated by that rascal and the element he controls. He tries to build a cotton mill to be run, without skilled labor, but he doesn't know how to adjust the niceties involved in employing workmen of two colors. He proceeds upon theories and forgets facts. In short, with the best intentions in the world he makes a mess of things. Finally he shakes the dust of the place from his feet and returns to the North, hopeless of overcoming the prejudice of that class of whites which is in political control, equally hopeless of any help from the other whites.

It must be acknowledged that the author does not spare the faults of the negro any more than he spares those of the white man—and in both cases many of his pictures are true.

Reprinted from *New York Times Saturday Review of Books* 54 (16 September 1905): 605.

Books New and Old

ANONYMOUS

. . . Having already signalized his devotion to the colored people through the writing of several novels in their defence, Mr. Charles W. Chesnutt plunges still more deeply into the problems of the present with *The Colonel's Dream*. His latest story is both truth and fiction. It explains the disadvantages under which a reformer labors, and it evidences the prejudices encountered by anyone—no matter if he be Southern born—who attempts to better Southern conditions in ways that do not accord with time-honored principles and prejudices. *The Colonel's Dream* is well written and well told, and it should accomplish a mission of enlightenment that the South and the Southerners sorely need. It is especially worthy of attention and consideration in these days of the rampant and intolerant Thomas Dixon, Jr. The volume is issued by Doubleday, Page & Co., who, in the exigencies of the bookmaking trade, are also the pervasive Dixon's publishers.

Reprinted from *Boston Evening Transcript,* 21 November 1905, part 2, p. 12.

The Colonel's Dream

Nahum Daniel Brascher

Charles W. Chesnutt has added another book to his already neat list of productions. He has previously written *The Conjure Woman, The Wife of His Youth and Other Stories, Frederick Douglass, The House Behind the Cedars,* and *The Marrow of Tradition.*

The name of his latest book is *The Colonel's Dream,* which came from the press fresh and beautiful this fall. The story is one of race conditions in the south as found by Colonel Henry French, a native white southerner who in early life came to New York City where after years a great fortune was made.

When Colonel French returns south for his health with his motherless son and heir, Philip, it was only with the expectation of remaining a few months. But finding an opportunity for vast improvement in Clarendon, and being of a charitable disposition, he begins a noble work of reformation and rejuvenation. Alas, his broad views of life clash with the narrow, prejudiced ideas of his native town people. Around the colonel's efforts to "take the light" is woven a charming story of love, romance and tragedy.

Charles W. Chesnutt has written with such vigor and earnestness as appeals to the mind of high ideals. He has told a story that will be interesting to children generations ahead. He has written with remarkable fairness bringing to light strange notions of the oppressor and hidden virtues of the oppressed. Charles W. Chesnutt knows human nature "from the cradle to the grave" and his characters are true to life in all their actions and words. In every page or two he injects bits of fine philosophy on the race situation in America and the dullest reader will ask the question, "Does he not reason well?"

Charles W. Chesnutt, the leading author among colored people, is misunderstood by a great many people and consequently unjustly criticised. The criticism is for the most part local and due to the fact that Mr. Chesnutt is not a "mixer," in the political sense of that term. He is seldom seen at any gatherings among colored people and, for this reason, there is an impression that he is an enemy of the race and not a friend. Nothing could be farther from right. The race has no truer friend or better informed member on current conditions

Reprinted from *Cleveland Journal,* 9 December 1905, 1.

than Charles W. Chesnutt. Whether he is a "mixer" or not, is none of our business. Every man has a right to choose his company. Mr. Chesnutt is a national man and not a local man; our esteem for him should be based on his national faithfulness to our cause. Through all his books, essays and addresses, as a member of the "Committee of Twelve," and in divers quiet ways, Mr. Chesnutt is loyal to the race. He works while others sleep and talk. Above all Mr. Chesnutt is a real man; he has brains, a great heart and ministering hands. His fame, as is often the case, does not exceed his true worth and ability; on the other hand, his modesty limits his fame. His books should be in every home.

The New Books

ANONYMOUS

In this quiet but intense story, *The Colonel's Dream,* Charles W. Chesnutt sets forth powerfully many of the problems that confront the South to-day. He writes as one who feels deeply every situation he describes, yet at no time does he become a fanatic. . . .

The story is wonderfully interesting, and so full of important information that it should be read by every student of sociology and economics in the country. Its pictures of mill life in the South, of the convict-labor situation, negro problems, and the prejudices of the more ignorant people against the new ideas are vividly impressed upon the reader's mind. But Mr. Chesnutt is not altogether pessimistic. With loving sympathetic touch he depicts the more enlightened people whose whole interest is unselfish in behalf of their own country. The book is a tragedy, but the author would have us believe that better things are bound to come.

Reprinted from *Indianapolis News,* 20 January 1906, 7.

INTERVIEWS AND
PERSONAL STATEMENTS
◆

An Aboriginal Author

Pauline Carrington Bouvé

It was Coquelin, the great French actor, who said once in epitomizing the art of acting: "Coquelin the man must stand behind and match Coquelin the actor."

Sometimes in literary art the detachment of the personality of the writer from the personality of his created people seems as distinct as though the reader saw the dual process of the man standing behind the author and directing the work step by step.

This ability to eliminate oneself, for the time being, from the actual conditions of personal environment is an evidence of creative power, the first element of that rare force, genius. Now to entirely appreciate how much or how little of personal experience is transcribed in a work of fiction, it is necessary to know something about the writer and his life, so after reading a man's book there is a natural desire to read the man himself.

Some months ago there appeared in the *Atlantic Monthly* a short story, entitled "The Wife of His Youth," which was signed by Charles W. Chesnutt.

The story, which touches upon a new phase of American life in fiction— the phase of the cultured "colored" man—was a strong one, possessing ethical and dramatic qualities, and showing the development of a distinct social system among us—a system of educational and social culture among that class of American citizens who belong in varying degrees of shade and color, to both the white and black races. In reading of the educated man's struggle, when, just on the eve of proposing marriage to a woman of his own strain of blood, and who, like himself, had received the illumination of knowledge, an old negress comes to the village, and making her way to the "colored gentleman's" house, asks him to help her in her search for her husband, who was lost in slavery days by a change of ownership. The old woman has searched for the husband, in whose faith and loyalty to herself she has no shadow of doubt, for nearly thirty years. The man of property and position hears her story and knows that the crucial moment of his life has come. He is bound by no legal obligation to this old negress, for with freedom came a new dispensa-

This interview, conducted on 14 August 1899 at the Hotel Oxford, Boston, Massachusetts, is reprinted from *Boston Evening Transcript,* 23 August 1899, 16.

tion of the law regarding slave marriage; she would never guess his identity, hidden under a new name and totally different conditions. He thought of the other woman, the woman who was so fitted to be his helpmate and companion, and then he looked at the bent form of the woman before him, who had spent so much of life in search of him, she believed to be as faithful as herself—and there was a battle in his soul.

Out from the strife he comes the victor, and the following night he bids his friends come to an entertainment, where he tells the story of the faithful soul, puts the vital question of the husband's duty to his guests, and then, while there is a confused murmuring of sympathy among his audience he rushes in and presents to them, the half-dazed, half-frightened old black woman as "The Wife of his Youth."

Hearing afterward that Mr. Chesnutt was comparatively a young man and that a slight strain of negro blood flowed in his veins, the writer of this article was gratified recently to meet this new author.

Mr. Chesnutt's keen gray eyes had at times the grave, severe expression that is seen in certain portraits of Gray Eagle and Sitting Bull, and it was when discussing certain conditions of Southern life that this look of calm, but concentrated bitterness was most noticeable. After watching these gray eyes it does not seem strange when the author speaks of the traditional Indian blood he inherits from an aboriginal ancestor, for Mr. Chesnutt is a descendant of three races, and owes, perhaps, a great deal of his mental and temperamental personality to this treble mixture of bloods.

Although the percentage of Caucasian blood is overwhelming, still, there are certain mental qualities belonging to him that may be attributed to the admixture of tropical and aboriginal race traits.

One cannot read *The Conjure Woman* without appreciating the humor of the author of these tales, and if one knows anything of the Southern negro, the distinctively negro humor is recognized, for the Afro-American invariably possesses humor—sometimes of the subtlest sort. To this same sixteenth, or thirty-second degree of "colored" blood much of the dramatic quality of his work is due, for the negro is naturally dramatic as well as humorous.

Looking at this man it would be quite impossible to detect that little drop of African blood if he himself did not claim it with a quiet dignity, that had the royalty of truth in its simple candor.

"You know my connection with the race," he said, speaking of his pictures of slave life. "For many generations there has been no slave, but the pressure against free negroes, as all who had a trace of African blood were called, became very great in 1858–9, and my mother's family moved to the West. My father, who was of the same strain as my mother, followed her and married her in the West, where I was born. I went back to Georgia [i.e., North Carolina] when I was ten years old, and stayed there until I was twenty-five, so that I know the life there in all of its aspects."

A shadow crossed his face as he spoke, and for a moment he was silent.

"You see," he continued, a bitter smile playing about his lips, "the words of the negro song, 'All Coons Look Alike to Me' express the sentiment of the whole people of that section. The educated man or woman, no matter what his character and ability may be, who has one-sixteenth, or one-thirty-second, or one sixty-fourth part of African blood is counted a negro and is debarred from the privileges of a white man or woman."

"Of course, Mr. Chesnutt," suggested his hostess, "wherever the race that has been for generations dominant suddenly finds the dominated race, whether fit or unfit for the promotion, put upon the same basis with it, there will be friction. Don't you think that a good deal of the hostility between the races in the South is due to the too sudden change in the conditions of both?"

Mr. Chesnutt reflected before he answered slowly: "Yes, that change was too sudden. It is natural enough that there should be a struggle for social supremacy—that would adjust itself—but there should be no legislation providing different coaches on the car lines for the colored passenger, if he be clean and decent; different places for him everywhere."

"That seemed hard, certainly; and yet in certain sections where the colored population greatly outnumbers the white it is not altogether unnatural for the minority to take extreme measures against the encroachments of the majority, especially when that majority is, considered collectively, inferior in intelligence. In some instances this knowledge of superiority of numbers breeds an aggressiveness of manner that is hard to bear."

"I know that," replied Mr. Chesnutt to some such consideration. "I am a Southern man and I have felt with the Southern white man. I have his blood too, and one of the pleasantest recollections of my life in Georgia [i.e., North Carolina] is the expressions of regret that I heard when I gave up teaching there. One white man told me he regretted my departure because he believed that I had been and would be the means of establishing a clearer understanding and a better relation between the black man and the white man, but the conditions there do not tempt a man of intellectual aspirations to stay."

When Mr. Chesnutt was asked what he thought would be the ultimate result of the situation, he answered gravely: "It is hard to tell; but there is already a 'race war' begun—spasmodic and intermittent, but in progress—but the victory will come only through education and enlightenment. Looking at the general masses of my people, the case seems almost hopeless, but when a great movement once begins, it may halt, but it does not retrograde."

The expression, "my people," sounded oddly from the lips of this man, but one was reminded of Booker Washington's words, "It takes 100 per cent of Caucasian blood to make a white American. The minute it is proved that a man possess one-hundredth part of negro blood in his veins it makes him a black man; he falls to our side. We claim the 99 per cent of white blood counts for nothing when weighed against 1 per cent of negro blood." Only in this case the 99 per cent of white blood was claiming the 1 per cent of negro blood.

Another question led to an interesting talk about his literary work. "I wrote my first story when I was an impressionable lad of fourteen years old, and it was published in Georgia [i.e., North Carolina] by a colored man who had a paper there. That was the beginning of my great desire to write, but I had to get my living and so I became a stenographer—but always I had the hope of some day turning to a literary life. I thought, too, that perhaps I would write better when I was older, so I was content to plod on."

As court stenographer, Mr. Chesnutt earns a very large salary in Cleveland, O., where he lives, and his quiet, patient pursuit of a business life, when his tastes and abilities made the field of letters appear so alluring, is not only an example to a host [of] less gifted aspirants to literary fame, but is evidence of the possession of sound judgment and that uncommon gift of "common" sense.

"I'll tell you how I happened to write the first story in 'The Conjure Woman' series," he said. "My father-in-law had made enough to buy one of the old Southern houses—a town house it was—but there was a great garden around it. One day an old colored man came to work in this garden, and as he leaned on his hoe he told me of an old man who had anointed his bald head with scuppernong grape-juice, which had the remarkable effect of producing a luxuriant crop of hair. This hair grew with the rising sap of the scuppernong vines and fell away periodically with the shrivelling of the grapes, occasioning a yearly repetition of the anointing process. That was the foundation of 'The Goophered Grapevine.' With the exception of 'The Wife of His Youth,' for which I had a slight basis in reality, as far as the hero of the story went, and 'The Goophered Grapevine,' all of my stories have been works of the imagination."

It is this purely imaginative quality of his work that makes Coquelin's words recur to the mind. Here is an educated, cultivated man, able to thoroughly project himself into the experiences and feelings of the most unlettered, superstitious old negro men and women of the slave regime. Portraying with the effect of actuality a period of which he can have no personal knowledge, he is Chesnutt the man, behind Chesnutt the author. The genius of the conception of these stories is directed by the skill of judgment, and when these two work together they produce art.

Take, for example, the story of "Sis' Becky's Pickaninny." There is humor and pathos and imagination in that story, and it, like all the tales in which the "Conjure Woman" figures, is hung on the thread of old John's [i.e., Julius'] diplomacy and shrewdness, for each one of his stories is told with a distinctly personal end in view.

This is a bit of characterization that is both strong and subtle: " 'Julius,' I observed, half to him and half to my wife, 'your people will never rise in the world until they throw off these childish superstitions and learn to live by the life of reason and common-sense! How absurd to imagine that the forefoot of a poor, dead rabbit, with which he timorously felt his way along through a life surrounded by snares and pitfalls, beset by enemies on every hand, can promote happiness or success, or ward off failure of misfortune!' "

And Princess [i.e., Julius] rises to the occasion: "Dat's w'at I tells dese niggers roun' heah. De fo'-foot am got no power. It has to be de hin'-foot, suh—de lef' hin'-foot er a grabe-ya'd rabbit, kilt by a cross-eyed nigger on a da'k night in de full er de moon." The pathos of little Moses, who, when his mother "wuz tuk' 'way 'mence ter git res'-less, en bimby w'en his mammy didn' come he sta'ted ter cry for her, en finally he des cried an' cried 'tel he cried hisself ter sleep," is infinite, when one knows that the mammy was sold and could never come back. But the "Conjure Woman" is at hand with her conjurings, and she effects "Sis' Becky's" return by sending a hornet to sting the legs of the master's horse, for which "Sis' Becky" had been traded, and by causing "Sis' Becky" to fall sick, by which means the horse and the woman were traded back again, and little Moses had his mammy once more.

"I have another lot of stories," confided the author at last, "and I want to find a title for them. 'The Wife of His Youth' is to be the leader, and I want a sub-title that will show that these stories touch upon the contact of the two races in many ways as parent and child, teacher and pupil, and other relations. And I have just signed a contract with Small, Maynard & Co., for another book—'The Life of Frederick Douglass,' for the Beacon Biography Series," he added. "I have promised it this fall." The life of Douglass by one who belongs to his race will be an interesting book apart from its value as a biography, for in this work Mr. Chesnutt will unconsciously set the mark not only of his ability in a new line of literary effort, but of his present and future attitude toward the two races to which he belongs. Despite the fact that Mr. Chesnutt shows a bitterness sometimes toward the white people of the South, he is evidently a man who has a broad vision of things, and his book on Frederick Douglass will be one of the most significant ones to be issued by Small, Maynard & Co. Together with *The Future of the American Negro,* by Booker T. Washington, to be issued by the same firm this fall, it will inaugurate a new line of thought among colored men of letters. These two books, like these two men, may be regarded as "signs of the times," and they and their works deserve very careful consideration.

That there are evils in the South and terrible evils, too, cannot be denied, but both races have had much to bear. The remedy for such evils lies in following the advice of the wisest man of his race: "Christianize the white man, christianize the black man!"

[Chesnutt's 'The Negro in the South': A Summary]

ANONYMOUS

M̲r̲. Charles W. Chesnutt, author of the popular story book *The Conjure Woman* and other fascinating Negro stories, was the speaker on the above topic, and in introducing this absorbing theme he said that the Negro problem was an old one, having its beginning when the first slave was landed at Jamestown, and men of a race whose instinct and struggle had always been toward liberty and light planted beside themselves on the soil of the Old Dominion, representatives of a vastly older race, widely divergent in outer aspect and in general training and development, a race crushed and brutalized by an unfriendly climate and by centuries of superstition and oppression at the hands of other men. The new-comers at that time were but raw material as compared with their still despised descendants. They were entirely alien in blood, speech, religion, thought; in everything but their common humanity, which was not recognized, and to all intents and purposes they were alien in that. It was said that the Negro was alien in religion, but that did not count; for they were believed to have no souls. Many crimes had been done in the name of religion, yet religion had never been made a pretext for the enslavement of the Negro race, though it had been used as a cloak to cover and uphold it. The Spaniards enslaved the Indians and baptized them in the name of God, and ostensibly for the good of their souls. The English colonists imported slaves solely from greed. There was nothing good about slavery. Conceived in iniquity, born in sin, cradled in shame, drowned, it had been believed, in blood, and buried beneath the Constitutional Amendments, slavery still rears its noisome head and poisons the air of this republic. That it did not destroy the republic and humanity, too, was due, not to any good in slavery, but to the spark of divinity in human nature, which even slavery could not entirely extinguish, and was due vastly more to the hosts who went forth from the hills of New England, from the Atlantic seaboard, from the plains of

This summary of a speech delivered by Chesnutt at some time between 6 and 12 August 1899, during the sixth annual Greenacre Conference in Eliot, Maine, is reprinted from "The Greenacre Season," *Boston Evening Transcript,* 20 September 1899, 16.

the West, and gave their lives for liberty and union, one and indissoluble, then and forever!

The problem of Negro labor in slavery had, from time to time, taken on many phases. One point early considered was: Would the labor be profitable? Then: How could enough of it be obtained; how could such a thing as slavery be made to harmonize with free institutions? These difficulties were early foreseen and discussed, for the principles underlying the Constitution as applied to the white and colored races were involved and presented serious difficulties. In time it was hoped the traffic in slaves would die out, and provision was made for its abolition. This, however, encouraged domestic slave herding. The abolition movement took form at a very early date, and assumed substantial proportions as the influence and arrogance of the slave power increased. What the abolitionists undertook was to arouse the conscience of the nation—or of the North, that part of the nation which had a conscience on the subject. In this they succeeded; the public conscience was aroused. The great statesman whose fame is bound up forever with the abolition of slavery said, long before he had the power to change existing conditions, that this country could not permanently remain one-half in slavery, the other half free. And what he thus declared eventually became a fact. The civil war took place, which resulted in the preservation of the Union and the abolition of slavery. But with the emancipation of the Negro race came a harder problem still. To make them free required a few years of agitation, a few years of war, the stroke of a pen. Then came the problem of the future—to protect them in the freedom thus bestowed, which was sure to be combated, not only by the sullen hostility of the vanquished South, but also by the powerful inertia of the social forces so long turned against them. To become a citizen in fact as well as in name, was the problem, and as an attempt at its solution the Negro was given the ballot, and every State was forbidden by Constitutional enactment to pass any laws that would curtail his rights by reason of his race and color. A further problem presented itself: to make those Constitutional amendments operative. That problem is now before the bar of public opinion, and has to be dealt with, and like problems are rapidly coming to the front. The question of paramount importance at present is whether or not the results of the Civil War shall be nullified by race prejudice, embodied in the form of laws and judicial decisions which are contrary to the Constitution and principles of our Government, or whether these principles shall be steadily adhered to until, under their beneficent operation this vexed question shall be finally and correctly solved.

Ever since the Constitutional amendments affecting the status of the emancipated Negroes had been on the statute book there has been a struggle going on. The North had struggled to enforce them, while the South had tried in every way to nullify them. To many it had long been a source of surprise and pain that the North should permit the fruits of the war to be destroyed. As slavery was the real cause of the war, the South could have been placated by yielding to it on that point.

It seemed as if a united country now as then meant to let the South work its will with the Negroes, and to pat it on the back, praise it for the wisdom and humanity with which it bears its burden—a burden of its own seeking, to which it fondly clung and fought to maintain, in spite of the effort made by its apologists to saddle the responsibility on their ancestors.

The lecturer then cited various facts illustrative of the conditions now prevailing throughout the Southern States, and the means adopted by the white population to circumvent the constitutional amendments which conferred the rights of citizenship on the Negroes and entitled them to the same political rights enjoyed by the whites. Quoting the well-known aphorism that "no man is good enough to govern another without his consent," he showed how the colored race is practically unrepresented and governed against its consent. In some States the system of registration and certificates, in others property and educational qualifications, are such that the Negroes have no show whatever. In justification of the irregularities practised against colored voters the cry of Negro domination had been used, while in one notable case a candidate for governor had run on a platform, the chief plank in which was opposition to Negro education.

Humiliating discriminations against Negro citizens were common everywhere, and the right to hold office by a colored citizen had been challenged in a blood-curdling manner in more than one recent instance. So bitter had Southern prejudice towards the Negro become that in some of the largest cities of the South conditions prevailed almost as bad as in South Africa, where a Kaffir cannot walk on the sidewalk.

Chief among the remedies for all these anomalies and unjustifiable conditions was education, and this was accomplishing a great deal and would accomplish much more. And it must be all-round education of the hand, brain and heart. The hands of the Negroes must be trained that they may be able to live and be adequately rewarded for their labor and be something more than servants; their brains should be educated that they might cultivate true manhood, and strive for the highest excellence. Nothing should be unattainable for any free man in a free country.

Alluding to lynching, Mr. Chesnutt declared that all such sanguinary and diabolical methods were based on falsehoods and misconceptions. As a remedy for crime such brutal exhibitions were worse than the disease they sought to stamp out. Lynching must be stamped out by force of public opinion, voiced in every way, and by legal enactment, for the Constitution as it now stands is no barrier against these deeds of murder.

The North can do much to put an end to all these things. It has done a great deal in the past and it must not allow its interest to die. It is quite apparent to every unbiased mind that the South cannot be trusted. The people in the Southern States are too blinded by prejudice. By prejudice even good men are overborne and reason blindly from false premises. The North can influence and direct public opinion because it is entirely unbiased, while the South is too sensitive. In a word, there was only really one remedy for all the racial trouble, and that was the enjoyment of equal justice by both races and equal opportunity in every phase and circumstance of life. Better days were about to dawn for all, but when the Negro race in this country was allowed to enjoy its privileges and its rights just as the white race does, then it would be discovered that the Negro had been undeservedly misunderstood and cruelly wronged for sins he had never committed.

Mr. Chesnutt at Work

Max Bennett Thrasher

I recently met Mr. Charles W. Chesnutt, the well-known writer of Southern stories, in Alabama, and enjoyed the opportunity which I had there to learn something of his methods of work.

Mr. Chesnutt told me, when I asked him about his literary work, that his stories, as a general thing, develop gradually in his mind, sometimes taking a long time in the process, and that even then they are usually written out slowly. "The March of Progress," which was printed in the *Century,* "was an exception to this, though," Mr. Chesnutt said. "I wrote the whole of that out one forenoon, copied it on the typewriter in the afternoon, and sent it off that same evening.

"Sometimes I write a story out complete, as I think at the time, and yet, after it is completed I have a feeling that it lacks something. Perhaps the story may lie around for months before I am able to tell just what there is about it that does not satisfy me. It was that way with 'The Wife of His Youth,' probably the most widely read story I have written—my best story, some people say. I wrote that story, complete, as I thought, and then it lay in my desk for a year because I was not satisfied with it. As the story was written then I made the little old black wife appear to her prosperous and cultured husband as he was getting ready to entertain a company of guests, before whom he eventually acknowledged her.

"There was something lacking in the story, though, and I knew it. One evening after dinner, when the manuscript was more than a year old, I picked it up and read it through, and at once there came to me a knowledge of what was wanting. The story lacked the element of conflicting interest. I saw that there ought to be another woman in it, by contrast with whom the little old black wife should be made more striking. I wrote the story over, and wrote into it the second woman—the young, educated, attractive woman whom the man was to have married if 'the wife of his youth' had not returned. Then the story was complete.

This interview, conducted during the tenth annual Tuskegee Negro Conference, 20–21 February 1901, is reprinted from *Boston Evening Transcript,* 4 September 1901, 13.

108

"I have been greatly interested," Mr. Chesnutt continued, "to see how women feel about the way in which I made that story end—whether they think that the man ought to have acknowledged the unattractive old woman to whom he was bound by ties of sentiment and gratitude, rather than by legal bonds, or whether he did not owe it as a duty to himself to marry the other woman, the one who was a much more fitting mate for him, and who, with himself, was entitled to happiness. I have asked a good many women, cultivated, intelligent women, what they thought, the man ought to have done—whether they thought he did right. The answer which I get almost invariably seems to depend on the age of the woman who gives it.

"Young women, those who are under twenty, reply promptly and enthusiastically, 'He did just right. He ought to have acknowledged the little old black wife whom he had loved years before, and who had loved and sought him through all those years.' Women between twenty and thirty stop to consider the question. They usually say, finally, in a deprecating sort of way, 'Ye-es, I think he did right. I suppose he ought to have married the woman he did.' When I ask the question of a woman over thirty, she does not take any more time for reflection than the very young woman did. She says promptly, 'He did not do right. He made a mistake. He ought to have married the other woman.'

"In all these cases I take it there is sympathy for both women in the story but the woman under twenty, looking out upon life through the rose-colored glasses of youth, allows her sympathy for the older woman to predominate. She thinks the young woman in the story can afford to be generous, because she has life before her, and one chance to marry will not matter to her among the many she will have. The woman of twenty-five has had more experience with life. She has learned that chances to marry well are not frequent enough so that any ought to be passed over without careful consideration. The woman who is still older reasons that a good matrimonial opportunity should not be let slip for anything."

Mr. Chesnutt had been spending some time in the Southern States getting impressions and collecting material which will doubtless find expression in future writings. "I was surprised," Mr. Chesnutt said, "after an absence of many years from the South, to note the fidelity with which my mind had retained the impressions received in youth. The old 'conjure woman' and 'conjure man' whom I have made it a point to unearth in my travels bear a faithful resemblance to old 'Aunt Peggy, the conjure woman,' and the roots and herbs still have in the minds of at least a few surviving relics of the past, their ancient potency. I interviewed a conjure doctor who furnished me with 'a hand,' a charm of mysterious significance which he guarantees will bring me good luck, and which he assured me would keep me 'from losing my job.' I also secured a genuine rabbit's foot, from a rabbit killed in a graveyard on a dark night. This is the 'real thing,' and not the spurious imitation which is marketed in Northern cities."

Mr. Chesnutt visited the neighborhood and the old house in which the scene of his recently published novel, *The House Behind the Cedars,* was laid. He says that the house has fallen somewhat into disrepair, and of the cedar hedge which once surrounded it only one tree remains. He secured a photograph of the house, and brought away with him as a souvenir a twig from the sole surviving cedar.

Mr. Chesnutt says that he was deeply interested in the study of racial conditions during his Southern sojourn, and while he saw much to depress, he also found here and there, and especially in the educational work at Tuskegee and elsewhere, good grounds for hope that some time, in some way, a just and rational solution may be found for the many and vexed problems which have grown out of slavery and the contact of the two races which make up in so nearly equal numbers the population of the South.

I asked Mr. Chesnutt, one day, if it was because he had a vein of superstition in his nature that he wrote such weird stories. "No, indeed," he said. "I have not a bit of superstition. Sometimes I think that I have not even a proper amount of reverence. My first literary ventures were along the lines of short stories for newspaper syndicates, and squibs for *Puck* and such papers as that. I wrote about Southern themes because at that time I was comparatively fresh from the South, and was more familiar with things there than at the North. I soon found that there was a greater demand and a better market for writings along that line.

"I remembered a remarkable yarn which had been related to me by my father-in-law's gardener, old Uncle Henry, to the effect that the sap of a pruned grapevine rubbed on a bald head in the spring would produce a luxuriant growth of hair, which would, however, fall out when the sap in the vine went down in the fall. To the creative mind this was sufficient material for the story 'The Goophered Grapevine.' That story resulted in several other involving the same idea, for instance, that of the man who was turned into a tree and by mistake chopped down, sawed into lumber and built into a house, which was ever afterwards haunted by the spirit of the unfortunate man. Those dialect stories, while written primarily to amuse, have each of them a moral, which, while not forced upon the reader, is none the less apparent to those who read thoughtfully. For instance, the story of the cruel master, who, through the arts of the conjure woman, was transformed into a slave and given for several weeks a dose of his own medicine, resulting in his reformation when he is restored to his normal condition of life, teaches its own story."

Mr. Chesnutt is an attorney by profession, and has been connected with the Ohio bar and the courts of the State for fifteen years. He lives at Cleveland. He has two daughters who graduated from Smith College last June, and two younger children. He spent ten years of his youth and early manhood as a teacher in North Carolina, and his daughters have fitted themselves for the work of teaching. Mr. Chesnutt's works have a deserved popularity, it seems to me, from the strength and delicacy with which they treat certain phases of the race question which are often avoided or neglected by other writers from lack of knowledge or want of courage. He writes frankly, and at the same time in a manner which commands attention and respect. He represents a new field in fiction. From his special knowledge, sympathy, and personal interest in his subjects, he is perhaps better qualified to discuss them than any other writer now before the American public.

ESSAYS AND ARTICLES
◆

[Chesnutt as a Mulatto Figure]

ALBERT BUSHNELL HART

. . . Many people say that there is no negro problem in the South—only a mulatto problem—and it is true that the mixed bloods are almost a third of the negro race, that they furnish most of the educated negroes and almost all the leaders, and that the lightest of them—often indistinguishable from whites to the uneducated Northern eye—feel passionately the injustice of excluding them from the society and the opportunities of the whites. Of the four negroes who have achieved literary distinction in the last decade, Washington, Du Bois, Chesnutt and Dunbar, only the last named is a pure negro. . . .

Reprinted from "Conditions of the Southern Problem," *Independent* 58 (23 March 1905): 644–49.

[A "Talented Tenth"]

Alfred Holt Stone

Here, then, it seems to me, is the first great problem of this people, the problem of the moral elevation of the masses, whose status will at last determine that of the race as a whole. No man is further than I from attempting to discount the value to a race or nation of its exceptional few—the wealth it has in the possession of a "talented tenth." But, after all is said and done, the race, it seems to me, must stand or fall by the character of the masses of its people. It cannot be saved by the poetry of Dunbar, by the novels of Chestnutt, by the music of Coleridge-Taylor, by the surgical skill of Williams, or by the culture and intellect of Du Bois. . . .

One of the greatest needs in the equipment of those who discuss the Negro from a distance is a better knowledge of the real Negro, and nothing would so promote this knowledge as a recognition of the fact that in crediting his race with the achievements of its mulatto element they but becloud the question. How may we reasonably hope to know what is best to be done for the Negro until we first truly grasp the facts of his moral and intellectual possibilities and limitations, as well as needs? And how may we hope to do this under our present method of treating the subject?

In reviewing the work of the most distinguished writer accredited to the Negro race—though [Chesnutt] has scarcely a visible trace of Negro blood in his veins—the foremost living American author [William Dean Howells] has used this language: "They [referring to the mulattoes] need not be ashamed of the race from which they have sprung, and whose exile they share; for in many of the arts it has already shown, during a single generation of freedom gifts which slavery apparently only obscured." This criticism develops the very foundation of the theory upon which all such discussions are based, and which we have referred to above—that the Negro is an undeveloped, not an inferior race—that in all essential particulars the white man and the black are by nature equally endowed. Thus is placidly ignored the truth that the Negro is one of the oldest races of which we have any knowledge, and that its very failure to develop itself in its own habitat, while the Caucasian, Mongolian,

Reprinted from *Studies in the American Race Problem* (New York: Doubleday, Page, 1908); 206, 428–31.

and others have gone forward, is in itself sufficient proof of inferiority. Conveniently disregarding the fact of the persistence of a racial status fixed several thousand years ago, they tell us that forty years of freedom are not enough to develop "gifts which slavery apparently only obscured."

The years, both of slavery and of freedom, passed by the Negro on this continent constitute but an insignificant span in the life of that people; yet if we blot out the achievements of the American Negro who has passed through slavery, what has the race left to boast of? And if we but go one step farther, and from the achievements of the "American Negro" obliterate all that the American mulatto has accomplished, what ground indeed would be left to those whose sentiment and sympathy have apparently rendered them so forgetful of scientific truth?

In 1902 a movement was inaugurated in Congress looking to the investigation of the suffrage laws of the various states. No attempt was made to conceal the real purpose of the movement and even though we go so far as to credit the proponent of the measure with honesty of opinion as to its necessity, what must be thought of his wisdom, and of the point of view from which he would have the so-called "investigation" made, when he himself, in the face of the facts of history and the experiences of recent years, calmly affirms that "there is no doubt that the Negro is capable of unlimited development," and declares his belief in the virtue of "participation in politics" as a means of "uplifting the race"? Yet such is our looseness of expression in discussing this question, that to challenge either the wisdom or correctness of such views is to hear, as their sole support, a recital of the achievements of "famous men of the Negro race," while, as a matter of fact, the names brought forward are merely those of well-known mulattoes—from Murillo's favourite pupil, down to Crispus Attucks, Benjamin Banneker, Douglass, Bruce, Lynch, DuBois, Washington, Chesnutt, and others.

I am well acquainted with the exceptions that may be urged here, but this is a plea for greater scientific precision in laying the foundations of race-problem study and treatment, and the student of Negro ethnology knows that these exceptions are more apparent than real. The traffic which furnished slaves to the Americas and the West Indies was no respecter of ethnic distinctions, and, while the great majority of those brought over were pure Negroes, through it a few of the higher types of Fulah and other stocks found their way into foreign servitude, and with their blood have occasionally transmitted some measure of their ability. Othman dan Fodio, the poet chief of the Fulahs, was no more a Negro than was Othello, nor was Abdul Rahaman, the Moorish chief, who was a Mississippi slave in the early part of the last century. Thus it will not answer to cite such sporadic examples as the revolutionary leadership of Toussaint L'Ouverture, the political cunning of Elliott, or the ballads of Dunbar.

Just as the crossing of the Spaniard upon the Indian has given us the mestizo of Central America and Mexico, so the blending of white and Negro blood has given us a type which combines some of the racial characteristics—good and bad—of both its progenitors. But in a sane treatment of the race question this hybrid can no more be regarded as typical of the potentiality of the Negro than can Porfirio Diaz be considered an index to the "undeveloped ability" of the native Mexican Indian whose blood he has in part inherited. It would certainly seem to be the part of wisdom frankly to recognise the Negro's own racial characteristics and honestly study them. But this cannot be done so long as in our consideration of the problem of what is best to be done for him we continue to confuse the great mass of American Negroes with the exceptional mulatto types, and point to the accomplishments of the latter as evidence in support of crass and preconceived notions as to the capacity of the former. . . .

The Mulatto: Problem of Race Mixture

RAY STANNARD BAKER

MOST LEADERS OF THE NEGRO RACE ARE MULATTOES

This much I know from my own observation: most of the leading men of the race to-day in every line of activity are mulattoes. Both Booker T. Washington and Dr. DuBois are mulattoes. Frederick Douglass was a mulatto. The foremost literary men, Charles W. Chesnutt and William Stanley Braithwaite, are mulattoes; the foremost painter of the race, H. O. Tanner, whose pictures have been in the Luxembourg, and who has been an honour to American art, is a mulatto. Both Judge Terrell and his wife, Mary Church Terrell, who is a member of the School Board of Washington, are mulattoes. On the other hand, there are notable exceptions to the rule. W. T. Vernon, Register of the United States Treasury, and Professor Kelly Miller of Washington, D. C., one of the ablest men of his race, both have the appearance of being full-blooded Negroes. Paul Lawrence Dunbar, the poet, was an undoubted Negro; so was J. C. Price, a brilliant orator; so is M. C. B. Mason, secretary of the Southern Aid Society of the Methodist Church.

Full-blooded Negroes often make brilliant school and college records, even in comparison with white boys. It is the judgment of Hampton Institute, after years of careful observation, that there is no difference in ability between light and dark Negroes. I quote from the *Southern Workman,* published at Hampton:

> The question as to the comparative intelligence of light and dark Negroes is one that is not easily settled. After long years of observation Hampton's records show that about an equal number of mulattoes and pure blacks have made advancement in their studies and at their work. While it is probable that the lighter students are possessed of a certain quickness which does not belong to the darker, there is a power of endurance among the blacks that does not belong to their lighter brethren.

Reprinted from *Following the Color Line* (New York: Doubleday, Page, 1908), 173–74.

As to the comparative accomplishment of light and dark Negroes after leaving school, the evidence is so confusing that I would not dare to enter upon a generalisation: that question must be left to the great scientific sociologist who will devote a lifetime to this most interesting problem in human life.

[More Caucasian than African]

Albert Bushnell Hart

In slavery days almost all the discussion of race questions came from the Whites, Southern or Northern. Now, there is a school of negro controversialists and observers, several of whom have had the highest advantages of education and of a personal acquaintance with the problems which they discuss, and thus possess some advantages over many white writers. About twenty years ago George W. Williams published his "History of the Negro Race in America" (1883), which, though to a large degree a compilation, is a respectable and useful book. Another writer, William H. Thomas, in his "The American Negro" (1901), has made admissions with regard to the moral qualities of his fellow Negroes which have been widely taken up and quoted by anti-Negro writers. Charles W. Chesnutt, in several books of collected stories, of which "The Conjure Woman" (1899) is the liveliest, and in two novels, "The House Behind the Cedars" (1900) and the "Marrow of Tradition" (1901), has criticised the rigid separation of races. No man feels more keenly the race distinctions than one like Chesnutt, more Caucasian than African in his make-up. One of the best of their writers is Kelly Miller, who has contributed nearly fifty articles to various periodicals upon the race problems; and in humor, good temper, and appreciation of the real issues, shows himself often superior to the writers whom he criticises. The most systematic discussion of the race by one of themselves is William A. Sinclair's "The Aftermath of Slavery" (1905), which, though confused in arrangement and unscientific in form, is an excellent summary of the arguments in favor of the negro race and the Negroes' political privileges. . . .

Outside of newspapers the Negroes have access to the written works of members of their own race, which are at the same time a proof of literary capacity and a means of teaching the people. Of course it is always urged that such men as Booker Washington, the educator and uplifter; Dunbar, the pathetic humorist; Chesnutt, author of stories of Southern life that rival Joel Chandler Harris and Thomas Nelson Page; DuBois, who in literary power is one of the most notable Americans of this generation; Kelly Miller, the keen satirist;

Reprinted from *The Southern South* (New York: D. Appleton, 1910), 14–15, 325.

and Sinclair, the defender of his people—prove nothing as to the genius of the races because they are mulattoes; but they and their associates are listed among the Negroes, included in the censure on negro colleges, and furnish the most powerful argument for the education of at least a part of the race. Few men of genius among the Negroes are pure blacks; but it is not true that the lighter the color the more genius they possess. So far as the effects of a prolonged and thorough education are concerned, those men from any point of view prove that the mulattoes, who are perhaps a fifth of the whole, are entitled to a thorough education. . . .

Charles Waddell Chesnutt

BENJAMIN GRIFFITH BRAWLEY

Charles Waddell Chesnutt, the foremost novelist and short story writer of the race, was born in Cleveland, Ohio, June 20, 1858. At the age of sixteen he began to teach in the public schools of North Carolina, from which state his parents had gone to Cleveland; and at the age of twenty-three, he became principal of the State Normal School at Fayetteville. In 1883 he left the South, engaging for a short while in newspaper work in New York City, but soon going to Cleveland, where he worked as a stenographer. He was admitted to the bar in 1887.

While in North Carolina Mr. Chesnutt studied to good purpose the dialect, manners, and superstitions of the Negro people of the State. In 1887 he began in *The Atlantic Monthly* the series of stories which were afterwards brought together in the volume entitled *The Conjure Woman*. This book was published by Houghton, Mifflin & Co., the firm which published also Mr. Chesnutt's other collection of stories and the first two of the three novels which he has written. *The Wife of His Youth and Other Stories of the Color Line* appeared in 1899. In the same year appeared a compact biography of Frederick Douglass, a contribution to the series of Beacon Biographies of Eminent Americans. Three novels have since appeared, as follows: *The House behind the Cedars,* in 1900; *The Marrow of Tradition,* in 1901; and *The Colonel's Dream,* in 1905.

Mr. Chesnutt's short stories are not all of the same degree of excellence, but the best ones show that he possesses mastery of the short story as a literary form, an art the requisites of which are completely uncomprehended by many of the younger aspirants for literary fame. One of the very best technically is "The Bouquet." This is a story of the devotion of a little Negro girl to her white teacher, and shows clearly how the force of Southern prejudice forbids the expression of simple love not only in a representative home, but even when the object of the devotion is borne to the cemetery. Most famous of all these stories, however, is "The Wife of His Youth," a simple work of art whose intensity is almost overpowering. It is a tale of a very fair colored man who, just before the Civil War, by the aid of his Negro wife, makes his way from

Reprinted from *The Negro in Literature and Art* (n.p., 1910), 21–28.

slavery in Missouri to freedom in a Northern city, Groveland (Cleveland?). After the years have brought to him business success and culture, and he has become the acknowledged leader of his social circle and the prospective husband of a very attractive young widow, his wife suddenly appears on the scene. The story ends with Mr. Ryder's acknowledging before a company of guests The Wife of His Youth. "Uncle Wellington's Wives" tells the story of a simple colored man who was attracted to the North by the marvellous stories he had heard of freedom of every sort, only to find after a disastrous experience as a coachman and as the husband of an Irish wife that he would have been a great deal better off if he had never strayed from Patesville, N.C., from the side of the faithful Milly, to whom he hastens his return. "The Sheriff's Children" is a tragic tale of the relations of a white father with his illegitimate colored son. Such stories as these, each setting forth a certain problem, working it out to its logical conclusion, excluding extraneous matter, and, as in "The Bouquet," selecting the title from the concrete means used in working out the theme, reflect great credit upon the literary skill of the writer.

In *The House behind the Cedars,* a story of Patesville (Fayetteville?), a young man, John Warwick, who might easily be mistaken for a white person, while still a boy, desirous of becoming a lawyer, goes from North Carolina to South Carolina and advances very rapidly in his profession, being to all intents and purposes a white man. The House behind the Cedars is the home in Patesville, N.C., in which John's mother and his sister Rena live. The story is chiefly concerned with the love affairs of Rena Walden. Across the street from the home, in a very humble little house, lives a young Negro, Frank Fowler, who loves Rena almost to the point of worship. He works with his father in a cooper shop at his home. When Rena was a little girl she used to play in his shop. One day a tool accidentally cut her arm, and her mother began to insist that she stay at home; but before long Frank came back into favor by saving the girl from drowning. Rena is now a young woman. Her brother from South Carolina appears on the scene one day to say that his wife is dead, and that he wishes to have her come and care for his little son. Rena now crosses the color-line, going first to spend a year in a school in Charleston, and later to her brother's home in Clarence, where she easily takes her place as the most beautiful and admired young woman in the town. Before long she becomes engaged to a young white fellow, George Tryon, whom John Warwick, as well as he could do so without disclosures, has sounded on the Negro question. A day or two before her marriage, however, Rena learns that her mother is sick, and she can not rest without going to see her. She departs very suddenly, leaving notes for her brother and for Tryon, saying to her lover that she has gone to visit an old and dear friend who has suddenly become very sick. Business now calls Tryon himself to Patesville, which is only a few miles from his own home in North Carolina. Of course he finally learns that Rena is colored and—rejects her. For two weeks the girl is very sick. When she recovers she gets employment as a school-teacher in the country a few miles from Patesville. This position she secures through the instrumentality of a man distantly connected with her by family ties, one Jeff Wain, a rather coarse, thick-set, hard-drinking mulatto who lives not far from the school, and whose past life, especially his marital relations, has been very questionable. Rena lives at his home, ostensibly under the care of his mother. She soon finds to her horror that her old lover, Tryon, lives very close to her school. She is of course afraid that her presence so near him, after his rejection of her, might be misunderstood. At this point, however, the love of young Tryon returns so nobly and passionately that he is anxious to have an interview with Rena. He sends her a letter; but of course, as she tells him in reply, she did not know that she was coming to his vicinity, and it is impossible for her to have anything to do with him without having a false construction put upon her conduct. In the meantime Rena is fearful of advances from another source, from the brutal Wain in whose home she is staying. One day this man attempts to caress her, and she flees for protection to the home of the old minister, Elder Johnson. One day, coming home from school, who should she find in front of her in the forks of the road but her two pursuers, Tryon and Wain? She turns aside and runs into some bushes just as a terrific storm bursts. Frightened nearly to death, she loses consciousness, and the rain beats upon her. She is found later by a party led by Elder Johnson, and taken home, where she is delirious. After a day or two, in her fever she dresses and slips out of the house, setting forth on the road to Patesville. After wandering for a considerable distance and going a few steps from the main road, she falls. Tryon attempts to find her, but fails. Frank Fowler, however, with his mule and cart, is more successful. In the last chapter, which is really a powerful piece of writing, Rena acknowledges the faithful love of Frank. Tryon, whose love for the girl has now overcome all scruples, goes to The House behind the Cedars only to find crepe on the door. The novel is Mr. Chesnutt's most sustained treatment of the subject for which he has become best known, that is, the delicate and tragic situation of those who live on the border-line of the races.

In *The Marrow of Tradition* the main theme is the relations of two women, one white and one colored, whose father, the same white man, had been married to the mother of each. The white woman is Mrs. Carteret, the wife of Major Carteret, editor of *The Morning Chronicle,* the chief daily of the Southern town of Wellington; and the colored woman is the wife of Dr. Miller, the chief colored doctor in the town. This novel touches on almost every phase of the Negro problem. Dr. Miller rides home from the North, and this leads to a discussion of the matter of railway accommodations for Negroes. Major Carteret's only baby gets sick, and a specialist is called from Philadelphia: this man has been one of the teachers of Dr. Miller, and his desire to have his old pupil assist him brings up the matter of Negro doctors attending white people. A local Negro newspaper comes under the ban in the campaign for white supremacy, and something of the tremendous influence wielded by a representative newspaper such as the *Chronicle* is shown forth. An old aristocrat's degenerate grandson, Tom Delamere, commits robbery, and by giving some coins to a trusted servant of his father's, Sandy by name, he shifts to this Negro the responsibility for his crime. Sandy barely escapes a lynching, but in the face of the worst exhibits the fineness of character possessed by some of the servants under the old regime, refusing to name his betrayer. Josh Green is a Negro giant who, when the election riot breaks out, pleads with both Watson, the colored lawyer, and Miller, the colored doctor, to become the leader of his little set of brave men. The last chapter, in which in the midst of slaughter and tumult Major Carteret's only baby again becomes very ill, and in which, no white doctor being near, both the Major and Mrs. Carteret implore Miller to come and save their child, is slightly extravagant; still it shows how in the face of eternity and God even Southern prejudice must fall. This novel is more bitter than others of Mr. Chesnutt's works. The Wellington of the story is very evidently Wilmington, N.C., and the book was written immediately after the race troubles in this city in 1898. It is a powerful plea for the Negro, but it is too much of a novel of purpose to satisfy the highest standards of art. The difference between *The House behind the Cedars* and *The Marrow of Tradition* is the difference between a simple little novel that gathers strength as its story advances and a work that was evidently intended to set forth to the American people almost every form of injustice visited upon the Negro in the South; accordingly the one is almost as far above the other artistically as *The Scarlet Letter* is above *Uncle Tom's Cabin*.

Better than either of these novels, however, is *The Colonel's Dream*. This story is somewhat more pleasant too. It does not undertake to discuss the specific problem set forth in the life of Rena Walden, but considers somewhat more generally, and at the same time artistically, matters of interest to the main body of Negro people, for instance, lynching and the convict lease system in the South, especially the latter. It is all a sad story of the failure of high ideals. Colonel Henry French is a man who, born in the South, achieves success in New York and returns for a brief season of rest in his old home, only to find himself face to face with all the problems that one meets in a backward Southern town. He becomes especially interested in the injustice visited upon the Negroes in court, with the resultant evils of the convict camps, and in the matter of the employment of white children in the cotton-mills. His dream is best stated in the author's own words: "He dreamed of a regenerated South, filled with thriving industries, and thronged with a prosperous and happy people, where every man, having enough for his needs, was willing that every other man should have the same; where law and order should prevail unquestioned, and where every man could enter, through the golden gate of hope, the field of opportunity, where lay the prizes of life, which all might have an equal chance to win or lose." It is needless to say that Colonel French encounters opposition to his benevolent plans, opposition which finally sends him back to New York defeated. Mr. Chesnutt writes in simple, clear English, and works with a high sense of art. He is to-day the foremost man of the race in pure literature, and his methods might well be studied by younger writers who desire to treat in the guise of fiction the many searching questions that one meets in the life of the South.

The Negro's Contribution to Literature, Music, and Oratory

WILLIAM H. FERRIS

Professor Albert Bushnell Hart's recent article in the *Independent*,[1] upon the Negro question, has attracted considerable attention. His position as a well-known professor of Harvard University, his reputation as an authority upon American history and the calm, judicial tone of his article commended it to thoughtful students of the so-called Negro problem.

The significant feature of his article to me lay in the fact that only four colored men loomed up before him in large enough proportions and commanded his attention to the extent that he could regard them as four colored leaders.

For three of these men, their title to fame lies wholly and solely in the fact that, in their poems, stories and essays, they have portrayed and revealed the soul-life of the Negro in a way to appeal to the American mind. One of these men partly won his reputation as a writer, who could tell the story of his life in a manner to command the attention of the country.

So we can say, then, that the Negro race, in America, has only produced four writers of note and distinction, and none of these has produced an immortal work that will go ringing down the ages and will ring forever in the hearts of men. In the judgment of posterity, these, with the possible exception of DuBois, will probably be classed as talented writers rather than men whose insight into the human soul and inimitable manner of uttering their thoughts ranks them as men of genius. These four Negro writers are W. E. Burghardt DuBois, Paul Lawrence Dunbar, Charles W. Chestnutt and Booker T. Washington. And of these, DuBois is the most gifted literary artist. And it must not be forgotten that we have other colored writers almost as talented as DuBois, Chestnutt and Dunbar.

I will endeavor to show . . . why the Negro, with his rich artistic equipment and endowment, has produced so many good talkers and so few good writers. I will endeavor to show why the four men whom Professor Hart characterizes as the "four Negro leaders" do not leap the chasm or bridge the gulf

Reprinted from *The African Abroad*, vol. 1 (New Haven, Conn.: Tuttle, Morehouse and Taylor, 1913), 255–56, 270–73.

that separates the clever from the great writers; and by a brief study of Homer, Dante, Goethe, Milton, Shakespeare and Carlyle, what the Negro writer must do, if he would not only artistically uncover to our gaze the inner life of the Negro, but would touch the throbbing heart of humanity, feel its pulse beat as it keeps time to the footsteps of the Almighty, as he writes his eternal laws of righteousness in the movement and march of human history, and would create those unforgetable phrases which haunt the memory and linger in our minds like—

> Music, when soft voices die,
> Lingers in the memory,
> Odors, when sweet violets sicken,
> Live within the sense they quicken. . . .

Chestnutt's "Conjure Women," "The Wife of His Youth," "The House Behind the Cedars," and "The Marrow of Tradition" are splendid productions. He is an interesting writer. What he lacks is a quality that even few white writers possess, and that is the quality possessed by Carlyle and Victor Hugo, the ability to paint heroes and heroines in flesh and blood colors. That is why we can't shake off the spell of Carlyle's French Revolution, or Hugo's famous battle picture of Waterloo. It may be questioned whether he has the vivacity of Dumas, the fascinating elegance of a Hawthorne, or the psychological insight of a George Eliot. But it is in the vivid word-painting qualities that Chestnutt is mainly lacking. Still his "Marrow of Tradition" is a burning protest against American race prejudice. And Chestnutt can not only feel and think and write as a Negro, but he can feel and think and write as an American citizen. In his "Conjure Women" Chestnutt's insight into Negro character and plantation philosophy and plantation life reminds us of Dunbar's unique poems and stories. But there is this difference: while Dunbar has preserved for us the relics of slavery days and interpreted the soul-life of humble colored people, of plain men and women, Chestnutt has in "The Wife of His Youth," "The House Behind the Cedars" and "The Marrow of Tradition," mirrored the thoughts, sentiments, and feelings of the intelligent and refined Negro, who has a large mixture of Caucasian blood in his veins. Chestnutt seems to have caught the spirit of "Uncle Tom's Cabin" and revealed the pathos in the lives of cultured colored people who are not full-blooded Negroes. Chestnutt possesses many of the characteristics that made Ik Marvel famous. A vein of true and sincere sentiment runs through his stories. And at times he almost moves us to tears.

Dunbar is a poet of genius when he writes in Negro dialect and reproduces the soul-life of the plantation Negro, and only a poet of high talent when he writes in pure English, and deals with the complex problems of modern life. He has not the passionate and commanding personality of a Byron, the aërial imagination of Shelley or the delicate beauty of phrase of a

Keats, but what he mainly lacks is the reflectiveness that characterizes the poetry of Goethe, Browning, Wordsworth, Tennyson, Clough, and Arnold. Still Chestnutt and Dunbar are in the front rank of living American writers, though I doubt whether they have grasped the significance of modern doubt regarding the verities of religious faith.

But we should not be too searching in our criticism of Dunbar and Chestnutt nor blame them for not doing what they did not aspire to do. Dunbar's first volumes were entitled "Lyrics of Lowly Life" and "Lyrics of the Hearth Side." He did not attempt to solve "the Riddle of the Universe." He essayed a humbler task, and he has succeeded admirably well. The same may be said of Chestnutt.

Dunbar's humor plays around his subjects just as lightly as the dancing sunbeams kiss the waving leaves. There is uproarious fun and merriment let loose in the "Party." In the "Ante-Bellum Sermon," we have the typical old-fashioned plantation preacher portrayed. There is a quaint fusing of Scriptural wisdom, history, and eloquence, with plantation philosophy and humor and nonsense in that sermon. And Dunbar has made live in that poem the John Jasper type of Negro preachers, which is passing away even in the South; while in "When Malindy Sings," "The Corn Pone's Hot," and a few other poems, there is an exquisite blending of humor and pathos and lofty sentiment that captivates us. We begin these poems with a smile, but before we know it we have left terra firma and are sweeping into the cloudlands of fancy and reverie upon the wings of Dunbar's genius. Dunbar's supreme greatness as a poet lies in the fact that he has done for his people what Robert Burns has done for the Scotch. He has touched the life of the lowly Negro with the transforming breath of poetry, transfigured it with the magic wand of his halo-shedding imagination and revealed its humor, its pathos, and hidden meaning.

In the poems of Phillips Wheatley, Rev. James David Corrothers, Frances Harper, A. A. Whitman, William Stanley Braithwaite, Mrs. Fordam, Still, Webster Davis and McGirt, in the books of William C. Nell, George W. Williams, Edward Blyden, Frederick Douglass, Alexander Crummell, Archibald Grimke and Dr. William Sinclair, in the novels of William Wells Brown, Frances Harper, Sutton Griggs, we see talented colored writers successful in clothing their thoughts in an attractive literary garb. I believe that Archibald Grimke's Lives of Garrison and Sumner are brilliant works. But these talented writers are not quite as unique and individual in their style and manner as Chestnutt, Dunbar and DuBois.

And now we come to the great DuBois. Both Dunbar and Chestnutt have artistically uncovered to our gaze the inner life of the Negro, but DuBois has done this and something more. He has not only graphically pictured the Negro as he is, but he has brooded and reflected upon and critically surveyed the peculiar environment of the Negro, and with his soul on fire with a righteous indignation, has written with the fervid eloquence of a Carlyle. If one desires to see how it feels to be a Negro and a man at the same time, if one desires to see how a sensitive and refined Negro mentally and spiritually reacts against social, civil and political ostracism, if one desires to see a Negro passing judgment upon his civil and political status, and critically dissecting American race prejudice as with a scalping knife, he must go to DuBois.

Note

1.   See "[Chesnutt as a Mulatto Figure]," in this volume.

The Negro in Literature

WILLIAM STANLEY BRAITHWAITE

The development of fiction among Negro authors has been, I might almost say, one of the repressed activities of his literary life. A fair start was made the last decade of the Nineteenth century when Chesnutt and Dunbar were turning out both short stories and novels. In Dunbar's case, had he lived, I think his literary growth would have been in the evolution of the Race novel as indicated in "The Uncalled" and the "Sport of the Gods." The former was, I think, the most ambitious literary effort of Dunbar; the latter was his most significant; significant because, thrown against the background of New York City, it displayed the life of the Race as a unit, swayed by the currents of existence, of which it was and was not a part. The story was touched with that shadow of destiny which gave to it a purpose more important than the mere racial machinery of its plot. In all his fiction, Dunbar dealt with the same world which gave him the inspiration for his dialect poems. It was a world he knew and loved and became the historian of without any revising influence from the world which was its political and social enemies. His contemporary, Charles W. Chesnutt, was to supply the conflict between the two worlds and establish with the precision of a true artist, the fiction of the Color Line.

Charles W. Chesnutt is one of the enigmas in American literature. There are five volumes to his credit, not including his life of Frederick Douglass for the Beacon Biography Series. From first to last, he revealed himself as a fictional artist of a very high order. The two volumes of short stories, "The Wife of His Youth and Other Stories," and "The Conjure Woman," are exquisite examples of the short story form equal to the best in American literature. Primarily a short story writer, Mr. Chesnutt showed defects in his long novels which were scarcely redeemed by the mastery of style which made them a joy to read. I recall the shock a certain incident in "The House Behind the Cedars" gave me when I first read the book at the time it was published, puzzled that human nature should betray its own most passionate instincts at a moment of the intensest crisis. I realized later, or at least my admiration for Mr. Chesnutt's art, led me to believe that the fault was not so much his art as

Reprinted from *Crisis*, 28 (September 1924): 204–10, with thanks to The Crisis Publishing Co., Inc., the magazine of the National Association for the Advancement of Colored People, for authorizing its use.

the problem of the Color Line. This problem, in its most acute details, was woven into the best novel Mr. Chesnutt has written called "The Marrow of Tradition." Certainly he did in that work an epic of riot and lawlessness which has served for mere pictorial detail as a standard example. In 1905 Mr. Chesnutt published "The Colonel's Dream," and thereafter silence fell upon him. I have heard it said that disappointment because his stories failed to win popularity was the cause of his following the classic example of Thomas Hardy by refusing to publish another novel. The cases are not exactly parallel because, while Hardy has refused to write another novel following the publication of "Jude, the Obscure," I have heard it rumored that Mr. Chesnutt has written other stories but will not permit their publication.

From the publication of Chesnutt's last novel until the present year there has been no fiction by the Race of any importance, with the exception of Dr. Du Bois's "The Quest of the Silver Fleece," which was published in 1911. . . .

The Negro as Writer

John Chamberlain

Negro fiction in America properly commences with Charles Waddell Chesnutt, a Clevelander who is still living, but whose writing falls mainly into the period of the 'eighties and 'nineties. One goes back to the archaic, quaintly-flavored novels and stories of this pioneer with mingled appreciation and esthetic blankness. Most of the Chesnutt plots hinge on such adventitious circumstances that the works of Thomas Hardy seem the very soul of the natural by comparison, but even in the stretches where the antique machinery creaks the loudest one reads with nothing but admiration for Chesnutt as a man. If his plot structure is definitely dated, the fault resides with the white models with which he worked in that era when the novel was designed to tell a story at all costs; and the spectacle of a Negro of the time working with any models at all and producing fiction with many good points is sufficient to compel applause.

For it was the time (to use Chesnutt's own words from *The Marrow of Tradition*) when the "nation was rushing forward with giant strides toward colossal wealth and world-domination, before the exigencies of which mere abstract ethical theories must not be permitted to stand." In the North "a new Pharaoh had risen, who knew not Israel—a new generation, who knew little of the fierce passions which had played around the Negro in a past epoch, and derived their opinions of him from the 'coon song' and the police reports." The Negro of the South had hardly had a chance at schooling, save in the institutions set up by the Freedmen's Bureau and manned by the Yankee schoolmarms who came in the wake of the carpet-baggers; and the Negro of the North was too busy waging his economic battles to pay much attention to the arts.

But Chesnutt, a school-teacher who had lived in North Carolina in the turbulent Reconstruction era, and who had later been admitted to the bar in Cleveland, had the urge to write of his people. Traditionally, he is the first of his race to have "made" the *Atlantic Monthly*. He started out politely enough with folk material, and for a time people were generally unaware that the work of Chesnutt was not that of a white man. But he pressed on to more

Reprinted from *Bookman*, 70 (February 1930): 603–11.

tragic materials, and handled them as no white novelist could have succeeded at the time in doing. And before he lapsed into silence all the materials of the Negro novel and short story as a vehicle for dramatizing racial problems had made their appearance, either explicitly or through adumbration, in his work.

Chesnutt blinked nothing. The problem of the color line fascinated him. He wrote stories of the Blue Vein Circle of Groveland (Cleveland?)—stories of a society of Negroes of light color that sets itself up above the darker members of the race. He dramatized the results of miscegenation in the South; he wrote of the snags that await the Negro who is "passing." The high passions following the Civil War and the rule of the carpet-baggers are built into his novels, *The House Behind the Cedars* and *The Marrow of Tradition*. While the former novel is generally the more admired, it is to *The Marrow of Tradition* that we must turn for the widest use of the materials presented by the Reconstruction South. The problem of a Negro doctor of intelligence in a black-hating community (a problem which has received ampler treatment at the hands of Walter White) forms the skeleton of this work; but the skeleton is an excuse for a generalized picture of a whole town of post–Civil War North Carolina. The novel is not remarkable for its characterization (no more so than are the novels of Thomas Dixon), but its people are credible enough as objectively revealed types to pull the reader along. It is the by-the-way sparks that fly from the wheel that interest us today: the workings of the chagrined southern white gentlemen, slaveholders of old, to the end of stirring up race antagonism against the Negro and his ally, the Republican carpet-bagger. We are moved by the machinations, not by the machinery; for the absurd propagandic twist at the close of the story leaves us undisturbed.

The House Behind the Cedars, which came before *The Marrow of Tradition* or *The Colonel's Dream,* is also interesting largely for its incidentals. It, too, is solved by the clumsy intrusion of a man-manipulated Fate, but it is an honest attempt to deal with the dilemma of a good-looking white woman who has a streak of Negro blood in her without resorting to the standard happy ending that marred some of George Cable's stories built around similar situations. We can well believe in the situation of *The House Behind the Cedars,* even though the mesh of coincidence that traps Rena Walden in a tragic death is a little too elaborate to swallow. The novel impresses us as true in essence. It might not have happened this way, but it very likely would have happened some other way.

Chesnutt is at his happiest, from a modern point of view, in the whimsical, poetic folktales that comprise *The Conjure Woman,* which was reprinted last spring by Houghton Mifflin, who hold the copyright of most of Chesnutt's works. (*The Conjure Woman* is the only Chesnutt book easily available, for all the rest have long since been out of print.) The worst side of the writer crops up in the short stories of *The Wife of His Youth and Other Stories.* The tales of *The Conjure Woman* are the stock in trade of an old Negro Machiavelli, Uncle Julius, who tells them with ulterior motives. For example, he regales his white masters with some nonsense about the "goopher" placed upon a grape vine with the end view in mind of preserving the income he has been deriving from the scuppernong wine made from the fruit. Julius is a lovable old liar with a fine imagination; and, as J. E. Spingarn says, every story he passes on adds a stroke to his self-portrait—something that cannot be said for Joel Chandler Harris's entertaining Uncle Remus. We accept queer twists from Uncle Julius.

But in "The Wife of His Youth" we cannot accept queer twists. For instance, when the dean of the Blue Veins of Groveland is confronted by the forgotten wife of his plantation days, a little black wizened woman, we cannot believe in the wrench whereby Chesnutt makes it possible for the confounded man to accept the situation and present "the wife of his youth" to the assembled Blue Veins at a ball originally intended to mark his betrothal to a charming young woman. The inner conflict of Mr. Ryder is totally missing. "A Matter of Principle" is the best of the Chesnutt short stories in the realistic genre; it is too plotted, but irony saves it. "The Sheriff's Children," a story of North Carolina, is effective as melodrama, for the sheriff who saves a prisoner from the lynching mob finds himself confronted by his own mulatto son, a son who is willing to kill him to make good his escape. In other stories, such as "The Bouquet" and "Ciceley's Dream," Chesnutt can become as sentimental as any of the cheaper fiction writers of his day or ours; but it is a tribute to his artistic conscience that he lapsed only occasionally.

To turn from Chesnutt to his contemporary, Paul Laurence Dunbar, is to descend quite a number of steps. Dunbar's realm was his poetry; his novels are hopelessly inept. He wrote four: *The Uncalled, The Fanatics, The Love of Landry* and *The Sport of the Gods;* and two books of short stories, *The Strength of Gideon* and *Folks from Dixie.* The moralizing with which *The Uncalled* is larded is as unappetizing as the mechanistic moralizing in Dreiser's *Sister Carrie,* of the same epoch of American letters; and it has not the Dreiserian virtue of being gloomy in a time of treacly fiction. To read *The Fanatics,* a Civil War story, is to read an unconscious parody; it contains a father who speaks to his son as "You cur, you mongrel cur, neither Northern nor Southern," and other things quite in tone with such talk. The Dunbar short stories are mostly in the sentimental vein. And the prose in which the novels and stories are written is uniformly sullen, woolly, and of interest only to the archaeologist of letters. To appreciate Dunbar one must turn to the poems. . . .

In the post-Chesnutt novel there are three Negroes who have done genuinely good work: Walter White, Claude McKay and Rudolph Fisher. Fisher has also written some short stories in which his technical dexterity is apparent, and he is the only modern Negro novelist who does not distort Negro character to make it seem superior to white character. The short sketches in Jean Toomer's *Cane* move us as poetry moves us, and are therefore far from negligible, even though Toomer has failed to give us any credible characterization. Eric Waldron, in *Tropic Death,* gets some sharp effects through his elliptical way of presenting melodramatic conflicts in the Caribbean region.

The Chesnutt tradition is carried on by Walter White, who has gone to the South for most of his material. White is probably not a novelist at heart. Part of his job has been to investigate lynchings in the South for the National Association for the Advancement of Colored People, a work which has resulted in his *Rope and Faggot: A Biography of Judge Lynch.* His best novel remains *The Fire in the Flint,* a book which succeeds because of the inherent power of the theme. It is an improvement on the work of Chesnutt, for this story of a Negro doctor's reception at the hands of the whites in a southern town has an inner logic which is not open to scepticism. White's second novel, *Flight,* is not up to the first; its motivations are not always plausible; but it has one memorable passage, a description of the Atlanta riots of 1906. This phantasmagoric outrage has been chanted by Du Bois in verse.

The work of McKay in prose is always poetic, for McKay brings his Jamaica world of color to everything he writes. There is a racial rhythm out of Langston Hughes in his first novel, *Home to Harlem,* a book that is saved from the rut of naturalism by the undertone of brooding provided by an intellectual Negro who is probably one aspect of McKay himself. *Banjo,* McKay's second novel, shows both advance and retrogression—advance because it is substantially richer, retrogression because the material is spread so profusely that it tends to clog the movement. McKay's defects as a novelist lie in his deficiencies as a dramatist; he has not yet seized on a problem that must spend itself in time with serious effects upon the involved characters.

The most able craftsman among the Negro novelists is Rudolph Fisher. In *The Walls of Jericho,* his novel of Harlem, the dominant note is one of comic sincerity. Fisher both moves his characters and moves beside them in friendly pity. His ear is remarkable; he can catch all the gradations of slang; and in a different field he is the peer of Ring Lardner as a manipulator of native idiom. The same qualities that mark his novel are present in his short stories, one of which, "The City of Refuge," is available in Edward J. O'Brien's collection, *The Best Short Stories of 1925.* Another, "Blades of Steel," may be obtained in V. F. Calverton's very valuable anthology of Negro literature recently issued by the Modern Library. Each of these stories turns on a trick, but the tricks depend on character for their effectiveness.

If we are to call Johnson's fictional *Autobiography of an Ex-Coloured Man* the precursor of the Harlem movement, it deserves extended comment. Although it was written while the author was a United States Consul in Nicaragua, it is evident that Johnson's eye and ear were close to the problems of the Negro at home. There is a real sense of all phases of the Negro problem in it. Its sentences are smooth and shapely; and it has a remarkable analysis of ragtime, written at a period before jazz had grown out of such beginnings as "Alexander's Ragtime Band." Considered historically, the book is one that the Negro would do well to call epoch-making, for it certainly caught the tempo of the future, and it explored problems that remain as portentous today as they were in 1912.

Of the lesser fiction writers not much need be said. Nella Larsen, author of *Quicksand* and *Passing,* cannot yet sustain a novel, although she has some skill at tracing the involute processes of a mind divided against itself. Jessie Fauset, author of *There is Confusion* and *Plum Bun,* has evidently gone to school to dubious models. *Plum Bun* depends so much upon coincidence that it becomes more ridiculous than the most intricate short story of Chesnutt. Wallace Thurman, a playwright and critic, has written one novel, *The Blacker the Berry,* which is "literary" in the worst sense. Du Bois, who spans the whole time between the Chesnutt era and the present, is more at home in the sociological essay than in fiction. His early *The Souls of Black Folk,* written when he was teaching economics and history at Atlanta University, amounts to a sort of Magna Charta of Negro rights, and remains his most effective work. His latest novel, *Dark Princess,* which mingles reality, fantasy and satire in distressing proportions, bogs the reader before he gets well into it. Characterization eludes Du Bois, probably because he is more interested in the future of the Negro race as a whole than in the Negro as novelist.

Chesnutt

STERLING BROWN

Charles Waddell Chesnutt . . . deserves to be called a pioneer. Writing to counter charges such as those made by Page in *Red Rock,* Chesnutt is the first to speak out uncompromisingly, but artistically, on the problems facing his people. One careful critic has stated that Chesnutt "was the first Negro novelist, and he is still the best," and another has said that his books contain early drafts of about all of the recent Negro novels.

In Chesnutt's *The Conjure Woman,* seven tales based upon Negro superstitions, Uncle Julius recalls Uncle Remus and Page's Uncle Billy, but differs from them in his craftiness. He tells his stories not merely to entertain, or to bewail the beautiful past, toward which he is ironic, but to gain his point in the present. His dialect is worked out in great detail, but is not so readable as that of Uncle Remus. There is good local color throughout, and some interesting characters emerge.

The Wife of His Youth, and Other Stories of the Color Line (1899) deals mainly with problems of race. The title story tells of a successful Negro in Groveland (Cleveland), the "dean" of the "Blue-Veins," who, on the eve of his engagement to a beautiful widow, theatrically acknowledges a little old black woman who had been his wife in slavery days and had helped him to freedom. A Negro mother denies her octoroon daughter in order for her to marry a New Englander of Mayflower lineage in "Her Virginia Mammy," a story like Cable's "Madame Delphine" but less convincing and gripping. In "The Sheriff's Children" a mulatto prisoner, falsely accused of murder, is defended from a mob by a sheriff who turns out to be his father. Desperate and cynical, the son is about to kill his father to escape when he is shot by the sheriff's daughter. In "The Web of Circumstance" a Negro blacksmith, falsely accused of stealing a whip, is sentenced to five years in the penitentiary on the same day that a white murderer is sentenced to one year. "The Passing of Grandison" shows a cunning slave, pretending to despise the abolitionist North, returning to his "understanding" master. He does so, however, only to manage the escape of all his kith and kin. "A Matter of Principle" satirizes the color line

Reprinted from *The Negro in America* (Washington, D.C.: The Association in Negro Folk Education, 1937), 78–82.

within the race: Clayton, an uppercrust near-white Negro, who "declined to associate with black people," pretends that his house is quarantined in order to keep a black Congressman from calling on his daughter. The Congressman turns out to be a mulatto, "well worthy" of Clayton's daughter.

The House Behind the Cedars (1900), Chesnutt's first novel, is concerned likewise with the color line. Rena, another octoroon heroine, is insulted by whites and oppressed by her mother and a mulatto suitor. Honorable devotion comes to her only through an upstanding black hero, but this cannot forestall her pathetic death. *The Marrow of Tradition* (1901), less conventional, is better. White characters range from the aristocratic General Delamere to his debauched grandson Tom; Major Carteret, demagogue for white supremacy; and McBane, ex-slave driver who knows one solution: "Burn the nigger." Negro characters range from Dr. Miller, a skillful physician, to the militant Josh Green; the loyal Sandy, and Jerry, a "white man's nigger." Sandy is framed for a murder in the first part of the book. A bloody riot, based on the one at Wilmington, N. C., is described in the second part. The white demagogues whip up the mob to fury, because a Negro newspaper has denounced lynching. Josh Green, who is willing to die rather than be shot down like a dog, who puts aside "fergetfulness and fergiveness," leads the aroused Negroes, when the upper-class Negroes believe that nothing can be done. The novel closes, however, on a note of forgetting and forgiving: Dr. Miller, whose own child was killed in the riot, goes to the home of his wife's white half-sister, to save her child with his very great medical skill. With all of its melodrama, the story has power; badly plotted, it still tells a great deal about social life in the South. Chesnutt idealizes some Negro characters, but candidly faces the weaknesses in others. Most important, however, is his going beneath the surface to social causes.

Chesnutt's last novel was *The Colonel's Dream.* Colonel French, an ex-Confederate officer of "family," dreams of resurrecting his native section and bringing it into the ways of prosperity and justice. As in so many novels of the time, his dream is not realized. He has opposed to him William Fetters, convict labor contractor, mortgage shark and political boss, together with the reactionary traditions and the inertia of the South. When the casket of his aged Negro slave, who had given his life for the Colonel's son, is dug up from the family burial plot and placed on his porch with a K.K.K. warning that the color line must continue even in death, he sees that his crusade is doomed. After this novel Chesnutt fell into an almost unbroken silence. Perhaps he felt the doom of his own crusade to bring about justice.

Whether he was pessimistic about his crusade or not, his achievements in fiction were worthy. Answering propaganda with propaganda, he might be expected to have certain faults. He was overinclined to the melodramatic, to mistaken identity, to the lost document turning up at the right or wrong moment, to the nick of time entrance. His characters are generally idealized or conventional. His "better class Negroes" speak too literary a language and are generally unbelievable models in behavior. Although attacking the color line within the race, he makes great use of the hero or heroine of mixed blood, and at times seems to accept the traditional concepts of Negro character. Even so, however, his characters stand nearer to the truth than those of Thomas Page or Thomas Dixon; he does not force them into only two grooves. There is no gainsaying his knowledge of the southern scene, or of the Negro upper class in northern cities. Unlike Dunbar he is opposed to the plantation tradition, sharply critical of southern injustice, and aware of the sinister forces at work in Reconstruction. Deploring the abuses of that era, he still sees, like Tourgée, that the story of a South victimized by carpet-baggers and scalawags is only a convenient half-truth. He gives high praise to the Yankee schoolmasters and schoolmarms who swarmed over Dixie to lift a second bondage from the freedmen. He shows exploitation, riots and lynching mobs, as well as the more refined exercising of prejudice. Often pompous and roundabout, in the manner of his times, he nevertheless knew how to hold a reader's interest. We must concede that he was melodramatic in plotting, but evidences of a skillful master's hand can still be found. He knew a great deal, and all things considered, he told it well.

The Mulatto in American Fiction

Penelope Bullock

In its heterogenous population and the individualistic traits of its various inhabitants the United States possesses a reservoir teeming with literary potentiality. Throughout the years, the American writer has tapped these natural resources to bring forth products of value and interest. Even though the characters whom he has depicted are not always lasting literary creations, they are significant in that they are social and sociological indices. Wrought from American life, they reflect the temper of the times and the actualities and the attitudes surrounding their prototypes in life. One of these characters is the mulatto. In this study[1] the portrayal of the mulatto by the nineteenth-century American fictionist is presented.

Who and what is the mulatto? According to Webster, he is, in the strictly generic sense, ". . . the first generation offspring of a pure negro and a white. . . ." The popular, general conception is that he is a Negro with a very obvious admixture of white blood. (In this study the persons considered as mulattoes are selected as such on the basis of this definition.) But the sociologist more adequately describes the mulatto as a cultural hybrid, as a stranded personality living in the margin of fixed status. He is a normal biological occurrence but a sociological problem in the United States. In the brief span of one life he is faced with the predicament of somehow resolving within himself the struggle between two cultures and two "races" which over a period of three hundred years have not yet become completely compatible in American life.

Two hundred years after the Negro-white offspring became a member of the population of the United States he made his advent into the American novel. How was he portrayed by the nineteenth-century writer?

The treatment accorded the mulatto in fiction was conditioned to a very large extent by the social and historical background out of which the authors wrote. The majority of them wrote as propagandists defending an institution or pleading for justice for an oppressed group. In depicting their characters, these writers very seldom approached them as a sociologist, or a realist, or a literary artist. They wrote only as partisans in national political issues. They wrote as propagandists: they distorted facts and clothed them in sentiment;

Reprinted from *Phylon* 6 (First Quarter 1945): 78–82.

they did not attempt to perceive and present the truth impartially. The persons of mixed blood pictured by these authors appealed to the emotional, prejudiced masses. But they are not truthful re-creations of life and of living people. Only a minor number of nineteenth-century writers were concerned with the actual, personal problems which the mulatto had to face because of the circumstances of his social environment.

The first group of propagandists to portray the mixed-blood in fiction were the Abolitionist writers. Outstanding among them were Richard Hildreth; Harriet Beecher Stowe; the Negro author, William Wells Brown; W. W. Smith; J. T. Trowbridge; and H. L. Hosmer. Playing upon the race pride and sentiments of the Caucasian group, these novelists placed in the forefront the near-white victim of slavery and asked their readers: Can an institution which literally enslaves the sons and daughters of the dominant race be tolerated?

From their novels emerges in bold, simple outline a major, stereotyped figure. He is the son or daughter of a Southern white aristocratic gentleman and one of his favorite slave mistresses. From his father he has inherited mental capacities and physical beauty supposedly superior to that of the Negro race. Yet despite such an endowment, or rather because of it, his life is fraught with tragedy. What privileges and opportunities he may enjoy are short-lived; for he is inevitably a slave. Suffering the degrading hardships of bondage, he becomes miserable and bitter. The indomitable spirit of his father rises up within him, and he rebels. If he is successful in escaping to freedom he becomes a happy, prosperous, and reputable citizen in his community. But even if his revolt against slavery fails, he meets his tragic death nobly and defiantly.

Following Emancipation, the era of Reconstruction brought the conflict between the Negro's assumption of rights which were legally his and the white man's continued monopoly of privileges. Here again was opportunity for the propagandist to take up his pen. And he did. This time, however, there were two groups of such writers, one representing each side of the issue. The pro-slavery writer had been silent concerning the mulatto, for miscegenation was a thrust at Southern society (although it was a phase of Northern life as well.) But the white Southerner now felt impelled to protect the lily-white South from the encroachment of the freed black man.

Representing the South in fiction were Thomas Nelson Page and Thomas Dixon, who pictured the mulatto as a dangerous element among the freedmen. Their sensational caricatures presented him as the despoiler of white womanhood, the corrupter of the white gentleman, and the usurper of political power. In *The Leopard's Spots* (1902) and *The Clansman* (1905), Dixon portrays three significant persons of mixed blood. Through George Harris, a Harvard graduate who wished to woo a white woman; Lydia Brown, the housekeeper and mistress of a radical Reconstruction leader in Congress, whose sinister influence over him threatens to ruin the nation; and Silas

Lynch, a bestial brute, he exhorts the South to preserve its racial integrity and prevent future America from being mulatto.

On the other hand, the cause of the freedman was pleaded by such Negro novelists as Mrs. Frances E. W. Harper, Sutton E. Griggs, George L. Pryor, and Mrs. Pauline E. Hopkins. They were at variance in their portrayal of the mulatto. But they did agree that his duty is to ally himself with the Negro group and sincerely and unselfishly aid in the fight for race betterment. In Mrs. Harper's novel, *Iola Leroy; or Shadows Uplifted* (1892), every significant Negro is a mixed-blood who, indistinguishable from white, is confronted with the question: To pass or not to pass? Each is eventually identified as a Negro, thereby upholding the thesis of the novel, which is: the mulatto is a tragic person only because and only so long as he fails to cast his lot with the minority group. But once the shadows are uplifted, once he proudly admits that he is a Negro, he rises above his tragedy and dedicates himself to the cause of the dark American.

Paul Laurence Dunbar, a contemporary of the Negro authors named above, was an outstanding writer in his brief life; but his contribution to the depiction of the mulatto was negligible. His stories of Negro life show only fleeting glimpses of persons of mixed blood.

A facetious yet significant portrayal of the mulatto is given by Samuel L. Clemens in *Pudd'nhead Wilson* (1890). In this story a mulatto slave and a white boy are exchanged in their cradles and grow up in reversed positions without their real identity being detected. Clemens demonstrates that social environment can discount parentage and legal edict in determining one's "racial allegiance." If in his formative years a mulatto has innocently lived as a white person, the discovery of his mixed blood cannot suddenly transform him into a Negro.

Such truth-penetrating analysis of the mulatto character as that by Clemens is rare in nineteenth-century fiction. The authors generally utilized him as an instrument for a cause—the abolition of slavery, a lily-white South, an equality of opportunity and rights for Negro and white citizen alike. There were, however, exceptions to the rule. There were writers to whom the mulatto himself was the cause. They were concerned with him as a human being living in a complex and paradoxical environment. These writers were A. W. Tourgée, a white Northerner; George W. Cable, a white Southerner; and Charles W. Chesnutt, a Northern Negro. In their approach to the mixed-blood they brought keen analysis, sympathetic interpretation, and sometimes literary artistry.

Tourgée portrayed the mulatto in two of his novels, *The Royal Gentleman* (1881) and *Pactolus Prime* (1890). Indicative of the understanding which he shows in his depiction of his subject is an incident described in the latter novel. A young girl lives as a white person until, on the eve of her father's death, she learns that he is a Negro. Realizing her situation, she cries out in agony to her father's lawyer. The lawyer is deeply moved by her reaction:

> It was the first time that he had ever realized the process through which the intelligent young colored American must always go, before our Christian civilization reduces him finally to his proper level of "essential inferiority."[2]

Here Tourgée shows that he is aware of a fundamental truth: the problem of the mulatto is to a very large degree but the problem of all Negroes—the desire for full and unqualified membership and participation in American society and culture.

Cable's convincing delineation of the *gens de couleur* of Louisiana and their peculiar juxtaposition in society was guided by intimate acquaintance with his subject and a sympathy that was neither gushingly sentimental nor politically partisan. Madame Delphine in the short story of the same name and Palmyre and Honoré Grandissime, free man of color, in *The Grandissimes* (1880) are tragic mulattoes. Cable, however, took his characters not from the stereotypes of previous literature but from life; and he developed them into three-dimensional characters. As Pattee says, "They are true to the fundamentals of human life, they are alive, they satisfy, and they are presented ever with an exquisite art."[3] Cable's sympathetic attitude toward the mixed-blood is expressed through one of the white characters in *The Grandissimes* (pp. 184–85):

> "Emancipation before the law . . . is to them [mixed-bloods] little more than a mockery until they achieve emancipation in the minds and good will of all . . . the ruling class."

Chesnutt was the outstanding delineator of the Negro-white offspring at the turn of the century. Exhibiting an obvious predilection for the mulatto character, Chesnutt gives him a prominent place in most of his short stories and novels. In *The House Behind the Cedars* (1900), the psychological analysis of the reactions of John and Rena to their situations as mixed-bloods indistinguishable from white probes deeply into the minds of these characters and lays bare the thoughts which were fermenting there. Rena believes that it is wrong to live under a veil of concealment when such an important issue as marriage is involved and finally decides that it is her duty to dedicate her life to the uplift of the downtrodden Negro. John's attitude is in direct contrast:

> Once persuaded that he had certain rights or ought to have them, by virtue of the laws of nature, in defiance of the customs of mankind, he had promptly sought to enjoy them. This he had been able to do by simply concealing his antecedents and making the most of his opportunities, with no troublesome qualms of conscience whatever.[4]

Himself a near-white, Chesnutt was keenly sensitive to the position of the mulatto in American life and creates characters convincing in their realism.

The portrayals of the mixed-blood by Cable and Chesnutt are the outstanding delineations of this character in nineteenth-century American fiction. To his disadvantage the mulatto entered fiction, at the pen of the advocate of Abolition, as an instrument of propaganda. Unfortunately, the majority of his succeeding portrayers were also zealous partisans of some cause, in whom were lacking the tempering and subtly interpretive attributes of the sociologist and the literary artist. Thus a series of types emerged—such as the beautiful but ill-fated victim of injustice and the extremely race-conscious leader of the minority group—and these patterns of portrayal developed into stereotypes. In the treatment of the mixed-blood the broad outline of actuality was sketched, but seldom was reality re-created. Rarely did the nineteenth-century writer probe beneath the surface to ascertain the truth underlying the fact and the cause effecting the result.

With the literary production of Chesnutt, however, the portrayal of the mulatto in the nineteenth century ends on a redemptive note and gives hope for a promising characterization in twentieth-century literature. Since 1900, inter-racial attitudes have become more intelligent and tolerant, and those members of American society who may be maladjusted have been given more humane consideration. The American fictionist has brought forth a quality of writing dealing with the mixed-blood during this period. The quality of the treatment thus accorded this character remains to be appraised.

Notes

1. This article is a summary of "The Treatment of the Mulatto in American Fiction from 1826 to 1902," unpublished Master's thesis, Department of English, Atlanta University, 1944.

2. A. W. Tourgée, *Pactolus Prime* (New York, 1890), p. 206.

3. "The Short Story," *Cambridge History of American Literature,* edited by W. P. Trent and others (New York, 1993), II, 384.

4. C. W. Chesnutt, *The House Behind the Cedars* (Boston, 1900), p. 78.

Social Realism in Charles W. Chesnutt

RUSSELL AMES

Helen Chesnutt's story of her father's life [in *Charles Waddell Chesnutt: Pioneer of the Color Line*] tells us a great deal about what it meant to be a Negro intellectual in the late nineteenth and early twentieth centuries. It is a straightforward, human account of the efforts, success in business, and "failure" in literature of a fine but little-known American writer. Reasonably enough, Miss Chesnutt does not attempt a full evaluation of his short stories and novels, for this would require discussion of the substantial erasure of Negro writers from the history of literature in the United States, and would bring into question the standards of criticism prevailing today. Some consideration of these matters, however, is necessary to an appreciation of this unusual biography and this unusual writer. Chesnutt was the first distinguished American Negro author of short stories and novels. He remains in certain respects the best. Neglect of his life and work represents, therefore, a general neglect of Negro literature.

Both *The Cambridge History of American Literature* and Parrington's *Main Currents in American Thought* ignore Chesnutt altogether, and hardly mention any Negro authors. The recent *Literary History of the United States* (edited by Spiller, Canby, and others, 1948) "discusses" Chesnutt in a fourteen-line paragraph given mainly to Paul Laurence Dunbar. Both are restricted to the status of dialect writers, "followers in the wake of Harris." The paragraph makes the trivial or inaccurate points that Chesnutt was an Ohioan, that his "legal training involved a number of years in North Carolina" (in fact he got his legal training in Ohio; North Carolina was the place where he grew up, taught school, and the scene of most of his fiction). It is stated that he and Dunbar enriched "that branch of nineteenth century literature which relates to the old-time Southern Negro," and this is a reference to his first and least important book. His major work is passed over with the remark that "his career included also three novels which expose the consequences of racial prejudice." (Vol. 11, p. 854 f.)

The best of these novels, *The Marrow of Tradition* (1901), was based on first-hand investigation of the Wilmington, North Carolina, riots of 1898,

Reprinted from *Phylon* 14 (Second Quarter 1953): 199–206.

and it describes a conspiracy to rob Negroes of the vote that ends in a tragic drama of mass lynching and courageous resistance. It is this novel that is summed up as being "about the struggles of Negro and white half-sisters" in a concisely inaccurate article on Chesnutt in *The Oxford Companion to American Literature* (1948). Among the rare studies by white scholars that give some attention to writing by Negroes, John H. Nelson's *Negro Character in American Literature* (University of Kansas *Humanistic Studies*, 1932, Vol. IV, No. 1) is typical:

> Only one negro, in fact—Charles W. Chesnutt—can seriously lay claim to the title of novelist, and for the most part, Chesnutt was more propagandist than literary artist. He dissipated his energies in working for the social betterment of his people. . . . *The Marrow of Tradition* . . . is unfair in tone, crudely partisan in design, inflammatory in suggestion, and worthless except as a polemical tract. Southern whites, so the novelist contends, not only engage in mob riots, but enjoy them. . . . (p. 135).

One might ask, in passing, if Mr. Nelson believes that it is artistically sound to portray lynchings as long as the lynchers do not enjoy themselves? In any case, it is interesting to note that the well-known Negro critic Alain Locke, as we shall see below, considers Chesnutt's work to be objective, balanced, and accurate, though Locke is sternly opposed to polemics and propaganda in fiction. One is tempted to say that propaganda is what we dislike, and objectivity is what we agree with.

Mr. Nelson concludes his "objective" study by saying that

> The pure black has been, at best, only wistful or mildly pathetic; usually he has appeared amusing even in his ambitions and strivings; nearly always he provokes a laugh or at least a smile. Thousands of readers of American literature have been entertained by his drollery, his incongruous display of civilization and savagery, his poetical outlook on the world. Without exemplifying exalted qualities or filling the position of epic hero, he has proved a great comic type, and for many decades has lent to much of American fiction a raciness, an enlivening element, a savor of the natural and primitive which could ill be spared. (p. 137.)

Nelson is right in one thing at least: it is true that the Negro has been restricted in the arts to the roles of clown, child, and primitive. Very rarely indeed has he been allowed the "exalted qualities" of an "epic hero," even though an American writer could best turn to Negro history, to such figures at Nat Turner, Harriet Tubman, and Frederick Douglass for the exalted heroes of epic stories.

For a Negro hero of full stature, I believe, we must go back to Frederick Douglass's little-known "The Heroic Slave" (published in *Autographs for Freedom,* 1853; reprinted in part in *The Negro Caravan,* 1941)—a long story about

Madison Washington and his leadership of a successful uprising on the slave-ship *Creole* in 1841. When, after fifty years in which there was not much fiction written by Negroes, we come to Chesnutt's stories and novels, the heroes and heroines are less exalted and more frustrated. They are not typical of the Negro people: half or more than half white in color of skin and, in one major work, *The Colonel's Dream,* not Negro at all; chiefly from the middle or upper classes. They indicate the possibilities of achievement and progress, but their role is defensive and half-defeated. In the period when U.S. capital first took part in the drama of world empire and shared the control of new millions of colored peoples, the Negroes in the South were re-subjugated by a parallel process. Speaking ironically to the people of the Philippine Islands, Finley Peter Dunne's Mister Dooley said: " 'We can't give ye anny votes, because we haven't more thin enough to go round now; but we'll threat ye th' way a father shud threat his childher if we have to break ivry bone in ye'er bodies. So come to our ar-arms,' says we." At the same time and with the operation of similar ideas, Negroes in the South were losing the vote, political office and jobs, through laws, terror, and lynchings. This process Chesnutt described. His main theme could not be liberation but had to be resistance and retreat. His protagonists could not be very large, victorious, or forward-moving.

Nevertheless, Chesnutt's Negroes are larger and more admirable than most of their successors in fiction written by Negroes—though it should be noted that this fiction, in the twentieth century, has in general showed people working and striving in a way that fiction by non-Negro writers has not. Chesnutt expresses some of the hidden heroic history of his people, for example, in minor characters in *The Marrow of Tradition*—through mention of an editor who risks lynching to write against lynching, and through the fuller portrait of Josh Green, the stevedore who would "rather be a dead nigger any day dan a live dog."

Chesnutt believed, however, that it was necessary to make concessions to the prejudices of the well-to-do white book-buyers. Among his characters there was more than a "fair" share of well-meaning and liberal white South-erners, of disreputable Negroes. His method was first to disarm his readers with conventional scenes and seeming stereotypes—for example, with idyllic relations between servants and aristocrats—and then in lightning flashes to reveal the underlying facts of injustice and rebellion. Chesnutt had long pondered his purpose, audience, and method as letters and diaries quoted by his daughter show. As early as 1880, when he was twenty-one, he wrote in his journal:

> I think I must write a book. . . .

> The object of my writings would be not so much the elevation of the colored people as the elevation of the whites. . . . Not a fierce indiscriminate onset, not an appeal to force, for this is something that force can but slightly affect, but a

moral revolution which must be brought about in a different manner. The subtle almost indefinable feeling of repulsion toward the Negro, which is common to most Americans—cannot be stormed and taken by assault; the garrison will not capitulate, so their position must be mined, and we will find ourselves in their midst before they think it.

No doubt it was with this indirect, persuasive method in mind that Chesnutt began, about 1884 in Cleveland, to write stories for newspapers and magazines including, within a few years, the Olympian *Atlantic Monthly*. His tales of Negro life during slavery, Reconstruction, and the "Counter-Revolution," were written with such restraint and with such a skillful blending of melodrama and realism that finally two volumes of them were published in 1899 by Houghton Mifflin and Company, and William Dean Howells said, in *The Atlantic* (May, 1900), that

> for the far greatest part Mr. Chesnutt seems to know quite as well what he wants to do in a given case as Maupassant, or Tourguenief, or Mr. James, or Miss Jewett, or Miss Wilkins. . . . and if he has it in him to go forward on the way which he has traced for himself, to be true to life as he has known it, to deny himself the glories of the cheap success which awaits the charlatan in fiction, one of the places at the top is open to him.

Chesnutt did have it in him to go forward on the way of truth, but his country did not have it in the civilization to value his work adequately. He gave up a lucrative business as lawyer, court reporter, and stenographer to devote himself to a high purpose in literature. He went on to write, with ever-increasing scope and depth, realistic novels about the South. But the "passionless handling," "the delicate skill," and the "quiet self-restraint" that Howells had praised were not enough to overcome the revulsion of many critics and the indifference of most book-buyers when *The House Behind the Cedars* was published in 1900, *The Marrow of Tradition* in 1901, and *The Colonel's Dream* in 1905. Even those who have read these novels seem, often, unable to understand what is written. For example, *The House Behind the Cedars* is described in *The Oxford Companion to American Literature* as "concerned with a light-complexioned Negress who is undecided whether to enjoy comfort as a white man's mistress or the sincere love of a Negro"; but the fact is that she does not at any time even remotely consider becoming the white man's mistress. It seems that a mind warped by prejudice automatically turns a high-principled Negro woman into a woman of loose morals. *The Marrow of Tradition* compelled admiration from William Dean Howells, but he found it too bitter for his taste. Paul Elmer More complained that in it Chesnutt had tried "to humiliate the whites" and that the last chapter was "utterly revolting." It is remarkable that so many critics, over the years, suddenly develop a sense of "fair play" when white people are "maltreated" by Chesnutt; and it is equally remarkable that no critic appears to protest when he shows Negroes in an unfavorable light. "The American Mind" has never welcomed such unpleasant truths as those told by Chesnutt, and racist attitudes were at a peak when his books were published. The muckrake of the reformers did not reach to the worst-smelling muck. This was a major period in American fiction in which substantial social novels, comparable to Chesnutt's were directed against monopoly—Norris's *The Octopus,* Dreiser's *Sister Carrie,* London's *The Iron Heel,* Sinclair's *The Jungle.* These novels did not, however, comprehend the relation of monopoly to imperialism or the use of racism to both. At a time when "the blessings of civilization," ironically praised by Mark Twain, were being extended to colored people in China, Cuba, the Philippines, and the United States, the best-sellers on the Negro question were racist novels like those of the Reverend Thomas Dixon—*The Leopard's Spots* and *The Clansman,* from which the motion picture *The Birth of a Nation* was made.

This particular motion picture, it so happens, brings up very sharply certain central questions and paradoxes concerning art that deals with Negroes or is created by Negroes. There is much "objective" art criticism that pleads a case for Griffith's "masterpiece" although it is admittedly propaganda for slavery and the Ku Klux Klan. Here, as in the British cinema's *David Copperfield* and the verse of Eliot and Pound, where anti-Semitism flourishes, "Art" triumphs over propaganda. Why is it, then, that the same or similar critics mechanically discover that pro-Negro, progressive, and radical propaganda unfailingly and fatally destroys "Art"? Here we have a strange formula: Art is impervious to reactionary propaganda; Art is blighted by radical propaganda.

Chesnutt's books have received just appraisal only from Negro scholars like Hugh Gloster, in *Negro Voices in American Fiction,* or the editors of *The Negro Caravan.* But even such critics have accepted the current preference for "Art." The decline of the Negro "purpose" novel, with its "crude propaganda," "racial hypersensitivity," and "race-conscious idealization of Negroes" has been welcomed. In a recent symposium on "The Negro in Literature: The Current Scene" (PHYLON, Winter, 1950), most, though by no means all, of the leading Negro writers involved condemned racial "propaganda" and favored "objectivity," "universality," and "artistry."

Chesnutt's "objectivity"—which is apparent to Negro observers but not to whites—is praised by the Dean of American Negro literary critics, Alain Locke, in "The Negro in American Literature," (*New World Writing,* 1952). Locke, however, considers Chesnutt an imitative, old-fashioned writer of very limited artistry: he "quite successfully modeled his short-story style on Bret Harte, his novel technique on Cable's, but with decidedly less success." It was not till the Twenties that Negro writers outgrew "the handicap of allowing didactic emphasis and propagandistic motives to choke their sense of artistry." Locke thinks that Richard Wright "climaxed the development" and, with others, "brought Negro writing abreast of contemporary American realism and within hailing distance of cultural maturity." It is suggested that full cultural maturity inhabits William Faulkner with his "brave introspection," "his unexcelled, intensive portrayal of Southern life," and his "honest liberal-ism."

If literary history in the United States is looked at in this way—if we have been advancing toward Faulkner instead of decaying toward Faulkner, if Negro writing has always lagged behind that of whites and is yet to grow up—then a writer like Chesnutt is a worthy but clumsy ancient whose work is merely of historical interest, for it was crippled by problems and purposes. If, on the other hand, one considers most fiction today, and typically the fiction of Faulkner, to be decadent, both in what it says and in the garbled way in which it is said, then the social realism of Chesnutt represents a peak from which our fiction has declined. It can certainly be argued that Chesnutt's portrayal of Southern life is far more inclusive, truthful, complex, interesting, and artistic than Faulkner's. But this argument can carry weight only if we abandon the pervasive "modern" belief that artistry consists in obscurity, the torturing of language, impressionism, the avoidance of story-telling, and concentration on madness, lust, and despair.

Faulkner portrays, if we have the patience to puzzle him out, the symbolic decay of aristocracy (Comptons, Sartorises) and rise of commerce (Snopses) while strange Negroes are a tragic chorus and a symbol of the white Southerner's guilt. Chesnutt showed us far more of the South and its history—the web of its economy, its semi-colonial relation to the North, its mills and farms and stores, its politics and courts, its peonage and forced labor camps—in short, the relations between its rulers and its workers—with a broad gallery of living, typical characters.

Decadent fiction is propaganda for the view that life is a bad dream in which the trapped human animal is a victim of his own "instincts" and of history's bad jokes. It is a poor, narrow form of naturalism. It is thin, disorderly, and unreal compared to the naturalism of Norris and Dreiser or the realism of Chesnutt and London. The writing of Chesnutt is propaganda for reason, for the understanding of society, for the development of human beings. It is artistic in the large, sound meanings of the term. He did not have the modern, artistic gift for scattering impressions—leaving the organization of fragments to the initiated reader who has the Freudian and symbolic tools needed to do the job. He told stories, traced the connections between people and events.

Chesnutt is a man very much worth knowing, through his books and through the record of his life which his daughter has made with careful and loving labor. Her biography will be an important experience for any American, Negro or white, who reads it. From it we can learn much about how to work, how to think, how to be a human being; and from it we can learn a great deal of informal social history of the United States. Chesnutt, unable to go to college, became at twenty-two the principal of the State Normal School at Fayetteville, North Carolina, taught Latin, singing, and the organ to young colored people, studied Greek, Latin, French, German, stenography, and music in addition to history, economics, and French and English literature. By comparison Jack London's and his Martin Eden's heroic efforts to master culture seem ordinary. And yet he found time to be such a husband that his wife wrote him, when he was seeking work, and a home for her, in the North:

> You were a companion, and you knew me better than even my father or mother, or at least you were more in sympathy with me than anybody else, and my failings were overlooked. No one can tell, my dearest husband, how I miss that companionship.

He was a man who wrote, in language like that of Mark Twain, to George Washington Cable, advocating federal enforcement of the Negro's right to vote:

> It is easy to temporize with the bull when you are on the other side of the fence, but when you are in the pasture with him, as the colored people of the South are, the case is different. . . . The ever-lengthening record of Southern wrongs and insults, both lawless and under the form of law, calls for whatever there is of patriotism, of justice, of fair play in the American people, to cry "hands off" and give the Negro a show, not five years hence, or a generation hence, but now, while he is alive, and can appreciate it; posthumous fame is a glorious thing, even if it is only posthumous; posthumous liberty is not, in the homely language of the rural Southerner "wu'th shucks." . . .

And Chesnutt, though "white" in appearance himself, wrote that

> Judge Tourgée's cultivated white Negroes are always bewailing their fate and cursing the drop of black blood which "taints"—I hate the word, it implies corruption—their otherwise pure race.

We may learn something about the obstacles faced by Negroes and women as writers when we read: "Self-confidence I believe as essential to success in literature as in acrobatics." We may better understand that truth exists in motion and develops out of conflict when we read Chesnutt's remark to Booker T. Washington: "Let the white man dwell upon the weakness of the Negro race; it is a matter which neither you nor I need to emphasize."

Chesnutt's work was the forerunner of a substantial body of fiction written by Negroes which has maintained an unusual level of social realism. A broad sampling of Negro fiction in this century indicates that it has been less escapist, more concerned with world history and culture, with working people and women, with courage and hope, than comparable fiction written by non-Negro authors.

A further, somewhat subjective point should be made. Character has almost disappeared from contemporary literature. Everyone knows that the characters of Shakespeare can be discussed as if they are real people whom we know, whose actions we can judge, whose decisions we can reconsider, whose individuality we retain. And we all know that this is also true of the people in what are universally recognized as the great novels. But in this sense there are no people in the books of Hemingway, Dos Passos, Faulkner, Joyce, and most of Steinbeck. It is the chief value of the writing of Thomas Wolfe that he creates living characters when he can get away from himself. A remarkable quality of Chesnutt's novels—and a quality we have got out of the habit of looking for—is clarity and liveliness of characterization. Not only his major characters but nearly all of his minor ones are distinct, memorable, and individual. They are not the author and they are not ourselves. They are not universal in the empty modern sense of the term. They are real social beings tied to a particular social fabric.

Charles W. Chesnutt: Novelist of a Cause

Carol B. Gartner

It is a depressing project to read the novels of Charles W. Chesnutt today, not because of the quality of the novels, but because we are reading the still appealing documents of a lost cause. Apart from the demands of an active and prosperous business in law stenography, Chesnutt devoted most of his life-long efforts to the cause of Negro rights and advancement. Although he did not always admit to a social purpose behind his fiction, he wrote from the beginning with a mixture of indignation, sympathy and idealism calculated to encourage the acceptance of Negroes as people. As the hopes and rights of Negroes in the South declined and abuses became rampant, Chesnutt wrote with horror of the new servitude and increased brutality. Despite new laws and certain advancements, we can still, unhappily, more than half a century later, read these books as documents on the Negro Question.

His career as a fiction writer started slowly, but promised enough during the first few years of the new century for him to give up his business and attempt to make a living as a lecturer and writer. But moderate success was not enough for him, and he soon moved on into new ways to promote his cause. His novels are not great, for Chesnutt dipped lavishly into sentiment, melodrama and coincidence, elements which mark the second-rate fiction of his period. But he wrote with enough realism, power and craft to make one regret that he stopped when he did, and that he allowed his proportion of polemic to grow with his craftsmanship as a writer.

Charles W. Chesnutt has little recognition today in the area of American literature. Most studies either ignore or summarily dismiss him. Larzer Ziff, in his recent book *The American 1890s,* which covers in detail the period when Chesnutt was beginning to attain recognition, does not mention him at all.[1] There is a full biography written by his daughter Helen M. Chesnutt, but this is largely impersonal and adulatory. It contains considerable information, and provides a good account of the problems faced by a colored man seeking education and success. Most interesting are the many journal entries and letters which his daughter has included.[2] The only recent articles on Chesnutt are those with a special purpose, the investigation of folk literature.[3] These con-

Reprinted with permission from *Markham Review* 1, no. 3 (1968): 5–12.

centrate on his first collection of stories, *The Conjure Woman,* which are not folk tales but are modelled on them. In a 1962 dissertation, Sylvia Lyons-Render discussed Chesnutt's craftsmanship and emphasized the value of his books as social documents.[4] Chesnutt has received extended notice only in surveys of Negro literature. In 1930 John Chamberlain surveyed his work, with which "Negro fiction in America properly commences," giving him moderate admiration and stylistic criticism.[5] Two recent surveys of Negro literature place Chesnutt above his Negro contemporaries as a fiction writer, but to David Littlejohn, who characterizes all Negro literature before Richard Wright's *Native Son* (1940) as the "Dark Ages," Chesnutt is "still very small beer."[6] To Herbert Hill, Negro writing was until recently, "with a few important exceptions, mainly interesting as sociology." Chesnutt, he feels, did not belong to the sociology or protest school, but was a "writer of originality" with "profound insight into Southern life." He ranged beyond the literary fashions and tastes of his time.[7]

Chesnutt viewed himself primarily as a colored writer, not just a writer, although he wanted his productions to be accepted as serious literature. He seems to have vacillated within himself between writing for the purpose of exploring race problems and advancing the colored people and writing to create fine literature. When he first wrote to Houghton, Miffin & Co. in 1891 to enquire about the publication of a volume of his short stories, several of which had already appeared in *The Atlantic Monthly* and other magazines, he commented:

> There is one fact which would give this volume distinction—though I must confess that I do not know whether it would help or hurt its reception by critics or the public. It is the first contribution by an American of acknowledged African descent to purely imaginative literature.
>
> In this case, the infusion of African blood is very small—is not in fact a visible admixture—but it is enough, combined with the fact that the writer was practically brought up in the South, to give him a knowledge of the people whose description is attempted. These people have never been treated from a closely sympathetic standpoint; they have not had their day in court. Their friends have written of them, and their enemies; but this is, so far as I know, the first instance where a writer with any of their own blood has attempted a literary portrayal of them. If these stories have any merit, I think it is more owing to this new point of view than to any other thing.[8]

Having stated his identification, he moved immediately to the other side of the picture.

> I should not want this fact to be stated in the book, nor advertised, unless the publisher advised it; first, because I do not know whether it would affect its reception favorably or unfavorably, or at all; secondly, because I would not have the book judged by any standard lower than that set for other writers. If some

of these stories have stood the test of admission into the *Atlantic* and other publications where they have appeared, I am willing to submit them all to the public on their merits.[9]

Chesnutt repeated the claim that he was the "first Negro novelist" in the United States in an article written late in his life.[10] In a footnote to the Houghton, Mifflin letter, however, his daughter points out that he had "overlooked the little-known *Clotel,* by W. W. Brown" (p. 68). They both overlooked other forgotten productions, such as *My Southern Home,* another novel by the author of *Clotel,* William Wells Brown, the first American Negro to devote his life to literature and earn his living that way, and abolitionist novels, like *The Garies and Their Friends,* 1857, by Frank Webb.[11] Chesnutt was more accurate in his 1931 article when he claimed that before *The Conjure Woman* broke into print in 1899, "no American colored writer had ever secured critical recognition except Paul Lawrence Dunbar . . . poet," and Phillis Wheatley, the Colonial poet who gained attention because she was an African-born slave.

Chesnutt had some early encouragement to be a writer, for when he wrote his first story, at fourteen, it was published in a small weekly newspaper run by a colored man in Fayetteville, North Carolina (H.M. Chesnutt, p. 8). In order to continue his education, he very early became an assistant teacher, and by the age of seventeen, a full-fledged teacher in country schools. In November, 1880, at twenty-two, he became principal of the Normal School at Fayetteville. Just a few months earlier in May, 1880, he had already formulated his aspirations as a writer. His journal reads, "I think I must write a book." His purpose was "high, holy," the elevation of not the colored but the white people, "for I consider the unjust spirit of caste which is so insidious as to pervade a whole nation . . . a barrier to the moral progress of the American people." He would not appeal "to force, for this is something that force can but slightly affect, but a moral revolution." The Negro had to prepare for recognition and equality, "and it is the province of literature to open the way for him to get it" (H.M.C., quotation from journal, May 29, 1880). These aspirations, and even this youthful idealism remained with Chesnutt for over twenty years, although they became somewhat less positive and tenable. He worked all his life to promote that moral revolution, but the publication of *The Colonel's Dream* in 1905 marked the end of his dream of moving white America through literature.

The authorities at Fayetteville had expressed their desire to keep Chesnutt as principal at the Normal School by paying him the unusual salary of $75.00 per month, but despite this inducement to stay he felt an "inner compulsion," and in May, 1883, resigned to go North (H. M. C., p. 32). He had been born in Cleveland, but returned with his parents as a young child to their home, Fayetteville, North Carolina. After trying a few other northern cities, Chesnutt returned to Cleveland, sent later for his wife and children, and lived there for the rest of his life. Although he always identified himself as colored, and moved socially in largely colored groups, he gradually became a part of the Establishment. His very prosperous law stenography business brought him into contact with all kinds of people, and his literary reputation brought even wider contacts with such prominent white literary figures as George W. Cable and Walter H. Page. He was active in organizations like the white-sponsored Open Letter Club, to which Cable introduced him, and which attempted to stimulate discussion and disseminate information on the race question, and later, the colored-sponsored NAACP. Despite grave differences of opinion, especially on the question of Negro suffrage which they argued by letter over the years, Chesnutt got to know Booker T. Washington, with whose family his own became very friendly. Washington believed in accommodation to white wishes in the South, even to accepting constant encroachment on Negro rights and abridgement of suffrage, as long as they allowed him to continue his development of Negro industrial education. He believed economic improvement was the first step up, after which others would successfully follow. Chesnutt did not agree and argued for Negro rights in lectures, letters and books.

Chesnutt gradually became a member of many of Cleveland's exclusive social and literary societies, although it sometimes took more than one proposal. This acceptance by white society and even the relationship, although slight, with Booker T. Washington may be part of the reason why neither Chesnutt's ideas nor writings have played any part in the more recent movements toward Negro rights. Although things have changed, all too many of the inequities Chesnutt wrote about still exist, and prejudice and brutality, although not lawful and open as in his time, have not disappeared. He was somewhat of a prophet, although things have improved much more slowly than he expected. In a letter to Edgar Dean Crumpacker in the House of Representatives Chesnutt wrote:

> The race question is doubtless destined to receive a great deal of attention on the part of the public for a long time to come. The Southern people, white and black, are likely to be tangled up in it for several generations, and it is a matter in which the North is under obligation to intervene, in one way or another, and at such times as are propitious, to see that justice is done to all concerned, and that the spirit of our institutions is not sacrificed merely to promote the selfish interests of any one faction of the people—whether the factional line be that of race or anything else. I am . . . entirely convinced that under the constitution of the United States, the government should not in any way draw or recognize a color line. (May 9, 1902, H.M.C., p. 181)

He was generally a moderate on the race question. Although he felt that the North must intervene, he had earlier written in his journal that he would not "appeal to force" (May 29, 1880).

The most likely reason that Chesnutt's writings have played no part in the continuing rights movement is that he simply was forgotten. His works were well received but did not sell well and went quickly out of print. By 1930 all his books were unavailable except *The Conjure Woman,* which had been reissued in 1929 (Chamberlain, p. 604). There was new interest in his work when he received a medal from the NAACP in 1928 for his "pioneer work as a literary artist depicting the life and struggles of Americans of Negro descent, and for his long and useful career as scholar, worker, and free-man of one of America's greatest cities."[12] Except for *The Conjure Woman,* books were not available to satisfy the new interest.

Chesnutt's real literary career began in Cleveland in 1885. S.S. McClure had organized the first newspaper syndicate in the United States and spon-sored a contest to attract new and inexpensive material. Chesnutt entered "Uncle Peter's House" which did not win, but was published in the *Cleveland News and Herald.* He sold other stories to McClure, published poems in a weekly, *The Cleveland Voice,* and in 1886 began writing for *Family Fiction.* None of these pieces appeared in his collected stories, but in 1887 came his big break. *The Atlantic Monthly* accepted the first of his conjure stories, "The Goophered Grapevine." "Po' Sandy" also appeared in the *Atlantic,* in May, 1888, and Chesnutt was launched. This story began his association with George W. Cable, who befriended and sponsored him, bringing him into con-tact with Richard Watson Gilder, editor of the *Century.* Cable offered Ches-nutt a position as secretary and assistant, in which he could work with Cable in the cause of Negro advancement and continue his writing. Chesnutt's busi-ness was too profitable to leave, and he regretfully declined.[13]

Publication brought him gradually into a personal relationship with Walter Hines Page, editor of the *Atlantic,* who counselled and encouraged him for many years. With Page's encouragement, Houghton, Mifflin & Co. finally agreed to put out a book of his conjure stories, *The Conjure Woman,* which appeared in 1899. Not long afterward they published a second book, *The Wife of His Youth and Other Stories of the Color Line,* also 1899.

The Conjure Woman contains Chesnutt's most delightful writing. There is serious purpose but it is submerged so that the stories remain light and humorous. They are in the form of the Western tall tale, with a serious-minded frame narrator, and a dead-pan spinner of folk tales. The narrator is a white gentleman from the North who has moved to North Carolina for his wife's health. He and his wife are the audience for the tales of Uncle Julius, an old Negro they find on the plantation they are buying. The man employs Julius, formerly a slave on the plantation, and he spins them tales suggested by current happenings. They are in Negro dialect, which provides some dif-ficulty but adds to the local color. The stories deal with incidents from the days of slavery. "In every instance," Chesnutt wrote later (*Colophon* article), "Julius had an axe to grind; for himself or his church, or some member of his family, or a white friend." These motives provide the only sour notes, for they undercut the effect, and spoil our suspension of disbelief. The contem-porary reviewer in the *Nation* felt that the stories "lose in effectiveness only by the deep policy imputed to their relater ... [which] calls his own credulity in question. The reviewer suggests that "Uncle Julius's scepticism cannot rob one of the belief that this was the real religion of the old plantation; the goopher "mixtry," not the overseer's lash, the dreaded power."[14] These endings reflect Chesnutt's own need to offer a rationalistic explanation, no matter how unconvincing, for the supernatural tales. He is unwilling to let them stand on their own, and perhaps is himself distrustful of their narrator, a polite old family-retainer type, left over from the days of slavery. The stories reveal their serious purpose as they gently bring out the horrors of slavery and the injustice of treating Negroes as if they have no feelings. The reactions of Miss Annie, the Northern gentleman's wife, would seem to be what Chesnutt wanted to produce in his audience. She is sympathetic, not harshly incredulous as her husband is. Near the end of "Sis Becky's Pickaninny" we find:

> "That is a very ingenious fairy tale, Julius," I said, "and we are much obliged to you."
> "Why John!" said my wife severely, "the story bears the stamp of truth, if ever a story did."
> "Yes," I replied, "especially the hummingbird episode, and the mocking bird digression, to say nothing of the doings of the hornet and the sparrow."
> "Oh, well, I don't care," she rejoined, with delightful animation; "those are mere ornamental details and not at all essential. The story is true to nature, and might have happened half a hundred times, and no doubt did happen, in those horrid days before the war."[15]

In this story the ulterior motive is to cure Miss Annie of her illness by inducting belief in a rabbit's foot. Miss Annie is duly cured. The differing attitudes of husband and wife toward Uncle Julius and his stories are underlined by the way they address the old Negro. To the wife he is always "Uncle Julius," to the husband simply "Julius."

In "The Goophered Grapevine," "Ol Mars Dugal' McAdoo" hires Aunt Peggy to conjure the vineyard so that the Negroes won't eat all his grapes. A new hand named Henry unknowingly eats the goophered grapes and must be unconjured. From that time on he goes through strange cycles of vigor and decline with the growth and decline each year of the grape vines. This is one of the most amusing of the stories and the dialect includes delightfully twisted words, such as, "en de han's on our own plantation wuz all so flusterated dat we fuhgot ter tell de noo han' 'bout de goopher on de scuppernon' vimes," and "En Aun' Peggy say dat bein' ez Henry did n' know 'bout de goopher, en et de grapes in ign'ance er de quinseconces."[16] This was the *Atlantic* version. When the story was included in *The Conjure Woman* "quinseconces" became plain old "conseq'ences," to me not an improvement (p. 20). At the end of the tale in the new version, Uncle Julius's ulterior motives became definite rather than suggested.

In "Hot-Foot Hannibal" Chesnutt showed that white people had no monopoly on cruelty, for slaves sometimes used the maltreatment and inequities of the system against each other. In a rage of jealousy, when fooled by Hannibal, Chloe tells the master of Jeff's part in a conjure scheme, and gets him sent away and sold. In "Po' Sandy" Chesnutt again shows the horrors of slavery and of treating Negroes as if they had no human feelings. The story almost nullifies its own point, however, when it seems to be merely a figment of Julius's cupidity. In the story "Dave's Neckliss" (*Atlantic*, 1889), told by Uncle Julius but not included in *The Conjure Woman* because it is not a conjure story, the author writes entirely from the white point of view. Of Uncle Julius he says that "his curiously undeveloped nature was subject to moods which were almost childish in their variableness." He continues:

> His way of looking at the past seemed very strange to us; his view of certain sides of life was essentially different from ours. He never indulged in any regrets for the Arcadian joyousness and irresponsibility which was a somewhat popular conception of slavery; . . . While he mentioned with a warm appreciation the acts of kindness which those in authority had shown to him and his people, he would speak of a cruel deed, not with the indignation of one accustomed to quick feeling and spontaneous expression, but with a furtive disapproval which suggested to us a doubt in his own mind as to whether he had a right to think or to feel, and presented to us the curious psychological spectacle of a mind enslaved long after the shackles had been struck off. (p. 501)

Chesnutt shows his mastery of the tall-tale form by his skillful creation of three semi-superman figures, Henry in "The Goophered Grapevine," Sandy in "Po' Sandy," and Dave in "Dave's Neckliss." His twisting of words is clever as well as funny when he implies double meanings, as in "Dave, w'en yer en Dilsey gits ready fer ter git married, I ain' got no rejections" (p. 502). He is master also of the sharp characterization. "Wiley was one er dese yer shiny-eyed, double headed little niggers, sha'p ez a steel trap, en sly ez de fox w'at keep out'n it" (p. 503). Chesnutt was not merely using folk tales. He wrote to Walter H. Page on April 4, 1898 about his "Konjah' stories." "They are made out of whole cloth, but are true, I think, to the general 'doctrine' of conjuration, and do not stray very far beyond the borders of what an old Southern Negro *might* talk about" (H.M.C., p. 93). The only one of the stories which foreshadows the more obvious polemic of Chesnutt's later work is "Mars Jeem's Nightmare," which to David Littlejohn "for all its charm and corn . . . is one of the more powerful allegorical fantasies of race-war literature" (p. 28).

Folk elements occasionally appear in Chesnutt's later books, but the author is always rationalistic and unbelieving. In *The Marrow of Tradition* Mrs. Carteret discovers a charm put in her child's bed by old Mammy Jane. She does not remove it. It might not help, she feels, but it can't do any harm. Her attitude is like that of Miss Annie, especially toward the rabbit's foot in "Sis Becky's Pickaninny." In *The House Behind the Cedars*, Rena gets a premonition of her mother's illness by dreaming three times of her being sick. This premonition is not really discounted by the author, but becomes a part of the tissue of coincidence. When she gets a further premonition about walking home from school with the little Negro Plato, it again proves valid, but the author writes it off rationalistically. "Her presentiment was probably a mere depression of spirits due to her condition of nervous exhaustion. A cloud had come up and threatened rain, and the wind was rising ominously" (p. 270). His own attitude toward superstition was expressed in his journal as early as August, 1875, at the age of seventeen.

> Well! uneducated people are the most bigoted, superstitious, hardest-headed people in the world! These folks downstairs believe in ghosts, luck, horse shoes, cloud-signs, witches, and all other kinds of nonsense, and all the argument in the world couldn't get it out of them. (H.M.C., pp. 14–15)

Although the conjure stories and the color-line stories of *The Wife of His Youth* had been written during the same period, the publication of the latter marked a change in Chesnutt's work. The humor diminished as the author more directly presented the problems of the colored in his own post-bellum America. As Chesnutt wrote in 1931, "substantially all of my writings, with the exception of *The Conjure Woman,* have dealt with the problems of people of mixed blood, which, while in the main the same as those of the true Negro, are in some instances and in some respects much more complex and difficult of treatment, in fiction as in life" *(Colophon)*. About his second book, Chesnutt wrote to his publishers, "I should welcome the thought that the book might be made to contribute in any degree to the 'enlightened and civilized treatment' of a subject, the handling of which has shown tendencies to lapse into unspeakable barbarism." "The book was written," he continued later in the letter,

> with the distinct hope that it might have its influence in directing attention to certain aspects of the race question which are quite familiar to those on the unfortunate side of it; and I should be glad to have that view of it emphasized if in your opinion the book is strong enough to stand it. (H.M.C., pp. 128–129)

Although the title story made a sensation when it appeared in the *Atlantic,* it seems today a combination of coincidence and melodrama, with no psychological development to make the hero's change of heart at all believable. It does explore the place and ideas of people of mixed blood, as do the other stories in the volume. The reviews were generally good. One writer happily asserted that the stories "present the negro simply as a human being, without the exaggerated pathos of the 'purpose novel' " (H.M.C., pp. 134–135). Hamilton Wright Mabie in *Outlook* praised the fine "psychological study of the negro in his new life" in the title story! (H.M.C., p. 135). John Chamberlain, thirty years later, saw *The Wife of His Youth* as showing the worst side of the writer. "We cannot accept queer twists" here as we can in *The Conjure Woman*. In the title story, "the inner conflict of Mr. Ryder is totally missing" (p. 604).

Howells gave Chesnutt's two volumes a favorable review in *The Atlantic Monthly* of May, 1900. He emphasizes Chesnutt's color, but insists that the stories are "worthy of unusual notice" no matter who the author. He finds in them "the delicate skill possible only from a love of truth." Howells praises the passionless handling of a tense part of our common life, the characterization and the stylistic skill, although he deplores the infrequent lapses. Chesnutt wrote later, "Imagine the thrill with which a new author would read such an encomium from such a source" *(Colophon)*.

It is not surprising that Chesnutt chose the subject of passing for his first extended work, the story "Rena Walden" which was eventually expanded further and published as *The House Behind the Cedars*. Charles W. Chesnutt was nearly white himself and could have passed. He was, as Littlejohn puts it, a "voluntary" Negro, Negro only by Southern legal definition, who could have led the life of a white man, but chose not to. "This," Littlejohn feels, "may help to explain the detached cool ease of his narrative voice, the voice of an urbane white (or near white) Northern observer viewing the battered and demoralized post-bellum South." Littlejohn has probably not read Chesnutt's biography, for his life was not free from the effects of prejudice, though they were, in his later life, largely diluted. Littlejohn attacks the melodrama of *The House Behind the Cedars,* which involves the ruin of a girl's life by the discovery by her fiancé of her Negro blood. "One can see the appeal of this theme to the sensation-hungry white gentility; but the adoption of it by Chesnutt strikes me as rather low, and perhaps reveals him as not altogether happy in his choice of a racial adoption" (pp. 27–28).

Chesnutt had considered passing. He wrote in his journal on July 31, 1875 (age seventeen):

> Twice today, or oftener, I have been taken for "white." At the pond this morning one fellow said he'd be damned if there was any nigger blood in me. . . . I believe I'll leave here and pass anyhow, for I am as white as any of them. (H.M.C. p. 13)

In editorial comment on sociological papers Chesnutt had written for the *Boston Transcript,* called "The Future American" (summer, 1900), the *Washington Times* wrote that "He faces the possibility of race amalgamation squarely, and speaks more frankly on the subject than most other writers have dared to do." He felt that " 'The races will be quite as effectively amalgamated by lightening the Negroes as they would be by darkening the whites.' " The editorial concluded that it was only natural for colored people to pass if they could as long as it had advantages for them. The only way to stop it was to give colored workmen and artists a chance to succeed without having to pass (H.M.C., pp. 149–150). Chesnutt himself decided not to try. He was idealistic enough to believe that things were different up North and that he could succeed as a colored man. After a talk with the doctor, while waiting for his first child to be born, Chesnutt wrote in his journal (April 23, 1879) that the doctor thought he could succeed in the North, "for there are more opportunities and less prejudice." They both believed "that when a young man starts out in life with a purpose, and works for that purpose, he is more than apt to accomplish it" (H.M.C., p. 17). He believed that he could live down prejudice and exalt his race (p. 17). For himself, he was right, but as he himself learned, it was not so for all the colored who came North. The teacher Mr. Taylor, at the end of *The Colonel's Dream,* must take a position way below his intelligence and training until helped out by the Colonel. Dr. Miller in *The Marrow of Tradition* is even more idealistic than Chesnutt himself. He believes that he can live down prejudice in the South.

> He liked to believe that the race antagonism which hampered his progress and that of his people was a mere temporary thing, the outcome of former conditions, and bound to disappear in time, and that when a colored man should demonstrate to the community in which he lived that he possessed character and power, that community would find a way in which to enlist his services for the public good. (p. 65)

He is proved wrong. In a 1916 letter, Chesnutt shows his satisfaction with his own life but a much less idealistic attitude toward Northern life.

> Indeed in this liberal and progressive Northern city we get most of the things which make life worth living, and this in spite of the fact that everyone knows our origin, and in spite of the fact that this is the United States and that there is plenty of race prejudice right here. . . . In the North, race prejudice is rather a personal than a community matter, and a man is not regarded as striking at the foundations of society if he sees fit to extend a social courtesy to a person of color. (H.M.C., p. 268)

Chesnutt wrote to Houghton, Mifflin about *The House Behind the Cedars.*

> I rather hope it will sell in spite of its subject, or rather, because of its dramatic value apart from the race problem involved. I was trying to write, primarily, an interesting and artistic story, rather than a contribution to polemical discussion.

Later in the letter he shifts position a bit.

> I hope the book may raise some commotion. I hardly care in what quarter, though whether, from the nature of the theme it will, I don't know. (Sept. 27, 1900, H.M.C., p. 152)

This novel and the two which followed it did contribute to polemical discussion and raise some commotion. The last two are better plotted and somewhat less melodramatic, but all three present strong pictures of the problems facing Negroes in the South and the inequities of their position. *The Marrow of Tradition* and *The Colonel's Dream* also show with detail and power the calculated viciousness and brutality of the Southern whites. *The Marrow of Tradition* pictures a riot in Wellington, caused by white jockeying to take over the government of the town and prevent Negro voting. It was based on the recent riot in Wilmington. Chesnutt had visited the town and thoroughly interviewed the people on their experiences. *The Colonel's Dream* is an exposé of the vicious convict labor system, which was creating a new slavery, under the law. By 1905, when Chesnutt published his last novel, he no longer pretended not to be writing a purpose novel. In his Dedication, he wrote

> To the great number of those who are seeking, in whatever manner or degree, from near at hand or far away, to bring the forces of enlightenment to bear upon the vexed problems which harass the South, this volume is inscribed, with the hope that it may contribute to the same good end.

All three novels involve considerable discussion of the matter of race. Some of this is from his characters' points of view, some straight argument. In *The House Behind the Cedars,* Judge Straight, who befriends the Negroes and expresses an enlightened attitude, is made eccentric, old and childless. The author seems afraid to have ordinary white men express such opinions. In the later books, there are groups of strong-minded men who try to do the right things and treat Negroes with humanity. They are in the course of the novels defeated by the benighted racists. George Tryon and Mrs. Carteret, through some melodramatic wrenching, are made to see the light and perhaps deplore their prejudices, but if life had gone on beyond the end of their respective books, it is doubtful whether their enlightened states would have continued.

Chesnutt was basically humanitarian. As a young school teacher he tried to avoid corporal punishment (H.M.C., p. 14, journal entry). In his books, however, he tried to present all sides of the race question fairly. Even white racists get a thorough hearing, although Chesnutt manages to make any moderately open-minded reader thoroughly indignant at their views. Southerners attacked him in any case, but even Howells, who had commented on the passionless attitude of his earlier books complained that *The Marrow of Tradition* was "bitter, bitter. . . . I am not saying that he is so inartistic as to play the advocate; whatever his minor foibles may be, he is an artist whom his step-brother Americans may well be proud of."[17] ("Step-brother!" Ah Howells, Ah Chesnutt.) *The Marrow of Tradition* was a literary success, but not as much of a financial success as Chesnutt and his publishers had expected. Chesnutt was disappointed in Howells's review and took issue with his earlier remark that there was no color line in literature. Chesnutt wrote to his publishers, "I am pretty fairly convinced that the color line runs everywhere so far as the United States is concerned" (H.M.C., p. 178). The reviewer in the *Nation,* unlike Howells, thought that Chesnutt was "calm, acute and just . . . surprisingly so."

In *The House Behind the Cedars,* Chesnutt comments on slavery with the Melvillean attitude that slavery brings out the worst in masters as well as slaves. He says it seriously, "One curse of negro slavery was, and one part of its baleful heritage is, that it poisoned the fountains of human sympathy" (p. 118), and comically, "The corruption of the white people's speech was one element—only one—of the negro's unconscious revenge for his own debasement" (p. 9).

John Walden's ideas on race are very simple.

> His playmates might call him black; the mirror proved that God, the Father of all, had made him white; and God, he had been taught, made no mistakes,— having made him white, He must have meant him to be white. (pp. 15–16)

Dr. Green's ideas (and George Tryon's) are equally simple. "They cannot take away our superiority of blood and breeding. In time we shall regain control. The negro is an inferior creature" (p. 136). A much more elaborate case is presented in the racist article George reads in Dr. Green's office (pp. 105–106), and in the editorial of Major Carteret in *The Marrow of Tradition* (pp. 30–31). Judge Straight is in the middle.

> We make our customs lightly; once made, like our sins, they grip us in bands of steel; we become the creatures of our creations. By one standard my old office-boy should never have been born. Yet he is a son of Adam, and came into existence in the way ordained by God from the beginning of the world. In equity he would seem to be entitled to his chance in life. (p. 35)

Chesnutt defended what Gilder felt was wrong in his portrayal in a letter to Cable.

> There are a great many intelligent people who consider the class to which Rena and Wain belong as unnatural. . . . I say this gentleman remarked to me in substance that he considered a mulatto an insult to nature, a kind of monster that he looked upon with infinite distaste; that a black Negro he looked upon with some respect, but any laws which tended in any way to bring the two races nearer together, were pernicious. (H.M.C., p. 57)

Thus George Tryon might indeed think:

> A negro girl had been foisted upon him for a white woman, and he had almost committed the unpardonable sin against his race of marrying her. Such a step, he felt, would have been criminal at any time; it would have been the most

odious treachery at this epoch, when his people had been subjugated and humiliated by the Northern invaders, who had preached negro equality and abolished the wholesome laws decreeing the separation of the races. (*Cedars,* p. 143)

Chesnutt, like many white writers, paints a picture of the humble Negro of dog-like devotion, whom the Southern white appreciate. His portrait however is touched with the sardonic, and these Negroes rarely come to a pleasant end. In *The House Behind the Cedars,* after telling how Frank once saved Rena's life, the author comments:

There are depths of fidelity and devotion in the negro heart that have never been fathomed or fully appreciated. Now and then in the kindlier phases of slavery these qualities were brightly conspicuous, and in them, if wisely appealed to, lies the strongest hope of amity between the two races whose destiny seems bound up together in the Western world. Even a dumb brute can be won by kindness. Surely it were worth while to try some other weapon than scorn and contumely and hard words upon people of our common race. (p. 177)

In *The Marrow of Tradition* Mammy Jane and her grandson Jerry are both typical cringing, faithful creatures. Though neither of them is killed purposely, neither survives the riot, although the Carterets have promised Mammy Jane their faithful care, and Jerry is sure that he can depend on the Major. It was no use, Chesnutt had countered Booker T. Washington's arguments, to depend on the faith of the white people.

Chesnutt's towns, like Clarendon in *The Colonel's Dream,* are in a state of decay. The Colonel believes that the whole South is in a state of decay, and sets out to do something about it. Chesnutt must already have been considerably disillusioned about his own dreams, for he gives the Colonel's short shrift. "No compassionate angel warned him how tenacious of life that which Fetters stood for might be—that survival of the spirit of slavery, under which the land still groaned and travailed—the growth of generations, which it would take more than one generation to destroy" (p. 120).

Charles W. Chesnutt achieved considerable literary recognition, but without the concomitant financial success and progress in achieving his purpose which he found necessary. Without sufficient money coming in, he could not afford to concentrate on writing, and without success in advancing the acceptance of colored people, fiction was not sufficiently worthwhile. The *Nation* review of *The House Behind the Cedars* was generally favorable, but Chesnutt could not have been encouraged in his purpose by the reviewer's suggestion that "He probably has but faint hope of upsetting social beliefs, and indeed the catastrophe suggests that such tragedies as the sacrifice of Rena Walden seem to him inevitable, therefore all the more pitiful" (Feb. 28, 1901).

Chesnutt is an example of a minority writer in whom social purpose, group purpose, must be mixed with individual purpose. A life devoted to literature for the sake of literature did not fit his aspirations. Other concerns were too important. Before 1905 Chesnutt returned to his business and concentrated on organization work. He wrote no more fiction after *The Colonel's Dream* until just before the end of his life, when he wrote a novel based on a real incident, again involving the color line. The novel was not accepted for publication and Chesnutt did not have the vitality to rewrite it.

Herbert Hill writes today that

> The greater part of contemporary American Negro writing is characterized by a determination to break through the limits of racial parochialism into the whole range of the modern writer's preoccupations. . . . [Writers] have abandoned the literature of simple and unrelieved protest, and have made the creative act their first consideration. They continue to confront American society as Negroes, but increasingly without the conflict between social and literary aspirations . . . [of the] past. (p. 3)

This conflict was very much a part of Chesnutt's life. He too however at the end of his career, looked forward to that change.

> To date, colored writers have felt restricted for subjects to their own particular group, but there is every reason to hope that in the future, with proper encouragement, they will make an increasingly valuable contribution to literature, and perhaps produce chronicles of life comparable to those of Dostoievsky, Dumas, Dickens or Balzac. (*Colophon*)

He himself had been, for a while, a writer of his people and in their cause. "And so the colonel faltered, and, having put his hand to the plow, turned back. But was not his, after all, the only way?" (*The Colonel's Dream*, p. 293). He at least believed that it was.

Notes

1. Larzer Ziff, *The American 1890s* (New York, 1966).
2. Helen M. Chesnutt, *Charles Waddell Chesnutt: Pioneer of the Color Line* (Chapel Hill, 1952).
3. Robert A. Smith, "A Note on the Folktales of Charles W. Chesnutt," *CLAJ*, V (1962), 229–32; and Donald M. Winkelman, "Three American Authors as Semi-Folk Artists," *J Am. Folklore*, LXXVIII (1965), 130–35.
4. Sylvia Lyons-Render, *Eagle with Clipped Wings: Form and Feeling in the Fiction of Charles Waddell Chesnutt* (Unpublished dissertation, Peabody, 1962. *DA*, XXIV (1963), 1175–76. She has published an article, "Tar Heelia in Chesnutt," *CLAJ*, IX (1965), 39–50.
5. John Chamberlain, "The Negro as Writer," *Bookman*, 70 (1930), 603–11.

6. David Littlejohn, *Black on White: A Critical Survey of Writing by American Negroes* (New York, 1966), pp. 21 and 27.

7. Herbert Hill, ed, *Soon One Morning: New Writing by American Negroes, 1940–1962* (New York, 1963), Introduction by Herbert Hill, pp. 3, 11–12.

8. H.M. Chesnutt, pp. 68–69.

9. H.M. Chesnutt, p. 69.

10. Charles W. Chesnutt, "Post-Bellum. Pre-Harlem," *The Colophon,* Pt. 5 (1931), unpaginated.

11. Hill, p. 10.

12. Reported in *The Cleveland Plain Dealer,* quoted in H.M.C., p. 304.

13. H.M.C., pp. 39–46.

14. *Nation,* 68 (1899), 421.

15. Charles W. Chesnutt, *The Conjure Woman* (Boston and New York, 1899, 1929), p. 159.

16. Charles W. Chesnutt, "The Goophered Grapevine," *The Atlantic Monthly,* LX (1887), 254–60, this reference p. 257.

17. William Dean Howells, "A Psychological Counter-Current in Recent Fiction," *North American Review* (Dec. 1901), quoted in H.M.C., p. 177.

'he Art of *The Conjure Woman*

RICHARD E. BALDWIN

I

In *The Conjure Woman* Charles Chesnutt analyzes with balance and subtlety the paradoxes and tensions of American racial life. The penetrating insights of these stories he never matched in his realistic fiction. Here Chesnutt avoids stifling stereotypes while criticizing the myths of white supremacy and demonstrating the range and quality of black experience. Other early black writers sought to do the same, but not until *Uncle Tom's Children* did any succeed as fully as did Chesnutt, for in *The Conjure Woman* he developed and exploited a finely balanced technique which solved the major artistic problems faced by early black writers.

The central problem was the audience. The reading public was predominantly white, and the audience that most early black writers cared most to reach was white, for it was to whites that they needed to tell the truth about the black experience in America. The need and the difficulty were one, for the problem of the black in America arose from the refusal of whites to perceive black experience accurately, and the artist's task was not simply to present the truth to white minds but to change those minds so that they could perceive the humanity of the black and the inhumanities which he suffered in America. The sentiments of white Americans could easily enough be touched, but the important and difficult task was changing their perceptions. Whites had to be trained to perceive black experience from the black point of view, for until the white man was so changed no serious black literature could receive a hearing because it would not be understood. The situation held dangers for the artist, since the task of reeducating America could not be completed quickly and the pressure of circumstances easily led writers to hasten the process by recourse to the melodramatic moral simplicity of propaganda.

From *American Literature* 43, no. 3 (November 1971): 385–98. Copyright 1971, Duke University Press. Reprinted with permission.

Chesnutt began his career with a clear understanding of the problem and of the necessary response of the artist. In 1880, before he began writing fiction, he noted in his journal that "if I do write, I shall write for a purpose, a high, holy purpose. . . . The object of my writings would be not so much the elevation of the colored people as the elevation of the whites." A little later in the same entry, in an observation basic to the strategy of *The Conjure Woman,* he noted that in the struggle of the Negro to win "recognition and equality" it was "the province of literature to open the way for him to get it—to accustom the public mind to the idea [of Negro equality]; to lead people out, imperceptibly, unconsciously, step by step, to the desired state of feeling"[1] toward Negroes.

Chesnutt aimed to modify white minds to feel the equality of the black man, and with the conjure tales he developed a perfect vehicle for his artistic needs. Chesnutt's genius shows in the certainty of touch involved in the choice of Uncle Julius as his central character. Choosing a character so close to widely current pejorative stereotypes was a stroke as significant as Wright's choice of Bigger Thomas, for only by confronting and thus destroying the stereotypes could the black artist hope to alter the public mind. Further, Uncle Julius resolves for Chesnutt the black artist's problem of creating a black character in a situation in which significant dramatic incident is possible. To demonstrate the equality of blacks and whites, a black character must be presented in dramatic conflict with whites in a situation which allows the black not only to survive but to succeed with dignity. The difficulty of imagining such situations was clearly formulated by William Couch, Jr., in an essay on "The Problem of Negro Character and Dramatic Incident": "Serious dramatic situation necessitates consequential action committed by a protagonist with whom we can sympathize and admire. The assumptions of American culture, on the other hand, are not congenial to emphatic and uncompromising action on the part of a Negro. This is especially true when white interests are involved. Therefore, a dramatic situation, capable of producing a powerful effect, will usually suffer a distortion of that effect when the agent of action is a Negro character."[2] In the face of this dilemma black artists have frequently relied on a conflict of virtuous blacks against vicious whites, thus accentuating the dilemma rather than resolving it.

Chesnutt's conjure stories, on the other hand, resolve this basic problem. The tales which Uncle Julius tells stand in the tradition of subterfuge, indirection, and subtle manipulation of whites developed by the slaves as a strategy for surviving in the face of oppression. Chesnutt's conjure stories turn the strategy of "puttin' on ol' massa" into effective dramatic action through parallels and tensions between the frames established by the white narrator and the tales told by Uncle Julius. In "The Goophered Grapevine," Chesnutt's first conjure story, Julius's attempt to use the tale of the goophered grapevine to place a new "goopher" on the vineyard in order to keep the white man from depriving him of his livelihood provides the most obvious parallel between frame and tale. Julius emerges from this dramatic conflict with a qualified success, for while he loses the vineyard he gains a more stable livelihood in the white man's employment.

The limitations of his success are illuminated by another parallel between frame and tale, however. An important part of the tale centers on the experiences of Henry, a slave of Dugald McAdoo, antebellum owner of the vineyard. McAdoo purchased Henry after the success of the fatal conjure Aunt Peggy had placed on his vineyards had so increased his crop that he needed more help. Henry ate some of the grapes before he could be warned of the conjure, and his life was saved by an antidote which involved his anointing himself with sap from one of the vines. From that time on Henry's life followed the rhythms of the growing season; he became strong and supple in the spring and summer, then withered up during the winter months. McAdoo made a great deal of money exploiting Henry by selling him when he was strong and buying him back cheap when he weakened in the fall. During the winter months McAdoo coddled Henry to protect the valuable chattel. Although Henry enjoyed this comfortable life, he was more than ever at McAdoo's mercy, for his life depended on the life of the vineyards. When McAdoo's greed led him to follow foolish advice which killed the vines, Henry paid with his life for his master's folly.

Henry was about Uncle Julius's age when McAdoo purchased him, and the narrator's hiring of Julius ominously parallels that transaction. Julius had been a free entrepreneur, and although his new job may pay more than the vineyard could yield to him, it represents a new form of slavery in which Julius loses a significant measure of his freedom in return for security; Julius's love of grapes, like Henry's, places him in the power of the white man. Yet this judgment must in turn be qualified by the implied parallel between the narrator and McAdoo, for it is obvious that the narrator is in some ways a wiser man than his slave-owning predecessor, a fact which mutes the threatening potential of his hiring of Julius while the mutual service of each to the other emphasizes the ways in which the story demonstrates the inescapable connections between the lives of black and white, a central theme in much of Chesnutt's work.

"The Goophered Grapevine" gains additional richness through the complicated nature of Julius's motivation. While he wants very much to preserve his vineyard, he simultaneously wants to strike out at the racial superiority assumed by the narrator. The tale which he tells consistently presents white men bested by blacks or acting in ways whose folly is clearly perceived by the blacks. Both in the broad outline of his tale of the goophered grapevine and in numerous minor points, such as the inability of the best white doctors to cure the goopher that Aunt Peggy has placed on Henry, Uncle Julius asserts the humanity of the black and his equality with, or superiority to, whites. Julius thus has the pleasure of effectively calling the white man a fool to his face, yet he fails to make any impression because the narrator is too blinded by racism to be able to perceive what Julius is up to. Ironically, that failure, while it underscores the truth in Julius's point, is vital to his success at preserving his livelihood, since the narrator would not likely have hired Julius had he perceived the insults. The concluding frame thus generates multiple ironies which illuminate the complex tension between the black's need to deny and attack white supremacy and the hard fact that while whites are not superior beings they nevertheless have very real power.

Chesnutt's success in dealing with this tension in *The Conjure Woman* depends not only on the complex motivation of Uncle Julius but also on the two white characters of the frame, the Northern narrator and his wife Annie. The two white people are crucial to Chesnutt's rhetorical strategy for leading white America "imperceptibly, unconsciously, step by step, to the desired state of feeling" toward blacks. The narrator, a basically decent sort of man, takes a typical paternalistic attitude towards Uncle Julius and his tales. He accepts Julius's attempts at manipulating him yet remains blinded by his own sense of superiority. His understanding of black life has been molded more by Uncle Remus and the plantation school than by Uncle Julius. As Julius begins the tale of the goophered grapevine, for instance, the narrator observes that "As he became more and more absorbed in the narrative, his eyes assumed a dreamy expression, and he seemed to lose sight of his auditors, and to be living over again in monologue his life on the old plantation."[3] This evocation of the plantation tradition reveals the narrator's blindness to Julius's revelations about slavery, for life on the McAdoo plantation had nothing of the dreamy quality of the idyls of Harris. The statement becomes richly ironic when the conclusion shows that Uncle Julius has had his eyes very much on his auditors and the demands of the present moment. It is the narrator whose eyes are closed, and in an adumbration of the Invisible Man motif he is "beaten" by a man he never sees.

The narrator's posture has immense rhetorical value for Chesnutt, for it enables him to present his stories with detachment from the point of view of any of his characters. The framing narrative voice is that of a typical white American liberal, an unconscious racist who seems free of bigotry. In his reactions to Julius's tale the narrator is not so dull as to miss all that the black is up to, yet he misses enough that he can report the tale of slavery with no sense of the range of its meaning, especially those portions directed against him. The narrator thus appears as a mixture of sensitivity and callousness, and he can be treated sympathetically while his blindness to Uncle Julius's character and to the implications of his tales provides ironic commentary on his own character and on America's racial absurdities.

Chesnutt's technique relies heavily on irony, and like any ironic technique it runs the risk that readers will miss the point, Annie, the narrator's wife, is developed as a contrasting character in order to reduce this danger. Her permanent convalescent state underscores the feminine sensibility which leads her to respond more deeply to Uncle Julius than does her husband.

When Julius announces that the vineyard is goophered, for instance, the narrator observes that "He imparted this information with such solemn earnestness, and with such an air of confidential mystery, that I felt somewhat interested, while Annie was evidently much impressed, and drew closer to me" (pp. 11–12). The narrator's attitude toward his wife frequently is as condescending as his attitude toward Julius, and after the tale is finished he notes that she "doubtfully, but seriously" asked, " 'Is that story true?' " (p. 33). His own reaction to the tale appears only in his assertion that he bought the vineyard in spite of the purported goopher. Annie's question, however, allows Chesnutt to imply the presence of metaphoric meanings through the absurd literalness of Uncle Julius's response that he can prove its truth by showing her Henry's grave. At such levels the tale obviously is not true, but the nature of the question and answer implies that other levels of meaning can be discovered by any who care to look for them.

Chesnutt seems not to have fully grasped the value of his white characters when he first wrote "The Goophered Grapevine," for his second conjure story openly exploits the contrast, and when he prepared the first story for book publication he added to the opening frame several long sections which develop the narrator more fully. The opening frame of the second story, "Po' Sandy," points out the difference between the narrator and Annie. When she rises eagerly to Julius's hint of a story, her husband comments that "some of these stories are quaintly humorous; others wildly extravagant, revealing the Oriental cast of the negro's imagination; while others, poured freely into the sympathetic ear of a Northern-bred woman, disclose many a tragic incident of the darker side of slavery" (pp. 40–41). While the narrator has sufficient curiosity to listen to the tales with pleasure he has no patience for discovering meanings in them; rather than revelations about American life he sees only an "Oriental cast of the negro's imagination." Annie, on the other hand, instinctively leaps to at least some meanings. The resulting contrast helps Chesnutt bring a white audience to perceive events from the black point of view, for while the narrator reacts with a typical white obtuseness, Annie, by seeing through the surface of fantastic and supernatural machinery, points the reader to the vital human life behind.

Chesnutt uses this contrast most effectively in "Po' Sandy." Uncle Julius's tale tells of Sandy, a young slave devoted to his wife Tenie, a conjure woman. Mars Marrabo continually sends Sandy, an exceptionally good worker, to help out relatives on distant plantations, and when Sandy tires of this Tenie turns him into a tree to keep him near her. When Sandy disappears, the dogs track him to the tree, where they lose the trail. After the excitement of his disappearance passes, Tenie nightly returns Sandy to human form. But then Marrabo sends Tenie to nurse his daughter-in-law, and during her absence Sandy is cut down, and Tenie returns just in time to watch her husband sawn into lumber to build a new kitchen on the plantation. The kitchen remains haunted by Sandy's ghost, so it is eventually torn down and the lumber used to build a schoolhouse. The narrator now plans to tear down the school and use the lumber to build Annie a new kitchen.

After Julius finishes his tale, the following exchange between Annie and the narrator occurs:

> "What a system it was," she exclaimed, when Julius had finished, "under which such things were possible!"
>
> "What things?" I asked, in amazement. "Are you seriously considering the possibility of a man's being turned into a tree?"
>
> "Oh, no," she replied quickly, "not that"; and then she murmured absently, and with a dim look in her fine eyes, "Poor Tenie!" (pp. 60–61)

The narrator as usual sees nothing but the surface of the tale, but with his insensitivity as a contrast Chesnutt needs no more than Annie's murmured "Poor Tenie" to alert us to the story of the pain caused by the inhuman violations of personal life and the brutalities endured by slaves. The narrator believes in the beauty of the Old South and the quaintness of Negro folktales, but through Annie we see the horrors of slavery.

Had Annie's role ended with "Poor Tenie!" the story would have verged on the sentimentality which so quickly destroys the effect of tales of pathos. But the sentimentality of the "dim look in her fine eyes" and the quiet murmur are the narrator's, not Chesnutt's. Annie has a sentimental streak, but Chesnutt nevertheless uses her to help effect a most unsentimental change of tone from the pathos and horror of the tale to the grotesquely incongruous, anticlimactic humor of the concluding frame. Through Annie's agency Chesnutt modulates the story from the grim brutalities of a man sawn into lumber to end on a note of gentle, ironic humor.

The humor of the conclusion is vital to the overall effect of the story, avoiding sentimentality and creating an impact more tautly complex than pathos. The humor of the frame relieves the pain of the tale itself, emphasizing the similar effect created by the incongruity between the horror experienced by the characters of the tales and the improbability of the conjure elements. The final effect has the complexity described by Ralph Ellison as the blues, the transcendence of pain "not by the consolation of philosophy, but by squeezing from it a near-tragic, near-comic lyricism."[4] At their best, Chesnutt's conjure stories require a response which sustains that type of tension between the tragic and the comic. The tension is most striking in "Po' Sandy," yet Chesnutt's third conjure story, "The Conjurer's Revenge," exploits it in an equally effective and perhaps more sophisticated way. In "The Conjurer's Revenge" the narrator needs a draught animal, and Julius hopes it will not be a mule; he hates to drive a mule for fear it may be a human being, and thereby hangs a tale. The tale tells how Primus, a slave, stole a shote from a conjure man who revenged the theft by turning him into a mule. A large portion of the tale deals with Primus's escapades as a mule—eating tobacco in the field, guzzling a huge quantity of wine, attacking the man who had taken over his woman. When the conjure man neared death he got religion, and feeling guilty about Primus summoned him in order to return him to human form. He lived long enough to turn back all of Primus except for one foot, which remained clubbed.

When Uncle Julius finishes the tale it appears that he knows a man with a horse to sell. Shortly after the narrator buys the horse Uncle Julius sports a flashy new suit, apparently purchased with his share of the money paid for the horse. Within three months, the animal dies of diseases brought on by old age, and while the entire affair makes fine comedy, the comedy has a harsh, vindictive quality unknown in the two earlier tales. The tale itself is a disconcerting mixture of the comic escapades of a man turned into a mule and the story of a slave who, to take the view of Primus's master, " 'had runned erway, en stay' 'tel he got ti'ed er de swamps, en den come back on him ter be fed. He tried ter 'count fer de shape er Primus' foot by sayin' Primus got his foot smash', er snake-bit, er sump'n, w'iles he wuz erway, en den stayed out in de woods whar he couldn' git it kyoed up straight, 'stidder comin' long home whar a doctor could 'a' 'tended ter it' " (pp. 126–127). Either way this tale lacks the compelling quality of the tale of Po' Sandy, and Annie's reaction to it is negative: " 'That story does not appeal to me, Uncle Julius, and is not up to your usual mark. It isn't pathetic, it has no moral that I can discover, and I can't see why you should tell it. In fact, it seems to me like nonsense' " (p. 127).

There is a moral, although not the sort that would dim Annie's fine eyes. The moral is enunciated by the narrator when, after discovering that the fine looking animal he bought is half blind and thoroughly broken down, he exclaims, "But alas for the deceitfulness of appearances" (p. 130). The story underscores this point. Julius's tale is pointless by comparison with the earlier two, but his telling of the pointless tale was a deceitful appearance intentionally used to cover his own motives and set up the narrator for the sales pitch made at the end.

Chesnutt's concern reaches beyond the sales of horses and mules, though, and "The Conjurer's Revenge" provides a broad commentary on the American racial situation. The title suggests that Uncle Julius's intentional swindling of his employer amounts to revenge. As in the tale Primus felt the wrath of the conjure man because he stole a shote, so in Chesnutt's story the narrator is bilked because Julius has had a valuable possession stolen—the dignity, freedom, and equality which are the components of his humanity—and works a goopher on the white man in revenge. The story focuses on "the deceitfulness of appearances" which lies at the heart of race relations, and in part on the deceitfulness of appearances in Chesnutt's earlier two stories. The earlier stories had glossed the moral turpitude of race relations by implicitly justifying Uncle Julius's behavior—in "The Goophered Grapevine" on grounds of practical necessity, in "Po' Sandy" on grounds of service to a communal group. "The Conjurer's Revenge" strips all romantic gloss from Southern life and presents the hard core of racial conflict, that mutual dehumanization which eliminates all moral compunctions from the black man's dealing with whites and which enables the white man to hide from himself the fact that the black man is a human being. If the white man becomes vulnerable to the deceitfulness of appearances, the appearances are his own creation, the self-delusions spawned by his denial of the black man's humanity. In this situation the black man quite naturally becomes a conjure man, using his wits to exploit and encourage the deceitful appearances which the white man has created. There is nothing moral or pathetic here, just a bald power struggle which is comically, tragically human, the deepest reality of American racial conflict.

II

Nearly ten years intervened between the publication of "The Conjurer's Revenge" and the appearance of *The Conjure Woman* in 1899. None of the additional four stories appeared previously in periodicals; so the sequence in which they were written is unknown. Each of these later stories, while it follows the original frame-tale pattern, reveals Chesnutt reaching the limits of the form's usefulness. The later four stories lack the complex balance of the earlier three. In "Sis' Becky's Pickaninny," for instance, the tight relation between frame and tale is lacking. By itself the tale fails to develop significant dramatic action, and unlike the tale in "The Conjurer's Revenge" it is not an integral part of a larger conception. "Hot-Foot Hannibal," on the other hand, has a frame and a tale technically well matched. Here, however, Julius has no significant role in either tale or frame. The parallels between tale and frame thus remain mechanical, and Chesnutt's point seems to be simply to demonstrate by the parallel that blacks feel the same pains, joys, and sorrows as whites. "Hot-Foot Hannibal" comes closer than any other conjure tale to the special group pleading of the propagandist.

The weakness of "Hot-Foot Hannibal" appears clearly when it is compared with "The Gray Wolf's Ha'nt." Nothing in *The Conjure Woman* surpasses Uncle Julius's tale of the gray wolf's ha'nt. This story of love, jealousy, and murder among the slaves achieves tragic stature and has no taint of propaganda. The tale is perfect in itself, but it is badly marred by being forced into a trite and irrelevant frame. The tale deals with conflict within the slave community and lacks the interracial conflict on which vital parallels between tale and frame depended in the three earlier stories. The tale does not need a frame, and its strength indicates that the conjure story could have been developed into a vehicle for exploring black culture. Interracial conflict was essential to the vitality of the form as Chesnutt initially conceived it, however, and his willingness to place this magnificent story in an unsuitable frame suggests that he was uninterested in forms which did not deal with such conflict.

The remaining conjure story, "Mars Jeems's Nightmare," suggests in fact that Chesnutt had reached the limits of the form even as a vehicle for exploring racial conflict. "Mars Jeems's Nightmare," which focuses on racial conflict with the unrelenting rigor of "The Conjurer's Revenge," is the only one of the later stories that creates something like the balanced tone, the intellectual strength, and the imaginative integrity of the early stories. The frame drama centers around Uncle Julius's grandson Tom, formerly employed by the narrator but fired for laziness and carelessness; Julius's aim in telling this tale is to get his grandson rehired. The tale tells how a vicious master is turned into a Negro and delivered into the hands of his own sadistic poor-white overseer until he is beaten into sympathy for his slaves. Moved by this tale Annie effects the desired change (in the concluding frame) by taking the boy back. Her act angers the narrator, but he lets the boy stay. Implicit in his acquiescence are the effects on him of the story of Mars Jeems's being turned into a slave. At the end of the tale the narrator acknowledges that the changing of a white man into a Negro was "powerful goopher," an ironic admission of the power of the tale on him and Annie, for it has in effect put them through the experience of Mars Jeems and has acted as a "powerful goopher" on them.

More than any other story, "Mars Jeems's Nightmare" examines the psychology which gives Uncle Julius power over the narrator. At the beginning of the story Chesnutt has the narrator characterize Uncle Julius at length in a passage which reveals more about the narrator than about Uncle Julius:

> Toward my tract of land and the things that were on it—the creeks, the swamps, the hills, the meadows, the stones, the trees—he maintained a peculiar personal attitude, that might be called predial rather than proprietary. He had been accustomed, until long after middle life, to look upon himself as the property of another. When this relation was no longer possible, owing to the war, and to his master's death and the dispersion of the family, he had been unable to break off entirely the mental habits of a lifetime, but had attached himself to the old plantation, of which he seemed to consider himself an appurtenance. We found him useful in many ways and entertaining in others, and my wife and I took quite a fancy to him. (pp. 64–65)

As an analysis of Uncle Julius this passage is accurate only in its assumption that the mental habits of a lifetime could not be cast off. It is dead wrong on the nature of those habits, however. The other stories in *The Conjure Woman* reveal how little Uncle Julius sees himself as another's property, while the tales reveal how little the slaves themselves had thought that way. The narrator's error reveals the patronizing attitude which blinds him to the reality of Uncle Julius's activities and which amounts to a wish to consign the freed slave to a new subservience.

The passage also reveals how the guilt created by this attempt to create a new slavery manifests itself in a sense of responsibility for blacks. Uncle Julius understands this psychological complex thoroughly enough to be able to exploit it cynically. At the conclusion of his tale about Mars Jeems he points the moral of the tale: "Dis yer tale goes ter show . . . dat w'ite folks w'at is so ha'd en stric', en doan make no 'lowance fer po' ign'ant niggers w'at ain' had no chanst ter l'arn, is li'ble ter hab bad dreams, ter say de leas', en dat dem w'at is kin' en good ter po' people is sho' ter prosper en git 'long in de worl' " (p. 100). This sententious moralizing reveals Uncle Julius's awareness of the white man's guilt and his willingness to exploit that sense of guilt unscrupulously. Uncle Julius has no interest in having his grandson educated; he asks only that allowance be made for him. Uncle Julius wants the patronizing whites to pay for their sense of superiority by supporting the blacks whose shiftlessness they have created by their attitudes and actions. In this story Uncle Julius emerges as an opportunist like Ellison's Bledsoe, and his relation to the narrator in many ways resembles that of Bledsoe to Norton. The situation Chesnutt draws is virtually hopeless, a vicious circle of mutual exploitation with no will on either side to break the cycle.

Although the situation "Mars Jeems's Nightmare" exposes is nightmarish, the story avoids pessimism and bitterness. While it does not achieve that lyrical tension between tragedy and comedy which made "Po' Sandy" a prose blues, "Mars Jeems's Nightmare" nevertheless does balance the hopelessness of the situation with the humor of Uncle Julius's manipulation of the whites and Annie's active complicity in his success. The balance vital to the conjure stories is also threatened from another quarter, however. From the beginning Chesnutt has been the ultimate conjure man, hoping that by "wukking de roots" of black culture he might be able to work a powerful goopher on white America and lead it to accept the equality of the black. The indirection of the conjure stories enabled him to pursue his goal with consummate artistry but without sufficient power to save America from bad dreams.

His desire to deal more directly with racial problems shows in "Mars Jeems's Nightmare" in its concern with an issue with broad social implications, the questions of employment and education for blacks and of white responsibilities therefor. The indirection of the conjure story was ill adapted to such concerns, and "Mars Jeems's Nightmare" inevitably raises questions which the limits of the form prevent it from dealing with. The crucial relation of the drama—the relation between the narrator as employer and Tom as employee—is peripheral rather than central. We can never learn about Tom, the nature of his purported laziness and carelessness, the possible causes, or the possible ways of dealing with the situation. The point of the story, of course, is that the situation precludes either party from dealing directly with these issues, and the story quite properly does not attempt to examine them. Nevertheless, such questions arise simply because the frame drama and the point of Uncle Julius's tale both enter the realm of practical social problems where these questions exist and demand attention. The grim vision of "Mars Jeems's Nightmare" registers the hopelessness of America's racial life and reveals the limitations of the indirect approach to racism which the conjure story provided. On the one hand, the conjure story provided a subtle instrument which could portray with a terrifying accuracy and clarity the functioning of American racial life, but it offered no imaginative way out for either author or audience. The lesson of the white narrator—that whites are too blind to perceive the truth about race—may have suggested to Chesnutt that it was not enough to show race relations in action but that what was needed was an art which would outline explicitly the white misconceptions about blacks and the forces responsible for their formation and perpetuation. In any event, Chesnutt's concern shifted from working a subtle goopher on white minds to attacking specific social problems and clearly laying bare the mechanics and consequences of racism, and the conjure story ceased to be a useful vehicle. After *The Conjure Woman* was published Chesnutt gave full attention to the realistic fiction he had been working with throughout the 1890's.

If Americans were too blind for subtle methods, they were no more amenable to direct confrontation. White Americans would not allow themselves to perceive life from a black perspective, and Chesnutt's turn from the complex art of the conjure story was unavailing. Realism did give Chesnutt room to explore additional dimensions of racial life in America, but the ultimate irony is that his realistic fiction never achieved sharper insights than those of "Mars Jeems's Nightmare" and the early conjure stories, while losing their balance, control, and clarity. It is through the marvelously subtle conjure fiction, which transcends the nightmare of American racism in a near-tragic, near-comic lyricism, that Chesnutt works his most powerful goopher.

Notes

1. Helen Chesnutt, *Charles W. Chesnutt: Pioneer of the Color Line* (Chapel Hill, N.C., 1954), p. 21.

2. *Phylon*, XI (Second Quarter, 1950), p. 128.

3. Charles W. Chesnutt, *The Conjure Woman* (Ann Arbor, Mich., 1969), pp. 12–13. Subsequent references to this work will appear in the text.

4. Ralph Ellison, "Richard Wright's Blues," in *Shadow and Act* (New York, 1964), p. 90.

The Evolution of Charles Chesnutt's
The House Behind the Cedars

ROBERT P. SEDLACK

For Charles Waddell Chesnutt, the decade between 1889 and 1899 was one of the busiest, most productive, and apparently most satisfying of his life. Besides pursuing his flourishing career of stenographer and court reporter in Cleveland, Chesnutt participated in the public discussion of what was then termed "the Race Question," turned out a series of stories, including the highly-successful "The Wife of His Youth," and worked on two distinctly different novels. Moreover, this intense literary activity was crowned with success in 1899 when two collections of tales, *The Conjure Woman* and *The Wife of His Youth,* were published by the prestigious Boston firm of Houghton, Mifflin.

Yet anyone who reads his daughter's biography of Chesnutt will recognize that this period was not so deeply satisfying as this brief summary would suggest.[1] For throughout the period Chesnutt struggled to revise for publication a story (originally entitled "Rena") that he cared about more deeply than any other. Initially conceived and composed as a short story in 1889, "Rena" was revised at least three times between 1889 and 1891, set aside for several years, turned into a novelette by 1895, and finally a novel by 1899. Despite this continual effort, Chesnutt was unable to get it published and, in a *cri de coeur* to his editor in March 1899, he revealed the depth of both his concern and his frustration: "Your house has turned down my novel Rena [*sic*] in great shape. They have condemned the plot, its development, find the distinctions on which it is based unimportant, and have predicted for it nothing but failure. I have not slept with that story for ten years without falling in love with it, and believing in it. . . ."[2]

Still determined, Chesnutt sat down once more to revise his manuscript, tightening the plot and eliminating some major weaknesses so that by the following year the improved version attracted the attention of the younger, more aggressive New York firm of Doubleday & McClure. Recognizing the improvements and reluctant to lose an author whose books were selling well, Houghton, Mifflin agreed to bring out the novel in 1900 under the new title, *The House Behind the Cedars.*

Reprinted with permission from *CLA Journal* 19 (December 1975): 125–35.

For Chesnutt, of course, the publication of this, his first novel, was a genuine triumph because it allowed him to explore in depth the subject that most concerned him, the lives of people like himself, mulattoes, who lived on "the color line" between two worlds. For our purposes, however, this long period of gestation provides an important chapter in Chesnutt's development as both a polemicist on the Race Question and as an artist. Indeed, the five manuscript versions of "Rena"/*House* deposited in the Fisk University Library[3] reveal both Chesnutt's growing militance as a polemicist and his increasing competence as an artist.

Although the Fisk manuscripts are not dated, it is possible to identify three stages in the development of this work: an 1889–91 short story of a tragic mulatto, Rena Walden, who forsakes a young black man to marry a lighter-skinned, but treacherous villain; an 1895–99 version that both expands the original story and complicates it by adding the love affair between Rena and a white Southerner, George Tryon; the final novel that integrates, though not altogether satisfactorily, the two different relationships. During this evolution, Chesnutt's story changes from an account of a relatively simple love triangle to the more complex picture of an entire society that emerges in the novel.

The 1889–91 version begins with a narrator reminiscing about his boyhood in Patesville, North Carolina; he describes the town, explains Mis' Molly Walden's background as the antebellum mistress of a wealthy white man, and then mentions two of her mulatto children: "All of Mis' Molly's children but one had left the shelter of her roof, and gone out into the world. One went South, changed his name, and was lost to his people."[4] The one who remains at home is Rena, the central figure of this story; the other, a son who plays no role here, is later resurrected and appears in subsequent versions as John (Walden) Warwick.

At this point the narrator disappears and attention focuses on Rena, an idealized young woman of seventeen, "bright" enough to pass for white. Although content, she is a worry to her mother who is concerned about the future of this nubile girl in the unsettled years of early Reconstruction. Marriage would provide Rena some degree of protection, but Molly will not permit her to marry just anyone. Because she has inherited the color prejudice of her world, she scorns a young neighbor, Frank Fuller (later Fowler), with his ebony skin and "strongly marked African features," who had grown to love Rena deeply when they were allowed to play together as children, but must now worship her from afar.

With the setting, characters, and central theme established, Chesnutt then introduces a mysterious stranger, well dressed and well equipped with a sturdy horse and fine carriage, who is visiting Patesville in quest of a mate. This stranger is soon revealed as Washington (later Jeff) Wain, an apparently prosperous plantation owner with a manor house and servants in a neighboring county. Because Wain is "light brown," Molly urges Rena to set her cap for him, and she plans a party to bring them together. At the party, to which only the fairest Negroes in the community are invited, Rena enjoys dancing with Wain while Frank, invited to sit on the back porch, can only watch in anguish.

The next morning, Wain returns to court Rena. During a carriage ride he professes his love, proposes, but is put off. When they return home, however, Molly overcomes Rena's instinctive aversion to Wain, and she agrees to marry him. Within four days they wed and leave Patesville. On the way, Wain reluctantly admits that he is really not so prosperous as he appears, that his situation is somewhat less ideal than he had pretended. In fact, he reveals that his manor house is a cabin with two rooms and a kitchen and that the other occupants are not servants at all, but his mother, two children by a former wife, a sister and her four children!

Shocked by these revelations and depressed by the "general air of shift-lessness and squalor" about Wain's home when they arrive, Rena is further shaken to realize that her husband's horse and carriage, even his clothes, have been borrowed. After these incidents, the subsequent knowledge that the land is worn out and the property heavily mortgaged deepens her grief. Thoroughly wretched, Rena endures in the hope of returning to visit her mother. Months pass and Wain at first procrastinates, then refuses to allow her to leave; meanwhile, Rena weakens physically and spiritually.

One day as Rena is working listlessly around the cabin, a wealthy white woman, Mrs. Carter, stops for a drink of water. Engaging Rena in conversation, she reveals that she is the former owner of Wain's first wife and, more ominous, she implies that the woman is not dead, but has run off because of her husband's cruelty. For Rena, this suspicion precipitates a crisis: she confronts Wain's mother that evening and collapses when the old woman seems to confirm her suspicion. Later that night, Wain's mother tries to poison Rena, but she refuses the potion and, awakening from a feverish sleep, flees towards Patesville. Meanwhile, the ever-faithful Frank, hearing an unfavorable report of Wain, has decided to see how Rena is faring. On the way to Wain's he happens on Rena prostrate beside the road; comforting her as best he can, he carries her home, where she dies.

In this earliest version of his story, Chesnutt followed the "high, holy purpose" that he had vowed to follow at the beginning of his literary career in 1880:

> The object of my writings would be not so much the elevation of the colored people as the elevation of the whites—for I consider the unjust spirit of caste . . . a barrier to the moral progress of the American people; and I would be one of the first to head a determined, organized crusade against it. Not a fierce indiscriminate onset, not an appeal to force . . . but a moral revolution which must be brought about in a different manner. The subtle almost indefinable feeling of repulsion toward the Negro, which is common to most Americans—

cannot be stormed and taken by assault; the garrison will not capitulate, so their position must be mined, and we will find ourselves in their midst before they think it.[5]

As important in this statement as Chesnutt's purpose—a moral revolution in white America—is his technique: he hoped to succeed not by *assault,* but by more subtle tactics, *mining* and *infiltration.* And the method of the 1889–91 version of "Rena" corresponded to this exactly: it was an attempt to awaken the conscience of America by showing that color consciousness *within* the Negro community destroys Rena. Of course, any reflective reader would recognize the great moral evil of racial prejudice just beneath the surface, but no white reader—and Chesnutt's audience was primarily white—needed to feel immediately threatened because of Chesnutt's oblique approach here.

Unfortunately, at this stage "Rena" was clearly an inferior piece of fiction. The use of a first person narrator who reminisces about events that occurred in Patesville between 1866 and 1870—years that correspond exactly to Chesnutt's return from Cleveland to Fayetteville, North Carolina, with his family—suggests that he was using incidents that were familiar to him as a boy, but that his imagination had only just begun to fashion into fiction. More important, Chesnutt's characters were poorly drawn. Indeed, in a July 1890 cover letter to his literary mentor, George W. Cable, Chesnutt noted that he had tried to improve this element in the accompanying revision: "I have given the mother more heart. . . . I have also shaded Wain down so that he is not quite so melodramatic a villain, and Rena's speech and so forth so that she is not quite so superior a being. . . ."[6] But Cable, after examining these changes, was unimpressed and discouraged Chesnutt from resubmitting the story.[7]

After an unsuccessful attempt the following summer to have "Rena" published as the title story of a collection of short pieces, Chesnutt put his manuscript aside for several years. Then in April 1895, he announced to Cable: "Several days before I received your letter I had taken up the MS of 'Rena Walden' with a view to re-writing it. . . . I have re-cast the story, and in its present form it is a compact, well-balanced novelette of 25,000 to 28,000 words."[8] Despite this reworking of the story into a novelette roughly twice the length of the earlier version, Chesnutt still could not find a publisher; so he continued revising his manuscript until, by 1899, he had a novel-length manuscript to submit for publication.

During this period, Chesnutt both expanded and added new material to his original story. To begin with, he filled in the background of his narrator, the setting, Molly's history, and Rena's relationship with Frank. More important, he then prefaced his original Frank-Rena-Wain triangle with a new plot involving George Tryon, a young white Southerner who falls in love with Rena before learning of her racial heritage. To do this, Chesnutt resurrected John Walden, Molly's son who had been lurking in the author's subconscious, to provide the necessary bridge between the world of Rena Walden and that of George Tryon.

In adding new characters and an altogether new plot, Chesnutt began to change his purpose. To be sure, he was still critical of racial prejudice *within* the Negro community: "To be white had been so long synonymous with wealth and position and so strongly emphasized in relation to them that Rena bowed to the symbol without any special thought of what it signified. She and her colored friends were not the only ones to whom a white skin had become a fetish; they but reflected the sentiment of the community in which they had been reared."[9]

However, with the addition of George Tryon, Chesnutt began to shift his criticism of prejudice from the black to the white world. In the longest of the transitional manuscripts, Tryon is depicted as a loud, blustering bigot. Early in his relationship with Rena, she asks him, point blank, if he would love her if she were a mulatto, and he replies, "I never could have looked at you,"[10] revealing that he too has inherited the prejudice of their world. Clearly, Chesnutt's purpose here was to show that the malignancy of racial prejudice also infects the white world. And, by presenting this white bigot as *partially* responsible for Rena's downfall, he made a much more direct attack on racial prejudice than he had in the original short story. Nevertheless, he softened this attack by making Tryon, like Rena, a victim of inherited prejudice and by keeping Wain as the chief villain who deceives, marries and destroys her.

At this stage in the evolution of the novel, Chesnutt's artistry was still weak. Besides the flawed point of view noted above, his characters were stereotypes: Rena, the tragic mulatto who naively hopes that racial prejudice will somehow not affect her own life; Wain, the treacherous villain of late nineteenth century melodrama; and Tryon, the white bigot who rejects the woman he professes to love. In addition, the story now had two distinct, unintegrated movements—the first involving Rena and Tryon, the second involving Rena and Wain—though Chesnutt struggled throughout the period to fuse them.[11] Under the circumstances, it is not surprising that Houghton, Mifflin turned Chesnutt down in 1899 when he tried to get this work published.

When the novel appeared in late 1900 as *The House Behind the Cedars,* however, Chesnutt had made several changes that reveal a final, more dramatic shift in purpose and a more competent, if flawed, craftsmanship. To begin with, he eliminated the first person narrator who appeared in all of his earlier versions and substituted a third-person privileged narrator. Further, he moved away from the stereotyped characters of the transitional stage toward *relatively* more complex and credible characters. And he subordinated the original plot, involving Rena with Wain, so effectively that the casual reader would be surprised to learn that Wain played a key role in the original story.

Although these changes are clear evidence of Chesnutt's more mature artistry, they must first be examined for what they reveal about his final, polemical purpose. For here, instead of the oblique criticism of the early short story or the even-handed attack of the transitional manuscripts, Chesnutt made an overt, direct assault on *white* racial prejudice, specifically that of George Tryon, while muting his criticism of prejudice within the black community. This is particularly evident in characterization and in the subordination of the plot involving Wain.

In presenting Rena, Chesnutt deleted entirely the passage quoted above describing Rena's "fetish" for white skin and, instead, suggested that her affection for Tryon arises as much from personal as from social reasons. Indeed, in a key passage when she is trying to learn Tryon's attitude toward miscegenation, the privileged narrator implies that personal reasons are more powerful than social ones, for he notes that "love blinded her"[12] when Tryon answers ambiguously. Wain, on the other hand, underwent a more complete change. Instead of being the chief antagonist, he does not even appear until two-thirds of the way through the novel and then only as a man seeking a teacher for a Reconstruction school, not as a potential mate. He does not marry Rena and, in fact, never seems much of a threat except in her sometimes fervid imagination. With these changes, Chesnutt obviously intended to shift the burden of his criticism to the white bigot, George Tryon, who cruelly rejects Rena when he discovers her racial identity. And, indeed, Tryon's immediate response to this discovery makes him an odious figure: "The full realization of the truth, which followed speedily, had . . . reversed his mental attitude toward her, and love and yearning had given place to anger and disgust."[13]

But, unlike the earlier version described above, George Tryon is no longer the one-dimensional figure of a blustering bigot. To perceive this, one need only examine the letter that Tryon sends to Rena's brother after the recognition scene. In an earlier version, Tryon concludes: "I wish you all good luck, your sister every happiness; but by God! . . . I *cannot marry* her—you know I cannot marry her!" And then he signs himself: "Your former friend, George Tryon."[14] This declaration comes from an angry young bigot whose innate sense of superiority has been threatened. The more moderate letter of the novel,[15] on the other hand, comes from a young man who begins, for the first time in his life, to question the bigotry he has ignorantly, unthinkingly accepted. By the end of the novel, though he has pursued Rena for a complex of mixed and confused reasons, he is determined to marry her: "He would find her; he would tell her that he loved her, that she was all the world to him, that he had come to marry her and take her away where they might be happy together."[16] But he arrives in Patesville just as Rena dies, and the reader sympathizes at the end with both Rena and Tryon.

At this point an obvious question arises: if Chesnutt was launching a more direct attack on *white* prejudice as these several changes in characterization suggest, why did he make Tryon a more moderate and a more sympathetic figure? The answer is that this is precisely the point where Chesnutt's polemical purpose and artistic skill converge. By making Tryon responsible for Rena's destruction, Chesnutt placed the blame where it belonged—on white racism; by making him sympathetic, Chesnutt could appeal much more effectively to his predominantly white audience.

This consideration, then, leads us back to Chesnutt's literary skill in *The House Behind the Cedars*. By eliminating a first person narrator who merely introduced the story but never participated in it, Chesnutt moved his novel from the realm of memory into the realm of the imagination. Unfortunately, his privileged narrator is often too obtrusive in commenting on the action, but this is a flaw that the novel shares with a great many late nineteenth century stories, and Chesnutt can be applauded for eliminating the more egregious weakness.

With regard to characterization, Chesnutt altered his main figures to emphasize his attack on white racism. In this final version, Rena is no longer the tragic mulatto victimized by her inheritance; though still idealized, she is much more astute about her situation and her relations with other people. Wain, on the other hand, ceases to be a major figure and appears instead as a shadowy character in the sub-plot. And Tryon, no longer the near caricature of the Bigot, is a troubled young man awakened to his own biases and struggling to overcome them. Of course, for modern readers accustomed to the psychological depth and complexity of twentieth century fiction, these characters will seem flat and perhaps unconvincing. But for Chesnutt, they are distinct improvements.

Lastly, instead of two loosely-related stories involving Rena first with Tryon and then with Wain, Chesnutt focused on her love affair with Tryon and turned the relationship with Wain into a sub-plot. But subordinating that story was not eliminating it, and Chesnutt still had the problem of relating plot and sub-plot. To solve this he resorted to the use of coincidence, a device more generally accepted in his time than in ours. As a result, *The House Behind the Cedars* often seems contrived, as for example in Chapter 24 when Tryon approaches Rena's home at the precise moment when she is dancing with Wain. Nevertheless, this is preferable to a broken-back piece of fiction.

In retrospect, then, *The House Behind the Cedars* evolved from a sketchy short story that attacked racial prejudice obliquely by revealing it within the black community of Patesville through a broken-back novelette with stereotyped characters that revealed prejudice in both black and white worlds to a more integrated novel with more credible characters that placed the blame for the tragic unhappiness of both black and white characters squarely on white racism. And, in a sense, Chesnutt came full circle in his technique: though he intended to achieve his purpose—"a moral revolution in white America"—through the guerrilla tactics of mining and infiltration, his overt attack on racial prejudice in the person of a white man, George Tryon, would suggest an abandonment of those methods. But by making Tryon a more credible and sympathetic character, Chesnutt returned to his earlier, more subtle tactics; for he would surely have affected more whites by showing that Tryon destroys his own happiness because of racism. To achieve this through Tryon, however, provides a final ironic twist to Chesnutt's decade-long struggle with this story—for *his* deepest concern from the original short story through the novelette and into the novel had always been with Rena, a bright mulatto like himself in a world infested with racism.

Notes

1.   See Helen M. Chesnutt, *Charles Waddell Chesnutt* (Chapel Hill: University of North Carolina Press, 1952), chs. 6–13, for a detailed account of Chesnutt's activities during this decade.

2.   Helen M. Chesnutt, pp. 107–08.

3.   In the Fisk catalogue of the Charles Waddell Chesnutt Collection, the five manuscript versions of "Rena Walden" are listed as "39p., 91p., 55p., 51p., 231p." For the sake of brevity, these versions will be referred to as R-39, R-91, R-55, etc., in the endnotes. At this point I wish to acknowledge the cheerful cooperation of the Fisk Library staff and to the Head of the Special Collections for permission to quote from the Chesnutt Collection.

4.   R-51, p. 8.

5.   Helen M. Chesnutt, p. 21.

6.   Helen M. Chesnutt, p. 59.

7.   George W. Cable to Charles W. Chesnutt, August 18, 1890.

8.   Helen M. Chesnutt, pp. 72–73. In her biography, Miss Chesnutt incorrectly states that this letter was written in 1894.

9.   R-231, p. 104.

10.   R-231, p. 106.

11.   An example of this effort to fuse the two plots appears in R-39, where the name of the woman who tells Rena about Wain's first wife, Mrs. Carter, is crossed out and "Mrs. Tryon" pencilled in.

12.   Charles W. Chesnutt, *The House Behind the Cedars* (New York: Collier Books, 1969), p. 79.

13.   Charles W. Chesnutt, p. 129.

14.   R-231, p. 130.

15.   Charles W. Chesnutt, pp. 137–38.

16.   Charles W. Chesnutt, p. 263.

A Better Mousetrap:
Washington's Program and *The Colonel's Dream*

Susan L. Blake

Charles Chesnutt was often called upon, both by individuals and by his sense of duty as a spokesman for the cause of racial equality, to comment on the views of Booker T. Washington. In his letters and essays, Chesnutt always struck between firm opposition to Washington's politics and polite regard for the man—a balance that has led one recent critic to consider his position essentially ambivalent.[1] But Chesnutt also commented on Washington's ideas in the less personal medium of fiction, which he had always considered a vehicle for social ideas, and there his ambivalence is much deeper than the distinction between politics and persons.

The Colonel's Dream, Chesnutt's strangely neglected last novel, is a systematic and thorough refutation of Washington's program for the advancement of blacks in the South. Colonel French's dream for the economic development of the town of Clarendon is founded on Washington's principle and follows Washington's methods. Although Chesnutt gives French the advantage of every favorable circumstance, the Colonel's project fails. The reasons for this failure are the reasons Washington's program cannot succeed. They reveal the false assumptions on which it is based and detrimental effects it may have.

The heart of Washington's political philosophy, reiterated throughout *Up From Slavery,* is that "the whole future of the Negro rested largely upon the question as to whether or not he should make himself, through his skill, intelligence, and character, of such undeniable value to the community in which he lived that the community could not dispense with his presence."[2] The way to the white man's sense of justice, in short, is through his economic advantage. This theorem, if you will, has several corollaries. First, that the interest of black people is best served by first serving the white community. Washington repeatedly advised black people, "where no principle is at stake, to consult the interests of their local communities, and to advise with their friends in regard to their voting" (*TNC,* 102). Second, that industrial education must precede more abstract higher education, for "the community may

Reprinted with permission from *CLA Journal* 23 (March 1979): 49–59.

not . . . be prepared for, or feel the need of, Greek analysis, but it may feel the need of bricks and houses and wagons" (*TNC*, 113). Third, that in "all things purely social," blacks and whites can remain "as separate as the fingers" until blacks have proved themselves worthy of white acceptance (*TNC*, 148). Fourth, that the Negro can afford to forgo political claims temporarily "depending upon the slow but sure influences that proceed from the possession of property, intelligence and high character for the full recognition of his political rights" (*TNC*, 156). Washington's theorem and all of its corollaries rest on two important assumptions. First, that black people have both the ability and the responsibility to attain standards set by whites unaided by the rights and resources whites enjoy. Second, that white people, the judges of this effort, are rational—that the "best people" are motivated by a sense of justice and the others at least by rational self interest.

In his letters, to Washington and others, and particularly in an essay entitled "The Disfranchisement of the Negro," published in 1903 in a collection of essays by leading black Americans called *The Negro Problem*,[3] Chesnutt consistently rebuts Washington's thesis and the premises on which it is based. Without political rights, he argues that the Negro remains under an economic handicap, deprived of public employment, taxed more heavily than whites in proportion to services (such as education) received, and worse, subjected to persistent slavery in the form of a legal peonage system (*NP*, 89–92). He addresses the premise that black people can be required to uplift themselves despite this handicap when he says in a letter to Supreme Court Justice Wendell P. Stafford, "A man cannot breathe without air, or eat without food, or develop without opportunity."[4] And as for white people, Chesnutt wrote Washington in 1903, "I have no confidence in that friendship of the whites which is to take the place of rights, and no expectation of justice at their hands unless it is founded on law."[5] In *The Colonel's Dream*, Chesnutt dramatized these arguments. As Washington had used the success of Tuskegee to illustrate his ideas; Chesnutt used the failure of Colonel French's plan for the economic development of Clarendon to refute them.

Colonel French, back in his hometown after more than twenty years in New York, is charmed by the grace and simplicity of Southern life, but dismayed by the idleness and decay he encounters, and revolted by the influence of Bill Fetters, who, with his symbolic name, his plantation run by convict labor, and his mortgage on every piece of property in town, represents the persistent spirit of slavery. French determines to "do something for humanity, something to offset Fetters and his kind":

> It required no great stretch of the imagination to see the town, a few years
> hence, a busy hive of industry, where no man, and no woman obliged to work,
> need be without employment at fair wages; where the trinity of peace, prosper-
> ity and progress would reign supreme; where men like Fetters and methods
> like his would no longer be tolerated.[6]

French, like Washington, expects to achieve humanitarian ideals by economic means. He hopes to improve the lot of the black people he has seen hanging around without work and being sold into virtual slavery on Fetters' plantation for the crime of unemployment, but, like Washington, he plans to do so by improving the economy of the whole community. French undertakes to build a cotton mill on the site of a long-since abandoned one. He will build the mill with local labor and local brick to stimulate other industries. He will run it with wages high enough to allow parents to send their children to school instead of work and with hours short enough to give workers time to spend in fresh air and family life. There will be plenty of work for blacks as well as whites, so blacks can have a chance to earn a decent living without incurring the jealousy of whites. The profits of the mill will be used to improve the schools and build a library. With prosperity achieved, the people of Clarendon will have the resources and motivation to pursue peace and progress, and Fetters—who owns not only the plantation run by convict labor, but also the controlling share of a cotton mill that works white women and children from the age of six twelve to sixteen hours a day for fifteen to fifty cents—will, as the Colonel tells Judge Bullard, come up to French's standards or lose his business (*CD,* 120).

In all matters peripheral to his main project, French also follows Washington's principles. The school for black children that he plans to support is to be an industrial school, and he presents it to a committee of black citizens in words that both echo and apparently refer to Booker T. Washington:

> "What your people need," said the colonel to the little gathering at the school-house one evening, "is to learn not only how to read and write and think, but to do these things to some definite end. . . . To make yourselves valuable members of society, you must learn to do well some particular thing. . . . Take advice from some of your own capable leaders in other places. Find out what you can do for yourselves, and I will give you three dollars for every one you can gather, for an industrial school or some similar institution." (*CD,* 161)

When Laura Treadwell objects that whites would not want to use a library that was also used by blacks, French readily agrees to build two—convinced that "we need not strain our goal by going too fast" (*CD,* 163). When the town's leading citizens argue for the disfranchisement of the Negro, French quietly presents Chesnutt's position for Washington's reasons—"that any restriction of rights that rested upon anything but impartial justice, was bound to re-act, as slavery had done, upon the prosperity and progress of the State" (*CD,* 194–195). And when his auditors do no more than listen politely, French remains, like Washington, "content to await the uplifting power of industry and enlightenment, and supremely confident of the result" (*CD,* 195).

If Washington's principles hold, French cannot fail; Chesnutt has given him every advantage of character and circumstance. French is a reformer drawn to give least offense to the South. He is not black, not a Northerner, not even at first a reformer. He is a son of Clarendon itself, a member of the aristocracy, a former Confederate officer, who has gone North after the Civil War, made a fortune, and returned to his hometown for a vacation. He in fact fits the description of one of the philanthropists Washington singles out in *Up From Slavery:* "Dr. Curry is a native of the South, an ex-Confederate soldier, yet I do not believe there is any man in the country who is more deeply interested in the highest welfare of the Negro than Dr. Curry" (*TNC,* 133). French both subscribes to and embodies the ideals the South claims. His first actions in Clarendon demonstrate his reverence for Southern ideals and traditions. He seeks the company of Laura Treadwell, a true Southern lady whose grace, simplicity, and goodness all but conceal her poverty. He buys back his old family home, restores it to its former condition and style, and gives an old-fashioned housewarming party intended to recreate the antebellum era. His relations with blacks are the sort that the town approves or idealizes. He revives the relationship of benevolent master to faithful slave when he "buys the time" of his old "boy" Peter, who has been apprehended for "vagrancy," and gives him the task of looking after his son Phil as Peter has looked after him when he was a boy. Although he sticks to the principles that black men should have a chance to succeed in society, he shares the prejudices of white society in general. In private, he wonders what has happened to "the loquacious, fun-loving Negroes" of his youth (*CD,* 113); in debate with his neighbors he carefully distinguishes his principles from his personal feelings: "I am no lover of the Negro, *as* Negro—I do not know but I should rather see him elsewhere. . . . But they are here, through no fault of theirs, as we are. . . . they are men, and they should have a chance—at least *some* chance," (*CD,* 165). To the virtues of civility, gentility, and kinship, Colonel French adds the characteristic Washington most admires in his philanthropists—businesslike behavior. If any man can placate the South into industry and enlightenment, it is Henry French.

French also has circumstances on his side. The people of Clarendon agree that they need just what he has to offer. In the fulsome welcoming article in the local newspaper, the *Anglo-Saxon,*

> the hope was expressed that Colonel French, who had recently sold out to a syndicate his bagging mills in Connecticut, might seek investments in the South, whose vast undeveloped resources needed only the fructifying flow of abundant capital to make it blossom like the rose. (*CD,* 86–87)

The industry French chooses to invest in is admirably suited to its location, for the mill can be built on the foundations of an old one available at a bargain for payment of back taxes. It will use the local resources of cotton, which otherwise has to be shipped North with diminished value, and it will use water power which has been going to waste. The slavery French wishes to combat is white slavery as much as black, for the women and children employed in Fetters' cotton mill are white. And French's first investments in the town, before he even starts work on the mill, have a noticeable and beneficial effect on its economy that foretells the benefits of the mill itself. The money put into circulation by the purchase of his family home from the barber

> soon permeated all the channels of local enterprise. The barber, out of his profits, began the erection of a row of small houses for coloured tenants. This gave employment to masons and carpenters, and involved the sale and purchase of considerable building material. General trade felt the influence of the enhanced prosperity. Groceries, dry-goods stores and saloons, did a thriving business. (CD, 88–89)

The old-fashioned housewarming party he gives provides enough work for the local tailor (among others) to support him for an entire year. When construction on the mill actually begins, French pays three times the going wage. If Southern whites are susceptible to their economic advantage, they cannot help but cooperate with Colonel French.

But they do not. Accommodating as he is toward Southern racial prejudices, French keeps running into a wall of racism that yields to neither a sense of decency nor economic self-interest. His effort to free Bud Johnson, one of Fetters' convicts and Laura's maid's husband, illustrates. Johnson has been apprehended, unjustly, for "vagrancy" while visiting his wife, contracted out to Fetters, provoked into behavior that has extended his sentence and could obviously do so indefinitely, and marked as the "bad nigger" to be made an example of. Fetters not only refuses to sell Johnson's contract to French "to please a lady"; he also refuses to sell it for five, even fifty, times its worth (CD, 224–225). The principles motivating Fetters in this contest are the same that motivate the public in general in the two events that finally make French give up and go home to New York—the lynching of Bud Johnson and the exhumation of Old Peter.

The violation of Peter's grave shows that white people cannot be counted on to reward service or sacrifice. Peter has been buried, despite some controversy, in the French family plot in the white cemetery, next to, and at the specific request of, little Phil, whom he has died trying to save. Peter has given his all to the white community. True to the plantation's traditional stereotype of the faithful darky, he has retained his owner's name when other freedmen changed theirs; he has kept up the French family graves when the family themselves moved away and neglected them; and he has made the ultimate sacrifice of his own life for his master's child. If faithfulness and sacrifice count for anything, they should let Peter rest in peace. But the mob digs him up and dumps his casket on the colonel's porch, with a note specifying, "Niggers by there selves, white peepul by there selves, and them that lives in our town must bide by our rules" (CD, 281).

The lynching of Bud Johnson, the result of the complex relationship of law and economics, shows that white people cannot be counted on to pursue their economic advantage. Johnson, whom French and his lawyer have helped to escape from Fetters' plantation, has been apprehended for attempting to murder two of Fetters' guards. By the time he is lynched, he is a criminal, but it is Fetters who has made him one. When French investigates the laws that can allow this brutalization, he finds that not only are the state's laws pertaining to vagrancy, debt tenancy, and convict labor exceedingly harsh and "clearly designed to profit the strong at the expense of the weak," but that "the law, bad as it was, had not been sufficient for Fetters' purpose, but had been clearly violated" (*CD,* 229). When he tries to fight this injustice, he comes up against the power of Fetters in both the judicial and legislative determinants of law. The witnesses he can get against Fetters are all employed by him or mortgaged to him, as is the judge who denies French's plea of *habeas corpus* on Johnson's behalf. The convict labor laws, whose terms are "exceedingly profitable to the State" and to private contractors like Fetters but "disastrous to free competitive labor," that is, the citizens of the state, have been made by lawmakers of whom "more than one . . . besides Fetters was numbered among these contractors" (*CD,* 229). Thus the whole society, not only the unfortunate blacks, is in legal as well as economic bondage to Fetters. But people are unwilling to trade the influence of Fetters for that of French because Fetters upholds their dearest white-supremacist principles. In a discussion of politics, old General Thornton, one of the leading citizens French looks to for support, clarifies this point. Although, he says, he felt in the last election that the Republicans stood for sound money and the Democrats for financial repudiation, the thought of voting the same ticket as "the triflingest nigger in town" made him vote against his "better instincts" because "we had to preserve our institutions, if our finances went to smash" (*CD,* 167). The mayor applies this same principle to the case of Peter's burial: "We all appreciate the colonel's worth, and what he is doing for the town. But . . . we do not want to buy the prosperity of this town at the price of our principles"(*CD,* 264).

The defeat of Colonel French's plans for Clarendon has shown that Washington's thesis is false. The "individual who has learned to do something better than anybody else—learned to do a common thing in an uncommon manner—" will be rewarded, as Washington had asserted, but not "regardless of the colour of his skin" (*TNC,* 137). His ingenious model for a different and better kind of cotton gin gets young Ben Dudley a chance to start a business in New York, and thus to marry his ambitious sweetheart; but Dudley is white and, more important in this case, the one who recognizes his genius is French, the Northern businessman. Economic power does create political power. The case of Fetters shows that it does. But Fetters is white and a supporter of white supremacy. The point is that economic interests do not outweigh racism. Washington has ignored or denied the overwhelming strength of racism.

French's plan and Washington's program fail because the premises under them do not hold. French's experience shows not only that ordinary white people are not motivated by rational self-interest, but also that the so-called "best people" cannot be relied on for a sense of justice. The Presbyterian minister, representative of Christianity as well as gentility, maintains (in words Chesnutt himself heard from "the Superintendent of Schools of a Southern city" and reported in "The Disfranchisement of the Negro" [NP, 105]) that "there is no place in this nation for the Negro, except under the sod" (CD, 164). When the colonel tries to find a contingent of prominent men to prosecute Bud Johnson's murders, "they became increasingly difficult to find as it became known he was seeking them" (CD, 278). And although the aristocratic members of the trustees of the cemetery have prevailed upon the mayor to allow French to bury Peter there, when the mob digs up his casket no one censures the action. "The best people," the colonel concludes,

are an abstraction. When any deviltry is on foot they are never there to prevent it—they vanish into thin air at its approach. When it is done, they excuse it; and they make no effort to punish it. So it is not too much to say that what they permit they justify, and they cannot shirk the responsibility. (CD, 283)

As the best people are an abstraction, so are the ideals they supposedly represent. The only instance in the novel in which justice is done is when Fetters pays a note owed to Laura Treadwell's father's estate that Colonel French's able young lawyer manages to call due minutes before the twenty-year statute of limitations has run out. A clear law—and only a clear law, as Chesnutt wrote to Washington—makes even Fetters do his duty.

The other premise, that responsibility for their elevation can be left to black people themselves, is attacked through the experience of Henry Taylor, the schoolteacher, who is Henry French's counterpart in the black community. Taylor, trusting French's confidence and his ability to insure that justice be done, has given the information that saves Ben Dudley, an innocent suspect in the murder case, and leads to Bud Johnson's arrest. When Johnson is lynched, Taylor loses his job and is called an enemy of his race; the industrial school project French has promised to support dies for lack of enthusiasm and leadership. As French has been discouraged by a racism that transcends both justice and economic self-interest, Taylor has been driven away by a negative kind of racial solidarity that, though ultimately damaging to the black community, is perfectly understandable since the kind of justice Taylor has staked his reputation on is seldom available to a people who, in Taylor's words, "have no hand in makin' the laws, or in enforcin' 'em . . . are not summoned on jury; and yet [are] asked to do the work of constables and sheriffs who are paid for arrestin' criminals, an' for protectin' 'em from mobs, which they don't do" (CD, 244). If people cannot "breathe without air, or eat without food," neither can they be expected to revere a law that does not protect them.

Chesnutt's answer to Washington in The Colonel's Dream is direct, logical, and unequivocal, but the form of reply itself reveals the author's dilemma. Chesnutt shares the colonel's dream. As the hopeful paeans at the end of both The Colonel's Dream and "The Disfranchisement of the Negro" attest, he would like to believe in "a new body of thought . . . [visible] to the eye of faith . . . favourable to just laws and their orderly administration" (CD, 294). While French builds according to Washington's plan for economic development, he voices Chesnutt's principles of political equality. There is no reason in French's mind, or in the novel's logic, why the two cannot go together. And while French is defeated, the very presentation of his defeat shows the reasonableness of his goals. Chesnutt seems to be trying to convince well-meaning white people to let Washington's program work at the same time he is persuading Washington and his followers that it won't work. And in this goal he runs up against the same barrier that stops Colonel French—reliance on the conscience and rationality of white people. But if he doesn't rely on white people, he has to rely on the ability of black people to get what they don't have without help from those who have it. In "The Disfranchisement of the Negro," Chesnutt distinguishes between the opportunities of Northern and Southern blacks to exercise political power and calls for positive racial solidarity to combat disfranchisement: "When this race develops a sufficient power of combination, under adequate leadership,—and there are signs already that this is near at hand,—the Northern vote can be wielded irresistibly for the defense of the rights of their Southern brethren" (NP, 120). But even here, where Chesnutt is not accommodating to the prejudices of a white audience in drawing his black characters—as he no doubt is in The Colonel's Dream—he concludes that the fight for full citizenship for blacks "will be, after all, largely a white man's conflict, fought out in the forum of the public conscience" (NP, 124). Strong as he makes the position of Henry French, who gives up on persuasive philanthropy, Chesnutt seems to be left inevitably in the slightly more ambivalent position of Henry Taylor, who "is fully convinced that his people will never get very far along in the world without the good will of the white people, but . . . is still wondering how they will secure it. For he regards Colonel French as an extremely fortunate accident" (CD, 293).

Notes

1. Arlene A. Elder, "Chesnutt on Washington: An Essential Ambivalence," Phylon, 38 (March 1977), 1–8.

2. *Three Negro Classics* (New York: Avon, 1968), p. 137. Subsequent references will be identified in the text by the initials *TNC* and the page number.

3. (Rpt. New York: Arno Press and the New York Times, 1969.) References will be identified in the text by the initials *NP.*

4. Helen M. Chesnutt, *Charles Waddell Chesnutt: Pioneer of the Color Line* (Chapel Hill: University of North Carolina Press, 1952), p. 232.

5. *Ibid.,* p. 193.

6. *The Colonel's Dream* (1905; rpt. Miami, Fla.: Mnemosyne, 1969), pp. 117–18. Subsequent references will be identified in the text by the initials *CD.*

Rena Walden: Chesnutt's Failed "Future American"

SallyAnn H. Ferguson

In his first published novel, *The House Behind the Cedars* (1900), Charles W. Chesnutt develops the theme of racial passing largely through Rena Walden, the main character. While generally complimenting the author on his artistry, scholars usually dismiss this protagonist as a weak and stereotyped mulatto. But a series of newspaper articles by Chesnutt entitled "The Future American" and published in the *Boston Evening Transcript* from August 18 to September 1, 1900,[1] places Rena and the passing theme in proper perspective and affirms her importance. Significantly, the publication dates of this series and *The House* virtually coincide. Moreover, a later speech by Chesnutt, "Race Prejudice: Its Causes and Its Cure" (1905), which was originally presented before the Boston Historical and Literary Association and then published in *Alexander's Magazine*,[2] expands on the views expressed in the *Transcript* series. In all these articles, Chesnutt argues that if America is left free, like Europe, to follow natural patterns of racial evolution, it will eventually develop a "Future American" formed from America's three "broad types"—white, black, and red. This new ethnic type will be "a people who look substantially alike, and are moulded by the same culture and dominated by the same ideals."[3] In the postbellum setting of *The House,* Chesnutt provides a fictional prototype of this "Future American" in Rena's brother, John Walden, a minor character in the novel. At the same time, the author also portrays its fictional antitype in Rena herself, who self-destructs in her attempt to achieve Chesnutt's racial ideal.

In the first "Future American" article, Chesnutt asserts that any dream of a pure Anglo-Saxon type for the United States should be abandoned even though the future race will be predominately white, call itself so, and will likely conform closely to the white type. But this race will have absorbed and assimilated the other two races. After making note of the many blacks and whites who are already mixed, he then introduces a formula which, if followed under laws that encourage miscegenation, would achieve complete racial admixture over a period of three generations. Assuming that one-

Reprinted with permission from *Southern Literary Journal* 15 (Fall 1982): 74–82.

eighth of the population is black, he would have this number marry an equal number of whites to produce a first generation of which one-fourth would be mulatto. These mulattoes, in turn, would marry whites to form a new generation half of which would be quadroons, or people who are one-fourth black. Finally, by the third generation, the entire population would be composed entirely of octoroons, with the pure whites being eliminated and no perceptible traces of blacks left. Chesnutt admits that this rather mechanical process will never happen, but argues that the same result will be brought about slowly and subtly. Citing slavery as a great advancer of a mixed race and then identifying prominent "white Europeans" like Aleksander Pushkin, Robert Browning, and Alexandre Dumas, who are in fact his imperceptible blacks, Chesnutt documents race-mixing in the Western world throughout the second "Future American" article. He deems racial amalgamation absolutely necessary in order to rid the country of the racial discord and strife with which a composite and homogeneous people would not have to contend. In the third article, therefore, Chesnutt states: "There can manifestly be no such thing as a peaceful and progressive civilization in a nation divided by two warring races, and homogeneity of type, at least in externalia, is a necessary condition of harmonious social progress."[4]

In *The House Behind the Cedars,* Chesnutt presents a fictional version of his non-fictional theory when he mates Molly Walden, already a second generation quadroon admixture of black and Indian blood, with her white lover. Their offspring, John and Rena, become the third generation of white/blacks who are supposed to continue the author's racial evolution with marriage to and children by whites. John Walden follows the pattern so perfectly that he has been recently called "the dramatic epitome of Chesnutt's ongoing commentary on the question of racial assimilation in America."[5] Specifically, Chesnutt characterizes John as a mulatto opportunist destined to marry a white woman and father her child. First, the author gives him a big scene in which fifteen-year-old John realizes that ". . . God, the Father of all, had made him white; and God . . . made no mistakes—having made him white, He must have meant him to be white."[6] Early in the novel, then, Chesnutt establishes that John has no identity problems whatever; if whiteness is a way of thinking, feeling, and behaving, then John Walden *is* white.

Additionally, while still a youngster in the black world, John gets educated in white culture, first and crucially through library books his father leaves at Molly's home. These volumes so delineate the differences between white social, economic, and political freedom on the one hand and the poverty and oppression of his own existence on the other that John rejects black life without regret and, instead, shrewdly prepares to meet the criteria for recognition and equality in a white setting. Later Judge Straight directs John to South Carolina, where more liberal passing laws make this action safer. He does this using, verbatim, the lines that Chesnutt writes in the second *Transcript* essay. " 'The term mulatto,' he read, 'is not invariably applicable to every admixture of African blood with the European, nor is one having all the features of a white to be ranked with the degraded class designated by the laws of this State as persons of color . . .' " (p. 154). Finally, after completing law school in South Carolina, John is placed in the white world where he simply keeps a vigilant eye for the opportunity—marriage to the rich, recently-orphaned daughter of a Southern plantation owner—that catapults him permanently into the white economic and social power structure. When he returns to Patesville as the successful brother come home to conduct his sister on a similar venture, he points proudly to all he has acquired: his deceased wife's connections, her good family name, and—most importantly—"their" son. John surreptitiously manipulates influential whites in order to attain racial harmony and economic and social equality for himself immediately—in the postbellum setting of *The House*. In so doing, he becomes the novel's standard for black success, and his near-white, octoroon son becomes the picture-perfect fictional representation of Chesnutt's non-fictional racial theory.

In the first *Transcript* article, Chesnutt also recognizes that "The real problem . . . the only hard problem in connection with the future American race, lies in the Negro element of our population."[7] Unlike the Indian, the black faces both external problems of assimilation caused by white prejudice against black skin and internal pressures from his own personal weaknesses. Chesnutt does indeed deal with the external black problems in *The House*, as most critics of the novel have documented.[8] Equally important but almost entirely unremarked, however, is Chesnutt's fictional treatment of those internal shortcomings that keep blacks from amalgamation—"Their poverty, their ignorance and their servile estate,"[9] all of which the author, in contrast to John, associates with Rena. Although her white looks should have guaranteed that she, like him, also gain equality with whites through passing, Rena is kept ignorant; thus, she both fails to assimilate and remains poor and servile. More simply, although she possesses an "innate taste and intelligence" (p. 55), Rena is given an inadequate, sexist education that teaches her to walk regally, but not to think and reason. Although she is expected to bring off the challenging deception of passing, an act requiring a sharp wit and intellect, she is cast as a typical Southern belle, a type not known for her native intelligence. John gets a mulatto teacher in his early years, his father's library after he learns to read, and a law degree after that; but Rena's formal education amounts to the "simpler stories" (p. 47) read to her by John when she is a little girl, sentimental novels from her father's library, and one year of boarding school at age seventeen. Certainly little in Rena's academic background is calculated to develop her higher cognitive skills of analysis and synthesis. Apparently, the author takes the rather chauvinistic view that the men around her—either her brother or husband—will always be there to think for Rena. Chesnutt sends them away, however, in those crucial days preceding her marriage to white George Tryon, when Rena needs good, sound sense in order to shake off the false dreams that plague her about Molly's being ill.

Since she has no one around to protect her from her own ignorance, Rena makes the ultimately fatal decision to return to Patesville—where George discovers she is black—on the "evidence" of her dreams. Or, to put it another way, she gives in to superstition because of her inability to reason. Chesnutt once condescendingly said of women: "Even should their judgment be at fault . . . they have fine intuitions, which are many times a safe guide to action. . . ."[10] But Rena, unfortunately, possesses little or no intuitive ability. In fact, when left to her own devices, Rena shows strong emotional ties to her black roots and a lack of total commitment to passing. She does exactly what Chesnutt's intrusive narrator earlier warns against: "Men who have elected to govern their lives by principles of abstract right and reason, which happen, perhaps, to be at variance with what society considers equally right and rea- sonable, should, for fear of complications, be careful about descending from the lofty heights of logic to the common level of impulse and affection" (p. 26). Thus because of her superstitious ignorance—a stereotypical charac- teristic of blacks—Rena cannot become a "Future American" like her brother.

Chesnutt repeatedly turns to the ignorance theme and to the personal weaknesses of blacks that inhibit their social fusion with the other ethnic types. He, therefore, consistently portrays Rena as a postbellum naif who unknowingly stops short on the color line and cannot move forward because she does not understand her own position there. Soon, Rena's ignorance that she remains psychologically black while trying to pass becomes her greatest fault. Chesnutt dramatizes this problem by contrasting the self-awareness of his two central characters. Shortly after Rena joins John in South Carolina, the intrusive narrator notes that "Her months in school had not eradicated a certain self-consciousness born of her secret. The brain-cells never lose the impressions of youth, and Rena's Patesville life was not far enough removed to have lost its distinctness of outline. Of the two, the present was more of a dream, the past was the more vivid reality" (p. 55). The author's virtual admission that Rena is still black despite her education contrasts sharply with his giving John an identity-establishing "God-made-me-white" scene and an education that figuratively "cleanses" him of his black heritage. Moreover, it also contrasts with Chesnutt's treatment of Mandy Oxendine, his one other female character to pass willingly. Much like John, she declares: " 'I wouldn'n be a nigger, fer God made me white . . . an" I 'termined ter be what God made me, an' I *am* white."[11] Rena, on the other hand, never asserts her white- ness, but Chesnutt alludes to her blackness through reference to the wave in her hair that Molly says " 'I've never be'n able to git . . . out' " (p. 20). Rena never once examines who she really is until George Tryon discovers her true color and halts her charade. Before, others tell her she is white while her behavior suggests just the opposite.

Furthermore, Chesnutt places in the black world those things Rena desires most, but puts the objects of John's wishes in the white. Several decades ago, Benjamin Mays alluded to this fact when he wrote that "Rena seeks the satisfaction and emotional security that comes from mingling with her own people."[12] Chesnutt certainly illustrates this idea by contrasting the Rena Walden-George Tryon affair with the other interracial "love" relationships in the novel—Molly Walden and the father of her children, and John and his wife. Although each of these latter two liaisons is mutually satisfying, they are for the blacks involved definitely based on economics, not love. Molly, for example, willingly becomes a white man's concubine when her father unexpectedly dies and leaves his family in dire poverty. As a result of her decision, ". . . while scarcely more than a child in years, Molly was living in her own house. . . . Her mother nevermore knew want. Her poor relations could always find a meal in Molly's kitchen" (p. 142). Still, Molly feels nothing more than gratitude for her white hero. Although she lacks even Rena's meager education, Molly is not ignorant about the South and its ways and knows that the white man is capable only of sleeping with the black woman, not of loving her. Molly, accordingly, never asks her lover for what he cannot freely give. Similarly, John understands the white's inability to love a black and thus carefully conceals his racial identity from his wife. He views marriage in rational, unsentimental, even businesslike terms and feels nothing but pride at getting a prosperous white woman in return for doing a good job as manager of her late father's plantation. Indeed, she would not have interested him had she been poor and black. John is practical and unemotional; he recognizes an opportunity to move up and takes it. Rena, on the contrary, seeks a deep, personal fulfillment from a white man that reaches beyond the conventional trappings of race and economic and social success to touch the soul. Before their marriage, she wants proof that George loves her despite her blackness, and would have revealed her true identity to him had her brother not convinced her to do otherwise. She fails to realize that the love and honesty she craves exist in the black, not the white, world of the novel—in the servile, poverty-stricken world of Frank Fowler. Chesnutt, therefore, makes Rena aspire to John and Mandy's goals of wealth and position, but gives her little of their understanding of racial realities and personal ambition. By keeping his protagonist black and confused as she moves into the white world, Chesnutt dooms her to failure while demonstrating his theory.

Nevertheless, Rena emerges as a likable person, mainly because Chesnutt subtly distracts the reader from her intellectual shortcomings by constantly referring to her fine feminine attributes—her "stately beauty," "admirably proportioned" figure, a walk "that revealed a light heart and the vigor of perfect health," a "soft and sweet and clear" voice, and a "singularly pretty face" with patrician features (pp. 8, 9, 10)—all qualities that enable her to become a beauty-contest winner, the epitome of female "success." When Rena is crowned Queen of Love and Beauty, she in effect becomes the idealized virgin, symbol of abstract goodness and purity—in short, the perfect Southern belle. In the course of the novel, this paragon of gentility evolves into a blameless, innocent victim battered by a cold, unfeeling, racist

South, as Rena seems when she finally dies. Through a combination of sexism and romantic allusion, Chesnutt encourages the reader to believe that external forces are responsible for Rena's death, since such a good-looking female specimen must surely be flawless.

Of much consequence at the book's end is the fact that Chesnutt kills off his heroine and does not allow her to marry Frank Fowler, who she acknowledges on her deathbed " 'loved me best of them all' " (p. 264).[13] Furthermore, one is led to question those critics who claim that racism alone brings on Rena's "tragedy," when considering that Chesnutt's intrusive narrator makes frequent references to the Walden children's having to atone for their parents' adulterous miscegenation, but then puts the entire burden for this atonement on Rena. More important, an ironic pun on Frank Fowler's last name suggests the influence of Chesnutt's racial theory in these matters and thus provides another reason the author could not send her back to him. Although good, candid, and direct, Frank is also a dark-skinned black man who would "foul her" with identifiably, black "fouler" children. Chesnutt, however, believes that the black race could paradoxically uplift itself by slowly phasing itself out through fusion with white blood—that is, through self-extinction. In his *Transcript* essays, he states that different racial types trying to survive in the same country create constant racial strife. In his later piece on "Race Prejudice: Its Causes and Cure," he uses this assumption to justify amalgamation. Race prejudice, Chesnutt claims, stems from racial differences, mostly physical "antagonisms" of color, form, and feature. Removal of these "antagonisms" will eliminate racial conflict. He concedes that prejudice will then still exist, but notes that it will not be of racial origin.

Chesnutt supports this conclusion with a contrast of blacks and whites that suggests how prejudices arise. He states: "They differed physically, the one being black and the other white. The one had constituted for poets and sculptors the ideal of beauty and grace: the other was rude and unpolished in form and feature. The one possessed the arts of civilization and the learning of the schools, the other, at most, the simple speech and rude handicrafts of his native tribe, and no written language at all. The one was Christian, the other heathen. The one was master of the soil; the other frankly alien and himself the object of ownership."[14] No matter how questionable its "facts," this passage provides sufficient evidence of Chesnutt's general belief in a white superiority and black inferiority caused by environment. Rena's marriage to Frank would have exacerbated the racial problem that marriage to Tryon would have ameliorated. Her death, however, punishes one who cannot conform to Chesnutt's racial ideas.

Most critics ignore Chesnutt's eschewal of the identifiable black, as Trudier Harris notes in a recent article on Frank Fowler, to whom she says little notice is given. "They have assumed that Chesnutt's discussion of the color line is well rendered on the basis of the mulatto or 'coloured' characters."[15] Moreover, these critics take lightly J. Saunders Redding's observations that

Chesnutt held himself at a great distance from the masses of blacks and related to them more through sympathy than anything else. While in the South, he did not share their common circumstance, environment, and habit, nor a common destiny.[16] Finally, James Gecau explains: "While Chesnutt could expose the overbearing attitudes of his characters, he could not escape looking down on those characters whose lifestyle was black. To him black culture and lifestyle was beneath serious consideration, a result of ignorance legislated by the black man's enslavement. Blackness as a structural quality did not exist in Chesnutt's sensibility, and if it did actually exist in the real life of black people, it was to be hastily gotten rid of through education."[17] Indeed, Chesnutt himself says the same in "Race Prejudice": ". . . I take no stock in this doctrine [of racial integrity]. It seems to me a modern invention of the white people to perpetuate the color line. It is they who preach it, and it is their racial integrity which they wish to preserve: they have never been unduly careful of the purity of the black race."[18] He goes on to add that "I can scarcely restrain a smile when I hear a mulatto talking of race integrity or a quadroon dwelling upon race pride. What they mean is a very fine thing, and a very desirable thing, but it is not at all what they say. Why should a man be proud any more than he should be ashamed of a thing for which he is not at all responsible? Manly self-respect, based upon one's humanity, a self-respect which claims nothing for color and yields nothing to color, every man should cherish."[19] Chesnutt's position is based on an apparently unshakable belief in the principle of unitary racial development: "I ask you to dismiss from your mind any theory, however cherished, that there can be built up in a free country, under equal laws, two separate sorts of civilization, two standards of human development."[20] But when Rena Walden retains her black qualities after complete acceptance in the white world, she is set at odds with Chesnutt's theory of racial development. Her ignorant bungling of the opportunity to marry white and well retards the evolutionary process that leads to higher black status in society. Rena, therefore, commits a crime against society when she fails to pass, because racial suffering continues when miscegenation does not. Her crime—refusal to miscegenate—makes her elimination inevitable. Because Rena does not stop being black, she dies.

Thus, Chesnutt programs his heroine to fail, as the comparison and contrast that develop between Rena and John throughout the novel make clear. The protagonist's white looks and boarding-school education are consistently undermined by stereotypical feminine and racial traits that inhibit her progress. Her brother, on the other hand, not only *looks* but also *acts* more white than black. Inevitably, when the test of passing arrives, John succeeds but Rena does not. Although critics claim that *The House Behind the Cedars* is the most artistic of Chesnutt's published novels, they ignore the extent to which the author uses it as a vehicle for racial propaganda, as he does later with *The Marrow of Tradition* (1901) and *The Colonel's Dream* (1905). Charles Chesnutt is primarily concerned with making a case for racial amalgamation in *The House Behind the Cedars,* which provides a fictional forum for ideas less subtly advanced in his non-fiction.

Notes

1. "The Future American: What the Race Is Likely to Become in the Process of Time," *Boston Evening Transcript,* 18 August 1900, p. 20; "The Future American: A Stream of Dark Blood in the Veins of Southern Whites," *Boston Evening Transcript,* 25 August 1900, p. 15; "The Future American: A Complete Race-Amalgamation Likely to Occur," *Boston Evening Transcript,* 1 September 1900, p. 24.

2. 1 (July 1905), pp. 21–26.

3. *Boston Evening Transcript,* 18 August 1900, p. 20.

4. *Boston Evening Transcript,* 1 September 1900, p. 24.

5. William L. Andrews, *The Literary Career of Charles W. Chesnutt* (Baton Rouge: Louisiana State University Press, 1980), p. 165.

6. Charles W. Chesnutt, *The House Behind the Cedars* (1900; rpt. New York: Collier-Macmillan, 1969), p. 145. All future references will be to this edition and be cited parenthetically in the text.

7. *Boston Evening Transcript,* 18 August 1900, p. 20.

8. For example, Robert P. Sedlack argues that *The House* evolved through three versions which move from blaming intra-racial prejudice for the "tragedies" in the novel to making white racism totally responsible. See "The Evolution of Charles Chesnutt's *The House Behind the Cedars,*" *CLA Journal,* 19 (December 1975), pp. 125–35. William L. Andrews also discusses the impact of a racist tradition on the "tragedies" in this novel in "Chesnutt's Patesville: The Presence and Influence of the Past in *The House Behind the Cedars,*" *CLA Journal* 15 (March 1972), pp. 284–94.

9. *Boston Evening Transcript,* 1 September 1900, p. 24.

10. "Women's Rights," *Crisis,* 10 (August 1915), p. 182.

11. Charles W. Chesnutt, "Mandy Oxendine," The Charles Chesnutt Collection, Fisk University Library.

12. *The Negro's God as Reflected in His Literature* (Boston: Chapman & Grimes, 1938), p. 151.

13. According to Robert Bone, Rena's death is arbitrary and a way for Chesnutt to avoid his artistic responsibilities. See *The Negro Novel in America,* rev. ed. (New Haven: Yale University Press, 1965), p. 37.

14. *Alexander's Magazine,* 1 (July 1905), p. 21.

15. "Chesnutt's Frank Fowler: A Failure of Purpose?" *CLA Journal,* 22 (March 1979), p. 216.

16. *To Make a Poet Black* (1939; rpt. College Park, Md.: McGrath Publishing Co., 1968), p. 68.

17. "Charles W. Chesnutt and His Literary Crusade," Diss. State University of New York at Buffalo 1975, p. 84.

18. *Alexander's Magazine,* 1 (July 1905), p. 25.

19. *Ibid.*

20. *Ibid.,* p. 26.

Charles W. Chesnutt's *The Wife of His Youth:* The Unveiling of the Black Storyteller

LORNE FIENBERG

I

At the pivotal moment in Charles W. Chesnutt's "The Wife of His Youth" a mysterious old black woman walks through a doorway and tells her story. For twenty-five years she has been carrying this simple tale of the brutality of slavery and of her faithful love; each retelling of the story is a critical act of self-identification. Now she has found the ideal audience for whom the act of listening and re-telling will also constitute an acknowledgement of the past and a re-creation of the self. 'Liza Jane's passage over the threshold of Mr. Ryder's home and the narrative act which they share proclaim both the metaphor and the theme which unify Charles W. Chesnutt's second collection of short stories. *The Wife of His Youth and Other Stories of The Color Line* (1899). As the characters define themselves through their negotiation of barriers of race, so Chesnutt's experiments with the short story form mark his own process of creating a positive identity for himself as a black author at the turn of the twentieth century.

The publication in March 1899 of *The Conjure Woman* signaled Chesnutt's entry into the literary marketplace, and through Uncle Julius he explored the dynamics of the relationship between a black storyteller and his white listeners. Uncle Julius's various strategies of veiling were an essential first step for Chesnutt in entering into creative negotiations with his own audience.[1] But although veiling secures for Uncle Julius certain powers and material advantages, it is essentially a self-negating rather than a self-affirming move, the muffling rather than the amplification of an authorial and authoritative voice. Significantly, Houghton Mifflin never revealed the racial identity of the author of *The Conjure Woman* at any point in their publicity for

Originally published in *ATQ,* vol. 4, no. 3, September 1990. Reprinted by permission of The University of Rhode Island.

the volume. By September 1899, the publishers were sufficiently encouraged by the reception of Chesnutt's first collection that they were hastily preparing a second volume of stories for the Christmas season. In this volume, Chesnutt would directly confront issues of racial identity and the unveiling of his own authorial voice.

Although the stories in *The Wife of His Youth* were written at intervals throughout the 1890s, even as Chesnutt was composing the Uncle Julius tales, taken as a collection they constitute a quite different strategy of presentation. In a letter to his publishers, Chesnutt explained one aspect of his intent:

> I should like to hope that the stories, while written to depict life as it is, in certain aspects that no one has ever before attempted to adequately describe, may throw a light upon the great problem on which the stories are strung; for the backbone of this volume is not a character, like Uncle Julius in *The Conjure Woman,* but a subject, as indicated in the title—*The Color Line* (Andrews 74)

Not simply a "problem" or "subject," "the color line" operates in each of the stories as a metonymy for the system of racial exclusion and the multiple barriers of oppression erected within American society. Unlike the veil, which inscribes silent vision and the subversive manipulation of hidden motives as versions of heroic action, the color line demands the more forceful assertion of identity which lies in crossing over the boundaries which inhibit and confine. And the characters' efforts to cross over, to devise new roles for themselves as social actors, parallel the unveiling of Chesnutt's own narrative voice.

The metaphor of the color line derives its historical complexity from the passage of the Thirteenth Amendment to the U.S. Constitution. For the freed slaves, this redefinition of their status as citizens amounted to the creation of a kind of new republic in which they might test the core values of the culture which had for so long excluded them. In particular, these new citizens were freed to test the enabling power of ideas such as individualism, autonomy, and self-help in the shaping of their social identities.

The black aspiration towards participation in a new republic assumed several dimensions: political responsibility and voting rights, education, the acquisition of property and wealth, and the cultivation of manners and cultural refinement. Success in any of these areas served as a badge of admission into a privileged world which had previously been barred to them. It is little wonder, then, that in the period following the Civil War blacks were the most ardent apostles of the transforming power of republican virtue.

While the Thirteenth Amendment outlawed the most obvious forces of enclosure, it by no means articulated the way abstract rights and an adherence to civic and personal virtue might overcome the multiple barriers which remained. The stories which Chesnutt selected for *The Wife of His Youth* inscribe the potential for self-identification even as they test the limits of a newly-won autonomy. The collection never ventures into the political arena, and only "Cicely's Dream" and "The Bouquet" treat education as an avenue for self-improvement. Still, Chesnutt's early journal entries clearly link his literary aspirations to a range of social and economic motives:

> I want fame; I want money; I want to raise my children in a different rank of life from that I sprang from. In my present vocation I would never accumulate a competency, with all the economy and prudence, and parsimony in the world. In law or medicine, I would be compelled to wait half a lifetime to accomplish anything. But literature pays the successful. (Andrews 9–10)

Although Chesnutt had asserted elsewhere in his journal that his mission was to expose the confining ideology of race and to reform the racial attitudes of a white audience, his personal aspirations must have been founded upon a belief that there already was a degree of equity in American society which extended its promise of mobility and economic success to its black citizens. And in fact, as he was enjoying the early successes of authorship, his family was establishing its standing in the rising mulatto society of Cleveland, Ohio, in the 1880s and 1890s. Out of this ambivalence emerges the dialectic of enclosure and open space, of fixed and contingent values, of socially prescribed roles and the autonomous creation of identity in the stories.

Readers who turn from the antebellum conjure tales of Uncle Julius to "The Wife of His Youth" must reposition themselves in time and place. They also face the challenge of attuning themselves to Chesnutt's narrative voice and to his shifting point of view. The story begins with the barest of assertions, that "Mr. Ryder was going to give a ball," and encourages the reader to anticipate an enumeration of "several reasons why this was an opportune time for such an event" (1). Instead of a straightforward list, however, the narrator introduces a complex set of social conditions and relationships:

> Mr. Ryder might aptly be called the dean of the Blue Veins. The original Blue Veins were a little society of colored persons organized in a certain Northern city shortly after the war. Its purpose was to establish and maintain correct social standards among a people whose social condition presented almost unlimited room for improvement. By accident, combined perhaps with some natural affinity, the society consisted of individuals who were, generally speaking, more white than black. Some envious outsider made the suggestion that no one was eligible for membership who was not white enough to show blue veins. The suggestion was readily adopted by those who were not of the favored few, and since that time the society, though possessing a longer and more pretentious name, had been known far and wide as the "Blue Vein Society," and its members as the "Blue Veins." (1–2)

This early parenthesis which delays the unfolding of the action marks the narrator's control over the tale's evaluative apparatus. This is a decisive shift from the conjure tales of Uncle Julius, in which the privilege of judging the narrative repeatedly falls to John and Annie, Uncle Julius's white listeners. The language of the parenthesis is itself at marked variance with the simplicity of the first paragraph, and it characterizes a narrative voice which hedges, qualifies, and even evades direct assertion in its process of explanation.

The purpose of the Society itself is clear: "to establish and maintain correct social standards" and boundaries of exclusivity which will demarcate the domain of "the favored few." The effect of the narrative voice, however, is everywhere to undermine the validity of the Blue Veins' social stance, as it calls into question all fixed positions and standards. The first verb in the passage, "might aptly be called," with its conditional passive voice and embedded adverbial qualifier, subtly undercuts Mr. Ryder's position of leadership. There is an archness to the narrator's initial refusal even to name the "certain Northern city" in which the Blue Veins' social successes are being played out. Their hope that they can improve their social condition is qualified by the insight that the potential for mobility is "*almost* unlimited." Similarly, the racial standard upon which membership in the Blue Vein Society is based is subtly compromised. Qualifiers such as "by accident," "perhaps," and "generally speaking" suggest that the terrain where racial distinctions are made, among the Blue Veins and in Chesnutt's fictive world, will be shadowy at best. Although the social program of the Blue Veins is devoted to the separation of insiders from outsiders, the sacred circle itself is marked by a name which signifies both the envy and the contempt of those who are on the outside.

Moreover, the ranks of the little society are constantly subject to invasion. Chesnutt evokes the ongoing process of judging the social elite in a single dazzling sentence which itself enacts the process of crossing over the Blue Veins' lines of exclusion:

> There were those who had been known to assail it violently as a glaring example of the very prejudice from which the colored race had suffered most; and later, when such critics had succeeded in getting on the inside, they had been heard to maintain with zeal and earnestness that the society was a lifeboat, an anchor, a bulwark and a shield,—a pillar of cloud by day and of fire by night, to guide their people through the social wilderness. (2)

Here the narrator delicately places all judgments in the mouths of an unidentified group ("there were those") who view the Society from both sides of its color line. But what appears at first glance to be an ironic exposure of the hypocrisy of their evaluation is complicated by the likelihood that Chesnutt (who was himself a member of the Cleveland Social Circle upon which the Blue Vein Society was patterned) held both views to be true. The Blue Veins have become implicated in the very strategies of racial exclusion which have oppressed them, and the piling up of the metaphors of survival, stability, and protection clearly suggests the insecurity of an indefensible position. The allusion to Exodus and to the struggles of a recently enslaved people in the wilderness seems more complicated, however, because Chesnutt was, like W. E. B. DuBois, deeply committed to the social and intellectual leadership of a small group of the best black citizens, or a "talented tenth." And the Blue Veins constitute for Chesnutt such an elite.

The Blue Veins, and Chesnutt among them, face the dilemmas inherent in any society when a group of people are given, for the first time, the promise of mobility and the autonomy to create social roles for themselves. For such people, the social structure must simultaneously embody openness and closure. The openness creates the potential for progress upward, but without levels and barriers of exclusion there is nothing to make the rise meaningful. When the autonomy to create one's social roles involves a denial of origins and the obligations of the past, exhilaration may be accompanied by a profound state of anxiety.

In "The Wife of His Youth," Mr. Ryder is able to shield himself from these conflicting emotions only until external forces intrude to exert the influence of memory and prior identity. To his credit, Ryder is uniquely susceptible to the transformative powers of the tale which the old black woman tells. He must sense that his claims to gentility and high economic standing are limited; this is one reason why he is seeking to improve his social position through marriage to a woman who is lighter-skinned than he is. He is prompted by more than polite condescension to admit the stranger into his home. The hope that hearing her story will "refresh [his] memory" (11) is an invitation to the storyteller to break down the barriers between the present and the past, and to admit the listener to a recognition of his origins.

For her part, the wife of Ryder's youth moves with consummate assuredness of her identity. The very first act of her narrative is to name herself, " 'My name's 'Liza, . . . 'Liza Jane' " (12), and to give an account of her slave experience. She is utterly confident about her entitlement to pass into Ryder's kitchen and tell her tale, and she never doubts that her example of fidelity must command respect. The dialect of her tale has the jarring quality of truth, when placed beside the polite locutions with which Ryder masks his linguistic past. So straightforward is the story, that it is possible to gloss over the brutalities which it recounts: the intended enslavement of the free black apprentice; the whipping and the punishment of being sold down the river which she endures to save her husband. After such sacrifice, Ryder's intimation that her husband may have forgotten or "outgrown" her is unimaginable to her. Her repeated assertions of fidelity accentuate Ryder's own life of denial, and he is finally compelled to confront his true identity: once when he beholds his own faded daguerrotype which 'Liza Jane wears around her neck; and then after she departs, as he "stood for a long time before the mirror of his dressing-case, gazing thoughtfully at the reflection of his own face" (17).

It would appear that the story's revelations either deal a shattering blow to Ryder's expectations, or they condemn him to a life of deceit and hypocrisy. In fact, the opportunity to retell and to complete 'Liza Jane's story becomes for Ryder the means of recasting his identity and creating the terms under which he will remain an admired center for the Blue Veins. In the process, *Ryder* becomes a figure for the *writer*, Chesnutt himself, who yokes literary authorship with the achieving of social pre-eminence.

Ryder's ball has the trappings of a courtly theatrical occasion. He intends it to be a celebration of his own social triumph, accompanied by singing, dancing, and a prepared toast to "The Ladies" which he has larded with quotations from Tennyson, his favorite poet. The intrusion into the festivities of the wife of his youth and his decision to tell 'Liza Jane's story destroy the prepared script for the event, but he simultaneously gains greater freedom to manipulate the ball's theatrical effects. His narration of the story commits him to a full revelation of his past, but he retains the power to shape his own role within the narrative and his audience's response to it.

Where 'Liza Jane's story achieves its impact through openness and a straightforward exposition of fact, Ryder's performance is an elaborately structured dance of the veils, which relies upon concealment and several kinds of artifice to insure that his truth will be received as he wishes it to be. When Ryder begins his revelation, he appears to be playing his role according to the original script which calls for a sentimental paean to the "fidelity and devotion" (19) of the Blue Vein ladies. He then artfully strips off the veil of linguistic cultivation by duplicating 'Liza Jane's tale "in the same soft dialect, which came readily to his lips" (20). The "responsive thrill" which greets this improvisation offers evidence that each of the Blue Veins is susceptible to the powers of the memory of great suffering.

Ryder proceeds by indirections with an "imagined . . . case" (20) which is, in fact, the story of his own life rendered in the third person, introducing each element with the word "suppose" to cast the cloak of hypothesis upon it. Having recounted his life without yet acknowledging it. Ryder challenges his listeners to judge the case: " 'My friends, what would the man do?' " (22). His manipulation of the terms of the evaluation—this was a man "who loved honor and tried to deal justly with all men"—ought to underscore the critical nature of the narrative moment: the future course of the teller's life depends upon his audience's reply. Mrs. Dixon, the wife who will never be, speaks for all of the Blue Veins: " 'He should have acknowledged her.' " Only then does Ryder approach the final "closed door" to introduce the wife of his youth and to announce his own identity: " 'Ladies and gentlemen . . . this is the woman, and I am the man, whose story I have told you' " (24).

Ryder's narrative ends where 'Liza Jane's began, with an acknowledgement of identity, but it is much more than a confession. His skillfully enacted drama of self-revelation calls upon the Blue Veins to examine and redefine the foundations of their own exclusivity. Ryder's performance proposes that henceforth not property, nor the veneer of culture, nor specious distinctions of race will constitute the dominant values of their little society, but eloquence, theatricality, moral responsibility, and human compassion. His story of identity inscribes justice and a more egalitarian code of ethics upon his social group, and establishes himself as a leader precisely because of his abundant possession of those values. Through Ryder's act of storytelling, Chesnutt can celebrate the exemplary behavior of the Blue Veins, even as he creates the possibility of a community of virtue which embraces rather than excludes.

Ryder is a more supple and versatile storyteller than Uncle Julius, and his narrative strategies announce a very different program for Chesnutt's second collection of short stories. While he understands the powers of concealment and silence, the vestiges of the "economies of slavery," his goal is finally openness and the affirmation of identity (Baker 21–33). For Uncle Julius, storytelling offers the unusual opportunity to manipulate an audience for psychological power and economic gain, and his art represents Chesnutt's own first negotiations with his readership. For Ryder, however, the potential for authoring the self through narrative carries the additional power to reshape his audience and to create its values. The most enduring stories in *The Wife of His Youth* comprise Chesnutt's exploration of the black author's more self-affirming roles.

II

In the arrangement of the nine stories in the collection, there is a ceaseless oscillation across boundaries: from present to past, from North to South, from freedom to slavery and back again. This fluidity, which is both structural and thematic, upsets the reader's assumptions about the dialectics of openness and enclosure which shape the characters' lives. "A Matter of Principle" is apparently a story about freedom and about the capacity to cross over social barriers. Chesnutt once again examines the Blue Veins' attempts to define the racial and cultural standards of their small society. But the very freedom to determine principles of exclusion makes "A Matter of Principle" the most rigidly bounded story in *The Wife of His Youth*. The story's central character, "Brotherhood Clayton," fails to see that the barriers he erects to protect his privileged position will eventually oppress and confine him. And the narrative structure and metaphors of the story reinforce Chesnutt's awareness that enslavement may be both socially- and self-imposed.

"A Matter of Principle" is bounded in several ways. Within the collection, Chesnutt places this story of free black society evolving in the urban North following the Civil War between two stories, "The Sheriff's Children" and "Cicely's Dream," which deal explicitly with slavery and its residue in the rural South. The narrative itself is framed by the voice of Brotherhood Clayton expressing his racial "principles" in nearly identical words at the beginning and the end. Clayton achieves only a limited measure of self-knowledge from his humiliation and social failure, and his own words and beliefs are the forces which inhibit his growth as a character. Within this enclosure, Chesnutt's narrator occupies a delicate position, simultaneously distancing himself from the racial attitudes Clayton expresses, even as he acknowledges the legitimate aspirations of the social elite to which he belongs.

Clayton's attempt to name his own racial status is an act of self-denial: "The fundamental article of Mr. Clayton's social creed was that he himself was not a negro" (94). His explanation of his racial principle consists of a variety of contradictory impulses:

> I know . . . that the white people lump us all together as negroes, and condemn us all to the same social ostracism. But I don't accept this classification, for my part, and I imagine that, as the chief party in interest, I have a right to my opinion. People who belong by half or more of their blood to the most virile and progressive race of modern times have as much right to call themselves white as others have to call them negroes. . . . Of course we can't enforce our claims, or protect ourselves from being robbed of our birthright; but we can at least have our principles and try to live up to them as best we can. If we are not accepted as white, we can at any rate make it clear that we object to being called black. (95)

Despite the passage's apparent indignation towards the color line, the reader quickly sees that Clayton's true racial agenda is to *redraw* the line so that he, himself, will be able to cross over. Only by defending the legitimacy of the *idea* of "the color line" can Clayton make the act of crossing over it personally significant. However, once he has established the barrier which separates him from those whom he considers "black," he has positioned himself in a racial no-man's land. His only hope for social recognition is to throw himself upon the mercy of " 'the Anglo-Saxon race [which] loves justice, and will eventually do it, where it does not conflict with their own interests' " (95).

Having allowed Clayton his rhetorical freedom, Chesnutt's narrator proceeds to undermine the authority of his racial views. Certainly, there is nothing contemptible about an appeal to standards of justice and equity in a republic which prides itself on such values. But the narrator immediately calls upon the judgment of "the discerning reader" who can perceive the selfishness of Clayton's selective application of his own principles. From a distance, this discerning reader observes the extravagant pretensions of Clayton's life and the difficult compromise which that pretense entails.

Despite all his hopes for breaking down social barriers, Clayton leads a miserable life of exclusion, much of it self-imposed. The process of excluding "black people" from their company deprives the family of numerous social pleasures. Far from moving freely in society, they take "refuge in a little society of people like themselves." They attend a predominantly white church and participate in several religious and benevolent associations

> where they came in contact with the better class of white people, and were
> treated, in their capacity of members, with a courtesy and consideration
> scarcely different from that accorded to other citizens. (96)

Such sanitized "contact" hardly constitutes a breaking down of barriers. In
fact, it tends to reinforce the Claytons' status as outsiders who have only the
impersonal contact of organization "members," and even then the courtesy
and consideration are "*scarcely* different" from the treatment accorded to all
members.

The true prisoner of this double process of social- and self-imposed
enclosure is Clayton's daughter Alice. Her father's minute gradations of racial
identity make the marriage market a barren economic space for Alice Clayton, where men darker than she are unacceptable, and where lighter-skinned
men find more attractive offers. The central action of "A Matter of Principle"
focuses upon the visit to Groveland of Congressman Hamilton M. Brown and
the presumption by Mr. Clayton that he has been delivered a man whose skin
color and social standing entitle him to marry his daughter. In the story's crucial scene, Clayton wrecks his daughter's chances by mistaking the Congressman for a different man, one who was "palpably, aggressively black, with pronounced African features and wooly hair, without apparently a single drop of
redeeming white blood" (117).

Clayton's racial ordeal is played out in the imposing Union Depot of
Groveland. It is one of Chesnutt's most detailed settings in the collection, and
it metaphorically reinforces the story's sense of the oppression of barriers created by society and by individuals. The Depot is described in terms of its
immensity and its mass; recurring lines of force and barriers of exclusion create an aura of officialdom and authority. The interior of the building is seg-
mented by "a dozen parallel tracks" running East and West. On either side of
the tracks, the various departments and administrative offices extend "in a
row for the entire length of the building" (114). A long open space is "separated from the tracks by an iron fence or *grille*." Access to the train area is
restricted to "two entrance gates in the fence at which tickets must be shown"
(114). This description clearly images the racial enclosure of Clayton's own
consciousness. Although a railroad terminal is by function a place of mobility,
of coming-and-going, this particular depot is rigidly bounded and only those
who possess proper credentials are allowed to pass the threshold. Clayton's
failure to identify the real Congressman Brown as he passes through the gates
follows from his inability to negotiate the lines of racial demarcation which he
has helped to create.

As a means of avoiding his obligation to entertain a "black" Congressman, Clayton has recourse again to his preferred strategy, the construction of
a barrier. The elaborate faking of the diphtheria quarantine shuts up his
house and his daughter, while Congressman Brown pays suit to another

woman. Clayton discovers his error in a newspaper column entitled "A Colored Congressman," which hurls the rhetoric of his own racism back at him:

> The bearing of this son of South Carolina reveals the polished manners of the Southern gentleman, and neither from his appearance nor his conversation would one suspect that the white blood which flows in his veins in such preponderating measure had ever been crossed by that of a darker race. (125)

The beneficiary of the story's mistaken identity is Mr. Clayton's shop assistant, Jack, who is left the master of Alice's affections. Jack is both the source of Clayton's error about the Congressman's identity and also the author of the quarantine plot which seals Alice off from his potential rival. But the text is silent about Jack's motives and his intent. If his flawed report is deliberate, then we may see in Jack a version of the wily trickster who, like Uncle Julius, knows and manipulates his employer's racial attitudes, and who can turn barriers of mis-communication to his own benefit.

The process of narrative judgment is both delicate and complex in "A Matter of Principle," because Chesnutt is dealing so closely with the aspirations of the social group with which he himself identified. In fact, the narrator's preferred strategy of evaluation is silence. The story particularizes Clayton's racial attitudes by placing them in direct discourse; then it uses the character of Jack and the "official" language of the newspaper accounts to bring him to an awareness of the way his racism has entrapped him. The ending seems to allow Clayton relief from his ignorance. But his wistful repetition of the creed of "Brotherhood" causes the work to close in upon itself, thus reinforcing the coffin-meaning of race in the story.

III

"Cicely's Dream," which follows, forms an unusual and troubling companion to "A Matter of Principle." Both stories establish the color line as a barrier which the main characters attempt to cross. For Cicero Clayton, society's promise of mobility proves to be a delusion, and the freedom to cross boundaries degenerates into an insistence on devising new forms of self-enclosure. Cicely, however, exercises extraordinary power to cross boundaries. So adept is she at negotiating the liminal world of Emancipation created by the Civil War, that she succeeds for much of the story in reversing entirely the terms of racial oppression in America. That Chesnutt finally denies Cicely the success of transforming her dream into reality may underscore his awareness of the powerful danger she would embody for the white readership he sought.

The opening paragraphs of "Cicely's Dream" create a significant fluidity of time, space, and situation. Chesnutt has plunged the action back from the urban North of the post-bellum period to an indeterminate rural landscape which is only marked indirectly by Cicely's submissive reference to " 'de w'ite folks up at de big house' " (138). The narrative never specifies Cicely's slave status, and the bonds which enslave her remain imperceptible until the mid-point in the story when Emancipation theoretically erases them.

Similarly, the opening paragraphs metaphorically situate the action at a threshold, and the story's initial impressions are of openness, illuminated vistas, and abundant potentialities. Old Dinah gazes out at her grand-daughter Cicely through "the back door of the cabin" shading her eyes from the sunlight which bathes the vast cornfield "stretching for half a mile" before her. The crop "just in the ear" bespeaks growth and fertility with "its yellow pollen-laden tassels over-topping the dark green masses of broad glistening blades" (132). The setting is replete with veils, lines, and barriers, none of which form any obstacle for the girl. Her first action is to climb "the low fence between the garden and the cornfield," where the long rows "vanished in the distant perspective." After picking down the lines of crops, Cicely reaches the "rail fence" which separates the cultivated terrain from "the thick underbrush of forest" (136), and she does not hesitate to climb this barrier in pursuit of "luscious blackberries" in their "wild state." In the early episodes of the story, Cicely crosses over the barrier repeatedly and unselfconsciously. When her grandmother cannot climb the fence, Cicely quickly replies " 'I'll take it down,' " and she dismantles the barrier in a matter of minutes (140). This exploration of the wilderness and the tasting of its luscious fruits is a rehearsal for the more serious testing of racial boundaries which is to follow.

The other dimension of Cicely's ability to cross over from the safely cultivated to the "wild state" is her dream vision. In it, Cicely imagines that she is loved and married by "a young man whiter than she and yet not all white" (139), the same dream that Cicero Clayton had for his daughter. In the case of "Cicely's Dream," however, Chesnutt provides the young girl with the materials—a wounded young man of indeterminate race and origins who has lost his memory—and the will to actualize her fantasy.

Realizing that the mysterious man's race will be the decisive factor in her future happiness, Cicely determines to *make* him black. Memory and the recovery of the past, the forces which redeem Silas Ryder in "The Wife of His Youth," are the only obstacles to Cicely's creation of a perfect lover. She "taught him to speak her own negro English, which he pronounced with absolute fidelity to her intonations" (147), and is able to make not only his speech, but also his manners and his daily life "an echo of [her] own" (147).

Only after Cicely has perfected her creation, secured his love, and shut the door on outsiders, does Chesnutt's narrator begin to interpret her work. The language of appropriation and possession prevails: "He was hers—hers alone" (148), and "She had found him; he was hers" (155). The narrator also offers a significant Biblical analogy:

She had found him, as Pharaoh's daughter had found Moses in the bulrushes; she taught him to speak, to think, to love. (149)

The analogy casts Cicely as the daughter of the master and her lover as the son of slaves. Cicely's fantasy has daringly reversed the colors of the racial oppression she has herself known. Nevertheless, her happiness depends upon the re-enactment of a system of appropriation of human beings which Chesnutt's short stories constantly repudiate.

It is unlikely that Cicely perceives the underside of the sentimental romance which she has authored. But Cicely's dream is clearly Captain Arthur Carey's nightmare, and a source of unease for the white reader who possesses comfortable preconceptions about racial difference. When the caprice of a temporary case of amnesia can shunt a man back and forth across the color line, skin color and the concept of "race" itself become the most arbitrary of signifiers.

From Carey's perspective, his melodrama of the discovery scene in which he regains his memory, Martha Chandler his beloved, and his whiteness is an agony of emancipation:

The imprisoned mind, stirred to unwonted effort, was struggling for liberty; and from Martha had come the first ray of outer light that had penetrated its dungeon. (164)

"And Cicely?" (167). At the end of the story, Cicely simply vanishes, and the narrator, ignoring her emotional devastation, philosophizes briefly about the pitiable condition of the jilted woman in a love triangle. The image of a daring reversal of the terms of American racial experience struggles against and finally succumbs to the imperatives of the sentimental romantic tale. Cicely's dream constitutes a thrilling experiment in the erasing of racial boundaries, but Cicely's failure is Chesnutt's retreat. While Chesnutt could link his own quest for an affirming narrative voice to the self-discovery of Silas Ryder in "The Wife of His Youth," he was, apparently, more reluctant to link the rebellious power of Cicely's romantic fantasy with his own fictional craft.

IV

"The Passing of Grandison" also seems poised between an affirmation of its hero's capacity to author his racial identity and his freedom, and Chesnutt's evasion of the extraordinary power involved in such an assertion. The title introduces the enigmas of identity and intention in the story. It explicitly reveals Grandison's ability to cross boundaries in his passing from slavery to freedom. But the title also carries with it the ambiguities of the very different practice of "passing" for white which constituted one of the most paradoxical ways of breaking the bonds of blackness at the turn of the twentieth century. As Michael Cooke has pointed out, "passing" is "self-assertion as self-denial, self-annihilation as self-fulfillment" (32).

Of the stories in Chesnutt's second collection. "The Passing of Grandison" bears the closest resemblance to the tales of Uncle Julius, not only in its slavery setting, but also in its hero's self-veiling. For several reasons, however, Grandison's veiling strategies are more mysterious and more laden with potential. His mask is at all points impermeable, not only to his masters, but also to the reader, who is repeatedly denied access to his motivation. Moreover, "The Passing of Grandison" is the only story in the collection in which the narrative voice largely suspends its adjudicative role. Finally, Grandison's veiling results in the most heroic form of self-identification available to a slave—his escape to freedom with his entire family.

In "The Passing of Grandison," we sense most clearly the absence in Chesnutt's second collection of the narrative frame which unifies *The Conjure Woman*. That frame in the first collection guarantees that the telling of each tale will be motivated by Uncle Julius's immediate material needs and then mediated by John's Yankee capitalism or Annie's genteel sentimentalism. The frame, moreover, establishes the limits of Uncle Julius's autonomy and powers of negotiation, limits imposed by his age, his attachment to the land, and his economic need. For all of his daring as a storyteller, within the frame, there are pattern, repetition, and a fixity of social condition beyond which Uncle Julius is unprepared to step. The absence of the frame in "The Passing of Grandison," and in *The Wife of His Youth* as a whole, bespeaks the characters' refusal to be bound by forms of identification and constraints upon action imposed by others. In the story, the crossing of boundaries is both metaphorically and literally a means of self-identification.

Nevertheless, the awareness of Grandison's greater potential dawns suddenly; within the story, the reader is held in narrative bondage. The passing to freedom of this docile slave and his apparent ecstasy for chains are viewed entirely through the eyes of his white masters. Readerly intuition might enable us to detect the irony in Colonel Owens' satisfaction at "this blissful relationship of kindly protection on the one hand, of wise subordination and loyal dependence on the other" (179). But Grandison's bowing and scraping, and the fearful invective he hurls at " 'dem ab'lishuners,' " preclude alternatives to the Owens' vision of their childlike, irresponsible, and ignorant chattel. For the duration of the story, the reader is shackled by the masters' delusions of perfect control over their slaves' minds and motives.

Grandison himself finds his ability to act freely confined by a double enclosure: not only by the slave system, but by the role he is designated to play in young Dick Owens' amorous theatricals. The plot is grounded in idleness and folly. The Colonel's son will take upon himself an absurd act—to lead Grandison into a situation where he will automatically embrace his freedom, masquerade it as heroic abolitionism, and then offer it to a superficial girl as a love token. Owens never ponders the value of freedom to those who are enslaved; he simply assumes that freedom is a "virus" which will inoculate the susceptible Grandison when he is placed in an infected environment.

The great imponderable of the story, for the young master and, inevitably, for the reader, is Grandison's refusal to play his part in this travesty of emancipation. Owens attributes the failure to Grandison's "stupidity" and the unaccountable fidelity of his race. Judging the slave only by the standard of his own selfishness and indolence, it never occurs to Owens that Grandison cannot place any value upon his personal freedom while his family remains in bondage. There is, in a sense, more freedom in Grandison's choice to cross back into slavery than in the trivialized gift of his master. In the act, Grandison demonstrates that the line which divides slave states from free states constitutes no barrier for him. Much more than his role in Dick Owens' farce, this reverse crossing of the slave border is a rehearsal for the genuine drama of emancipation which he will author for himself and for others.

But if Grandison repeatedly demonstrates his mastery of racial boundaries, Chesnutt grants no similar power to the reader in gaining access to his hero's mind. It is impossible to determine whether Grandison is simply a model of dogged family loyalty, or whether he is the calculating rebel, creating the role of the cowardly slave, fabricating tales of his escape from the abolitionists, mastering the masters through deceit in order to effect a mass escape. The story concludes with two powerful images. The first is the tableau of Grandison's family upon the fleeing Lake Erie steamboat, unified in their final gaze back into the place of enslavement. The second is the wave of derision by an anonymous sailor which mocks the slaveowner. In their flight, Chesnutt seems to merge two dominant nineteenth-century ideologies, the republican emphasis on freedom and the primacy of love and family bonding in the cult of domesticity. The essence of Grandison's "passing," however, is that his own motivation and power remain invisible to the end.

V

The concealment of "The Passing of Grandison" and its simultaneous affirmation of the heroism of crossing boundaries are an essential counterpoise to Chesnutt's intent in "The Web of Circumstance," which concludes *The Wife of His Youth*. Although the concluding story is set in the rural South following the abolition of slavery, the title's metaphor of entrapment suggests that the action will be played out within confining circumstances. The blacksmith, Ben Davis, does not wish to violate boundaries or to rebel against standards which exclude him. Rather, he believes that the laws of the land have placed him within the privileged circle, and he simply wishes to live out the promise of that privilege. His naive optimism about the egalitarianism of the Reconstruction South and his potential for self-making constitute the dangers which the white men in the story feel they must eradicate.

Ben Davis is not simply a victim of "circumstance" who succumbs to an unmerited doom. The white characters are correct in their assessment of him. Ben Davis *is* a dangerous man—dangerous because he dares to articulate a version of black pride and black striving which constantly exposes the fraudulence of a social and economic system which tantalizingly extends him membership and then denies him meaningful participation. As a means of overcoming this injustice, Chesnutt's narrator struggles to achieve an affirming voice. He takes up Davis's final imaginative vision, a dream of "purity and innocence and peace," and makes it, even at the moment of Davis's murder, the foundation for his own appeal for justice and a shared sense of humanity.

The story begins at the glowing forge of the blacksmith, a place of light emerging from dark shadows, of openness, and of intense industry. Ben Davis's given name invokes images of Franklin, of the accumulation of wealth through virtuous enterprise, and also of the goal of civic participation and responsibility. At the forge, the men of the community gather daily to discuss their affairs and their political beliefs. That Davis is a "blacksmith" speaks not only of his trade, but also of his potential as the "smith" or fashioner of a genuine "black" identity, following the agony of slavery. What Ben Davis demands of the economic system of the Reconstruction South is that it redeem its promise of the opportunity to better himself and to reap the rewards of his own industry and thrift. Because his dream of "self-making" is the dream of the American republic, it never occurs to him that fulfillment is available only selectively. But his assessment of economic conditions in the Reconstruction South and the potential for economic advancement are indeed a threat:

> We colored folks never had no chance ter git nothin' befo' de wah, but ef eve'y nigger in dis town had a tuck keep er his money sence de wah, like I has, an' bought as much lan' as I has, de niggers might a' got half de lan' by dis time. (293)

Ben's goal is a fundamentally American one, to pay off the mortgage: " 'den we won't owe nobody a cent. I tell you dere ain' nothin' like propputy ter make a pusson feel like a man' " (294). The version of himself which Ben wishes to fashion is not simply an economic one; it is a vision of virtuous conduct and citizenship in a thriving republic. At a more threatening level, however, it is a vision of southern society turned upside-down, of the possibility for self-mastery after twenty years as a slave. But the society in which Ben Davis lives will simply not make room for a black man who doesn't "owe nobody a cent." Significantly, the crime of which Ben Davis is falsely accused is the theft of the richly adorned whip of the former slaveholder, Colonel

Thornton. If Davis has not literally stolen the colonel's whip, then the white citizens of Patesville are surely correct that he has designs on the power of self-mastery that the whip represents.

In contrast to the special silence which pervades "The Passing of Grandison," Chesnutt re-asserts his narrative control and the authority of his judgment in "The Web of Circumstance." The abrupt shifts of scene create vulnerable readers who must struggle to fill the gaps of time during which Ben Davis has become ensnared in the web of circumstance. Since the appointed officers of the legal system are the primary agents of injustice, the narrator's commentary must assume the dimensions of the genuine inquiry into right and wrong which exposes the travesty provided for by the law.

The narrative repeatedly allows the reader access to the minds of principal players, such as the State's attorney who "was anxious to make as good a record as possible. He had no doubt of the prisoner's guilt." Behind the scenes we observe the "gentlemen" of the county advising a guilty verdict and stiff punishment to curb an outbreak of "petty thieving." We learn that Davis's own attorney "secretly believed his client guilty" (304). During the barrage of judicial bombast, the narrator's tone of superior judgment also extends to Davis's ignorance of the proceedings and the forces at work against him:

> He had never heard of Tom Paine or Voltaire. He had no conception of what a nihilist or an anarchist might be, and he could not have told the difference between a propaganda and a potato. (299)

Perhaps most significantly, the narrator places in the clearest light the single truth which the court has no interest in discovering—the identity of the real thief. The narrator's superior grasp of guilt and innocence in the case, as well as the ironic tone of his commentary, establish his position outside "the web of circumstance." He cynically eavesdrops on conversations between the lawyers and the judge which the accused himself cannot hear. He invades the judge's private chambers to listen to Davis's chief accuser, Colonel Thornton, plead for leniency, because " 'he's the best blacksmith in the county.' " The arrangement of other details highlights the irony of the verdict. Davis's outrageous five-year sentence is set against the sentencing of a white man to one year for manslaughter and another to six months for forgery. The judge bases this sentence, which he calls "light," upon the single standard that a "society rests upon the sacred right of property." The trial thus manifests a fundamental conflict at the heart of the republican ideology, between the desire to reward civic virtue and a capitalistic commitment to uphold the value of private property. Finally, Davis is convicted by the ideology which he once believed would protect his own efforts to prosper in a transformed southern economy.

During the proceedings, the narrator ironically observes that "the law in its infinite wisdom did not permit the defendant to testify on his own behalf"

(305). Ben Davis, always garrulous at the forge, is virtually silent in the court of law. Once deprived of a self-affirming voice, his only alternative is the self-negating construction of a barrier: "There was one flash of despair, and then nothing but a stony blank, behind which he masked his real feelings, whatever they were" (313).

This same veiling of identity characterizes his return from the penitentiary. Behind his mask, he derives a tortured delight from hearing his ignorant neighbors magnify his crimes. As they spread wild gossip about his children's deaths and his wife's infidelity, he fashions for himself a striking new identity to replace the failed role of the virtuous tradesman:

> he reasoned himself into the belief that he represented in his person the accumulated wrongs of a whole race, and Colonel Thornton the race who had oppressed them. A burning desire for revenge sprang up in him. . . . (318)

In the story's climax, however, Ben Davis experiences a vision of transformation in which he crosses the ultimate threshold from the anguish of hell to heavenly peace and comfort: "Suddenly the grinning devil who stood over him with a barbed whip faded away, and a little white angel came and handed him a drink of water" (320). When the angel, with her "halo of purity and innocence and peace" (321), turns out to be a child in fact, Davis casts off the mask of the black avenger only to be gunned down by Colonel Thornton. In a society which demands that men like Ben Davis be enslaved, imprisoned, or held powerless by laws and custom, even his smallest attempt to reach across the color line towards the angelic child necessarily seals his death warrant.

Had the story and the collection ended with Davis's ghastly murder, *The Wife of His Youth* might be viewed as depressing evidence that "the color line" is an insuperable barrier to the efforts of the characters in all the stories to author their own social identities. But "The Web of Circumstance" concludes, instead, with the narrator's prayer for the coming of "another golden age." With its recurring future tenses and language of anticipation ("hope," "foretaste," "hopefully await its coming") the passage represents an opening out rather than a sign of closure, and Chesnutt's resistance to fixed positions or strategies of presentation. For the black storyteller at the turn of the twentieth century, the process of unveiling moves beyond the heroic refusal to be enmeshed in the web of circumstance, and initiates the exhilarating challenge of affirmation and self-identification.[2]

Notes

1.   For an extended analysis of Uncle Julius's and Chesnutt's strategies of veiling, see Fienberg.

2.   The reading and research for this essay were carried out while I was a participant in a National Endowment for the Humanities Summer Seminar entitled "American Literature: Portraits in Black and White" (Yale University, 1989). My thanks go to Michael G. Cooke and the other participants in the seminar for their encouragement and intelligent response to my work.

Works Cited

Andrews, William L. *The Literary Career of Charles W. Chesnutt.* Baton Rouge: Louisiana State University Press, 1980.

Baker, Houston A., Jr. *Blues, Ideology, and Afro-American Literature: A Vernacular Theory.* Chicago: University of Chicago Press, 1984.

Chesnutt, Charles W. *The Wife of His Youth and Other Stories of The Color Line.* Ann Arbor: University of Michigan Press, 1968.

Cooke, Michael G. *Afro-American Literature in the Twentieth Century: The Achievement of Intimacy.* New Haven: Yale University Press, 1984.

Fienberg, Lorne. "Charles W. Chesnutt and Uncle Julius: Black Storytellers at the Crossroads." *Studies in American Fiction* 15 (1987): 161–173.

Voices at the Nadir:
Charles Chesnutt and David Bryant Fulton

WILLIAM GLEASON

Murder and lynchings have disgraced our land both North and South, . . . and we are thankful for every hand and every voice . . . that is raised in protest against such shameful outrages.

—Bishop Wesley J. Gaines[1]

In *The Marrow of Tradition* Charles W. Chesnutt raises not one, but two voices of protest against the ghastly violence of the 1898 Wilmington, North Carolina, race riot. Both William Miller, the pragmatic mulatto physician, and Josh Green, the vengeful black stevedore, clearly denounce the white-sponsored terrorism of the novel's Wellington. But the responses each offers are ideologically polar: Miller counsels patience, even meekness; Josh cries for militant resistance. Locating an authorial position on this question of the proper black response to white violence at the turn of the century has challenged critics since the novel's publication in 1901. Most of Chesnutt's contemporaries were deeply disturbed by the book's seeming endorsement, through Josh, of Afro-American rebellion. The intervening years, however, have given rise to a different view—that Chesnutt actually played "accommodationist literary politics . . . throughout his literary career."[2] Miller, critics now believe, is Chesnutt's more likely spokesperson.

Emerging coincident with this critical consensus, however—and threatening to destabilize it—is the argument that the novel's ideological contradictions go unresolved. Chesnutt's sympathies, this claim suggests, remain ambiguous; his own philosophy occupies a more subtle and shifting middle ground between Miller and Josh. In principle I am sympathetic to this sort of reading. It recognizes shades of meaning and resists critical pigeonholing. Yet I remain disturbed by the tendency in Chesnutt criticism (a tendency such a reading shares) to make *The Marrow of Tradition* talk out of both sides of his

From *American Literary Realism, 1870–1910*, volume 24:3 © 1992 by permission of McFarland & Company, Inc., Jefferson NC 28640.

mouth at the same time. Read one way—on the "conscious" level, according to a recent essay—the novel supports Miller's accommodativeness. Read another, seeking the repressed, "unconscious message," *The Marrow of Tradition* presents an equally "powerful" statement of militant "resistance and independence."[3] What this wanting to have it both ways actually represses are other voices that *consciously* endorse Josh's position at the turn of the century. There were Afro-American writers in 1900 less ambivalent about the proper response to white violence than Chesnutt. One in particular, David Bryant Fulton—pen-named "Jack Thorne"—also turned to a fictional account of the Wilmington race riot to make his case. Fulton's more consistently militant, progressive voice in that novel, *Hanover; Or the Persecution of the Lowly: A Story of the Wilmington Massacre* (1900), necessitates a reconsideration of Chesnutt's double burden.

On November 10, 1898, two days after statewide elections returned political control of North Carolina to white Democrats, armed whites invaded the black community of Wilmington and burned the offices of the black-owned newspaper, the *Record*. The rioting which followed left at least fourteen blacks dead, scores wounded, and thousands banished or homeless. White town leaders, moving quickly to shape public response to the violence, described the riot in Southern Democratic newspapers and sympathetic Northern journals as an orderly political rebellion. Wilmington, they claimed, had been legally liberated from the corrupt tyranny of incompetent blacks. "We took the city and went right to work," explained Colonel Alfred M. Waddell, leader of the white invasion, in the November 26 cover story of *Collier's Weekly*. "There is not a flaw in the legality of the government," Waddell continued. "It was the result of revolution, but the forms of law were strictly complied with in every respect."[4] *Collier's Weekly* reinforced Waddell's assertion of legitimacy by describing him in a subheading as the "Leader in the Reform Movement and now Revolutionary Mayor of Wilmington." A companion piece on the same page by a *Collier's* special correspondent hinted strongly that "the successful capsizing of Wilmington's municipal government . . . will be emulated in other communities where negro rule is oppressive."

Waddell's white, Democratic interpretation of the riot stood unchallenged by American historians until the 1951 publication of Helen G. Edmonds' *The Negro and Fusion Politics in North Carolina, 1894–1901*. Edmonds argues in one chapter that the riot was actually a thinly masked *coup d'état* by local Democrats, who in turn were supported by hundreds of armed men from throughout the state. While admitting that it would be virtually impossible to describe the riot itself in detail, Edmonds carefully reassembles the various tensions which contributed to the violent outburst. She concludes that a number of factors—notably "political confusion resulting from the Democrats' refusal to accept the city government of 1897, economic competition between white and black labor, the violent opposition of whites to Negro office-holding, . . . the yellow journalism of the press, . . . [and] the orators of the 'white supremacy' campaign"—made Wilmington "a veritable boiling pot."[5] Just before the election, a group of Democrats, led by Waddell and calling themselves the "Secret Nine," drew up a "Declaration of White Independence" asserting that Wilmington whites would no longer submit to the rule of blacks. The "Declaration," which was shown at the close of election day (November 8) to a gathering of thirty-two prominent blacks of the city, threatened violence unless the black-owned *Record* ceased publication and its editor, Alex Manly, left Wilmington. The black leaders had until 7:30 a.m., November 10, to respond. When no reply was received (a letter was written, Edmonds suggests, but arrived late), Waddell led shotgun-carrying whites in the burning of Manly's offices.

Edmonds' version of the ensuing riot differs markedly from the picture painted by participants like Waddell—and from the dramatic cover drawing of *Collier's Weekly*, which features a mob of black men firing pistols. Edmonds instead documents a white mob relentlessly pursuing "offensive" blacks and then killing them, with the demonstrated support of the state militia—who were ostensibly called to restore order after the burning of the newspaper offices. Waddell's subsequent explanation of the "legal" establishment of Democratic control of the city government she exposes as "specious." She claims that rather than a spontaneous act of justifiable revoution, the Wilmington riot was a symptom of a "malignant growth," a carefully planned yet indefensible "campaign of intimidation, misrepresentation, vilification, and violence" (p. 174).

In 1984 H. Leon Prather, Sr., produced a book-length study of the riot that reconsiders Edmonds' sources while introducing much new material. Arguing in his preface that "the definitive pen of the black scholar is needed to correct the distortions and to fill in the glaring omissions," Prather attempts his own careful "delineation and analysis of the political and socio-economic forces that generated this American tragedy."[6] Though Prather largely corroborates Edmonds' outline and interpretation of the events, he provides a more densely textured exploration of what happened before, on, and after November 10, both in and out of Wilmington. Hoping to produce more than just a scholarly history, Prather also strives to "capture the spirit of the drama" in order to expose the "horror" of the riot. He begins aptly by questioning the appropriateness of the phrase "race riot" itself to describe events like those in Wilmington. Prather suggests that "racial massacre"—a "macabre mixture of carnage and carnival"—would be more accurate (p. 11).

Chesnutt, who supposedly dedicated himself to a full-time writing career in 1899 in direct response to his shock over the violence in Wilmington, wrote *The Marrow of Tradition* after touring the South to collect material for the novel. Chesnutt's account of the riot roughly corresponds to the currently accepted outline, although he makes certain signal alterations. First,

Chesnutt shifts the action from November to September, placing it two months before the elections rather than two days following. Chesnutt's fictional riot occurs shortly after Major Carteret, owner and editor of the local white newspaper, reprints a provocative anti-lynching editorial that had appeared in the local black newspaper earlier in the year. In the real Wilmington, Alex Manly's editorial—which implied, according to Joel Williamson, that lynching was the result "not of black men assaulting white women, but of white women caught with their black lovers and crying rape to save their reputations"—had appeared in August.[7] White supremacists immediately called for Manly's resignation (and his neck) and tried to force the *Record* to shut down, but when the initial excitement waned, Manly was allowed to continue publishing. In October, however, three weeks before the elections, hundreds of thousands of copies of his editorial were reprinted and circulated around the state. Manly was vilified at huge Democratic rallies by fiery guest speakers such as Senator "Pitchfork" Ben Tillman of South Carolina. Armed bands of Redshirts, "a sinister Klan-like organization" of poor whites, were soon stalking the streets of Wilmington.[8] This gradual rekindling of tension helped create the proper atmosphere for the November riot. Chesnutt, however, compresses several weeks of activity into only a few days, heightening the sudden fury of the riot. And although he carefully alerts the reader that town leaders like Carteret, Colonel Belmont, and Captain McBane—representing three castes of Southern white society—secretly manipulate the riot, he does not let them control the direction of his anger. In the end, the mob of primarily lower class whites does its ghastliest work despite the protests of Carteret.

Chesnutt's second major change is to shift the beginning of the attack to the afternoon, with the worst of the violence occurring after dark, against a black background illuminated by Dr. Miller's burning hospital. By making this particular change, Chesnutt seems more interested in deepening the psychological and symbolic dimensions of the riot than in strict historical accuracy. The sheer audacity of a daylight massacre was certainly shocking. But the nighttime setting, for Chesnutt, powerfully suggests that Major Carteret's scheme is no different in intent or outcome from the hooded midnight murders of the Ku Klux Klan.

By contrast, Fulton's dates, times, and settings match the historical data much more closely. His riot takes place in the morning, on November 10, and is largely confined to the daytime. Manly's *Record* offices are burned, not the colored hospital. Portions of Fulton's mob roam uncontrolled through the city, while others are under careful military guidance—just as the actual rioters were assisted by the Wilmington Light Infantry, the naval reserves, and additional out-of-town military units. Fulton even notes the presence of a Gatling gun, tested in public for its "efficiency as a deadly weapon" before the election.[9] This detail, like most in *Hanover*—is confirmed by the written records.

And yet as one probes these records, disturbing questions emerge. How much of Fulton's account reflects reliable information and how much has his own story in fact shaped subsequent interpretation? Prather notes in his preface that the events in Wilmington "inspired two works of fiction," Fulton's and Chesnutt's (p. 10). Yet Prather himself cites *Hanover* half a dozen times as an historical source, then notes cryptically in his bibliographical essay that while Fulton "writes authoritatively about some aspects of the riot, . . . he does make some factual errors" (p. 207). In other instances—including the very first sentence of his opening chapter—Prather appears to lift material from *Hanover* without explicit acknowledgement, noting no other source. Edmonds cites *Hanover* as an historical source four times, once even using a sentence from the novel as the recorded speech of Colonel Waddell, the model for both Chesnutt's Colonel Belmont and Fulton's "Colonel." And a recent literary critic lists Fulton (along with, among others, Edmonds) as a "first-rank historian" who corroborates the accuracy of Chesnutt's story.[10]

Is this merely sloppy scholarship? Fulton had left Wilmington in 1887—a decade before the riot—and there is no evidence that he was any closer to it than, say, Chesnutt. Certainly the notion of examining a fictional work for factual information is inherently problematic. But what if that text takes special pains to authenticate itself? *Hanover* opens with an "Associated Press Market Report" that appears to be an actual news clipping, and the novel includes "Mrs. Adelaide Peterson's Narrative" (a letter supposedly written in December of 1899 to Fulton offering one citizen's eyewitness report of the massacre), plus a second news blurb. Using Robert Stepto's model of slave narrative authentication, *Hanover* would seem on its own to be a form of "integrated narrative," with its authenticating documents merged into the tale.[11] But when *Hanover* is used to verify another generic text (such as Edmonds' history, or Prather's, or Chesnutt's novel), it reaches the status in Stepto's formulation analogous to an "authenticating narrative."

Certainly that is how Fulton wanted *Hanover* to read. His scrupulous attention to the "facts" reflects his desire, as stated in his own introduction, to present a "truthful statement of the causes that led up to the doings of the 10th of November" (p. 10). Fulton names names; and although he changes certain identities and even invents entire characters and situations, he clearly wants *Hanover* to stand as an indictment of those responsible for the terror and bloodshed. In Fulton's own words, "It will be proven."

The burden of "proof" on an Afro-American novelist attempting to portray race relations as they "really" were at the turn of the century was extraordinary. As Rayford Logan has demonstrated, the twenty-five years following the end of Reconstruction amounted to a national betrayal of Afro-Americans. Acting with the implicit support of organized labor, agricultural interests, the Supreme Court, and American presidents from Hayes to McKinley, Southern white supremacists systematically (and often brutally) stripped away the tentative gains made by blacks following Emancipation. Where Afro-Americans had expected first-class citizenship, they were offered segregation, discrimination, exploitation, and contempt. This general repudiation of the "American Creed" crested in the 1890s, as state after state passed legislation to disfranchise blacks and lynchings escalated to nearly two hundred a year.[12] 1901—the year Chesnutt published *The Marrow of Tradition*—marked the nadir in the quest for equal rights.

In popular American literature, the escalation of political, social, and economic pressures that this reassertion of white supremacy presented for black Americans was mirrored by "the ascendancy of white, Southern writers . . . who attempted to sustain through their portrayal of black characters the myth of Negro inferiority that had long served the apologists of slavery."[13] The works of these plantation school writers—particularly Joel Chandler Harris, Thomas Nelson Page, and Thomas Dixon—were extremely popular with the primarily white, middle-class readership. While other post-bellum American novelists began experimenting with realism, the dominant modes of the best-selling plantation school continued to be romance and melodrama. With regard to their portrayal of blacks, however, the mythopoeic works of this latter school were frequently accepted as truthful chronicles. Moreover, newspapers and magazines in both the South and the North unremittingly pressed the stereotypes of the comic-criminal Negro into the daily American consciousness.[14] Thus Afro-Americans attempting to write at this time (and to the same readership) were faced with the dilemma of working within the plantation/journalist tradition, or unmasking its falsehoods and presenting their own "truer" versions of history.

Chesnutt clearly struggles with this dilemma in *The Marrow of Tradition*. On the one hand, a number of fairly traditional frameworks operate in the novel. Aunt Polly's secret chest, the two suppressed wills, and the love subplot entangling Tom Delamere, Clara Pemberton, and Lee Ellis, for example, seem borrowed from popular romantic fiction, while Mammy Jane's dialect history of the Carterets and the description of the cakewalk in chapter thirteen are plantation-school conventions. The novel is highly plotted, and many of its structural principles are fairly obvious (such as the daybreak birth that opens the book and the nightfall death that closes it). Yet even as Chesnutt uses these traditional forms, he intentionally challenges negative stereotypes of blacks and attempts to counteract them with his own positive images. *The Marrow of Tradition's* range of characterization, both white and black, marks in fact a noteworthy advance of the color line in American and Afro-American fiction. In the words of Addison Gayle, Chesnutt's very strength "lies in the contrast between old and new images of black[s]. . . . [He] presents the stereotype and its opposite side by side, and thus, for the first time in a black novel, balance in terms of black images is achieved."[15]

The powerful role of the Southern press in creating and perpetuating imbalanced black images also comes under rigorous scrutiny in *The Marrow of*

Tradition. Chesnutt pointedly moves his fictional version of the "voice and publicity organ" of North Carolina white supremacy from Raleigh—where Josephus Daniels' inflammatory *News and Observer* was actually located—to "Wellington" itself.[16] The offices of Major Carteret's *Morning Chronicle,* moreover, become the literal meeting place for Belmont, Carteret, and McBane to plot their campaign of intimidation and violence. Chesnutt is particularly sensitive as well to the North's complicity in the dissemination of Democratic propaganda. He is careful to make Carteret's paper, for example, a member of the Associated Press so that Carteret helps control the images of both whites and blacks received by the Northern press. As Belmont reminds the major, "Through your hands passes all the news of the state. What more powerful medium for the propagation of an idea? The man who would govern a nation by writing its songs was a blethering idiot beside the fellow who can edit its news dispatches."[17]

Chesnutt's blend of romantic convention and social critique has identifiable precursors in the Afro-American canon. One might think, for example, of Harriet Jacobs' simultaneous limitation by and transformation of the sentimental novel in *Incidents in the Life of a Slave Girl* (1861). The journalistic core of *The Marrow of Tradition* also links Chesnutt's narrative to a tradition in American realism initiated by William Dean Howells with the 1882 publication of *A Modern Instance.*[18] And yet, as Dickson D. Bruce, Jr., has stressed, many black writers at the turn of the century "began to look in directions that were quite different from those reflected in the works of their predecessors" (pp. 99–100). By writing an historical novel—one whose "history," moreover, was barely two years old—Chesnutt was attempting something distinctly new. Chesnutt's own earliest works were largely humorous and sentimental short stories, featuring both blacks and whites, though typically not in controversial situations. His shift to more serious themes began in the 1880s with his Uncle Julius tales, seven of which were published in 1899 in his first collection, *The Conjure Woman.* These stories, told in the familiar pre–Civil War plantation school style, conceal an ironic intensity that was probably lost on most of his white readers.[19]

In 1899 Chesnutt also published a brief biography of Frederick Douglass for the "Beacon Biographies of Eminent Americans," plus a second book of tales, *The Wife of His Youth and Other Stories of the Color Line,* the latter collection focusing more directly on post-Emancipation race relations. In 1900 appeared Chesnutt's first published novel, *The House Behind the Cedars,* an antebellum story of passing. Thus *The Marrow of Tradition* marks Chesnutt's first extended treatment of contemporary themes and his first explicitly historical text. But where his previous writings had been largely well received, Chesnutt's second novel "stepped over the bounds of racial decency and . . . shook his white audience's faith in him."[20] Discouraged by poor reviews and dismal sales, the pre-eminent Afro-American fiction writer at the turn of the century published only one more novel after *The Marrow of Tradition.*

What had Chesnutt done? Howells, previously an unqualified Chesnutt supporter, praised the novel's "power," "courage," and "justice," but lamented its bitterness and lack of mercy. Less sympathetic critics were outraged by its supposedly false and humiliating treatment of whites.[21] Perhaps readers also sensed that Chesnutt's "historical" novel didn't quite play up to their expectations of that very popular nineteenth-century literary genre. Historical novels, according to one recent theorist, typically invoke a usable and heroic past in an attempt to satisfy "a desire for national homogeneity."[22] *The Marrow of Tradition*'s usable past, however, is decidedly unheroic, and the novel implicitly indicts an invidious national desire for a return to discriminatory political, social, and economic hierarchies. Although Chesnutt's novel may indeed serve as "a vehicle for claiming and defining a national identity," a role which Philip Fisher suggests nineteenth-century historical novels commonly played, the identity that *The Marrow of Tradition* posits as "American" is almost entirely a negative one.[23] Chesnutt carefully and truthfully implicates, for example, most of white society—North and South alike—in what his narrator calls "the *American* habit of lynching" (p. 179, italics added). And yet Chesnutt's effort to present a realistic range of both white and black characterizations suggests that easy statements about essential "identities" are inherently suspect. Indeed, the tension between Chesnutt's indictment of the "American" character and his resistance to stereotyping the specific individuals in his narrative reflects the novel's deeper ambivalences. Chesnutt's text is no exception to Bruce's observation that tension and ambiguity provide "the key structural framework for black literary composition" at the turn of the century (p. xi). *The Marrow of Tradition* is full of what Bruce calls the "unresolved contradictions" generated by "the character of race relations that developed in America before World War I" (p. xii).

At the root of these contradictions may be Chesnutt's acute awareness of his own indeterminate status as an educated mulatto in the post-Reconstruction South. "I occupy here a position similar to that of Mahomet's Coffin," he writes in his journal in 1881. "I am neither fish, flesh, nor fowl—neither 'nigger,' 'white,' nor 'buckrah.' Too 'stuck up' for the colored folks, and, of course, not recognized by the white."[24] Thus, early on, Chesnutt felt estranged both intellectually and racially not only from whites—to be expected, given the harsh discrimination prevalent at the end of the nineteenth century—but also from blacks; who were frequently hostile to light-skinned mulattoes. According to one biographer, Chesnutt gradually became a nonracial "isolattoe."[25] His first fiction was published without specific mention of his race; not until 1900, when Howells reviewed his color line stories, did Chesnutt's own color become widely publicized.

Although Chesnutt was himself light enough to pass, he never seriously considered doing so as an adult. Yet he felt a strong attachment to Rena Walden, the Gothic heroine of his first novel, *The House Behind the Cedars*. In a letter looking back to the novel from the perspective of the late 1920s—when the early fervor of black nationalism in the United States was waning—Chesnutt refers to *The House Behind the Cedars* as "in a way, my favorite child, for Rena was of 'my own people.' Like myself, she was a white person with an attenuated streak of dark blood."[26] The distinctions Chesnutt prefers are clearly those of class, not race. This preference is dramatized in *The Marrow of Tradition* in the Jim Crow chapter, "A Journey Southward," when Miller is joined in the "colored" car by a party of black farm laborers:

> For a while Miller was amused and pleased. They were his people, and he felt a certain expansive warmth toward them in spite of their obvious shortcomings. By and by, however, the air became too close, and he went out upon the platform. For the sake of the democratic ideal, which meant so much to his race, he might have endured the affliction. . . . [But] personally, and apart from the mere matter of racial sympathy, these people were just as offensive to him as to the whites in the other end of the train. Surely, if a classification of passengers on trains was at all desirable, it might be made upon some more logical and considerate basis than a mere arbitrary, tactless, and, by the very nature of things, brutal drawing of a color line. (pp. 60–1)

Though not a farm laborer, Fulton did spend nine years as a Pullman porter, later working for a music publishing house, in a sugar refinery, and at the Central Branch of the Brooklyn YMCA.[27] Clearly of a lower social class than Chesnutt, Fulton was, moreover, not mulatto. The son of ex-slaves from North Carolina—Chesnutt's parents were free blacks from the same state—Fulton grew up in Fayetteville and then moved with his mother to Wilmington in 1867 at the age of six, only a year after Chesnutt had himself moved to Fayetteville with his family. Fulton was educated in American Missionary Association schools, and began his literary career as a newspaper writer, contributing to the same Wilmington *Record* that Manly would eventually edit in 1898. Later, while living in New York, Fulton contributed articles, poetry, and letters to various newspapers and magazines, including the *Standard Union,* the *New York Times,* and *Colored American Magazine.* Classifying Fulton remains difficult; he is alternately described in various sources as novelist, polemicist, pamphleteer, and literary gadfly. On the title page to *Eagle Clippings,* a 1907 collection consisting primarily of articles originally published in the *Brooklyn Daily Eagle* and a set of Pullman porter stories, Fulton calls himself a "newspaper correspondent and story teller."[28] He then further foregrounds himself as a protector of the black race, announcing in his introductory note that "after all, in all of my writings on the Race question, I have simply been on the defensive, answering traducers and endeavoring to ward off the blows aimed at my people by the enemy" (p. 3).

The enemy here includes both white supremacists and sycophantic Uncle Toms. In *Eagle Clippings* Fulton attacks Page and Dixon—typical targets for black writers—but also assails blacks who support white ideology, particularly those in positions of influence. In a 1903 entry titled "Jack Thorne Utters a Blast for Manliness" (possibly punning on Manly's brave anti-lynching stance a few years earlier), Fulton can scarcely conceal contempt:

> When a few years ago ex-Gov. Northen of Georgia invaded Boston armed with a typewritten defence of the burning of Sam Hose, the Congregational Club of that city paid two dollars a ticket to hear an African Methodist bishop refute the charges made by the Georgian against his people and defend them. The members of that club and their friends listened in disgust to a crawling Negro who joined Northen in his tirade of abuse. "Thou too Brutus?" That very bishop is supported in luxury by those low (?), vicious (?) Negroes, whom he was not man enough to defend. (p. 39)

In his fiction, Fulton equates this notion of race defence with race pride. Here we may draw some of the sharpest distinctions between Fulton and Chesnutt. In *The Marrow of Tradition* Josh Green's success as a model of militancy is ambivalent at best. Josh not only dies, but, as one critic points out, his race pride is in part a personal vendetta against McBane, suggesting that "Chesnutt is not always comfortable with the [militant] image."[29] Unable to portray Josh as a race patriot, Chesnutt gives only equivocal endorsement to the black nationalism in ferment in 1900. Fulton, on the other hand, makes race pride a consistent theme in *Hanover,* and adds a twist—his chief race patriot is a light-skinned mulatto. Molly Pierrepont, erstwhile high-class prostitute for the aristocratic whites of Wilmington, discovers her essential blackness when one of her lovers tells her of the secret plans to massacre the town's blacks. When he tries to convince Molly that her skin color will protect her, she bristles:

> "Of course we don't include such as you, Molly," he said, lightly tapping her on the shoulder. "You are no Nigger, you are nearly as white as I am."
> "Nearly as white," echoed Molly with a sneer. "Do you mean to try to choke it down my throat that my whiteness would save me should your people rise up against Niggers in Wilmington?" (p. 37)

Molly later plays a significant role during the massacre, challenging white ruffians in the streets and also warning the blacks at the Cotton Press of the gathering mob's intentions. But the most valorous hero in the novel is Daniel Wright, a character named for one of the blacks actually killed during the riot. Fulton likens Wright to Israel Putnam, the legendarily brave Revolutionary soldier of Bunker Hill. At the height of the mob's terror, Fulton asks:

> Was there a Putnam here to essay to inspire courage into these frightened negroes, who left their wives and children at the mercy of the mob, and were fleeing toward Hillton? Yes, there was one, and his name was DAN WRIGHT.

> Did Dan Wright fully realize the enormity of his act as he faced this mob of white men, armed to the teeth, now pressing down upon him? Did Dan Wright feel that death was to be his reward for this act of bravery? Yes, but this did not deter him or affect the steadiness of his aim. (p. 84)

According to Prather, several versions of Wright's death exist in the source material. Wright apparently kept himself well-armed—even as white store-keepers refused to sell blacks weapons or ammunition for weeks before the riot—and was accused of being the first to shoot a white man, which apparently triggered the further bloodshed. He certainly foreshadows Josh, and both Chesnutt and Fulton feel compelled to ask whether their militant hero dies in vain. Chesnutt is characteristically ambivalent: "One of the two [Josh or McBane] died as the fool dieth. Which one was it, or was it both?" (p. 309). But Fulton, after Wright has been riddled with bullets, crushed to the earth, and "dragged bleeding and torn through the streets" (p. 84), answers the same question quite differently:

> Died Dan Wright as a fool dieth? Was it right for him to stand alone against such fearful odds? Yes, that the chronicler in recording this terrible one-sided fight might be able to mention one act of true bravery; that among so many cowards there was one man. (p. 85)

Chesnutt, like Fulton, believed that his own influence as a writer could be brought to bear successfully on the race question, although he acknowledged to his journal that any impact he might have would be gradual, almost surreptitious:

> Not a fierce indiscriminate onset, not an appeal to force, for this is something that force can but slightly affect, but a moral revolution which must be brought about in a different manner. The subtle almost indefinable feeling of repulsion toward the Negro, which is common to most Americans—cannot be stormed and taken by assault; the garrison will not capitulate, so their position must be mined, and we will find ourselves in their midst before they think it.[30]

Thus when the rioting begins in *The Marrow of Tradition* Chesnutt has Miller advise Josh to be patient, not heroic. He counsels against resistance, arguing that "our time will come,—the time when we can command respect for our rights; but it is not yet in sight. Give it up boys, and wait" (p. 283). Because Chesnutt's riot comes before the election, Josh and his friends fight not only for social and economic rights, but also for the right to vote (even though, ironically, their fighting will likely destroy that right for the present). Thus Miller's cautious words seem to echo Booker T. Washington's 1895 Atlanta Compromise speech, in which Washington renounced immediate social equality and suggested that blacks were then too "ignorant and inexperienced" to be full participants in the South's political process.[31] The striking (though historically inaccurate) tableau near the end of Chesnutt's novel—Josh and the lower class resistance fighters waging a battle at night—should perhaps be read as an ironic endorsement of Washington's later position in *Sowing and Reaping* (1900): "Great responsibility rests upon the educated Negro of to-day," Washington states. "The great masses look to him for inspiration, for guidance, in plodding their way out of the darkness into the light."[32] Chesnutt thus may signal Josh's failure as a race leader by making him guide the black masses not into the light, but into a murderous darkness. With Josh in the dark (and eventually in the grave), Miller, the educated doctor, survives to seek the light.

Yet as John Reilly has persuasively argued, we cannot be too quick to assign polar values to complicated issues of black protest at the turn of the century. Active minds contain "a complex of subtly graded inclinations and conceptions which are continuously modifying and cancelling each other, conflicting and reorganizing themselves."[33] One might point out, for example, that in the novel itself, Miller—even if he represents Washington's "educated Negro of to-day"—succeeds no better than Josh in guiding the blacks "into the light." Evidence also suggests that Chesnutt disagreed sharply with Washington over black suffrage, though he shared Washington's economic conservatism. In the years following the publication of *The Marrow of Tradition,* Chesnutt was careful to steer a middle course; he generally supported the DuBois-backed anti-Bookerites, but at the same time refused to attack Washington publicly. Moreover, John Wideman demonstrates that Chesnutt's identification with Miller is more complex than a first reading reveals, especially considering that Miller's status at the novel's end is hardly enviable—his son has been killed, his hospital burned to the ground (p. 128). But Chesnutt's narrative suggests that he sees more promise in Miller's "Give it up boys, and wait," than in Josh's eagerness to fight. A look at Chesnutt's 1899 biography of Frederick Douglass may be revealing here, if we read his description of Douglass' refusal to join John Brown in his fatal raid on Harper's Ferry as a gloss on Josh and Miller: "John Brown went forth to meet a felon's fate and wear a martyr's crown: Douglass lived to fight the battles of his race for years to come. There was room for both, and each played the part for which he was adapted. It would have strengthened the cause of liberty very little for Douglass to die with Brown."[34] Aside from Chesnutt's disturbing flirtation with Social Darwinism here, he clearly suggests that Douglass' course, like Miller's, is more commendable than John Brown's—or Josh Green's.

Comparison to *Hanover* would be tidy, then, if Fulton consistently endorsed the positions of men like Brown, Green, and Wright. He does not. Or, I should say, he seems to affirm other forms of protest besides violent resistance. Or does he? Molly, despite her bravery, tells the chair of the Republican Executive Committee before the election to "keep the men away from the polls. Surrender everything. Better to lose a vote than to lose a life"

(p. 55). At the Cotton Press during the riot she warns the unarmed and frightened men—about to rush outside into the mob's death-trap—"Back! Don't rush like fools to death" (p. 83). Dr. Philip Le Grand fights his way to Colonel Moss, leader of one portion of the mob, to find out what the whites want the blacks to do. "We propose to scourge this black pest out of Wilmington," announces the Colonel. "If you can induce them to go to their houses and recognize the authority of the white people, you can prevent further bloodshed." "I will do my best," the minister replies (p. 90). Fulton describes other men of standing in the community (a minister, a fireman) who are forced to flee for their lives in the face of insurmountable odds.

One can read ironies into Fulton's characterizations to suggest that he damns where he seems to praise. To Le Grand, for example, the riot is "far more than he was prepared to grapple with" (p. 87). He later watches helplessly as a heroic black boy is gunned down by the mob. Reverend Selkirk (modeled on Allen Kirk, an actual Wilmington minister), who takes up Manly's cause in August and thus earns a place on the death list, refuses to "retract a single word said in defence of my people," but does agree to flee (p. 100). And fireman McDuffy, also marked out for death, "was a man without fear" (p. 106). Yet he also flees, leaving his wife and children to the mercy of the mob. (At least Miller in *The Marrow of Tradition,* criticized by some readers for putting concern for his family over concern for his race, doesn't simply flee. But then Miller wasn't one of the blacks the mob was trying to exterminate.)

Because *Hanover* has other identifiable artistic weaknesses—including a quirky, uneven style, poorly sustained characterization, and a string-thin narrative structure—one is tempted to dismiss Fulton as incapable of a subtly ironic voice. Yet his best nonfiction pieces in *Eagle Clippings* are charged with sarcasm and ironic humor. Fulton opens one letter, "Takes Issue with Thomas Nelson Page and the Rev. Mr. Dixon," for example, "ponder[ing]" the last installment of Page's "very interesting study of the Race problem." "Emerging slightly from the beaten path," Fulton writes, "Mr. Page divides the Negro race into three classes, i.e., the respectable, the middling respectable, and the very bad" (p. 36). At the letter's end, after exposing the hypocrisy of a white judge with "six mulatto children" who sentences a black man and a white woman to five years in prison for daring to marry, Fulton reflects: "It's a great thing to be a white man; it sugars over the grossest sins and vineers [*sic*] the roughest exteriors. No wonder ignorant, renegade Negroes are clamoring for face bleach" (p. 37).

If *Hanover* lacks structural force, certain recurring themes knit up the book's diffuse stories. One of these themes is race pride, whether manifested as violent race patriotism or simply nonviolent defence of the lives of one's people. This theme allows us to regard Fulton, unlike Chesnutt (who once claimed, "I never wrote or tried to write as a Negro"),[35] as a precursor to the aggressive black nationalism of Marcus Garvey. The connections are more than superficial, and some of the seeds of Garvey's thought—which Wilson Moses claims were present in many proto-Garveyist movements at the turn of the century—can be discovered in both *Hanover* and Fulton's other writing.[36] In one *Eagle* clipping responding to an attack by a white reader, Fulton emphasizes his pride in racial purity:

> The gentleman in referring to Jack Thorne has taken great pains all through his letter to stigmatize me as "Jack Thorne the Negro," Such modes of attack have been very disastrous to us at times. It is our privilege, however, to dignify that name. I would inform the gentleman that I am a Negro full-blooded. Thanks to my sainted mother there is not a drop of the blood of his race in my veins. (p. 53)

At times Fulton's pride in race veers toward literal militancy. In another *Eagle* selection written after the New Orleans riot of 1899, he declares: "The child should be taught that self-defence is as essential, as obligatory as self-respect, and the use of the rifle as the alphabet" (p. 41). And in 1906: "the Afro-American people should not be without the means of defence; every cabin could and should be an arsenal" (p. 56).

Fulton also admired T. Thomas Fortune's activist paper, the *New York Age* (to which the letter with the previous excerpt was originally sent), and as librarian to the Negro Society for Historical Research he probably met later Garveyite John Edward Bruce. The Society issued his *Plea for Social Justice for the Negro Woman* in 1912, and in 1913—the same year Garvey was in London contributing to Duse Mohamed Ali's *Africa Times and Orient Review*—Fulton's article "Race Unification; How It May Be Accomplished" was published by the same press. In this piece, according to William Andrews, Fulton "rejected the idea that the future of Negroes rested on amalgamation with or reliance on whites and emphasized the need for a knowledge of 'race history,' 'race achievement,' and 'race literature' as a stimulus to 'race pride' and advancement."[37] Chesnutt, however, argued in a series of articles for the *Boston Transcript* in 1900 that amalgamation of the races was not only likely, but desirable; elsewhere he rejected the principle of race pride out of hand (and possibly interjected his own "manly" pun): "Why should a man be proud any more than he should be ashamed for anything for which he is not responsible? Manly self-respect based upon one's humanity, a self-respect which claims nothing for color and yields nothing to color, every man should cherish."[38]

And every woman? There are no detailed analyses of Chesnutt's attitudes towards women as yet. But women do play crucial roles in both *The Marrow of Tradition* and *Hanover*. Chesnutt seems fully aware that women are at the very core of the race question in the South. Issues of genealogy and reproduction, for example, give the novel much of its substructure. The birth of Carteret's son (ironically tagged the "happy gift of god") stirs up the Major's "dormant hopes" that his family's "old name" will survive his death, but also kindles "new desires" (p. 28). Carteret wants his son to inherit money and property—and a South free from "nigger domination." It is no accident that he fires off his first anti-Negro editorial only a few days after Dodie's birth, or that the end of the book turns on the question of saving the child's life. Concomitantly critical for the novel's thematic structure are the interwoven issues of miscegenation and rape. Janet Miller, for example, is Olivia Carteret's unacknowledged half-sister, daughter of Olivia's father through "marriage" to his black housekeeper. Polly Ochiltree, Olivia's aunt, is largely responsible for Janet's social and fiscal disinheritance, though the papers Sam Merkell intended for Janet's mother would not necessarily have withstood Southern small-town legal scrutiny. Aunt Polly's own murder, presumably by a black attacker—actually the disguised Tom Delamere—who also (presumably) rapes her, sets off an explosion of racial hatred and nearly causes the lynching of Sandy. The mob's hunger for revenge is not sated until the riot.

However, despite the structural and thematic significance of women in *The Marrow of Tradition*, Chesnutt fails to shape consistently strong female images of the "New Negro." Janet certainly comes the closest; Chesnutt allows her to make the closing moral pronouncement in the novel. But Janet in certain ways also conforms to what Francis Keller terms Chesnutt's "Victorian predispositions" (p. 254). Although educated to be a school teacher, for example, she declines a career in favor of marriage. When she does appear in the book, she is primarily seen and not heard. Janet also secretly is ashamed of "the heritage of her mother's race . . . as part of the taint of slavery" (p. 66). The young "chip-on-the-shoulder stage" nurse is a potentially appealing model and perhaps suggests race advances to come, but her role is restricted to a single, unenthusiastic paragraph.

Chesnutt's reluctance to give black women more prominent roles in his retelling of the riot is highlighted by Fulton's insistence on making women of both races more strong-willed, intelligent, and morally sound than the men, Molly, for example, is not the only woman to brave the rioters; Lizzie Smith, in a bizarre display of courage, defies her would-be assailants by stripping completely nude and shaming them into retreat. Lizzie strips away the black sexual mystique that her attackers insist defines her: "Yo've got ter search me right . . . yo'll fin' I am jes' like yo' sisters an' mammies, yo' po' tackies" (p. 95). Mrs. West, Molly's independent foster mother and president of the all-colored, all-woman Union Aid Society, defends Manly's editorial, even though in historical Wilmington certain black men denounced it. After the massacre, a woman petitioner takes on the role of black priest to lead her church in a fervent prayer for protection from further persecution.

Fulton also gives two of the most vicious white racists—Teck Pervis (a fictionalized Mike Dowling, leader of the Redshirts) and Dr. Jose (probably Peyton Hoge, the minister whose sermon following the riot intoned "we have taken a city")—wives who counsel them against bigotry and violence. Mandy Pervis ridicules Teck's belief that the white aristocrats will actually keep their promises to poor whites once the riot is over, and Mrs. Jose assails her husband's reliance on scripture for his race hatred. Thus the strongest, most progressive women in *Hanover* are the moral equals of Alex Manly—or, to be more accurate, of Ida Wells, the "eminent heroine" to whom Fulton dedicated *Hanover.* One of Wells' own 1892 editorials against lynching brought an especially violent response: her newspaper office "was looted and burned to the ground, her co-owners, barely beating the mob, were run out of town; and Wells herself was warned that she would be hanged from a lamppost if she were to return."[39]

The most consistently strong-willed female character in *The Marrow of Tradition,* on the other hand, is Aunt Polly, the vindictive widow who would have "whipped to death" Sam Merkell's black wife (p. 138). Chesnutt's decision to name this bitter white woman after his own stepmother—and then place her shocking murder at the novel's center—is curious. Helen Chesnutt records no spite between them in her 1952 biography of her father. Yet she does note that on his mother's deathbed Chesnutt "had promised [her] that he would watch over his brothers and sisters, a promise which made Ann Maria's last days happy."[40] Shortly after Ann Maria died, however, her mother brought Mary Ochiltree, a family cousin (and scarcely five years older than Chesnutt) into the household. Mary soon took over the care of the children and married Chesnutt's father. While Chesnutt, according to his daughter, "idolized" his mother, Fulton's respect for women was more expansive. In addition to the 1912 *Plea for Social Justice for the Negro Woman,* in 1923 he presented "Mother of Mine; Ode to the Negro Woman" to the annual convention of New York Colored Women's Clubs. In a long chapter in *Hanover* Fulton has an outspoken white woman indict the destructive hypocrisy underlying what W. F. Cash has termed "the Southern rape complex";[41] she further asserts that white women are signatory partners to the ritualistic mutilations of black men—and by extension, black women:

> The lynchings and burning that are daily occurring in the South are intended as warnings to white women as well as checks to Negro men. Men who constitute these mobs care no more for virtue than so many beasts; . . . It is time for us to rise up and let our voices be heard against the making of our protection an excuse for crime. . . . [Women like] this poor wretch will rise up in the judgment and cry aloud against us as her unnatural sisters who stood upon her and trampled her in the mud and mire. (pp. 117–18)

We may assume that relatively few of Fulton's contemporaries, white or black, read these words. *Hanover* is strikingly different from the conventional narratives Chesnutt's readers expected. Its literary failings did not, however, keep it out of everyone's hands; Fulton hints in *Eagle Clippings* that *Hanover* contributed to his being "branded as a felon" and fired from at least one job (p. 3). He would likely have agreed with a later black critic who argues that, for early Afro-American writers, "literature was an instrument to be used in warfare against an oppressive society."[42] Indeed, in an *Eagle Clipping* memorial, while praising the dying poet Paul Laurence Dunbar for taking time to "dream of the beautiful," Fulton notes that "some of us, in our own strong love for the race and in our zeal for their welfare, have waged war to the knife, knife to the hilt, far beyond the skirmish line" (p. 58). Chesnutt, whose literary gifts allowed him to reach a significantly broader audience than Fulton, nonetheless waged a safer war. Yet perhaps, given the crushing forces on black Americans in 1900—a time when the race question was considered by many to have reached an irresolvable impasse—he waged the only war he could hope one day to win. Perhaps Chesnutt's ambiguous ending to *The Marrow of Tradition* (Miller hesitating at the foot of the stairs) is more realistic for blacks in 1900 than Fulton's optimistic Molly Pierrepont stepping up to God in a New York A.M.E. church. Perhaps Fulton's readers needed the more forceful talents of a DuBois or Garvey to make the black Christ (Fulton's final apotheosis of Dan Wright) into a truly redeeming image. But we must release Chesnutt of the burden of being the voice of both accommodation and militancy at the turn of the century. For other voices sang more fiercely, if less loud.

Notes

1. These remarks conclude Gaines' welcoming address to the 1896 General Conference of the A.M.E. Church, held in Wilmington, North Carolina. See James H. Handy, *Scraps of African Methodist Episcopal History* (1902; rpt. Ann Arbor, MI: University Microfilms International, 1982), pp. 306–7.

2. William L. Andrews, *The Literary Career of Charles W. Chesnutt* (Baton Rouge: Louisiana State Univ. Press, 1980), p. 174.

3. See Marjorie George and Richard S. Pressman, "Confronting the Shadow: Psycho-Political Repression in Chesnutt's *The Marrow of Tradition*," *Phylon*, 48 (Winter 1987), 298.

4. Colonel Alfred M. Waddell, "The Story of the Wilmington, N.C. Race Riots," *Collier's Weekly*, 26 November 1898, p. 5.

5. Helen G. Edmonds, *The Negro and Fusion Politics in North Carolina, 1894–1901* (Chapel Hill: Univ. of North Carolina Press, 1951), p. 165.

6. H. Leon Prather, Sr., *We Have Taken a City: Wilmington Racial Massacre and Coup of 1898* (Rutherford, NJ: Fairleigh Dickinson Univ. Press, 1984), pp. 11–12.

7. Joel Williamson, *The Crucible of Race: Black/White Relations in the American South Since Emancipation* (New York: Oxford Univ. Press, 1984), p. 197.

8. Prather, p. 83.

9. Jack Thorne [David Bryant Fulton]. *Hanover; Or the Persecution of the Lowly: A Story of the Wilmington Massacre* (1900; rpt. New York: Arno Press, 1969), p. 77.

10. Frances Richardson Keller, *An American Crusade: The Life of Charles Waddell Chesnutt* (Provo, UT: Brigham Young Univ. Press, 1978), p. 190.

11. Robert B. Stepto, *From Behind the Veil: A Study of Afro-American Narrative* (Chicago: Univ. of Illinois Press, 1979), p. 5.

12. Dickson D. Bruce, Jr., *Black American Writing from the Nadir: The Evolution of a Literary Tradition, 1877–1915* (Baton Rouge: Louisiana State Univ. Press, 1989), p. 3.

13. John Wideman, "Charles W. Chesnutt: *The Marrow of Tradition*," *American Scholar*, 42 (Winter 1972–73), 128.

14. See Rayford W. Logan, *The Betrayal of the Negro from Rutherford B. Hayes to Woodrow Wilson* (London: Collier Books, 1965), particularly chapters 10–13.

15. Addison Gayle, Jr., *The Way of the New World: The Black Novel in America* (Garden City, NY: Doubleday, 1975), p. 51.

16. See Prather, p. 55. According to Williamson, p. 197, Daniels' *News and Observer* reprinted 300,000 copies of Manly's editorial.

17. Charles W. Chesnutt, *The Marrow of Tradition*, (1901; rpt. Ann Arbor: Univ. of Michigan Press, 1969), pp. 82–3.

18. The two writers Chesnutt claimed he hoped to emulate were Harriet Beecher Stowe and Albion Tourgée. In a 1901 letter to Houghton Mifflin & Company. Chesnutt wrote that he wanted *The Marrow of Tradition* to "become lodged in the popular mind as the legitimate successor of *Uncle Tom's Cabin* and *A Fool's Errand*" (see Keller, p. 192). Fulton, too, emphasized the former connection in *Hanover,* as indicated by his subtitle, *The Persecution of the Lowly* (which seems an intentional echo of *Life Among the Lowly,* the subtitle to Stowe's novel in volume form) and by the constant references in his text to *Uncle Tom's Cabin.*

19. For a fuller treatment of Chesnutt's career, see chapter 3 of Sylvia Lyons Render's *Charles W. Chesnutt* (Boston: Twayne, 1980).

20. Robert M. Farnsworth, introduction, *The Marrow of Tradition,* p. xvi.

21. *Ibid.,* p. xv.

22. Ernest E. Leisy, *The American Historical Novel* (Norman: Univ. of Oklahoma Press, 1950), p. 4.

23. Philip Fisher, *Hard Facts: Setting and Form in the American Novel* (New York: Oxford Univ. Press, 1985), p. 15.

24. Chesnutt, Journal, 3 January 1881. Cited in J. Noel Heermance, *Charles W. Chesnutt: America's First Great Black Novelist* (Hamden, CT: Archon Books, 1974), p. 65.

25. Heermance, p. 68.

26. Chesnutt, Letter to John Chamberlain, 16 June 1930. Cited in Keller, p. 185n.

27. William L. Andrews, "Jack Thorne," *Dictionary of American Negro Biography,* eds. Rayford W. Logan and Michael R. Winston (New York: Norton, 1982), p. 590.

28. Thorne [Fulton], *Eagle Clippings* (Brooklyn, NY: D. B. Fulton, 1907), title page.

29. Gayle, p. 53.

30. Chesnutt, Journal, 29 May 1880. Cited in Heermance, p. 140.

31. Cited in Logan, *Betrayal,* p. 278.

32. Booker T. Washington, *Sowing and Reaping* (New York: Caldwell, 1900), p. 13.

33. John M. Reilly, "The Dilemma in Chesnutt's *The Marrow of Tradition,*" *Phylon,* 32 (Spring 1971), 37.

34. Chesnutt, *Frederick Douglass* (Boston: Small, Maynard, 1899), p. 87.

35. Chesnutt, Letter to John Chamberlain, 16 June 1930. Cited in Andrews, *Literary Career,* p. 139n.

36. Wilson J. Moses, *The Golden Age of Black Nationalism, 1850–1925* (Hamden, CT: Archon Books, 1978), pp. 197–8.

37. Andrews, "Jack Thorne," p. 590.

38. Chesnutt, "Race Prejudice: Its Causes and Its Cure," *Alexander's Magazine* (July 1905), p. 25. Cited in Heermance, p. 72.

39. Paula Giddings, *When and Where I Enter: The Impact of Black Women on Race and Sex in America* (New York: Bantam, 1984), p. 29.

40. Helen Chesnutt, *Charles Waddell Chesnutt: Pioneer of the Color Line* (Chapel Hill: Univ. of North Carolina Press, 1952), p. 6.

41. W. F. Cash, *The Mind of the South* (New York: Knopf, 1941). Cited in Gunnar Myrdal, *An American Dilemma: The Negro Problem and Modern Democracy* (New York: Harper, 1962), p. 1356.

42. Gayle, p. ix.

W. D. Howells and Race: Charles W. Chesnutt's Disappointment of the Dean

JOSEPH R. MCELRATH JR.

In 1900 William Dean Howells's essay "Mr. Charles W. Chesnutt's Stories" positively summarized Chesnutt's achievement as the author of three books published in 1899. *Frederick Douglass,* a slim and derivative volume in Small, Maynard & Company's "Beacon Biographies" series, was seen by Howells as not especially remarkable, except insofar as it was "the work of a man not entirely white treating of a great man of his inalienable race."[1] Race was as important a consideration when he turned to Chesnutt's collections of short fiction, *The Conjure Woman* and *The Wife of His Youth and Other Stories of the Color Line;* but at least as significant was the high order of artistry encountered therein: "the volumes of fiction *are* remarkable above many, above most short stories by people entirely white, and would be worthy of unusual notice if they were not the work of a man not entirely white" (p. 700). Indeed, Howells favorably compared the African-American author with Maupassant, Turgenev, Henry James, and Mary E. Wilkins. The appearance of the essay in the widely circulated and prestigious *Atlantic Monthly* doubly ensured the impact of this eulogy, in which quibbles concerning Chesnutt's occasional turns from characterization to satirical caricature and lapses into authorial self-consciousness were decidedly minor criticisms. In addition, Howells's recognition of Chesnutt resulted in the two men meeting each other before the piece was published and even before Howells had finished composing it; it also resulted in the formation of an epistolary relationship prized by Chesnutt, and in Howells's flattering solicitation of novelistic manuscripts for Harper & Brothers later that year, in the fall of 1900.

This historically significant nexus, in which a "not entirely white" *littérateur* and the entirely white Dean of American Letters achieved a rapprochement relatively uncommon in the Jim Crow Era, was, however, not so durable as those in which Albion W. Tourgée and George Washington Cable

Reprinted with permission from *Nineteenth-Century Literature* 51 (March 1997): 474–99. © 1997 by The Regents of The University of California.

had figured with Chesnutt from the late 1880s through the mid 1890s. In fact, the amicable relationship between Howells and Chesnutt lasted less than two years, from early February 1900 to December 1901, when Howells wounded Chesnutt with as positive a review of *The Marrow of Tradition* as he could muster, but one in which he had to make the now widely quoted comment that the novelistic exposé of white racism was flawed by Chesnutt's "bitter" tone. Although Chesnutt continued to exercise—more selectively than before—the bragging rights to which Howells's attentions entitled him, he never accepted this assessment of his hot-headed performance in *Marrow,* nor did he learn from Howells's about-face how his behavior required modification if he was to have a hope of being a more popular and influential writer. Howells was not so much a Negrophile as Cable (at least until 1894, when Cable took a different tack in *John March, Southerner*) and Tourgée; but that Chesnutt could alienate a sympathizer who championed as well Paul Laurence Dunbar and Booker T. Washington should have alerted Chesnutt to the fact that he had strayed radically from the course he had set in 1880 toward the goal of seducing, rather than browbeating, the white American readership into a more benign attitude toward the African American. When he continued on the new heading in his next novel, *The Colonel's Dream* (1905), he did so in spite of the caution sounded by his onetime fan, and he reaped the harvest of *Dream*'s more bitter denunciation of the South as unredeemable: its publication ended his career as a professional novelist.

Such, in brief, is the history of the Howells-Chesnutt relationship, in which Chesnutt's ambitions, repeatedly made clear in his journal of 1874–1882 and then in his correspondence through 1905, account for his ultra-solicitous attitude toward Howells. Three motivations stand in high relief. First, Chesnutt was an idealist who had given himself to the noble cause of African-American advocacy represented by Harriet Beecher Stowe, Tourgée, and Cable. Second, he was a pragmatist convinced that professional authorship in the service of high moral principle was compatible with, and in his case guaranteed to result in, the taking of hefty profits on a scale enjoyed by those literary reformers. And third, this self-made man was a self-confessed egotist convinced that his superiority to the mass of men—black, white, and mulatto—would be recognized; that is, he was unswervingly dedicated to achieving fame.[2] Howells was a means to these ends.

As influential reviewer and power-broker within the publishing industry, Howells promised to facilitate earnings as great as those that Chesnutt enjoyed as a stenographer in Cleveland. In May 1900 Howells, more than any other critic, had accelerated Chesnutt's ascent of Parnassus, and he might be counted upon later that year to maximize Chesnutt's renown by reviewing his first novel, *The House Behind the Cedars.* As important for Chesnutt-the-idealist, Howells had recognized and sanctioned the moral implications of *The Conjure Woman* and the more explicit themes of fictional "sermons" (Chesnutt's own term) in *The Wife.*[3] It was, to use today's phrase, a "dream team":

Chesnutt was having his needs met and, not to categorize Chesnutt as a self-aggrandizer and Howells as only a disinterested party, so was Howells—until autumn 1901 and the publication of *Marrow*. How this was so with Howells is not so transparent, though. With Howells one does not find the like of Chesnutt's extraordinarily candid journal and his many letters implementing his strategy when dealing with numerous correspondents who might advance his literary career. The data that are available are comparatively few in number, and yet it is possible to speculate with some confidence as to what Howells's motivations were.

A decade before Howells bestowed upon Charles W. Chesnutt the boon that almost all aspiring authors of the time desired—a public expression of his approval—the 1890 readers of *A Hazard of New Fortunes* had the chance to infer his attitude toward the racial group that Chesnutt would, in both senses of the term, represent. For us now it is important to seize upon the same opportunity, in that the short-lived relationship between the two men did not depend solely upon Howells's recognition of Chesnutt's talent per se in 1900. Rather, Negritude counted for Howells as much as it continues to count today for editors and critics similarly situated, and the gist of this historically significant intersection of the Anglo-American literary tradition and a newly emerging variant of it has much to do with the fact that Chesnutt wrote principally about African-American experience and had publicly identified himself with a minority for which Howells displayed a markedly sympathetic regard. They had that in common: both men, in their own ways, privileged the African American, just as both displayed a contrary attitude toward the Irish American.[4]

Early in *A Hazard* Isabel and Basil March are searching for an apartment in New York City, and we find them knocking upon the door of a house they wish to inspect. They are greeted by an African American, and Howells's language abruptly waxes sentimental as the couple acts in a way anticipating the behavior of the white liberal role-model figures, John and Annie, that Chesnutt would offer 1899 readers of his Uncle Julius stories in *The Conjure Woman* but in fact had already made available to readers like Howells in four tales published in the *Atlantic Monthly* and *Overland Monthly* between 1887 and 1889.[5] Perhaps revealing influences such as Joel Chandler Harris's lovable Uncle Remus, Chesnutt's ingratiating Uncle Julius, and who knows how many other attractive Uncles and Aunties featured in fictions set in the South, Howells made his own benign contribution to the mythology of color thus: "One of those colored men who soften the trade of janitor in many of the smaller apartment-houses in New York by the sweetness of their race, let the Marches in, or, rather, welcomed them to the possession of the premises by the bow with which he acknowledged their permit."[6] It immediately becomes clear that Isabel is impressed by the appearance of the first floor of the house, but it is soon more apparent that the chief attraction on the premises is the colored man whose gracious "sweetness" captivates her—so much so that she almost forgets to ask about one of her requirements for a second- or third-floor apartment, an elevator:

> He answered, "No, ma'am; only two flights up," so winningly that she said,
> "Oh!" in courteous apology, and whispered her husband [*sic*] as she followed lightly up, "We'll take it, Basil, if it's like the rest."
> "If it's like him, you mean."
> "I don't wonder they wanted to own them," she hurriedly philosophized. "If I had such a creature, nothing but death should part us. . . ."(p. 46)

That the apartment is unsuitable for them and the rent too high is not the conclusion to which she wants to come: having such a janitor is a near-irresistible attraction. Isabel, that is, plays a part like that assigned to Chesnutt's Annie in the Uncle Julius stories: she is a sentimental white female whose eminently Victorian maternalism manifests itself in affection for the "child race" to which Chesnutt alluded in his correspondence with Booker T. Washington.[7] Basil's more commonsensical appraisal of the situation, however, finally breaks the spell, as he assumes the empathetic but more paternal, authority-figure role that Chesnutt assigns to John in *The Conjure Woman*. No, they will not take the apartment solely because of Isabel's and, to a lesser degree, Basil's own sympathetic predisposition toward the African American.

As they leave, Isabel urges Basil to give the janitor a quarter, and a proper understanding of what thereupon transpires requires our recollection that neither Isabel nor Basil is a negatively conceived character. Basil is not here or elsewhere in *A Hazard* harsh in tone toward his wife; none of the caustic, dismayingly superior attitudes of Bartley Hubbard are his. Isabel is at least as good-hearted a woman as another female figure in the Howells canon, Marcia Hubbard. Basil immediately understands Isabel's reaction to the janitor not only because he too is sensitive to the man's charms but because, it appears, Isabel is not demonstrating Negrophilia for the first time:

> "I would have given half a dollar willingly to get you beyond his glamour," said March, when they were safely on the pavement outside. "If it hadn't been for my strength of character, you'd have taken an unfurnished flat without heat and with no elevator, at nine hundred a year, when you had just sworn me to steam heat, an elevator, furniture, and eight hundred."
> "Yes! How could I have lost my head so completely?" she said, with a lenient amusement in her aberration which she was not always able to feel in her husband's.
> "The next time a colored janitor opens the door to us, I'll tell him the apartment doesn't suit at the threshold. It's the only way to manage you, Isabel."
> "It's true. I *am* in love with the whole race. I never saw one of them that didn't have perfectly angelic manners. I think we shall all be black in heaven— that is, black-souled." (pp. 47–48)

Isabel being a Bostonian accounts to some extent, of course, for such enthusiasm. That Chesnutt should have found at the turn of the century his most receptive audience among others of a like mind in Boston—the onetime cauldron of abolitionist fervor and, postbellum, the locale in which Booker T. Washington repeatedly received bankable tokens of warmly felt interest in the African American—is not surprising if Isabel is, indeed, true to the type Howells had in mind. The "sweetness" in question Chesnutt did not neglect in several of the stories collected in *The Conjure Woman* and *The Wife.*

But the scene is telling in another way, particularly when one focuses not on Isabel but on Howells himself. As the Marches moved from Boston to New York City, so did Howells, taking with him the "Bostonian" attitude in question. The year after the book publication of *Hazard* he focused more closely on the African American, this time in female form, in a *Harper's Monthly* serial; and he did so in a much more thoughtful manner than in 1871, when he lightheartedly and, to some minds, condescendingly described in *Suburban Sketches* "the black pansies and marigolds and dark-blooded dahlias among womankind."[8] His new work of 1891, *An Imperative Duty,* was a study of the problems encountered by fair mulattoes whose sub-Saharan Africanness, like that of Rena and John Walden in Chesnutt's *The House Behind the Cedars* (1900) and of Chesnutt himself, was so attenuated that the classifications of black and white were rendered virtually meaningless, though they continued to carry weight in both black and white American social circles.

In *An Imperative Duty,* that is—the only novel by Howells that one finds in the remains of Chesnutt's personal library now at Fisk University[9]—Howells became a contributor to the "tragic mulatto" novelistic tradition whose principal mainstream American practitioner had been Albion W. Tourgée, one of Chesnutt's inspirations to authorship and afterward an early booster. Tourgée's *Hot Plowshares* (1883), in fact, provides a convenient point of reference when one notes the similarities between Howells and Chesnutt that served as the foundation for their friendly interactions at the turn of the century, in that all three authors manifested their concern for the vicissitudes faced by the mulatto. Tourgée's heroine, attending a school for girls in New England, is astounded to learn one day that she is not purely Caucasian, and her teachers and fellow students react in various ways to the appalling news that she is "tainted by Negro blood"—as Tourgée measures the ways in which racist attitudes manifest themselves not in the vicious South but the "enlightened" North. After the initial response of horror she resolves to bear the heavy burden of her mixed racial ancestry and to continue her studies—whereupon Tourgée eliminates her problem by means of another, more toothsome discovery: a mistake was made; she is wholly Caucasian after all. Having hammered home his point about racism, that is, Tourgée took the easy way out in this tragicomedy. In *An Imperative Duty* Rhoda has a similar experience in that she also finds that she is not wholly Caucasian. But the story develops in a much more credible and, because her black ancestry is not erased, meaningfully positive way. A white liberal role-model figure, Dr. Olney, accepts her as she is, marries her, and whisks her off to Italy, where her olive complexion suggests only southern Italian extraction. Thus is a real, personal problem solved in a commonsensical, humane, and believable way, albeit the American social problem actually faced by the mulatto in 1891 is not. While Dr. Olney wholly transcends race prejudice, Rhoda herself is ashamed of her lineage and swears him to secrecy.

Chesnutt consciously or unwittingly follows Howells's lead in one of two stories collected in *The Wife;* and he provides, if not a more satisfying conclusion for readers who had misgivings about "race mixing," then an eminently more practical one for those finding attractive the notion of putting an end to "tragic mulatto" experience among individuals who could not so easily emigrate to Mediterranean lands. It is ironic that much more of a "smiling aspects" of American life solution than Howells was able to concoct is effected by means of a simple and inarguably ethical deception that solves the immediate problem faced by the white hero and the fair mulatto heroine and that, in the larger social situation, may over time promise an end to social exclusion for many others with similar complexions and facial features. "Racial amalgamation," or intermarriage, was the panacea that Chesnutt would more formally propose in the *Boston Evening Transcript* in 1900;[10] but in "Her Virginia Mammy" of 1899 he was already giving the expedient a fictional consideration. Here the Caucasian Dr. Winthrop discovers that his fiancée, Clara, is a mulatto, and he models nobility by continuing to love her. Further, as though he had absorbed the ethical pragmatism of the Reverend Sewell in *The Rise of Silas Lapham,* Dr. Winthrop demonstrates his "economy of pain" moral reasoning by withholding the fact of her genetic background from Clara. Remaining oblivious to her mulatto status, Clara, it seems, will continue to "pass" like many another of Chesnutt's generation and to enjoy the happiness that is hers when we last see her; and unlike Howells's heroine, she will do so in the United States. Neither Chesnutt nor Howells can be termed optimistic about the "tragic mulatto" aspect of the "Negro Problem" they treat in their respective works; what they obviously did have in common, though, was the hope that by the act of writing about it, and by humanizing what was for the predominantly white readership a problem in the abstract, a positive contribution might be made to narrowing the social gap between blacks and whites.

In the second story, "Cicely's Dream," Chesnutt again echoes Howells by creating a mulatto heroine whose personal characteristics are so superior that any consideration of racial inferiority is rendered impossible for a right-thinking Victorian. Only a racist beast would entertain notions of inferiority when encountering the supernal "sweetness" that Chesnutt has infused into Cicely. But in the story's conclusion one finds that Chesnutt parts company with Howells—no happy ending here. Rather, Tourgée's markedly less sanguine point of view, seen in his tragic rather than tragicomical novel about another mulatto heroine, *Toinette* (1874), comes to mind. In "Cicely's Dream" the heroine, a veritable Ruth, is the perfect lover of a mulatto more fair-skinned than she who is being nursed back to health in Cicely's community following a Civil War battle. When she much later discovers that this man, an amnesiac, is already engaged to another, Cicely's thrice-times-happy tale becomes a pathetic one illustrating racial equality in the area of depth of feeling: the reader is shown that mulattoes such as she are as capable as Shakespeare's Juliet and Gounod's Marguerite of experiencing Romantic ecstasy and its antipode, Romantic agony. But, the reader also realizes, the relationship was doomed from the first in this tale, whose fatalism is grounded in the fact of racial bias: Cicely's loved one, it turns out, is not a mulatto but a white who, Chesnutt implies, would never have been even her companion had he not suffered memory loss. When his fiancée appears and he thereby regains his wits, Cicely is appreciated for her service—and abandoned. As would not become apparent to Howells until the publication of *The Marrow of Tradition*, Chesnutt was more prone to assume a distinctly negative, outraged fictional perspective on the "Negro Problem" than Howells imagined in 1900 and much of 1901—particularly when the victims of racism were the fair mulattoes like Chesnutt himself.[11]

Chesnutt's anger did not show in "Cicely's Dream." It was apparent, though, in one of the *Wife* stories that Howells did not mention in his essay, the ruthless indictment of Southern whites that is "The Sheriff's Children." Howells appears to have chosen not to respond to this story, filtering it out as he saw in *The Wife* what he wanted to see. Simply stated, Howells's behavior suggests that there was, indeed, much more of Isabel March in him than one would be inclined to suspect: he wanted to maintain his belief in the innate "sweetness" of the unresentful African American and to enjoy an optimistic view of a progressively improving race whose good qualities, when more widely recognized and acknowledged, would elicit a greater degree of acceptance on the part of white America.

Howells, of course, was aware of the considerable complexity and magnitude of "The Negro Problem," a formidable national one because whites and blacks of the Jim Crow Era were pitted against one another, with the former decidedly in the ascendancy despite the rhetoric concerning the threat of "Negro dominance" in 1890s newspapers and magazines. After all, in *An Imperative Duty* Rhoda did emigrate to Italy. Writing to Henry Blake Fuller on 10 November 1901 and turning his attention to Chesnutt, whose *Marrow* had been published in mid-October, Howells revealed in a remarkably succinct manner the depth of understanding he had achieved by then: "Good Lord! How such a negro must hate us."[12] But this insight into Chesnutt's animus, actually focused on Southerners rather than the class of whites represented by Howells and Fuller, was a new one. Howells appears to have been caught by surprise, even startled, by Chesnutt, whom he had not previously thought of as a man with a chip on his shoulder. In 1900 Howells had had no cause to suspect the presence of the deep-seated enmity observed by Pauline C. Bouvé when, in 1899, she interviewed Chesnutt in Boston and noted his attitude of "concentrated bitterness" toward the South.[13] The Chesnutt that Howells had met that year and whose short fictions he praised was altogether another person, one who had provided a second major "feel-good" experience of the African American, like that first provided by Paul Laurence Dunbar in 1896. Chesnutt had heightened his already more positive regard for the African American; and Howells's perspective on the race would become even more celebratory in August 1901, shortly before the publication of *Marrow,* when he touted Booker T. Washington in an essay prompted by a reading of *Up from Slavery.* Far from coincidentally did the word "sweet" appear when Howells alluded to Washington's fine, "brave" sense of humor; indeed, Howells was then nearly euphoric over the progress being made by his pet minority and its three spokesmen, who might have every reason to gnash their teeth but instead chose to demonstrate the "sweetness" that he was sure was theirs. Further, the emergence of these men as nationally visible indicators of the too-long-denied capabilities of African Americans was a development to which he had had the gratification of contributing mightily when he personally ushered the first, Dunbar, across the color line into the *de facto* segregated American publishing industry. Help had been needed to initiate the process of integrating the African American into the world of letters, and Howells's powerful influence had been an effective catalyst.

One of the more cunning, unfair twists of history resulting in the embarrassment of a major benefactor of the pioneer writers in the African-American tradition stems from the present perception of Howells's condescension and from an unwillingness to acknowledge that affirmative action, in the most positive sense, was occurring in American life long before it became public policy almost a century later. True, there was a payoff for Howells: like Chesnutt, he could have the heady experience of doing good that the abolitionists of the previous generation enjoyed when he seized opportunities to "exalt [the] race," as Chesnutt phrased it in his journal.[14] Still, the magnanimity of what Howells freely did to assist Dunbar, Chesnutt, and the group they represented cannot be gainsaid. As of 1896 African-American authors had little hope for popular success due to the fact that their writings were being published outside the mainstream by low-profile firms and, in Dunbar's case, even more insignificant print shops without any publisher's imprint. In the early to mid 1890s Francis E. W. Harper, Anna J. Cooper, William Easton, Sanda (i.e., William H. Anderson and Walter H. Stowers), and Paul Laurence Dunbar were necessarily negligible entities because they were handled by presses such as the one that guaranteed obscurity for Pauline Hopkins's novel *Contending Forces* in 1900, the Colored Co-operative Publishing Company. Booker T. Washington understood the problem completely and leapt at the chance to redo his 1900 *Story of My Life and Work*, first made available for subscription sale by J. L. Nichols and Company, publisher of the *Voice of the Negro* magazine, and thus destined to reach a minimal number of readers. When a major player in the publishing industry, Doubleday, Page & Co., offered to market his autobiographical *Outlook* serial as the book *Up from Slavery* (1901), Washington was suddenly a best-selling author. But that was several years after Howells had set a precedent for bringing a black author into the mainstream by casting the limelight on a volume produced by an obscure printing company in Toledo, Ohio, that white playwright James A. Herne had sent him. Howells enjoyed the poems in African-American dialect that it contained, taking a special but now politically incorrect liking to one, "The Pahty," which is today viewed as "reflecting the epitome of the 'happy darky' stereotype."[15] Worse today is Howells's explanation of why he chose to review Dunbar's *Majors and Minors,* for his kindliness now reads as the attitude of a racist who had the temerity to react as he did to the frontispiece portrait of an author so pronouncedly Negroid in appearance:

> There has come to me from the hand of a friend, very unofficially, a little book of verse, dateless, placeless, without a publisher, which has greatly interested me. Such foundlings of the press always appeal to one by their forlornness; but commonly the appeal is to one's pity only, which is moved all the more if the author of the book has innocently printed his portrait with his verse. In this present case I felt a heightened pathos in the appeal from the fact that the face that confronted me when I opened the volume was the face of a young negro, with the race traits strangely accented; the black skin, the woolly hair, the thick, out-rolling lips, and the mild, soft eyes of the pure African type.[16]

But, in a 13 July 1896 letter to Howells, the author of the pity-inducing foundling was anything but offended by these candid remarks: "from the very depths of my heart I want to thank you. You yourself do not know what you have done for me. I feel much as a poor, insignificant, hopeless boy would feel to suddenly find himself knighted."[17] While as politically incorrect as Howells, Dunbar's response was, in fact, appropriate. Given the real-world racial situation in 1896 and the more-than-humble garb in which his art had made its way to Howells's desk, Dunbar's elevation to prominence by Howells was a near-miraculous event.

Affirmative-action policy today is not grounded in "pity" or a theory of special privilege, and neither was its 1890s version expressed in Washington's 1895 Cotton States Exhibition speech. In *Up from Slavery* Washington identified as one of the chief causes of "The Negro Problem" the dearth of performance *expectations* for African Americans: how could *merit* be recognized if no one expected to find it in that quarter? His ideal society of the future was a meritocracy. Howells, we know (because he told us so in *Harper's Weekly*), was indeed moved by pity when examining Dunbar's book—which he knew was destined to oblivion, no matter what its intrinsic merits, unless someone like himself intervened. When he did intervene, Dunbar was rescued from the outer darkness: a mainstream firm, Dodd, Mead and Company, published *Lyrics of Lowly Life* the same year and the rest is history, thanks largely to Howells's certification of Dunbar's artistry. For as he explained in the introduction he wrote for *Lyrics,* drawing attention to Dunbar did not require suspension of his critical judgment for philanthropic purposes: "I thought his merits positive and not comparative; and I held that if his black poems had been written by a white man, I should not have found them less admirable."[18] Still, the significance of color could not be denied: Howells was, after all, celebrating the arrival of the first "American negro who had evinced innate distinction in literature." Chesnutt was the second, and once again Howells's motivation when calling attention to him was twofold.

The Conjure Woman and *The Wife of His Youth* were not, like *Majors and Minors,* bona fide first-discoveries by Howells. In the late 1880s the editorial staff of the *Atlantic Monthly* and, beginning in 1897, Walter Hines Page in particular had already done for Chesnutt what Howells had done for Dunbar: the two volumes arrived in New York in the casings of Houghton, Mifflin & Co., the prestigious Boston firm that published the *Atlantic.*[19] Yet Howells was moved to do his part in the good cause. Indeed, his essay for the *Atlantic Monthly* was not solicited by Houghton, Mifflin & Co.—he volunteered it. That is, his being paid for it did not obviate the gratuitous nature of the gesture nor its autobiographical significance in the context of turn-of-the-century racial politics. And Chesnutt made the task a pleasant one by rendering most of his African-American characters in *The Conjure Woman* as likeable as those imagined by Isabel March in *A Hazard of New Fortunes* and as those found by Howells himself in *Majors and Minors* and *Lyrics of Lowly Life.*

That Howells encountered "sweetness" like Dunbar's was no accident. As early as 1880 Chesnutt described in his journal his plan to seduce the white readership by overcoming "the subtle almost indefinable feeling of repulsion toward the negro, which is common to most Americans—and easily enough accounted for"; it was a repugnance that could not "be stormed and taken by assault." He would, "while amusing them," instead "lead [his white readers] on imperceptibly, unconsciously step by step to the desired state of feeling" (29 May 1880; *Journals,* p. 140). The method worked wonders with Houghton, Mifflin's Walter Hines Page, a transplanted white Southerner whose conception of how *The Conjure Woman* should be compiled dovetailed with Chesnutt's seduction plan. This utterly unthreatening, hostility-free book, by an African-American author who was the ingratiatingly witty master of the "soft sell" and capable of chuckle-inducing drollery reminiscent of Washington Irving's best work, perfectly manifested Chesnutt's 1880 theory of how to accomplish through art "the elevation of the whites" (29 May 1880; *Journals,* p. 139). Howells—who did not realize that the table had been turned and that it was he who was being "elevated"—was so disarmed by Chesnutt's charm that in the *Atlantic Monthly* essay he went so far as to characterize the tales in a way that few modern critics have, bestowing upon them the kind of praise he reserved for the highest kind of art. That is, he actually described the conjure stories as works of Realism: "They are new and fresh and strong, *as life always is,* and fable never is; and the stories . . . have a wild, indigenous poetry, the creation of *sincere* and original imagination, which is imparted with a tender humorousness and a very *artistic reticence*" ("Chesnutt's Stories," p. 700; emphasis added). Lifelikeness, sincerity, and authorial self-effacement—these are quintessential criteria of the Howellsian aesthetic.

Most noteworthy in the essay, regarding Howells's conception of Chesnutt, is another application of the Realist's gauge of truth in art; for Howells came to a conclusion that is sure to irritate those who today have noted that, rather than generating accurate representations of the African American, Chesnutt uses what are arguably racist stereotypes. For, *somehow,* Chesnutt is judged as having satisfied the criterion of fidelity-to-nature—by a critic who lacked the empirical data needed to come to such a conclusion:

> As far as his race is concerned, or his sixteenth part of a race, it does not greatly matter whether Mr. Chesnutt invented [his characters'] motives, or found them, as he feigns, among his distant cousins of the Southern cabins. In either case, the wonder of their beauty is the same; and whatever is primitive and sylvan or campestral in the reader's heart is touched by the spells thrown on the simple black lives in these enchanting tales. *Character, the most precious thing in fiction, is as faithfully portrayed* against the poetic background as in the setting of the Stories of the Color Line. (p. 700; emphasis added)

The *somehow* of Howells's verdict on Chesnutt's veraciousness regarding what motivates African Americans in *The Conjure Woman* need not be viewed as wholly mysterious, though. Howells's treatment of *The Wife of His Youth and Other Stories of the Color Line* as well leads one to the same speculation in light of a point that Howells made in *Criticism and Fiction* (1891) and elsewhere: that every individual is qualified to be a critic insofar as the main activity involved in evaluating art is a comparison between what one knows is true by experience and what one finds pictured as true.

In fact, Howells *was* drawing from his experience of the African American when dubbing Chesnutt a Realist; but that shallow experiential pool was mainly an imaginative one imbued with New Englandish moral idealism. In Dunbar's poems Howells found confirmation of what egalitarian humanists such as Emerson, Thoreau, and Whitman had previously proclaimed: according to his introduction to *Lyrics of Lowly Life* he saw "evidence of the essential unity of the human race, which does not think or feel black in one and white in another, but humanly in all" (p. 280); in the *Harper's Weekly* review he was moved to speculate that "perhaps the human unity, and not the race unity, is the precious thing, the divine thing, after all" (p. 630). And he found cause in Chesnutt's stories to generalize along the same lines. That is, the stories in *The Wife of His Youth* on which Howells concentrated his attention conformed to the a priori conceptions of African Americans already formulated by a benevolent Bostonian who only needed to expand the Dunbarian black paradigm in order to accommodate *The Wife's* mulattoes. *Le Voilà,* in these pictures of the "region" occupied by mulattoes, Chesnutt "has not shown the dwellers there as very different from ourselves" ("Chesnutt's Stories," p. 701). "The Wife of His Youth," for example, features a self-educated and self-made attorney, like Chesnutt himself, whose high-Victorian nobility eventuates in a self-sacrificial act worthy of the satirical treatment given *Tears, Idle Tears* in *The Rise of Silas Lapham;* but Howells does not blink, or wryly wink to his reader, as he treasures this short story in which the hero is made to demonstrate that African-Americanness is no obstacle to Christ-like self-denial.[20] Singled out for praise is "The Bouquet," the young heroine of which is of a darker complexion though no less noble. Sophy embodies what most present-day readers would find a cloying "sweetness" as she suffers without anger the outrages of social discrimination in a South so racist that it will not allow her to mourn properly for the deceased white teacher she admired and loved; still, Howells was not put off by the sentimentality of the tale. "The Web of Circumstance," also cited by Howells, features another self-made African American, who has built up a business by strict adherence to the Protestant work ethic but is caught in the web of circumstantial evidence planted by his wife's lover, then punished not only wrongly but too severely by the white judicial system in the degenerate South, and finally shot to death because of a distinctly "Southern" misreading of—once again—circumstantial evidence.

As is well known, Howells preferred art in which both the rose and thistle in the field of life received attention and the lighter moments were acknowledged along with the weighty. Chesnutt again rose to the occasion. Balanced against the works of high seriousness in *The Wife* were more risible stories, one of which Howells focused upon. He appreciated the comedy of "Uncle Wellington's Wives," which not only affords a vintage "shanty Irishwoman" cameo—she is a slattern given to alcoholic excess and even polyandry—but as waggishly admits the existence of the ne'er-do-well mulatto. One suspects as well that this unflattering portrait of an African American, like the satirical treatment in "A Matter of Principle" of intra-racial prejudice displayed by fair, or "blue vein," mulattoes, reinforced the notion that Chesnutt was a Realist, unflinchingly determined to tell the *whole* truth, at all costs, about his people.[21]

Yet one other conclusion is mandated by "Mr. Charles W. Chesnutt's Stories." It is that Chesnutt, who rushed down to New York from Boston when told at the Houghton, Mifflin & Co. offices that Howells was writing an essay about him,[22] evidently had considerable success in convincing Howells when he called at his apartment in The Dalhousie that he had the full scoop on the African-American community and particularly the mulatto caste featured in *The Wife*. After meeting the apparently white author who, he was given to understand, had voluntarily identified himself with African Americans in general and assumed the duty of serving as the special representative of mulattoes, Howells, like Cable before him, had good cause to assume that he was dealing with an "insider" who knew the African American in all varieties from the ground up.[23] That is, he had another reason to assume that he was evaluating the work of a Realist in *The Wife:*

> these stories, after all, are Mr. Chesnutt's most important work, whether we consider them merely as realistic fiction, apart from their author, or as studies of that middle world of which he is naturally and voluntarily a citizen. We had known the nethermost world of the grotesque and comical negro and the terrible and tragic negro through the white observer on the outside, and black character in its lyrical moods we had known from such an inside witness as Mr. Paul Dunbar; but it had remained for Mr. Chesnutt to acquaint us with those regions where the paler shades [i.e., mulattoes] dwell as hopelessly, with relation to ourselves [i.e., whites], as the blackest negro. ("Chesnutt's Stories," pp. 700–701)

No, Howells does not go so far as Isabel March when she declares that white souls will be perfected as black souls when they enter heaven; but for him, in the United States and in the brotherhood of mankind, black and mulatto souls are already the same as those of whites, and all are imperfect in varying degrees. Chesnutt's 1880 plan for the seduction of white readers, in other words, worked fully with Howells, who very much wanted to believe and see as true-to-life the positive image of the African American that he had encountered in the two volumes and in Chesnutt himself.

It is odd, given his enthusiasm for Chesnutt, that Howells did not take the opportunity to boost him once more when, later in 1900, Chesnutt sent him a copy of *The House Behind the Cedars* and then a suggestive follow-up letter reminding him of just how much he appreciated the *Atlantic* essay that Howells had published six months earlier.[24] In passing, one cannot help but wonder how this distinctly old-style romance might have affected Chesnutt's relationship with Howells. It features a mulatto heroine passing as white whose name, Rena or Rowena, signals the influence of Scott's *Ivanhoe,* as does a high-society fête and a literal chivalric tournament, at the end of which Rena is proclaimed the "Queen of Love and Beauty" by the knight-for-a-day who becomes her beau. Her racial background soon discovered by him, the rejected "tragic mulatto" experiences protracted psychological stress and a full-stops melodramatic death. And heard throughout *House* is an intrusive, moralizing author. It is especially peculiar that Howells gave no known sign of having read the novel since, at this time, he was courting Chesnutt, sending him three letters in which he solicited a novel dealing with the color line and agreeing to read another that dealt with white characters. Chesnutt seems to have then had three never-published, long manuscripts on hand. How many of them, if any, he sent to Howells is moot; the correspondence, unfortunately, documents only Howells's continued interest in Chesnutt.[25]

This interest surfaced more publicly in August 1901 as Howells paid tribute to Booker T. Washington, the "marvellous yellow man" whose Atlanta Exposition speech brought "the white race into kindlier and wiser relations with the black than they had known before."[26] Howells himself attempts to accomplish more of the same by highlighting what is explicit in *Up from Slavery:* that Washington is not interested in forcing social or political equality but in simply educating and providing the means of economic advancement to his people. Exercising a fine sense of humor like Dunbar's and Chesnutt's, Washington is the great communicator of African-American decency and commendable ambition because, like his more literary comrades, he is able to observe and describe his people clearly and truthfully, "to place himself outside his race, when he wishes to see it as others see it, and to report its exterior effect from his interior knowledge" (p. 283). "It is his unfailing sense of humor that saves him from extremism. At any rate, cool patience is not more characteristic of Mr. Washington than of Mr. Dunbar or Mr. Chesnutt or of" the one well-known militant among African Americans, Frederick Douglass (p. 284). Indeed, Howells rates this "calm" as "characteristic of the best of the race," for it "saves them from bitterness." It even enables these three men to "enjoy the negro's ludicrous side as the white observer enjoys it"—which leads Howells to wonder about a collateral possibility that would be more troubling were it not for his persistent faith in the "sweetness" of the polite race he had described eleven years before in *Hazard:* "What if their amiability should veil a sense of *our* absurdities, and there should be in our polite inferiors the potentiality of something like contempt for us? The notion is awful; but we may be sure that they will be too kind, too wise, ever to do more than let us guess at the truth, if it is the truth" (p. 284). Again he returns to the theme that Washington is no threat, a reassuring notion given Howells's long-term concern about the menace of anarchism in America. We can be "doubly sure," when thinking of Washington, "that the negro is not going to do anything dynamitic to the structure of society. . . . In his heart is no bitterness" (p. 285).

Two months later Chesnutt, who did not leave behind a record of his awareness of this encomium, had a copy of *The Marrow of Tradition* sent to Howells. Howells discovered in it something worse than a rendering of the "ludicrous side" and "absurdities" of whites. Contempt for the principal white characters, all of whom are measured as morally inferior to the exceptionally civilized mulatto hero and heroine, was expressed neither comically nor even satirically. A "dynamitic" black, Josh Green, mortally settles an old score with the virulently racist Captain McBane, who once preyed upon Green's relatives. A white Southerner murders a white woman and attempts to pin the blame on an inoffensive, even docile African American of the old school. A group of whites is allotted one hundred percent of the blame for a race riot. A white half-sister of the heroine deprives her of the inheritance their father left her; she will not acknowledge the heroine's existence, much less their kinship; and yet, as the novel closes, the scorned mulatto saves the life of her half-sister's child.

Howells's sympathy was not exhausted by his reading of *The Marrow of Tradition,* but when one considers his review in light of his previous comments on Chesnutt, not to mention those on Dunbar and Washington, one must conclude that *Marrow* was a profound disappointment if not a cause for temporary disillusionment. The tone of this early supporter of the N.A.A.C.P. in "A Psychological Counter-Current in Recent Fiction" was not bitter; the best he could do, though, was rise to ambivalence.[27] Howells acknowledged the power with which Chesnutt had presented his case for social equality in this mordant fiction demonstrating the intolerableness of life in the South; and he did not echo other reviewers who charged that Chesnutt had given his African Americans a monopoly on virtue while painting his whites with a tarbrush: "No one who reads the book can deny that the case is presented with great power, or fail to recognize in the writer a portent of the sort of negro equality against which no series of hangings and burnings will finally prevail" (p. 883). Chesnutt "stands up for his own people," yet he does so "with a courage which has more justice than mercy in it. The book is, in fact, bitter, bitter" (p. 882). And, as has been noted, Howells's heretofore ebullient sense that the gap between black and white would be diminished over time gave way to the chilling declaration he made to Fuller: "How such a negro must hate us." Chesnutt had erected a barrier between them: the "not entirely white" author of 1900 had made it clear in October 1901 that he was on the other side of the color line, a "negro." Howells is not known to have communicated with or mentioned Chesnutt again.

Chesnutt, it should be noted in closing, did not fully understand what had transpired. In a 9 December 1901 letter to Booker T. Washington he mentioned that Howells has "paid his respects" to the new novel, implying thus that the review was a positive one. On 30 December 1901 he wrote to Houghton, Mifflin & Co. inquiring about the sales of *Marrow;* assuming that the review was common knowledge there, he referred less confidently to his "friend Mr. Howells" who "has said many nice things about my writings— although his review of *The Marrow of Tradition* in the *North American Review* for December was not a favorable one, as I look at it." As late as 11 November 1905, when answering a request for information from a Mrs. W. B. Henderson, whose daughter, a high-school senior, was to write a paper on *Marrow,* Chesnutt still resisted acknowledging the strategic blunder in his campaign to win the hearts and minds of readers like Howells. He wrote about the book that he once believed would prove as popular and influential as *Uncle Tom's Cabin* thus:

> The book was received by the public with respect, but not with any great enthusiasm. By the public I mean the great reading public whose opinion is reflected by the newspapers and magazines which reflect public opinion. It had a fair sale, but was criticized as being bitter. I did not intend it to be so. Nor do I think it was. I would suggest to Miss Henderson, in her review of the book, that she eliminate anything that savors of rancor or bitterness. I have found by experience, that in writing on this subject, an attitude of fairness and impartiality is more likely to command attention than the partisan and personal view which it is so difficult to keep from taking.[28]

To Chesnutt's mind, that is, he had demonstrated fairness and impartiality, not to mention suppressed his bitterness.[29]

In the 30 December 1901 letter to Houghton, Mifflin & Co. Chesnutt unwittingly glossed the gist of the breakdown of his relationship with Howells. He pointed out that Howells "has remarked several times that there is no color line in literature. On that point I take issue with him." The critical development was that, as Howells was attempting to erase the line that had long been there in the United States, another had been drawn as—to quote William L. Andrews—Chesnutt became the "first African-American writer of fiction to enlist the white-controlled publishing industry in the service of his social message" and thus "reached a significant portion of the national American reading audience with his analyses and indictments of racism."[30] As has been seen, Chesnutt did reach Howells, who had already been "enlisted" by poet Dunbar, only to turn him away along with other reviewers and white book-buyers not interested in being pilloried for either the sins of their fathers or their Southern contemporaries. Howells had misjudged Chesnutt's capacity for "sweetness." Chesnutt had misestimated Howells's tolerance, not only for the "novel with a purpose" subgenre but for literary invective.

Notes

1. *Atlantic Monthly*, 85 (May 1900), 699–701.
2. The three motivations are clear in several entries in *The Journals of Charles W. Chesnutt,* ed. Richard H. Brodhead (Durham, N.C.: Duke Univ. Press, 1993); hereafter cited as *Journals.* For example, "I shall write for a purpose, a high, holy purpose. . . . The object of my writings would be not so much the elevation of the colored people as the elevation of the whites,—for I consider the unjust spirit of caste . . . a barrier to the moral progress of the American people; and I would be one of the first to head a determined, organized crusade against it" (29 May 1880; pp. 139–40). And, "It is the dream of my life—to be an author! It is not so much the *monstrari digito,* though that has something to do with my aspirations. It is not altogether the money. It is a mixture of motives. I want fame; I want money; I want to raise my

children in a different rank of life from that I sprang from. . . . [and] literature pays—the successful" (26 March 1881; p. 154). The same fixations will be seen repeatedly revealing themselves in *"To Be an Author": Letters of Charles W. Chesnutt, 1889–1905,* ed. Joseph R. McElrath, Jr., and Robert C. Leitz, III (forthcoming, Princeton Univ. Press). Please note that "mulatto" is the term used, in its secondary meaning, in this essay: Chesnutt was not the son of black and white parents but biracial ones, and he also claimed Native American ancestry.

3. On 10 December 1899 Chesnutt thus characterized *The Wife of His Youth* to Houghton, Mifflin & Co. after editor Harry D. Robins suggested that the advertisements might stress the moral-reform purpose of its stories: "The book was written with the distinct hope that it might have its influence in directing attention to certain aspects of the race question which are quite familiar to those on the unfortunate side of it; and I should be glad to have that view of it emphasized if in your opinion the book is strong enough to stand it; for a sermon that is labeled a sermon must be a good one to get a hearing" (Chesnutt Collection, Fisk Univ. Library).

4. Chesnutt's low opinion of the Irish will be apparent in the discussion of "Uncle Wellington's Wives," below. Howells's was especially clear in the *Harper's Monthly* serialization of *An Imperative Duty,* though not so apparent in the revised text of the book version; for example, excised was dialogue in which Rhoda Aldgate declares, "I'm sure the Irish are twice as stupid as the colored people, and not half as sweet!" Howells, of course, was not overtly declaring his point of view through Rhoda; but his portrayal of the Irish in this novel squares with Rhoda's assessment, and his attitude toward blacks is much more positive than hers. Other instances of such self-censorship can be seen in the textual variants listed in the "Emendations" to *An Imperative Duty,* in *The Shadow of a Dream and An Imperative Duty,* ed. Martha Banta, et al., vol. 17 of *A Selected Edition of W. D. Howells* (Bloomington: Indiana Univ. Press, 1970), pp. 108–9; see also Banta's introduction, pp. iii–xii, which succinctly describes the evidence of Howells's positive attitude toward African Americans and "public role in assuming part of the white man's burden in the historical struggle of the Negro for his social rights" (p. xi).

5. In the *Atlantic Monthly* appeared "The Goophered Grapevine," 60 (1887), 254–60; "Po' Sandy," 61 (1888), 605–11; and "Dave's Neckliss," 64 (1889), 500–508. "The Conjurer's Revenge" was published in *Overland Monthly,* 13 (1889), 623–29.

6. *A Hazard of New Fortunes,* ed. David J. Nordloh, et al., vol. 16 of *A Selected Edition* (Bloomington: Indiana Univ. Press, 1976), p. 46.

7. Chesnutt used the term in a 31 October 1903 letter to Booker T. Washington (Chesnutt Collection, Fisk Univ. Library). His attitude was not Isabel's, though, as he delivered one of many salvos against Washington's position on the franchise issue: "To my mind it is nothing less than an outrage that the very off-scourings of Europe, and even of Western Asia may pour into this Union almost by the millions annually, and be endued with full citizenship after a year or two of residence, while native-born Americans, who have no interest elsewhere and probably never will have, must be led around by the nose as members of a 'child race,' and be told that they must meekly and patiently await the result of an evolution which may last through several thousand years, before they can stand upon the same level of citizenship which any Sicilian, or Syrian or Turk or Greek or any other sort of European proletarian may enjoy in the State of Alabama."

8. "Mrs. Johnson," in *Suburban Sketches* (New York: Hurd and Houghton, 1871), p. 19.

9. Chesnutt's copy was the 1893 printing by Harper & Brothers. He owned two other volumes by Howells: *Literary Friends and Acquaintance* (1901), in which he perhaps expected to see a reference to himself; and *Literature and Life* (1902). See McElrath, "Charles W. Chesnutt's Library," *Analytical & Enumerative Bibliography,* 8 (1994), 102–19.

10. "The Future American: A Complete Race-Amalgamation Likely to Occur," *Boston Evening Transcript,* 1 September 1900, p. 24. Chesnutt's argument here is buttressed by two other articles with the same title and the following subtitles: "What the Race Is Likely to Become in the Process of Time," *Boston Evening Transcript,* 18 August 1900, p. 20; and "A

Stream of Dark Blood in the Veins of Southern Whites," *Boston Evening Transcript*, 25 August 1900, p. 15.

11.   As Howells, until the publication of *The Marrow of Tradition*, did not see the splenetic side of Chesnutt's personality reflected in the October 1903 letter to Booker T. Washington quoted above in n. 7, so Tourgée never learned how angry Chesnutt was about his novelistic treatments of the "tragic mulatto." Chesnutt's letters to Tourgée are laden with praise for his defenses of the African American; but he sang a different tune to George Washington Cable on 13 June 1890. After berating Thomas Nelson Page, Harry S. Edwards, Maurice Thompson, and Joel Chandler Harris for their characterizations of African Americans, Chesnutt complained that "Judge Tourgée's cultivated white negroes are always bewailing their fate, and cursing the drop of black blood that 'taints'—I hate the word, it implies corruption—their otherwise pure blood" (George Washington Cable Collection, Tulane University).

12.   *Selected Letters of W. D. Howells, Volume 4: 1892–1901*, ed. Thomas Wortham, et al., vol. 24 of *A Selected Edition* (Boston: Twayne Publishers, 1981), p. 274.

13.   See "An Aboriginal Author," *Boston Evening Transcript*, 23 August 1899, p. 16.

14.   "If I can exalt my race, if I can gain the applause of the good, and the approbation of God, the thoughts of the ignorant and prejudiced will not concern me" (12 October 1878; *Journals*, p. 93).

15.   Doris Lucas Laryea, "Paul Laurence Dunbar," in *Realism, Naturalism, and Local Color, 1865–1917*, ed. Matthew J. Bruccoli and Richard Layman, et al., vol. 2 of *Concise Dictionary of Literary Biography* (Detroit: Gale Research, 1988), p. 159.

16.   "Life and Letters," *Harper's Weekly*, 40 (1896), 630.

17.   Dunbar, quoted in *Life in Letters of William Dean Howells*, ed. Mildred Howells, 2 vols. (Garden City, N.Y.: Doubleday, Doran & Company, 1928), II, 68.

18.   "Paul Laurence Dunbar," in *Selected Literary Criticism of William Dean Howells, Volume II: 1886–1897*, ed. Don L. Cook et al., vol. 21 of *A Selected Edition* (Bloomington: Indiana Univ. Press, 1993), p. 280.

19.   Determined to see Chesnutt succeed, Page conceived *The Conjure Woman* on 30 March 1898 (Chesnutt Collection, Fisk Univ. Library), directing Chesnutt to write new Uncle Julius stories to be collected with three of the four already published (see n. 5).

20.   It is noteworthy that Howells did not suspect the fabrication in the emerging African-American tradition of what he described satirically in chapter 2 of *Criticism and Fiction* as an "ideal grasshopper," that is, a "sweet" African-American figure resembling the one constructed by himself and, before him, by writers such as Stowe, Tourgée, and Harris in the Anglo-American tradition (see *Criticism and Fiction*, in *Selected Literary Criticism, Volume II*, p. 301).

21.   Chesnutt's concession to the point of view of contemporary racists is extraordinary by any measure. Uncle Wellington is none other than the "shiftless nigger" archetype: he is lazy; he is a sneak-thief who pilfers his hardworking wife's meager savings in order to go North, with the intention of marrying a white woman; and he cohabits with "white trash," that is, an Irishwoman who, as is eventually discovered, is still married. And when the down-at-the-heels prodigal returns to the South, the seductive aroma of fried chicken and a wife willing to overlook his peccadillos make the transition back to his former way of life a pleasure.

22.   W. B. Parker of the *Atlantic Monthly* replied to Howells's offer on 5 February 1900—"We'll be glad to have it"—and related that Chesnutt was in his office on 2 February: "he hoped to see you before going West" (Houghton, Mifflin letterbooks, Houghton Library), Early in the morning of 3 February, well before Howells received Parker's letter, Chesnutt was in New York and left a note for Howells, asking to see him before 10 a.m. and relating that "Messrs. Houghton, Mifflin & Co. suggested that I see you on my way thro New York" (Rutherford B. Hayes Library). It is also possible that Howells met with Chesnutt the next month or shortly thereafter; in a 25 October 1900 letter to Chesnutt, Howells referred to the "pleasure of seeing you in the spring" (Chesnutt Collection, Fisk Univ. Library).

23.   Chesnutt was Cable's protégé in 1889–90, and Cable encouraged him to write a never-published essay first entitled "An Inside View of the Negro Question" and then "The Negro's Answer to the Negro Question." Cable apparently did the same with another African-American author, William S. Scarborough, who also developed the possibilities of being a sophisticated emissary to the white community who could explain what was actually occurring in black life. Another African American who, to Chesnutt's enragement, exploited his racial identity the same way was William Hannibal Thomas, whose *The American Negro* was published by Macmillan in 1901 and was so defamatory in its allegations that Chesnutt and other African Americans succeeded in getting Macmillan to suppress it.

24.   On 1 May 1900 Chesnutt had written Howells: "I want to thank you very cordially for your appreciative review of my books in the May *Atlantic*. It would have been pleasant coming from any source, and it has a very great value coming from you. I thank you especially for the few words of frank criticism where you call attention to lapses in style, and to the occasional 'look in the reader's direction.' I think I appreciate the force of these suggestions and shall be able to profit by them in the future—there would be little hope for me as a literary artist if I could not. I shall try to keep in mind the heights to which you point me, both by precept and example, and shall hope to meet the conditions which you prescribe for my success. I may not confine my studies to the 'paler shades,' but I shall endeavor always to depict life as I have known it, or, if I wander from this path, as I think it ought to be. I am very grateful for your kindly notice and encouragement, after which I feel that I can safely subscribe myself a man of letters and hope for a worthy career in that field of effort. Permit me to count myself among your friends as I have numbered you with mine . . ." (Houghton Library). The follow-up letter that was intended to suggest that a like essay on *House* would be appreciated does not survive; but Howells's 12 November reply to it, including the statement "I only did letters a service in praising your stories," indicates that Chesnutt made a timely allusion to the essay (Chesnutt Collection, Fisk Univ. Library).

25.   On 25 October 1900 Howells wrote "in behalf of Messrs. Harper & Brothers" for a novel "which you would like to show me with a view to its publication by them. We should like it to be . . . something about the color-line, and of as actual and immediate interest as possible—that is, of American life in the present rather than the past, even the recent past; but we would not bar anything you thought good enough to offer for our consideration." On 31 October he informed Chesnutt that there "is no chance for your novel here as a serial; and I would rather wait for the color-line story which your brief suggestion interests me in. At the same time, if you wish to show me the story of office-life I shall be glad to read it, with the understanding that it could be used only in book form." Finally, Howells thanked Chesnutt on 12 November 1900 for the copy of *House*, telling him not to "wait to send me the Color Line story. Let me see the other, if you can, at once." (All three letters are in the Chesnutt Collection, Fisk Univ. Library.)

26.   Howells, "An Exemplary Citizen," *North American Review*, 173 (1901), 282, 283.

27.   See Howells, "A Psychological Counter-Current in Recent Fiction," *North American Review*, 173 (1901), 872–88.

28.   The letter to Washington is in the Washington Papers collection, Library of Congress; the other two are in the Chesnutt Collection, Fisk Univ. Library.

29.   Francis J. Garrison, son of William Lloyd Garrison and a Houghton, Mifflin editor, thought so too. He wrote Chesnutt on 9 November 1901, praising him for a fairness in the treatment of both blacks and whites "as remarkable as was that of Mrs. Stowe in *Uncle Tom's Cabin*" (Chesnutt Collection, Fisk Univ. Library).

30.   William L. Andrews, introduction to *Collected Stories of Charles W. Chesnutt* (New York: Mentor, 1992), p. vii. For a different perspective on the Howells-Chesnutt relationship, see Andrews's "William Dean Howells and Charles W. Chesnutt: Criticism and Race Fiction in the Age of Booker T. Washington," *American Literature*, 48 (1976), 327–39.

Under the Upas Tree:
Charles Chesnutt's Gothic

CHARLES L. CROW

In the preface to *The Marble Faun,* Nathaniel Hawthorne provides a famous list of the things lacking for the artist in American life: "No shadow, no antiquity, no mystery, no picturesque and gloomy wrong, nor anything but a broad prosperity, in broad and simple daylight."[1] This is a stunning admission of blindness to the racial injustice that has indeed provided its gloomy subject for generations of American artists. In the twentieth century, of course, some of America's most celebrated authors have drawn on the gothic mode to explore the tragedy of racial relations in America: William Faulkner, Richard Wright, Toni Morrison, Leslie Marmon Silko, Louise Erdrich, and Cormac McCarthy, among others. These modern and contemporary explorers of the ghosts and shadows of America's racial landscape were anticipated by writers—black and white—in the 1800s who also used the gothic to enter this most vexed and most important of American subjects.[2]

This essay explores Chesnutt's use of the gothic in three fine stories: "The Marked Tree," "The Dumb Witness," and "The Sheriff's Children." The first two are "John and Julius" stories that use the same framing characters and setting as the tales in *The Conjure Woman* (1899), though they were not published in that volume. (They thus stand in the same relation to the story cycle volume as Sarah Orne Jewett's "The Foreigner" does to *The Country of the Pointed Firs.*) "The Sheriff's Children" is from *The Wife of His Youth and Other Stories of the Color Line* (also 1899).[3] The sequence in which I have arranged the stories represents not the order of composition but a scale from more to less obvious gothic elements: from a tale in which conjure (witchcraft) drives the plot, to a story that has clear signature traits of gothicism but no magic, to a story appearing squarely in the mode of realism, in which the gothic elements are so submerged that many readers may protest that the tale is not gothic at all. All three stories are united by recurring Chesnutt themes, or obsessions: paternity, language and silence, and miscegenation—though the latter theme, the master concern for Chesnutt, seems to have

This essay was written specifically for this volume and is published for the first time by permission of the author.

been overlooked in previous discussions of "The Marked Tree." In each story there are secrets held by black characters; in each there is a plot of revenge. And in each, the crime of slavery sends out ripples of complicity that implicate, ultimately, Chesnutt's white audience.

I

In "The Marked Tree," John, the white narrator, is driven by his coachman Julius to the site of the ruined Spencer plantation. Of the once mighty estate, the only relics are a blackened chimney and the stump of a tree—a still-sound stump, though with "a rotten heart."[4] This tree stump is the key image of the story, the remains of a huge oak that the last patriarch, "Marse Aleck" Spencer, was fond of identifying with his own thriving family. Yet it is not, Julius insists, really an oak stump. John should not sit on it if he has any trace of southern blood and thus any possible kinship to the lost family. It is a "U-pass tree," Julius says—reproducing, in dialect, the term applied to it by the doomed Aleck Spencer, near the end of the family's tragedy.

"The Upas Tree, the fabled tree of death," John recalls (196). The reference is not, as one might suspect, to Greek mythology, but to a legend introduced into English literature by Erasmus Darwin concerning a tree in Java so poisonous that it could "destroy all animal and vegetable life to a distance of fifteen or sixteen miles around it" (Oxford English Dictionary). Other nineteenth-century writers before Chesnutt, including Byron, Southey, Ruskin, and Emerson, had employed this rich image.

The fall of the House of Spencer, as related to John by Julius, began in a series of financial reverses that left the family strapped for cash on the eve of the wedding of Aleck Spencer's eldest son, Johnny. Rather than compromise the splendor of the wedding to the daughter of another prominent family (and thus admit the family's financial embarrassment, which the marriage is intended to remedy), Spencer raises cash by selling a young slave man, Isham. Isham's mother, Phyllis, is promised that her son will be treated well on a neighboring plantation. But he is abused, escapes, is wounded by pursuers, and dies on the wedding day in his mother's arms. Phyllis is not powerless, however: she is a conjure woman, a practitioner of magic, and she curses ("marks") the Spencer oak, and thus the family.

Then begins a series of misfortunes, recounted in colorful and perhaps sadistic detail, resulting in the deaths of all the male heirs of the family and many of the childbearing Spencer women: deaths all, in some way, involving the tree. When Aleck Spencer finally understands the connection, he has the tree—which he now calls the Upas tree—cut down. The falling tree kills Mars Aleck himself. The next winter a burning log from the tree rolls from an upstairs fireplace, and in the conflagration the last members of the Spencer household perish.

This story is unusual among Chesnutt's conjure tales. It is one of only two in which magic is used against white people (the other is "Mars Jeems's Nightmare") and the only one resulting in the deaths of whites. Moreover, it is unique in that the experience of John, the skeptical Ohioan, seems to validate the conjure. In negotiating to buy the remaining Spencer family land, John contacts a distant Spencer kinsman, who comes to the old plantation to meet John, sits on the Upas stump, and is stung to death by a rattlesnake.

The story that John tells comes to an apparently sensible resolution, however, as is typical of the conjure stories. John buys the estate, dynamites the stump, and installs his cousin's family on the now, as he believes, exorcised land.

John seems to feel (and the unwary reader will agree) that he has participated in a kind of political allegory proving the progress of American civilization. The energetic northerner, with no curse of southern heritage, has destroyed the Upas tree, even as the Civil War destroyed slavery. He brings progressive institutions to the South; the gothic southern heritage is replaced by the light of common day.

Yet as with all of Chesnutt's fiction, a reading reflecting John's easy liberalism should be suspect. John's self-defined rationalism reflects a refusal to enter imaginatively the world of African American experience. Surely, from Julius's perspective, the tragedy of the story is less in the fall of Aleck Spencer's family than in the destruction of the enslaved family of Phyllis. And there is more in this largely suppressed tragedy than John can, or most of his audience will, recognize. The father of Isham, the young man who is sold, is never mentioned; paternity, indeed, was often unrecorded on plantations. We should note, however, Julius's apparently casual comments after he mentions Isham's birth: "De mammy had worked 'round de big house de year befo', but she had give er mistress some impidence one day, and er mist'iss had made Marse Aleck sen' her back ter de cotton fiel' " (198). Mrs. Spencer continues to hate Phyllis, does not "like the look of Isham," and urges that he be sold. Chesnutt carefully constructs the parallelism between the two boys: Johnny and Isham are born on the same day; Isham pays, ultimately with his life, for Johnny's wedding. If to these hints one adds the punning name Isham—Is-Ham, recalling the disfavored son whom Noah cursed with slavery—Chesnutt's implication should be clear.[5] The boys are brothers. Aleck Spencer has sold his black son to insure the prosperity of his white heirs. Phyllis revenges her son's death on the boy's father, and on the descendants who had usurped Isham's patrimony. What she thinks about the fall of the Spencers, however, we do not know, for she has no voice in the story. The revenge and the silence of the betrayed mulatto will be seen again.

Because John has misunderstood key literal events of his story, we should resist his implied political allegory as well. Chesnutt certainly does not believe that the Upas tree (i.e., the poisonous legacy of racial oppression) has been eradicated, either in the post-Reconstruction era in which the story is set, or the 1920s, when it was published. When John installs his own kinfolk on the estate, he becomes, in a sense, the successor to Aleck Spencer. There is no reason to believe that the new white order will be more enlightened than the last.

II

Like "The Marked Tree," "The Dumb Witness" is based on conflicting layers of discourse and *unheimlich* family secrets left unspoken. John and Julius again visit a neighboring estate, and as they enter "the lane . . . by passing between two decaying gateposts," we realize that we are again hip deep in the overgrown landscape of southern gothic:

> As we drew nearer, the house stood clearly revealed. It was apparently of more ancient date than any I had seen in the neighborhood. It was a large two-story frame house, built in the colonial style, with a low-pitched roof, and a broad piazza along the front, running the full length of both stories and supported by huge round columns, and suggesting distantly, in its general effect, the portico of a Greek temple. The roof had sunk on one side, and the shingles were old and cracked and moss-grown; while several of the windows of the upper part were boarded up, and others filled with sash from which the glass had apparently long since been broken.[6]

On the veranda of this decayed mansion are an elderly man with hawklike features, seated on a massive oaken chair, and an elderly woman, whose similar features betray their kinship, but who is black. As the visitors draw closer, they witness a remarkable exchange. The old man approaches the woman and demands to know the whereabouts of "the papers." The woman rises from her seat and begins to speak,

> I thought at first [John says] in some foreign tongue. But after a moment I knew that no language or dialect, at least none of European origin, could consist of such a discordant jargon, such a meaningless cacophony as that which fell from the woman's lips. And as she went on, pouring out a flood of sounds that were not words, and which yet seemed now and then vaguely to suggest words, as clouds suggest the shapes of mountains and trees and strange beasts, the old man seemed to bend like a reed before a storm, and began to expostulate, accompanying his words with deprecatory gestures. (160)

Then the old man, imagining some meaning in the sounds, seizes a shovel and begins to dig in the yard.

Julius explains that "Dey's bofe 'stracted, suh . . . out'n dey min'. Dey's been dat-a-way fer yeahs an' yeahs" (161).

John eventually gathers the story of the House of Murchison from Julius and other sources, and correcting Julius's errors, as he tells us, he puts the "facts together in an orderly sequence" (162).

The Murchison family was prominent in the Carolinas from colonial times: a Murchison was a general in the Revolutionary War and delegate to the Constitutional Convention. His son was a distinguished jurist. But with the general's grandson, Roger, the family's decline begins. Roger never marries, has no heir, but turns the management of the estate over to a bright, energetic nephew, his prospective heir, while taking his pleasure in the fashionable cities. It is the nephew, Malcolm, whom we now see, crazed and elderly, on the veranda.

Like his uncle, Malcolm does not marry but stays on the family estate in the company of an old black cook and "the housekeeper, a tall, comely young quadroon," whose name is Viney—the other figure on the veranda. After some years on the estate, the young Malcolm courts a wealthy widow and wins her promise of marriage. Viney, jealous, speaks to the widow and tells her *something*—which leads her to break off the marriage. When Malcolm deduces Viney's actions, he cuts out her tongue.

This outrage recalls the similar abuse and murder of Lavinia in *Titus Andronicus:* "Viney" is probably a contraction of "Lavinia."[7] It also signifies on the rape and mutilation of Philomela by Tereus. These allusions prepare us for revenge, which events soon set in motion. A letter arrives from Malcolm's uncle Roger, who has been mortally wounded in an accident in Washington. The letter relates that he has left a will naming Malcolm as his heir, along with bonds and other documents and valuables, which will give the young man wealth and clear title to the estate: "I do not say here where they are, lest this letter might fall into the wrong hands; but your housekeeper Viney knows their hiding place. She is devoted to you and to the family—she ought to be, for she is of our blood—and only she knows the secret" (166). There is no mention, incidentally, of a legacy for Viney, who is not only a Murchison but the mistress of Malcolm—and, for all we know, may have been Roger's mistress as well, or his child, or both.

But Viney cannot speak: she has no tongue. Malcolm tries to teach the illiterate slave to write, but she proves a remarkably poor pupil. Distant heirs challenge the estate, legal fees eat funds and land, and Malcolm declines into the distracted figure seen in the narrative frame, endlessly questioning Viney, trying to find the secret in her storm of shapeless nonwords.

When old Malcolm dies, John goes to the plantation house, driven again by Julius, to conduct some business with the new owner, the brisk young Roger Murchison, nephew of Malcolm. John finds the place set in order, the gateposts repaired, windows again glazed. He is met at the door by Viney, and he asks if young Roger Murchison is at home:

> "Yas, suh," she answered, "I'll call 'im."
> Her articulation was not distinct, but her words were intelligible. I was never more surprised in my life.
> "What does this mean, Julius?" I inquired, turning to the old man, who was

grinning and chuckling to himself in great glee at my manifest astonishment. "Has she recovered her speech?"

"She'd nebber lost it, suh. Ole Viney could 'a' talked all de time, ef she'd had a min' ter. Atter ole Mars Ma'colm wuz dead, she tuk an' showed Mistah Roger whar de will an' de yuther papers wuz hid." (171)

The papers were in the great oaken chair in which Malcolm had been sitting all those years.

Any analysis of this complex story will quickly reveal how far Chesnutt is from the accommodating local colorist he is still sometimes taken for. As Eric Sundquist has argued in detail, Viney's babble—a verbal equivalent of a mask—accurately reproduces the discourse strategies of oppressed peoples.[8] We might also notice the opposition in the story of vernacular speech on the one hand, and writing, documents, on the other—the language of power, control, of Malcolm and of John. It was documents, such as the Constitution, at whose framing Malcolm's great-grandfather assisted, that deprived African Americans of citizenship and ratified their condition as slaves; legal documents, such as would have been employed by Malcolm's grandfather, the judge, that constructed whiteness and blackness according to law; wills that define some children as heirs and disinherit others. The history of the Murchison family is essentially that of the legal system of the United States. Viney's revenge is thus against an entire structure of written words that are instruments of oppression, to which she opposes silence and her impenetrable babble of shadow language.

How is the discourse war resolved? Not quite as John believes, with, again, restored order and a New South partaking of northern efficiency, the past forever buried, all mysteries dispelled. John does not notice that the terms with which he praises the young second Roger are exactly the terms used to describe Malcolm at the time he began managing the plantation for the first Roger. Both are good, responsible, energetic young administrators, better than the old uncles they succeed (compare 158, 163). The common language and recurring names suggest a cycle of corruption, not progress toward a New South. Moreover, John, in retelling the story and correcting Julius's "mistakes," does not acknowledge how well he has been taken in by the former slave's trickster discourse, for presumably Julius, and perhaps all the other former slaves of the neighborhood, knew that Viney could speak. When Julius told John, "Dey's both distract," he was concealing the truth, participating in Viney's long-term slave rebellion. In all of the John and Julius stories (the seven included in *The Conjure Woman* and the eight that were not), this is the clearest instance of Julius dropping his mask. And John does not see it.

How much, finally, can John know about a story that has so much silence and indeterminacy at its core? We do not actually know, for example, what Viney told the widow. We assume, guided by John's always-suspect narration, that she revealed her incestuous sexual liaison with Malcolm, but we don't know this. An alternative reading, unprovable but only slightly less plausible, is that Viney, "who is of our blood," reveals that Malcolm, son of a mysterious younger brother and some undescribed woman, is himself of African heritage. While I do not want to insist on this reading, or even to advance it very seriously, I would point out that the slave owner who is, knowingly or unknowingly, of the race he oppresses is standard fare in the southern gothic. This is one of the things that happens under the Upas tree, and it is used as a plot device by southern writers from Kate Chopin to William Faulkner; and of course, Chesnutt uses it himself in *The House behind the Cedars*. The point is that the ultimate authority for the story's meaning is not John's. The story belongs to the tricksters Julius and Viney, and they, not John, are closest to the imagination of Charles Chesnutt. Only they—the old woman who knew all the family's secrets and the old man who is the oral historian of the region's black community—know what tangle of relationships binds the inbred Murchisons. Whiteness and blackness are legal fictions of the country's ruling class. Viney and Julius will not help us (John and the reader) in drawing the color line in their tale.

III

These various themes of language and heritage and narrative authority, guilt and complicity and revenge, converge again in the final story under consideration, "The Sheriff's Children." The story opens with an apparently upbeat travelogue description of a postbellum rural community. The bland tone of the third-person narration, however, is subtly subverted by an undercurrent of imagery revealing the gothic mode:

> Ten years make little difference in the appearance of these remote Southern towns. If a railroad is built through one of them, it infuses some enterprise; the social corpse is galvanized by the fresh blood of civilization that pulses along the farthest ramifications of our great system of commercial highways.[9]

Is this praise of progress coming to the New South, or a threatening image of Frankenstein's monster stirring? Throughout the story, the apparently hearty description—the equivalent of John's perspective—will be undercut and contradicted by revelations from the secret life and history of Branson County.

The story at first seems to celebrate the sheriff of the title as a progressive man of the New South. A brave officer in the Confederacy, a college graduate, a man of some travel and broad outlook, he took the oath of allegiance to the Union soon after surrender and was elected sheriff. In this office, he is popular and respected. The story begins with a briskly paced account of the sheriff's defense of his jail against a mob that has come to lynch a young mulatto man suspected in the murder of a local citizen.

But after the mob is driven off, the sheriff discovers that his prisoner has scooped up a pistol placed aside during the defense of the jail. In the following confrontation, the prisoner reveals that he is the sheriff's son. He is, he explains,

> "Tom, Cicely's son. . . . Don't you remember Cicely—Cicely whom you sold, with her child, to the speculator on his way to Alabama?"
>
> The sheriff did remember. He had been sorry for it many a time since. It had been the old story of debts, mortgages, and bad crops. He had quarreled with the mother. The price offered for her and her child had been unusually large, and he had yielded to the combination of anger and pecuniary stress. (85)

In this moment, we confront the complex psychology and moral ambiguity of serious gothic fiction. The sheriff, to this point, may have seemed rather like the familiar hero of Western genre fiction; but readers identifying with him should find their responses suddenly conflicted. The cell has become the claustrophobic space of gothic fiction; the jailer and prisoner are discovered as the "inappropriate" family unit that some scholars find essential to the gothic mode.[10]

In the intense scene following the revelation, Tom rejects with contempt every claim that his father might have on his mercy and concludes that he must kill his jailer-father to escape. But as he raises his pistol, Tom is wounded by a shot fired by the sheriff's devoted white daughter, Polly, who has arrived in time to see her father menaced but has heard none of the dialogue. The sheriff bandages the wounds of his son, who has now lapsed into sullen silence. That night the sheriff confronts his conscience, condemns his own sins, and resolves to help Tom.

> He could . . . investigate the circumstances of the murder, and move Heaven and earth to discover the real criminal, for he no longer doubted the prisoner's innocence; he could employ council for the accused; and perhaps influence public opinion in his favor. An acquittal once secured, some plan could be devised by which the sheriff might in some degree atone for his crime against this son of his—against society—against God. (92–93)

He imagines many things, but (if we read closely) he does not imagine publicly recognizing Tom as his son, and making him the equal of Polly. When the Sheriff arrives at the jail, he finds that the young man has torn the bandages from his wounds and has died during the night. Like Melville's Babo, his final defiance is silence; like Viney, his revenge is in withholding the words of love he would once have given.

IV

Each of these stories assumes a well-meaning but limited reader who assumes and insists, like Hawthorne, that the light of common day and a broad prosperity are the essential truth of American life. But this innocence is bought at a terrible price. Polly's happy innocence is a representation of this bargain, essentially paid for by the sale of Cicely and Tom, as Aleck Spencer sacrifices Isham to his dream of a white dynasty, and Malcolm Murchison sacrifices Viney. As Cynthia Goddu recently observed, "American gothic literature criticizes America's national myth of new-world innocence by voicing the cultural contradictions that undermine the nation's claim to purity and equality."[11] Chesnutt dramatizes these contradictions as sharply as any American writer, as clearly as any of the great gothic novels of the twentieth century that his stories anticipate. Each of these tales tells us, though we do not want to hear it, that there are difficult and chilling truths that we ignore. The Upas tree still casts its poisoned shadow over the land.

Notes

1.   Nathaniel Hawthorne, *The Marble Faun: Or the Romance of Monte Beni* (Columbus: Ohio State University Press, 1968), 3.

2.   The scholarly dialogue on Chesnutt's use of the gothic mode begins with Robert Hemenway's 1973 essay "Gothic Sociology: Charles Chesnutt and the Gothic Mode," *Studies in the Literary Imagination* 7, no. 1 (1974): 101–19. Hemenway argues that the premises of the gothic render it inherently unsuitable for an African American author. Although the essay is well reasoned and contains accurate observations about *The Conjure Woman,* I depart from what seems to me a restrictive definition of the gothic and assert, on the contrary, that the gothic, like other European literary modes, was successfully subverted by Chesnutt—as it was and would be by many other authors of color—into a sophisticated tool for exploring the tragedy of the color line.

3.   During his lifetime, Chesnutt did not publish "The Dumb Witness," but a version of the material was worked into *The Colonel's Dream* (1905); "The Marked Tree" appeared in 1924.

4.   Charles W. Chesnutt, "The Marked Tree," in *The Conjure Woman and Other Conjure Tales,* ed. Richard C. Brodhead (Durham, N.C.: Duke University Press, 1993), 195. Hereafter cited in the text.

5.   See Genesis 9:20–27.

6.   Charles W. Chesnutt, "The Dumb Witness," in *The Conjure Woman and Other Conjure Tales,* 159. Hereafter cited in the text.

7.   I am indebted to Professor Frederick S. Frank of Allegheny College for this suggestion.

8.   Eric Sundquist, *To Wake the Nations: Race in the Making of American Literature* (Cambridge: Harvard University Press, 1993), 387–92. Sundquist's nearly book-length chapter on Chesnutt is by far the best study of the author to date and has influenced my approach in many respects.

9. Charles W. Chesnutt, "The Sheriff's Children," in *The Wife of His Youth and Other Stories of the Color Line* (Ann Arbor: University of Michigan Press, 1968), 61–62. Hereafter cited in the text.

10. For gothic psychology and ambiguity, see Robert D. Hume, "Gothic versus Romantic: A Revaluation of the Gothic Form," *Publications of the Modern Language Association of America* 84 (March 1969): 282–90; for the inappropriate family unit, see William Patrick Day, *In the Circles of Fear and Desire: A Study of Gothic Fantasy* (Chicago: University of Chicago Press, 1985), 5; see also Sundquist, 394, for a related point about taboos against the "monstrous."

11. Cynthi Goddu, *Gothic America: Narrative, History, and Nation* (New York: Columbia University Press, 1997), 4.

"The Growth of a Dozen Tendrils": The Polyglot Satire of Chesnutt's *The Colonel's Dream*

GARY SCHARNHORST

For a variety of reasons, Charles Chesnutt's third and last novel has been virtually ignored. Compared to *The House behind the Cedars* (1900) and *The Marrow of Tradition* (1901), *The Colonel's Dream* (1905) has seemed misbegotten, hastily or haphazardly written, a commercial and critical flop that effectively dashed Chesnutt's own dream of literary success. In context, the novel has seemed to Chesnutt's career what *The Confidence Man* was to Melville's—a last-ditch and ultimately failed attempt to shock readers into a kind of attention before the writer lapsed into a kind of silence. I want to propose an alternative reading of the text, however—one that regards it as a pastiche of "parodic-travestying forms," in Mikhail Bakhtin's phrase.[1] That is, I believe that *The Colonel's Dream* is a remarkably modern, multilayered experiment or "complex intentional linguistic hybrid"[2] that satirically rewrites many of the standard literary formulas popular around the turn of the century before the story implodes and collapses in the final pages.

The main thrust of the plot, such as it is, may be briefly summarized. Colonel Henry French, a former Confederate officer, sells his bagging mills in New York and with his young son Phil returns to his southern hometown of Clarendon (modeled on Fayetteville, North Carolina, where Chesnutt was reared). Like Albion Tourgée's hero Colonel Comfort Servosse in *A Fool's Errand* (1879),[3] the Reconstruction novel that apparently inspired Chesnutt's story, Colonel French travels south for his health but remains there because he wants to help revive the local economy and reform social abuses and inequities between the races. He joins the "life-and-death struggle for the soul of Clarendon"[4] with the lowborn nouveau riche scalawag and "Flem Snopes prototype"[5] William Fetters, whose surname suggests the economic shackles in which he holds virtually all the citizens, both black and white. Their virtual slavery is epitomized by the fate of Bud Johnson, a black man

This essay was written specifically for this volume and is published for the first time by permission of the author.

271

who is repeatedly convicted of petty crimes and sentenced to jail so that Fetters can "buy his time" under the convict-labor laws and consign him to work the fields on one of his plantations. Determined to change the social and economic climate of the town, French invests in property and begins to build a cotton mill, but he abandons his project in bitter despair when the body of Uncle Peter, his old family retainer, is exhumed in the night by a white mob from a cemetery reserved for white burials only. Meanwhile, French, a middle-aged widower, courts the flower of Old South aristocracy and propriety in the person of Laura Treadwell, who agrees to marry him but withdraws rather than accompany him back to New York at the close of the novel.

The episodic quality of the plot, with its several false starts, feints, and digressions, may no doubt be explained in part by Chesnutt's patchwork method of writing it. In May 1904, Houghton, Mifflin rejected the original version of the novel, which the author conceded was "hardly. . . . more than an elongated short story" (*Author,* 213), whereupon Chesnutt submitted the manuscript to his friend Walter Hines Page at Doubleday, Page. Page also thought it too slight to publish ("It is not long enough nor full enough") but urged Chesnutt to revise and expand it: "Can you give it more body? Make it of larger structure; introduce, if necessary, more characters, and round it out to something like a good hundred thousand words able bodied novel? I hope you can" (213, 214). In its original version, according to William L. Andrews, the story seems to have focused on French's "mission of economic stimulus and moral encouragement," which he abandons when "racists desecrate the grave of his black retainer" (Andrews, 236). Page also admonished Chesnutt not to "work the machinery of the alleged hidden treasure too hard"—a reference to a creaky subplot about a cache of gold coins presumably hidden on a decaying local plantation (*Author,* 214). In reply to Page's suggestions, Chesnutt agreed to develop "several threads of the story" (213), in particular by making French a more romantic figure. That is, he expanded the novel, as his narrator explains, with "the growth of a dozen tendrils" (*The Colonel's Dream,* 56). Chesnutt submitted a revised manuscript in late September 1904 ("It is not quite 100,000 words but is very close up in that neighborhood") that Page accepted six weeks later, and the author continued to tinker with the story, both in manuscript and in proof, before its publication on September 9, 1905. His changes in proof were so extensive that he apologized to the publisher for the expense of making them (*Author,* 222–23). In fact, the novel threatened to become a baggy monster with more loose ends than a frayed rope. Reviewers for the *Outlook* and the London *Morning Leader,* for example, indicted its crude construction, and the New York *Evening Mail* tried to turn its maelstrom of subplots into a virtue: "It abounds with incident and gives us quick vivid gleams of thrilling little side stories all along."[6] Not only were reviews mixed, but sales of the novel were disappointing. It went into only two printings, indicating that no more than a few thousand copies were sold.

Although Chesnutt continued to write intermittently until his death in 1932, he would publish no more books.

Unfortunately, no reader of *The Colonel's Dream* seems to have remarked on its unrelieved irony, the satiric and parodic mode in which it is written. Much as Nathanael West's *A Cool Million* travesties the success stories of Horatio Alger, or Walter Van Tilburg Clark's *The Ox-Bow Incident* parodies the formulaic Western, so Chesnutt's novel resolutely subverts or deconstructs each of the familiar formulas it deploys. To illustrate the point: one recurring trope in *The Colonel's Dream* seems to have been borrowed from such temperance novels as T. S. Arthur's *Ten Nights in a Barroom*. Several scenes in Chesnutt's novel are set in Clay Jackson's barroom, "a place with an evil reputation as the resort of white men of a low class. Most crimes of violence in the town could be traced to its influence, and more than one had been committed within its walls" (*The Colonel's Dream*, 58). Jackson sells "rotgut whiskey—a cheap brand of rectified spirits coloured and flavoured to resemble the real article, to which it bore about the relation of vitriol to lye" (60). The white men disgruntled with French's policy of hiring and promoting workers regardless of race gather in Jackson's saloon to air their grievances (191). There a white foreman fired for insubordination "hurled invectives at the colonel, to all who would listen, and with anger and bad whiskey, soon worked himself into a frame of mind that was ripe for any mischief" (241). There, too, intemperate white men or "riffraff" conspire to enslave black prisoners under the laws (242), hatch the plan to exhume old Peter's body after his burial (271), and plot to lynch Bud Johnson (277). The logic of the plot, in other words, would seem to commend strict temperance, given its repeated condemnation of the villainy executed under the influence of demon drink. By rights, that is, a temperance novel such as *The Colonel's Dream* appears to be on first glance should describe the closure of a tavern or two or depict the reformation of a drunk who purges his life of vice and dissipation. But Chesnutt's novel fails to follow the formula to its logical end. To the dismay of the reader who expects novels to offer such a progressive and reassuring message, nothing changes in this story. The rambling plot repeatedly frustrates expectations.

In similar fashion, the novel at one point travesties the sentimental Uncle Remus tales of Joel Chandler Harris. Publicly, as in his 1901 essay "Superstitions and Folklore of the South," Chesnutt merely observed that Harris, "in his Uncle Remus stories, has, with fine literary discrimination, collected and put into pleasing and enduring form, the plantation stories which dealt with animal lore."[7] Privately, however, Chesnutt was much more critical of the plantation tradition of popular fiction and Harris's brand of Negro folklore. As Chesnutt wrote to George Washington Cable in 1890, Harris and others of his ilk "give us the sentimental and devoted negro who prefers kicks to half-pence"; and as he wrote to Booker T. Washington in 1901, they "have furnished my chief incentive to write something upon the other side" of the race question (*Author*, 66, 167). In chapter 16 of *The Colonel's Dream*, Chesnutt overtly parodies Harris as Uncle Peter recounts the story "The Black Cat and the Haunted House." Once again, at first glance, much like Chesnutt's Uncle Julius stories, the episode seems to subscribe to the formula: an aged former slave reminisces to a white boy. As Uncle Peter explains, his story is of a piece with the other tales " 'bout Bre'r Rabbit and Bre'r Fox an de yuther creturs talkin' an' gwine on" (*The Colonel's Dream*, 147). In this case, however, the story is vapid and pointless: "Ole Mars' Tom Sellers" wagers five dollars that a black drover named Jeff won't stay the night in a haunted house. Late at night, a black cat suddenly appears and talks to Jeff, at which point he leaps out a window. "Is that all, Uncle Peter?" Phil asks "when the old man came to a halt" (149). It's difficult to imagine the docile little boy in Harris's tales asking Uncle Remus so impertinent a question. Whereas the anecdote rings true in the most general way—after all, both black cats and talking animals are common in black folklore—in fact I have been unable to find any record of genuine lore about a talking black cat. That is, the anecdote seems to be inauthentic in exactly the same way that many of Harris's Uncle Remus tales are inauthentic. Phil later recalls "Uncle Peter's story of the black cat" (257) and follows such an animal across a train track near his home, hoping to talk with it—when despite Peter's attempt to rescue him, both of them are struck by a railroad car. Phil and Peter are killed, in other words, as an indirect result of the pointless anecdote Peter has earlier narrated, in ironic contrast to the normal denouement of Harris's amusing Uncle Remus stories. As Andrews has noted, Chesnutt's Uncle Julius stories "observed the conventions of a popular genre only to manipulate and parody them" (Andrews, 261).[8] The same may be said of "The Black Cat and the Haunted House," which otherwise is an inexplicable digression in *The Colonel's Dream*.

The subplot about the missing treasure of gold coins—the storyline Page warned Chesnutt not to overwork—also fits this pattern of self-reflexive parody. Ben Dudley, scion of an old genteel family, hopes one day to find the $50,000 in gold his dead great-uncle Ralph presumably hid on the ancestral estate during the Civil War so that he may marry Laura's niece Graciella Treadwell. Ben's faith in the existence of the hidden treasure is buoyed by a yellowed letter written by his great-uncle that explains that he has confided the secret of its location to a housekeeper, the slave Viney. "It sounds like a letter in a novel," Graciella allows (127)—which is, of course, exactly the point. Unfortunately, Viney is illiterate and apparently mute as a result of a stroke she suffered during a whipping ordered by her owner (and former lover) Malcolm Dudley, Ben's uncle. Liable to fits of "hysterical violence" due to the "passionate strain of the mixed blood in her veins" (171), Viney at first glance seems to fit the stereotype of the tragic mulatto.[9] This part of the novel is, in fact, a revision of "The Dumb Witness," an Uncle Julius story

Chesnutt had written eight years earlier.[10] Much as "grave, unromantic men" dissect every old house in St. Petersburg "plank by plank" and dig around foundations in a vain search for hidden treasure after Huck and Tom recover the gold of Murrell's gang in *The Adventures of Tom Sawyer,*[11] Malcolm Dudley has spent a quarter century in a "fruitless search" for hidden gold:

> The yard had been dug over many times. Every foot of ground for yards around had been sounded with a pointed iron bar. The house had suffered in the search. No crack or cranny had been left unexplored. The spaces between the walls, beneath the floors, under the hearths—every possible hiding place had been searched, with little care for any resulting injury. (*The Colonel's Dream,* 176–77)

In the end, as it happens, Viney is not really mute, nor is she a type of the tragic mulatto. Whereas in the original version of the story Viney tells Malcolm's nephew where the treasure is hidden and so enables him to restore the plantation to its antebellum glory, in the novel she finally admits the treasure *does not exist.* Ralph Dudley had left two heavy bags of gold and the letter at the plantation, but he returned an hour later "*and took it all away,* except the letter! The money was here one hour," Viney explains, but because she was whipped on Malcolm's order during that hour, she exacts revenge. By her silence, she compels him to spend "twenty-five years in looking for nothing— something that was not here!" (274). Eric Sundquist contends that Chesnutt "diluted [the] import" of the story in revision, partly by discarding the suggestion of incestuous relations between Viney and Malcolm.[12] Yet Chesnutt, in changing the story, tended to valorize Viney, to invest her with more heroic attributes than those of the tragic mulatto, and so revised the stereotype. He also "unwrote" the more conventional plot of "The Dumb Witness," with its clichéd recovery of treasure, and so again deflated reader expectations. The mystery of the hidden gold, first mentioned in chapter 5 and carefully woven into the fabric of the novel, abruptly turns to ashes in chapter 35 when Viney reveals the treasure never really existed.

This complex strategy of ironic or parodic signification extends not only to isolated incidents or subplots in the novel but to its two main story lines: Colonel French's project of reforming and civilizing Clarendon and his romance with Laura Treadwell. On the surface, *The Colonel's Dream* seems a realistic, Howellsian study of the social and economic conditions in the post-Reconstruction South from the perspective of a progressive white protagonist. Colonel French buys the mansion where his family had lived before the war from a mulatto barber and hires a number of local contractors to restore it, priming the town's economy with his dollars:

> The stream of ready money thus put into circulation by the colonel soon permeated all the channels of local enterprise. The barber, out of his profits, began the erection of a row of small houses for coloured tenants. This gave employ-

> ment to masons and carpenters, and involved the sale and purchase of considerable building material. General trade felt the influence of the enhanced prosperity. (88)

An experienced and confident businessman, French plans to build the cotton mill to exploit the town's proximity to raw material, its water power, and its underemployed labor force. He proposes nothing less than "to shake up this lethargic community; to put its people to work, and to teach them habits of industry, efficiency and thrift" (106). The backwater town "offered a field for profitable investment. He would like to do something for humanity, something to offset Fetters and his kind" (117). Like a catalyst in a chemical reaction, he soon launches a variety of reforms. He offers to renovate the academy for white students. He pledges to match with three dollars of his own every single dollar raised for an industrial school for blacks modeled on Booker T. Washington's Tuskegee Institute.[13] Like Andrew Carnegie, he plans to build a public library, "a shrine of intellect and taste, at which all the people, rich and poor, black and white, may worship" (162). Above all, he tries to reform the convict-lease laws that permit a barbaric form of peonage.

The novel particularizes the operation of these unjust laws in the case of Bud Johnson, who is forced into virtual slavery.[14] Through his agents, Fetters buys Johnson's labor over a period of 18 months for little more than a hundred dollars. Henry Clay Appleton, the editor of the local newspaper, the Clarendon *Anglo-Saxon* (!), defends this system: "These convict labour contracts are a source of considerable revenue to the State" and finance most forms of "Negro education." Besides, Appleton argues, "niggers don't look at imprisonment and enforced labour in the same way white people do," and "convict labour is humanely treated" (76)—the very sort of claims made before the war by pro-slavery apologists. A secluded part of Fetters's plantation, in fact, holds "numerous" graves of "convicts who had died while in [his] service" (219). Through his lawyer, French submits a case against the convict-lease laws to a grand jury that fails to issue an indictment; he sues under a writ of habeas corpus for the body of Bud Johnson but loses in court; and he prepares "a memorial for presentation to the federal authorities" indicting the system that the bureaucrats ultimately ignore for political reasons (230–31). Desperate, French finally authorizes his lawyer to bribe one of Fetters's guards to allow Johnson to escape. On the surface, the colonel's actions are principled, even courageous. But Johnson, rather than leave the state, ambushes and nearly kills two white men complicit in his unjust imprisonment and forced labor. "With the best of intentions, and hoping to save a life," French realizes, "he had connived at turning a murderer loose upon the community. . . . With the best intentions he had let loose upon the community, in a questionable way, a desperate character" (246, 247). French reports Johnson's whereabouts to the authorities, who arrest the escapee. But in yet another ironic twist, Johnson is lynched in a riot of passions, and despite French's best efforts, not one person in the mob is ever brought to justice. In his campaign to "punish the lynchers," moreover, he stands "single-handed and alone; and without the support of public opinion he could do nothing" (279). What had begun as a reform novel along the lines of Tourgée's *A Fool's Errand* or Cable's *John March, Southerner* suddenly reverses course in its final pages. The entrepreneurial hero abruptly cancels every social palliative he had planned for civic improvement, abandons the town to its fate, and flees to the North (much as the author had in 1883). "Clarendon has had its chance, nor seems yet to have had another," Chesnutt's narrator observes in a coda (294). Even before his departure, as Andrews adds, "none of French's reforms has effected the slightest change in the Clarendon status quo" (Andrews, 252–53). Much as the ingrained racial intolerance, political corruption, and moral laxity of the town destroy Colonel French's dream, the end of the novel travesties the predictable denouement of most reform fiction.

In revising *The Colonel's Dream,* Chesnutt also fleshed out a plot that may best be read as an ironic sentimental romance or domestic melodrama. The progress of French's courtship of Laura Treadwell exactly parallels the progress of his scheme for social reformation. In chapter 10, for example, the colonel both receives the deed to his ancestral home and finds "pleasure in Miss Laura's sweet simplicity and openness of character." As a bachelor, "he did not lack for the smiles of fair ladies, of which the town boasted not a few," but the Treadwell home "held the first place in his affections" (90). In chapter 18, he both seeks out "new reforms" with "philanthropic zeal" and finds "much pleasure in talking over these fine plans of his with Laura Treadwell." He discovers, despite Miss Laura's genteel poverty, "how active in good works she was" (155, 156). Together they visit the academy French resolves to rehabilitate. The colonel repeatedly links the fate of his suit to his crusade to reclaim the town from Fetters. As he proposes marriage to Laura, he declares that "in you I find the inspiration for good deeds" (184). He fights to free Bud Johnson and to reform the convict-lease laws "to please Miss Laura" (231). And when his plans begin to sour, he takes comfort in the notion that the "dear, good woman he had asked to be his wife" with "her clear, spiritual vision" would join him in the struggle (276). He "could go forward, hand in hand with the good woman who had promised to wed him, in the work he had laid out" (279). In the conclusion of the novel, however, this familiar plotline collapses, too: the romance ends not with the happy union of hero and heroine but with their courtship suddenly dissolved. Miss Laura refuses to leave her aged mother in Clarendon to follow the man she might marry to New York. That is, though *The Colonel's Dream* follows the same basic trajectory of Tourgée's *A Fool's Errand* until its final pages, Chesnutt departed from his model at the close much as he resisted or revised popular formula throughout the novel. Whereas Tourgée's story ends with the marriage of Lily

Servosse and the Southern cavalier Melville Gurney (a symbolic reconciliation of North and South), Chesnutt's story does not sound so sentimental and unrealistic a note.

In truth, moreover, Laura Treadwell is a remarkably ambiguous heroine, the incarnation of both the best and worst attributes of the Old South. To be sure, she is musically talented and kind to little Phil, but she also exhibits the virulent racism that infects the town. Miss Laura is aghast when French buys his ancestral mansion from the barber William Nichols: "You could never *live* in it again—after a coloured family?" (84). Although she accompanies the colonel to the white academy, she is loath to visit "the coloured school" and is "secretly relieved" when he excuses her "from a trip so unconventional" (158–59). When French announces his plan to build a library for both blacks and whites, Miss Laura delicately protests: "I am afraid the white people wouldn't wish to handle the same books" that black people have touched. Rather than inspiring the colonel with her vision she often influences him to equivocate and compromise, as when she persuades him to build a separate (and inherently unequal) library for blacks lest "we strain our ideal by going too fast" (163). She is ashamed to admit that she is paid to teach music to the daughter of the mixed-race barber,[15] the same person from whom the colonel buys his family mansion. The barber's wife "belonged to us before the war," Laura explains, "and we have been such friends as white and black can be." The Nichols and Treadwell families have essentially switched social caste since the war, and the barber is able to hire Miss Laura as a type of servant with part of the profit on the house he sold to French. Ironically, though she is an indirect beneficiary of French's largesse, she is ashamed to work for a black family, toward whom she assumes a haughty superiority: her aged mother knows of her humiliation "but feigns that I do it out of mere kindness, and tells me that I am spoiling the coloured people. Our friends are not supposed to know it, and if any of them do, they are kind and never speak of it" (181–82). The hypocrisy and corruption epitomized by Fetters, in other words, taints even Laura Treadwell, the nominal heroine.

Finally, like many of Chesnutt's stories, *The Colonel's Dream* travesties the genre of race fiction popular at the turn of the century, which included, most notoriously, Thomas Dixon's *The Leopard's Spots* (1902) and *The Clansman* (1905). Dixon, a North Carolina minister, warns in his first novel:

> One drop of Negro blood makes a Negro. It kinks the hair, flattens the nose, thickens the lips, puts out the light of intellect, and lights the fires of brutal passions. The beginning of Negro equality as a vital fact is the beginning of the end of this nation's life.[16]

Similar racial arguments are voiced in *The Colonel's Dream* by the Reverend McKenzie, who figures as a Dixon type:

I have become profoundly convinced that there is no place in this nation for the Negro, except under the sod. We will not assimilate him, we cannot deport him. . . . To coddle them, to delude them with false hopes of an unnatural equality which not all the power of the Government has been unable to maintain, is only to increase their unhappiness. (164)

Chesnutt's Uncle Peter at first glance seems little more than a racist caricature like Nelse, the "black hero of the old regime" in *The Leopard's Spots*. Loyal to his old master, Peter waxes nostalgic about "de ole times" and smacks his lips at the thought of watermelon (26). As Laura Treadwell allows, again betraying her unreconstructed racial views, "There are few like him left, and there were never any too many" (32). As Andrews explains, Chesnutt revived the "familiar convention" of plantation fiction in the first third of the novel to "draw his reader into the story and to adumbrate the romantic quality of the South" (Andrews, 239). By the end of the novel, however, Peter is a more noble figure, transcending the comic or pathetic stereotype. He vainly attempts to rescue Phil from a moving rail car: the "bruised and broken old black man" sacrifices "his life to save him" (261). Whereas Dixon warns of the horrors of racial "amalgamation" and "equality" in the New South, Chesnutt indicts its racial separation and hostility:

White and coloured children studied the same books in different schools. White and black people rode on the same trains in separate cars. Living side by side, and meeting day by day, the law, made and administered by white men, had built a wall between them. (263)

Yet Phil's dying wish is to be buried near Peter, and the colonel is determined to honor both his son and his servant by interring them together. Whereas Dixon praises the Ku Klux Klan for bringing "order out of chaos" and protecting "the weak and defenseless,"[17] Chesnutt depicts the cowardice of the mob that exhumes Peter's coffin under cover of darkness. This sordid and brutal event at once triggers French's departure from Clarendon and signals both the collapse of his philanthropic schemes and the end of his engagement to Laura Treadwell. The colonel takes "his dead to the North" and reburies Peter and Phil "in a beautiful cemetery" overlooking New York harbor, where "there is none to question old Peter's presence or the colonel's right to lay him there" (290). However caricatured the black figures may seem in the beginning, Chesnutt's novel revises the stereotypes by the close.

Much as a trickster may ridicule tropes borrowed from blackface minstrelsy, *The Colonel's Dream* borrows incidents and characters from a variety of equivalent sources to both mimic and satirize them. Such a polyphonic or polyvalent approach, with its parodic voices, hybrid languages or "heteroglossia," and myriad subplots, is liable to entrap the unwary reader. The novel systematically deconstructs every literary formula it deploys before abruptly collapsing in the final pages in what Andrews has called an "unmitigated melodrama of despair" about the South (Andrews, 246). Like the evasion chapters of *Huck Finn,* however, such a contrived conclusion is not entirely artless. More than any other turn-of-the-century novel, *The Colonel's Dream* disrupts the familiar patterns of popular fiction and disdains the comforts of a happy ending.

Notes

1.   Mikhail M. Bakhtin, *The Dialogic Imagination,* ed. Michael Holquist, trans. Caryl Emerson and Michael Holquist (Austin: University of Texas Press, 1981), 61.

2.   Ibid., 81.

3.   As Joseph R. McElrath Jr. and Robert C. Leitz III remark, Chesnutt apparently "named his *idéaliste manqué* hero Colonel French" in tribute "to the recently deceased Tourgée, whose alter ego in the autobiographical *Errand* was a 'fool' with a Gallic surname, Servosse" (introduction to Charles W. Chesnutt, *"To Be an Author": Letters of Charles W. Chesnutt, 1889–1905,* ed. McElrath and Leitz [Princeton, N.J.: Princeton University Press, 1997], 20; hereafter cited in the text as *Author*).

4.   Charles W. Chesnutt, *The Colonel's Dream* (1905; reprint, Upper Saddle River, N.J.: Gregg, 1968), 158; hereafter cited in the text.

5.   William L. Andrews, *The Literary Career of Charles W. Chesnutt* (Baton Rouge: Louisiana State University Press, 1980), 248; hereafter cited in the text.

6.   Curtis W. Ellison and E. W. Metcalf Jr., *Charles W. Chesnutt: A Reference Guide* (Boston: Hall, 1977), 57–68.

7.   Chesnutt, "Superstitions and Folklore of the South," in *Mother Wit from the Laughing Barrel,* ed. Alan Dundes (Englewood Cliffs, N.J.: Prentice-Hall, 1973), 371.

8.   See also Robert C. Nowatzki, " 'Passing' in a White Genre: Charles W. Chesnutt's Negotiation of the Plantation Tradition in *The Conjure Woman," American Literary Realism* 27 (Winter 1995): 20–36.

9.   The other mulatto who figures prominently in the novel, the barber William Nichols, "a man of thrift and good sense" (82) who owns five houses and drives a tough bargain with French, also violates the stereotype.

10.   This story appears in *The Short Fiction of Charles W. Chesnutt,* ed. Sylvia Lyons Render (Washington, D.C.: Howard University Press, 1974), 153–63.

11.   Mark Twain, *The Adventures of Tom Sawyer* (Berkeley: University of California Press, 1982), 254.

12.   Eric J. Sundquist, *To Wake the Nations: Race in the Making of American Literature* (Cambridge: Belknap Press of Harvard University Press, 1993), 390.

13.   Susan L. Blake contends that *The Colonel's Dream* "is a systematic and thorough refutation of Washington's program for the advancement of blacks in the South" ("A Better Mousetrap: Washington's Program and *The Colonel's Dream," CLA Journal* 23 [March 1979]: 49)—a point well taken, even if the novel seems, in my reading, a much broader satire.

14.   Chesnutt also objected to the convict-lease laws in the South in his essay "Peonage, or the New Slavery," *Voice of the Negro* 1 (September 1904): 394–97.

15.   In 1878 Chesnutt married 19-year-old Susan Perry, the daughter of a prosperous barber in Fayetteville; that is, he apparently models the characters of the barber and his daughter in the novel on his father-in-law and his wife.

16.   Thomas Dixon Jr., *The Leopard's Spots* (New York: Doubleday, Page, 1902), 244.

17.   Ibid., 152.

Telling Genealogy:
Notions of the Family in *The Wife of His Youth*

CHARLES DUNCAN

Any consideration of the literary output of Charles W. Chesnutt must, of course, acknowledge race as a defining feature. Certainly, Chesnutt exhaustively probed the matter, examining in great detail both the sources of race consciousness in the United States and the far-reaching consequences of what has become our prolonged national mediation on the issue. As a means of exploring the broad social and cultural implications of post-Reconstruction race relations, his fictions, especially the works collected in *The Wife of His Youth and Other Stories of the Color Line,* repeatedly concentrate on individual families struggling to preserve or, more often, to remake themselves in the turbulent end-of-the-century American milieu. His interest in rendering American social conditions in microcosm by focusing on assorted versions of the family prompted Eric J. Sundquist to claim, in fact, that "[n]o writer before Faulkner so completely made the family his means of delineating the racial crisis of American history as did Chesnutt."[1] Indeed, Sundquist contends that the author's color-line stories, as well as *The House behind the Cedars* and *The Marrow of Tradition,* work precisely to refute "destructive charges" in circulation at the turn of the century, including the claim that "the 'failure' of the black family was a sign of racial degeneration."[2] But whereas Sundquist finds that Chesnutt, in his fiction, ultimately blames "the legacy of white dissipation" for leaving "the most visible mark of pathology—white pathology—on the black family,"[3] I want to suggest that the stories in *The Wife of His Youth* represent instead his attempts to reimagine the American family in a broader context, a family able to resist or, perhaps, even to transcend the racial and social pressures of American social history. And although a few of those fictions depict families nearly able to achieve such a transcendence, Chesnutt seems finally to conclude that the very cure for racial ills—an understanding of, or a coming to terms with, the past—constitutes a sort of poison pill. For, in his fictions, the past functions both to sustain and to over-

This essay was written specifically for this volume and is published for the first time by permission of the author.

281

whelm his characters as they seek to establish a place for themselves and their families in the American social universe.

As a self-made, highly successful businessman and largely self-taught writer and intellectual, Chesnutt had a deep investment in the notion of an America that would support, or at least tolerate, individuals who strove to *make* better lives for themselves, especially those who prospered, as he did, as a consequence of hard work and attention to education. But because he was no weak-kneed sentimentalist, virtually all the characters in *The Wife of His Youth* who attempt to reconstitute their families see their efforts conclude in varying degrees of failure. "The Sheriff's Children" and "The Web of Circumstance" both grimly depict, for example, how generally well-intentioned and talented figures repeatedly and depressingly fail to build families able to withstand the past as manifested in an array of blood conflicts and varied social forces.[4] And while comic in tone, "A Matter of Principle" and "Uncle Wellington's Wives" likewise trace the careers of those whose attempts to reformulate their families miscarry, in part because the characters fail to account sufficiently for the vagaries of racial history: the former satirizes the intraracial prejudices of a skin color–obsessed father trying to engineer his daughter's marriage and, by extension, a lighter-complected race; the latter comically deflates an unambitious man's belief that marrying a white woman would raise him socially.

Even in the works that come closest to ratifying the possibility of black families overcoming the constraining racial and social conditions of late-nineteenth-century America—works that will be the focus of this essay—Chesnutt still hints at the enormous costs and complications brought on by war and nurtured by the cultural disarray of Reconstruction and its aftermath. In "Her Virginia Mammy," for example, a black mother who has spent her life searching for her long-lost daughter must ultimately deny their relationship to protect the young woman's marital prospects; in "Cicely's Dream," the black protagonist falls in love with an amnesiac she has nursed back to health only to lose him when the (white) past reasserts itself in his life; and in "The Wife of His Youth," the central character must confront his own past in determining whether he can reconcile his urge to "advance" his race with his family duty.

These stories display obvious thematic and stylistic similarities, but none so pronounced as their shared interest in genealogy, an issue that, according to Kimberly W. Benston, resonates throughout African American literature: "For the Afro-American, then, self-creation and reformation of a fragmented familial past are endlessly interwoven: naming is inevitably genealogical revisionism. All of Afro-American literature may be seen as one vast genealogical poem that attempts to restore continuity to the ruptures or discontinuities imposed by the history of black presence in America."[5] If Benston is right about black literature forming "one vast genealogical poem," then Chesnutt contributes his best stanza with these three stories. For in them he foregrounds the crucial role played by storytelling in the healing (or overcoming) of "a fragmented familial past," a process that gestures toward a new, less restrictive, more interracial model of the American family.

Although several of Chesnutt's treatments of this theme—including "The Sheriff's Children," "The Web of Circumstance," and "A Matter of Principle"—explore issues of family from predominantly masculine positions, he more often illuminates the topic by reflecting on how late-nineteenth-century American women, both black and white, work to remake or protect their families.[6] "Her Virginia Mammy," for example, examines just how complex identity construction could be for a late-nineteenth-century woman with an uncertain family history. Like other Chesnutt fictions, the story explores race issues, but it suggests that although women must struggle, like men, to fashion personal and family identities during (and after) Reconstruction, the two sexes envision their problems in significantly different terms. First published in *The Wife of His Youth* (1899), the story features Clara Hohlfelder, the adopted daughter of German immigrants who refuses to marry until she can verify the worthiness of her blood family. "You know I love you, John," Clara tells the man who has just proposed to her, "and why I do not say what you wish. You must give me a little more time to make up my mind before I consent to burden you with a nameless wife, one who does not know who her mother was."[7] Clara's refusal to marry a man of "pure" blood—his ancestors include "the governor and the judge and the Harvard professor and the *Mayflower pilgrim*" (116)—derives from her fear that she comes from common stock.

While the light-skinned Clara dreads the possibility of having coarse ancestry, she never considers the true case: she is a mulatta. Clara ultimately meets the woman—Mrs. Harper, really her mother—who can answer her genealogical questions. But when Mrs. Harper learns that Clara's marital hopes depend on the purity of her blood, she does not refute her daughter's mistaken guess that the older woman is her "Virginia mammy." In another writer's hands, such a plot might easily devolve into mawkish sentimentality, but Chesnutt manipulates the story in such a way as to minimize the importance of the pair's coincidental discovery of each other after so many years of separation. Instead, he focuses on the way Clara and Mrs. Harper deliver their own stories to each other, forming what Susan Fraiman calls "a long, caressing conversation in which the two women piece together their common past."[8] But this scene has bite to it as well, which becomes clear when Mrs. Harper ultimately and purposefully subverts the conversation: by choosing to omit one crucial detail of her own story—her real relationship to Clara—she consciously permits her daughter to form an inaccurate conception of her race identity. Mrs. Harper's selfless act thus allows Clara to marry and therefore to build a family, at a huge cost to herself and her own dreams of family reconstruction.

By focusing on how Clara and Mrs. Harper exchange and reshape each other's narratives—and especially the latter's reluctant affirmation of her daughter's mistaken genealogical beliefs—Chesnutt examines the construction of family from a less literal perspective than elsewhere in his fiction. Through the telling of her carefully crafted narrative, which she modifies for Clara's benefit, Mrs. Harper *composes* a family for her daughter, even at the exclusion of herself. Rather than rely on literal "blood" connections—as an ex-slave, she had seen her own marriage condemned by her husband's family—Mrs. Harper (and later John) instead expands the very notion of family, translating a genealogical construct into a linguistic one. In thus fashioning a more inclusive model of family, one that takes its form from the narrative exchanges that lie at the heart of this story and others of its type, Chesnutt establishes a trope that likewise informs "Cicely's Dream," "The March of Progress," and "The Wife of His Youth."

Despite the maudlin nature of the plot, Chesnutt infuses "Her Virginia Mammy" with rich ironies, and in a context one rarely associates with irony. Throughout a story that initially appears to conform to the stereotypical "tragic mulatta" paradigm, Clara's actions and words provide a darkly comic foreshadowing of what the reader comes to learn. Clara teaches dancing, for example, to a class of black pupils, although the decision to do so has not been an easy one, as the narrator points out: "Personally she had no such prejudice, except perhaps a little shrinking at the thought of personal contact with the dark faces of whom Americans always think when 'colored people' are spoken of" (119). Once she accepts the class, her views grow more expansively liberal, and she tells John, "I hardly think of them as any different from other people. I feel perfectly at home among them" (121).

Other characters' comments similarly generate dramatic irony. Early in the story, for example, Clara's suitor attempts to placate his lover's "blood" concerns by telling her not to brood on the subject to the exclusion of life's pleasures: "It is a fine thing, too," John says, "to be able to enjoy the *passing* moment. One of your greatest charms in my eyes, Clara, is that in your *lighter* moods you have this faculty" (121, italics mine). Chesnutt here puns on passing,[9] a term often used in reference to African Americans who choose to live as white, and a subject about which few authors make such jests.[10] In addition to foreshadowing the culmination of the plot, these subtle (and almost uncomfortably comic) ironies also emphasize the extent to which Mrs. Harper's genealogical lie, when combined with Clara's light-colored skin, will ensure that the young woman enjoys a future made up exclusively of "passing moment[s]."

Mrs. Harper also articulates ironies—clearly with more self-consciousness than Clara or John demonstrates—by using the same term in consecutive sentences to reify vastly different realities. When Clara asks about her blood parents' backgrounds, for example, the older woman replies, "Your father was a Virginia gentleman, and *belonged* to one of the first families. . . . [and] Your mother—also *belonged* to one of the first families of Virginia" (127–28, italics mine). The second use of "belonged" has, of course, a more literal connotation here, one that reveals Mrs. Harper's past status as a slave. Finally, the story's most piercing irony comes after Mrs. Harper has delivered Clara's incomplete (and therefore misleading) family information, confirming the young woman's fantasy that she comes from "pure" bloodlines: "I knew it must be so," Clara tells Mrs. Harper, who must want either to giggle or to scream at her daughter's profound misreading of her heritage, "Blood will always tell" (127). Here Clara's fragile psyche and her future with John are secured, in fact, precisely because "blood" (Mrs. Harper) will not "tell."

Despite this ironic treatment of the heroine, the story ends with the betrothal of this racially mixed couple, an event that William L. Andrews suggests took "the question of miscegenation out of the realm of abstract moral prohibition and made it a matter of personal ethical decision."[11] The person who must decide this question, however, is neither Clara nor Mrs. Harper but John, the man who willingly chooses to marry a woman with black ancestry. Although no one expresses the idea openly, and Clara certainly misses the signposts, John clearly recognizes that Mrs. Harper and Clara share bloodlines: "Then she [Clara] told him Mrs. Harper's story. He listened attentively and sympathetically, at certain points taking his eyes from Clara's face and glancing keenly at Mrs. Harper, who was listening intently. As he looked from one to the other he noticed the resemblance between them, and something in his expression caused Mrs. Harper's eyes to fall, and then glance up appealingly" (130). Despite his recognition of the family resemblance, John neither reveals his understanding to Clara nor cancels the engagement.

This passage partly illuminates the web of Chesnutt's complex thematic and narrative intentions. The two women inextricably linked by blood but separated by circumstance are once more reunited here symbolically when Clara takes on the telling of Mrs. Harper's story. In the retelling, Clara becomes a surrogate narrator for her mother and simultaneously reveals her true genealogy to John, who "reads" both the story itself and the subtext Clara cannot decode. "Her Virginia Mammy" thus ultimately suggests that both extremes of the racial polarity—a Boston Brahmin and an ex-slave—can place the idea of "family" on a higher plane than race or "blood." And although Clara's obsession with the past forces Mrs. Harper and John to mislead her, Chesnutt seems here to devalue the importance of the past as a shaper of identity. Standing in marked contrast to Morrison's *Song of Solomon,* Walker's *The Color Purple,* and Griggs's *Imperium in Imperio,* among many other works by black writers that insist on the importance of tracing one's roots, "Her Virginia Mammy" stresses instead the advantages to be derived from de-emphasizing ancestry.

It seems likely, in fact, that John speaks for the author when he offers, long before learning of Clara's true heritage, this rebuttal to her concerns about her bloodlines:

> We are all worms of the dust, and if we go back far enough, each of us has had millions of ancestors; peasants and serfs, most of them; thieves, murders, and vagabonds, many of them, no doubt; and therefore the best of us have but little to boast of. Yet we are all made after God's own image, and formed by his hand, for his ends; and therefore not to be lightly despised, even the humblest of us, least of all by ourselves. For the past we can claim no credit, for those who made it died with it. Our destiny lies in the future. (118)

Significantly, although John had outlined this position while still under the impression that Clara's ancestry was "merely" common, he does not renounce this idealistic philosophy once he recognizes the truth.

Faced with the imminent marriage of John and Clara at the conclusion of "Her Virginia Mammy," modern readers have noted the potentially subversive qualities of the work. It might easily be read, as Andrews suggests, as an endorsement of miscegenation, a dangerous position for a turn-of-the-century black writer to take. In another recent reading, Fraiman foregrounds the importance of gender in "Her Virginia Mammy," a story that while "most overtly a tale of racial identity" is "also a tale of *female* identity. I suggest a reading that focuses less on black-white relationships than on mother-daughter relationships, less on race than on generation and gender. Such a reading should not diminish but, on the contrary, heighten our attention to race in this story; in Chesnutt the issues of gender and race overlap with and serve to amplify one another."[12] Fraiman's discussion of "Her Virginia Mammy" positions the work within a matrix of both gender and race, a locus that is dramatically apparent as well in such fictions as "Cicely's Dream," "White Weeds," and "The March of Progress."

But although Fraiman is right in seeing "Her Virginia Mammy" as an important and neglected work that encases the author's sensitivity to the importance of gender in identity construction, it also is one of Chesnutt's most pointed metacritical commentaries on his readers, both of his own day and ours. The story's ironies collude to establish Clara—whose name ironically suggests racial purity—as the proxy for late-nineteenth-century white readers. Like Sheriff Campbell in "The Sheriff's Children," Clara is a seemingly reasonable but befuddled reader of the world around her, especially when confronted with texts that challenge her preconceived notions of blackness (notions that insist, for instance, that an older black woman must be "mammy" rather than "mother").

Unlike the sheriff, though, Clara is protected from the consequences of her misreading, leading to what might seem to be a happy ending for her. Yet it is precisely within the nature of that protection that Chesnutt calls the story's ending—and benevolent white readers' sense of self—into question. Clara's happiness and ability to carry on with her life come only at enormous cost: her enforced and continuing ignorance of the most intimate details of her personal—and racial—history. Through the deceived but content Clara, Chesnutt thus mocks the very idea of a secure identity, thereby warning that the racial complacency of even the most sympathetic white reader may well have hidden costs. In a story whose "happy" ending would likely have appealed to readers who had unexamined assumptions about racial identity, then, Chesnutt dramatically embeds an incisive satire of those readers.

Just as provocative, though, is the manner in which Chesnutt calls attention to the very nature of the family formed at the end of "Her Virginia Mammy." By the conclusion of the story, the apparently liberal-minded John has suddenly transformed into an ominous and magisterial presence. As Clara celebrates her newfound identity—" 'Clara Stafford,' mused the girl. 'It is a pretty name' " (130)—John immediately usurps it: "You will never have to use it," he tells her, "for now you will take mine" (130). Even Clara, not the most astute of readers, seems to intuit her future husband's intentions here when she laments, "Then I shall have nothing left of all that I have found" (130). And John's final act in the narrative—he puts "his arm around [Clara], with an air of assured *possession*" (130, italics mine)—resonates suspiciously with the diction of slavery. Thus whereas John appears satisfied with the outcome of events, the two women pay differing but profound costs for the formation of this particular family.

If the optimism raised by Clara's impending marriage is tempered by the price at which she achieves it, "Cicely's Dream" articulates still more pessimistic readings of its protagonist's chances of creating or preserving a workable family for herself. The story might easily be read as an answer to "Her Virginia Mammy," in that both consider interracial love. But whereas the latter story concludes with a marriage, the former depicts how Cicely, a young black woman, must confront the grim consequences of her falling in love with a white man, although the circumstances of the story collude to hide his race from her until it is too late. The plot has Cicely finding a badly wounded young amnesiac of indeterminate race—an adult tabula rasa—in the field near her house, and, with her family's help, nursing him back to physical health. Because he has lost his memory and other brain functions, she also has the rare opportunity of constructing an identity for him. In an inversion of what Reconstruction generally meant for blacks, here an African American woman is enabled to form an identity for a white man, an act of love on her part that seems likely to result in the marriage of the two characters. The story thus seems on course to articulate the author's reconception of the American family, one unconcerned with race and blood. But in ways both similar and dissimilar to what transpires in "Her Virginia Mammy," Chesnutt interrupts (and finally terminates) the possibilities for this kind of fruitful social transgression. In "Cicely's Dream," the past—in the form of a white woman who had been engaged to marry John—reasserts itself in the lives of the two protagonists and effectively disallows Cicely's attempts at social engineering.

As with many of his works, Chesnutt sets "Cicely's Dream" in the South during a time of political and social regeneration, and the story mirrors that process on a far more personal level. He focuses on how Cicely re-creates John—her family names him after John the Baptist—as an ideal mate for herself, and John becomes a masculine double of his benefactor. In typical fashion for his canon, Chesnutt here highlights the extent of this doubleness by focusing on voice: "As time went on Cicely found that he was quick at learning things. She taught him to speak her own negro English, which he pronounced with absolute fidelity to her intonations; so that barring the quality of his voice, his speech was an echo of Cicely's own" (176). Not surprisingly, the story emphasizes the degree to which these two characters share speech patterns. For Chesnutt, voice and identity often overlap, and in "Cicely's Dream," the author contrives an inverted tale of "passing," as a white man who speaks "negro English" is accepted into the black community. John's learned identity (and his impending marriage to Cicely) is finally displaced only when he has contact with another voice from his past.

Ultimately John is "restored to reason and to his world" (185) by listening to the embedded narrative of his long-lost fiancée, who just happens to be Cicely's white teacher, a transplanted northerner named Martha Chandler. Martha's moving narrative, ostensibly of how she came to teach blacks in the South, penetrates the fortress of his amnesia and strips away Cicely's reconstructive efforts. In her farewell address to the schoolchildren and their families, Martha's story (purportedly an autobiographical one, which begins "I want to tell you how I came to be in North Carolina") evolves into a tribute to her lost love:

> so that if I have been able to do anything here among you for which you might feel inclined, in your good nature, to thank me, you may thank not me alone, but another who came before me, and whose work I have but taken up where *he* laid it down. I had a friend,—a dear friend,—why should I be ashamed to say it?—a lover, to whom I was to be married, as I hope all you girls may some day be happily married. His country needed him, and I gave him up. He came to fight for the Union and for Freedom, for he believed that all men are brothers. He did not come back again—he gave up his life for you. Could I do less than he? I came to the land that he sanctified by his death, and I have tried in my weak way to tend the plant he watered with his blood, and which, in the fullness of time, will blossom forth into the perfect flower of liberty. (185)

In effect, John—or Arthur, the name by which Martha knows him—is the subject of narratives by two women who love him. First Cicely re-creates him as a black companion for herself, and then Martha's eulogy of him as a valiant martyr for freedom reawakens his dormant memory. But the story essentially concludes by defining him once more in relation to a woman: "From that moment his memory of the past was a blank until he recognized Martha on the platform and took up again the thread of his former existence where it had been broken off" (185). His identity therefore remains completely a feminine (and linguistic) construct as two women try to reformulate their social and familial roles in a country attempting to come back together.

Chesnutt's narrative construction of the story in many ways mirrors that of "Her Virginia Mammy," in which Clara and Mrs. Harper compose family identity through the exchange of their stories.[13] Although "Cicely's Dream" initially follows that pattern by foregrounding the personal narratives of Cicely and Martha, the two stories differ in one provocative way. Indeed, the very telling of Martha's story, which allows her to refashion her family by restoring the narrative of her fiancé's past, interrupts Cicely's own successful composition of a family bond for herself and John. A literal embodiment of the past thus overwhelms Cicely's voicing of the present and the future in a way that evokes the central tension of "Her Virginia Mammy." But recognizing the potential ruptures that would result from her own role as an incarnation of her daughter's history, Mrs. Harper chooses to shield Clara from the past and its consequences. Although "Cicely's Dream" renders Cicely's ultimate loss of John, it—like "Her Virginia Mammy"—nevertheless hints at the guardedly optimistic message that if not for a confrontation with the burden of the past, a young, black, turn-of-the-century woman might very well succeed in forcefully articulating her own place in the world.

If "Her Virginia Mammy" and "Cicely's Dream" represent Chesnutt's acknowledgment that turn-of-the-century America was not quite ready for a radical reenvisioning of the family, then "The Wife of His Youth" seems, at first glance, to fashion a more optimistic message. Whereas those stories seriously question readers' preconceptions of family, "The Wife of His Youth" concludes with the reunion of a long-separated couple, a reunion that symbolically fuses several polarities—the North and the South, the white and the black, the rich and the poor—by means of an apparently harmonious marriage. But the very nature of that reunion might well suggest yet another hesitation on Chesnutt's part.

The protagonist of this story, Mr. Ryder, is "dean" of a society of African Americans that has come to be known as the "Blue Veins." The purpose of this organization (which William L. Andrews suggests may have had as its source the Cleveland Social Circle, Chesnutt's own club) "was to establish and maintain correct social standards among a people whose social condition presented almost unlimited room for improvement" (102). That the Blue Veins' membership is composed of "individuals who were, generally speaking, more white than black" (102) the narrator ironically attributes to accident. Despite the opportunities for divisive commentary, however, the narrator's depiction of these Blue Veins—a group of light-skinned, well-educated African Americans with whom Chesnutt had much in common—remains gently ironic.

Indeed, "The Wife of His Youth" features a primary narrator who might most accurately be described as a wry but sympathetic commentator whose role as ironist diminishes as the voices of his characters gain strength. By the midpoint of the story, in fact, he becomes as much of an arranging presence as a narrator, and he devotes most of his energy to orchestrating the embedded narratives of the two protagonists. Thus Chesnutt gradually effaces his primary narrator until the voices of his characters finally articulate their own identities without any external mediation from the narrator. In this way, the author fashions one of his best realistic fictions: the narrator merely directs the reader's attention to vital information rather than attempting to interpret events and actions for his audience. Early in the story, however, the narrator establishes the tone by undercutting the pretensions of Mr. Ryder and the other members of the Blue Vein club.

Encased in this mildly critical treatment of those who would redraw racial boundaries in their own favor is a remarkably sentimental love story. While Mr. Ryder prepares a marriage proposal to a young, light-skinned widow named Mrs. Dixon—a proposal he plans to deliver publicly at a Blue Vein function that evening—his meditations are interrupted by an elderly ex-slave named 'Liza Jane. She has come to him seeking help in locating her long-lost husband, separated from her by the random cruelty of slavery. She has been looking, she tells Mr. Ryder, for "Sam Taylor" for the past 25 years, but without success. Even the epitome of snobbery, Mr. Ryder, cannot easily dismiss the loyalty and determination of this woman. At the Blue Vein dinner that evening, Mr. Ryder repeats to his guests the woman's story, onto which he grafts an apparently hypothetical conclusion. Suppose the man she seeks had since raised himself to a respected position within the community, he wonders aloud. He further asks them to suppose that the man has learned that his wife, whom he thought dead, had been seeking him for all those years. And finally, Mr. Ryder asks, "Suppose that perhaps he had set his heart upon another. . . . What would he do, or rather what ought he to do, in such a crisis of a lifetime?" (112). After his guests tearfully respond that this hypothetical man ought to acknowledge her, Mr. Ryder introduces to them the wife of his youth.

Chesnutt spends nearly half of the story establishing the daunting odds that this long-separated couple must overcome to achieve their reunification. He takes great pains to emphasize the extent to which 'Liza Jane embodies what Mr. Ryder has spent most of his adult life trying to avoid. She violates the two primary unwritten principles that the Blue Veins have formulated, that members be light colored and of free birth. As an ex-slave, she obviously fails the latter criterion, and as to the former, the narrator offers a definitive description: she is "very black,—so black that her toothless gums, revealed when she opened her mouth to speak, were not red, but blue" (106). This physical description of 'Liza Jane captures Chesnutt's meticulous handling of imagery: Mr. Ryder, the dean of a club that allegedly permits into their society no one who "was not white enough to show blue veins" (102), ultimately acquiesces to the most intimate society possible with a woman so black that her gums appear blue. The description also emphasizes the physical disparity between 'Liza Jane and Ryder, whose "features were of a refined type," and whose "hair was almost straight" (103).

In addition to the profound difference in appearance between the two, Chesnutt likewise stresses other impediments to their reunion. 'Liza Jane delivers her speech to a man who, the narrator tells us, lamented the "growing liberality" in social matters that had forced him "to meet in a social way persons whose complexions and callings in life were hardly up to the standard which he considered proper for the society to maintain" (105). Indeed, the narrator suggests that as "one of the most conservative" members of the Blue Vein Society, Ryder had become "the custodian of its standards, and the preserver of its traditions" (103). To that end, Ryder hopes his social ball for the Blue Veiners "would serve by its exclusiveness to counteract leveling tendencies, and his marriage to Mrs. Dixon would help to further the upward process of absorption he had been wishing and waiting for" (105).

Although their differences in social station and appearance seem overwhelming, the profound disparity in voice most emphatically divides Ryder and 'Liza Jane early in the story. Chesnutt arranges to have them speak in what appear to be two different languages. Ryder's diction and vocabulary do not differ materially from that of the articulate and well-educated narrator, as evidenced by this passage in which the dean of the Blue Veins describes his feelings on the race question:

> "I have no race prejudice," he would say, "but we people of mixed blood are ground between the upper and the nether millstone. Our fate lies between absorption by the white race and extinction in the black. The one does n't want us yet, but may take us in time. The other would welcome us, but it would be for us a backward step. 'With malice towards none, with charity for all,' we must do the best we can for ourselves and those who are to follow us. Self-preservation is the first law of nature." (105)

This passage, constituting the first instance in which the protagonist is quoted in the story, establishes Ryder's voice: his polished, elevated language nevertheless calls attention to the obvious philosophical shortcomings of the speech, as well as its utter(ed) hypocrisy.

Compare Ryder's elevated diction to the dialect of 'Liza Jane, whose speech elicits from the elite Blue Veiner an attitude of "kindly patronage" (107): "'scuse me, suh," she tells him, "I's lookin' for my husban'. I heerd you wuz a big man an had libbed heah a long time" (107). To dramatize even more emphatically the disparity in locution of the two characters, Chesnutt juxtaposes 'Liza Jane's speech with Ryder's reading aloud of Tennyson's poetic description of feminine beauty. Ryder wonders whether the woman to whom he will propose more nearly resembles "A daughter of the gods, divinely tall" or "a part of joyous Spring" (105–6). The scene his ex- and future wife walks into, then, establishes a context of verbal expression that apparently excludes her from his milieu.

Paradoxically, however, 'Liza Jane effectively penetrates Ryder's hypocrisy through her compelling account of her search for "Sam," as told in her own voice:

> "Den de wah broke out, an' w'en it wuz ober de cullud folks wuz scattered. I went back ter de ole home; but Sam wuz n' dere, an' I could n' l'arn nuffin 'bout 'im. But I knowed he 'd be'n dere to look fer me an' had n' foun' me, an' had gone erway ter hunt fer me."
>
> "I's be'n lookin' fer 'im eber sence," she added simply, as though twenty-five years were but a couple of weeks, "an' I knows he's be'n lookin' fer me. Fer he sot a heap er sto' by me, Sam did, an' I know he's be'n huntin' fer me all dese years,—'less'n he's be'n sick er sump'n, so he could n' work, er out'n his head, so he could n' 'member his promise. I went back down de ribber, fer I 'lowed he'd gone down dere lookin' fer me. I's be'n ter Noo Orleens, an' Atlanty, an' Charleston, an' Richmon'; an' w'en I'd be'n all ober de Souf I come ter de Norf. Fer I knows I'll fin' 'im some er dese days," she added softly, "er he 'll fin' me, an' den we'll bofe be as happy in freedom as we wuz in de ole days befo' de wah." (108)

Despite the potentially ominous reference to the couple's happy days "befo' de wah"—Chesnutt rarely makes such allusions lightly—this moving description of 'Liza Jane's physically and emotionally devastating odyssey inspires in Mr. Ryder a personal odyssey of his own.[14]

But for him to complete his journey, he first must undergo a step-by-step process that emphasizes the importance of voice in forming or re-forming identity, both individual and family. He successfully completes the first stage of his conversion back to "Sam Taylor" when he listens to 'Liza Jane's narrative. He accomplishes the second when he, like Clara of "Her Virginia Mammy," takes on the telling of another's story, by repeating 'Liza Jane's story to the Blue Veins. "The Wife of His Youth" goes beyond "Her Virginia Mammy" in that although the protagonists of the latter story trade narratives, no final merger is possible because the mother withholds a crucial piece of information, and the daughter cannot "read" her mother's subtext: Mrs. Harper thus remains "Mammy" rather than "Mother." But Mr. Ryder and 'Liza Jane fully share their stories, and their lives become once more intertwined, their family restored.

Their reunification demands more, however, than merely Ryder's willingness to listen to his long-lost wife: he must also acknowledge his past self. Along with accepting his past—and the consequences of that acceptance— Ryder embraces an earlier incarnation of himself, and one that must be particularly painful for a Blue Vein to admit. This reversion manifests itself in a very public shift of voice as he retells 'Liza Jane's story to the Blue Vein Society:

> He then related, simply but effectively, the story told by his visitor of the afternoon. *He gave it in the same soft dialect, which came readily to his lips,* while the

company listened attentively and sympathetically. For the story had awakened a responsive thrill in many hearts. There were some present who had seen, and others who had heard their fathers and grandfathers tell, the wrongs and sufferings of this past generation, and all of them still felt, in their darker moments, the shadow hanging over them. (111, italics mine)

This passage stresses the ways Chesnutt brings together several polarities. First, 'Liza Jane's dialect springs readily to Ryder's lips; the years he has spent subordinating the speech patterns of his youth slip away as he narrates his wife's story. Second, the usually distant and snobbish Blue Veiners, who pride themselves on their "lightness," suddenly discover a broader community of feeling while listening to a story that highlights their "darker moments."[15]

But Ryder does not commit himself fully even by speaking her story. He takes a final step in that direction by offering a "hypothetical" exploration of Sam Taylor's options. By recasting his own life into these apparently speculative terms, Ryder can function as narrator and thereby create a distance from his past self from which to study this confusing array of issues. In putting the case to his guests, Ryder once more emphasizes the polarities that separate 'Liza Jane from her hypothetical husband:

Suppose that he was young, and she much older than he; that he was light, and she was black; that their marriage was a slave marriage, and legally binding only if they chose to make it so after the war. Suppose, too, that he made his way to the North, as some of us have done, and there, where he had larger opportunities, had improved them, and had in the course of all these years grown to be as different from the ignorant boy who ran away from fear of slavery as the day is from the night. (112)

After stressing these additional polarities—in age, in color, in training, and in geography—Chesnutt bridges them by having Ryder acknowledge, at the urging of the Blue Vein Society, the wife of his youth, an act that also affirms his own identity.

The juxtaposition of these two narratives likewise reveals that Chesnutt has reversed the verbal hierarchy that the early parts of the story had established, a strategy he uses to good effect in *The Conjure Woman* and "The March of Progress" as well. Because much of the story until the appearance of 'Liza Jane's embedded narrative is focalized through Ryder's perspective, readers might also tend to adopt his attitude of condescension toward the apparently illiterate old woman who shows up at his door. But when we witness, or rather "hear," how 'Liza Jane's embedded narrative is a far more persuasive social commentary than the polished hypocrisy of Ryder early in the story, we have to reevaluate our notions of "articulateness." Confronted with 'Liza Jane's powerful narration of her own life, in which she lays bare the profound commitment of her quest in her own compelling voice, readers might suddenly find themselves dislocated. Mr. Ryder does, of course, find himself dislocated, or rather *relocated,* after listening to her stirring oration. Indeed, her story triggers the events that ultimately result in the two protagonists working toward reunification by trading and finally combining narratives in a complex matrix of identity building that culminates in their creating one shared life narrative.

The very telling of 'Liza Jane's story allows Ryder to recapture a powerful voice of his own. Gone is the suave hypocrisy that characterizes his speech early in the story. It has been replaced by Ryder's forceful "old" voice, a conversion that suggests that true articulateness need not spring from social refinement. And when Ryder's voice begins to revert to dialect, his audience of Blue Veins—moved to tears by his compelling evocation—are more affected, the reader might speculate, than they would have been by the highbrow poetry he had originally planned to read.

Chesnutt self-consciously positions storytelling at the center of "The Wife of His Youth" as he does in *The Conjure Woman.* But where Julius appears on the scene as raconteur, Mr. Ryder *becomes* a storyteller as a means of reconstructing his past. His successful transformation has a direct and proportionate relationship to 'Liza Jane's influence, as Lorne Fienberg notes: "Ryder's narrative ends where 'Liza Jane's began, with an acknowledgement of identity, but it is much more than a confession. His skillfully enacted drama of self-revelation calls upon the Blue Veins to examine and redefine the foundations of their own exclusivity."[16] Once more, Chesnutt's meticulous structuring of his fiction is apparent. Where 'Liza Jane had announced her identity to open her embedded narrative, Ryder closes the story (and his own embedded narrative) with a definitive assertion of his long-suppressed identity and a commitment to share the rest of his life with the woman from his past.

Ryder's final acknowledgment of his wife and his own identity affirms Chesnutt's conflation in this work of the many polarities that inform most of his canon. As in *The Conjure Woman,* he places two dissimilar voices in dialogue. But where the first collection emphasizes the tension between the two culturally polarized voices and only hints at the possibility of mutual understanding, "The Wife of His Youth" suggests that the rift need not remain permanent. When the twain do meet, as they do in the reunion of Mr. Ryder and 'Liza Jane, other polarities—racial, geographic, and economic—are similarly reconstructed. In "The Wife of His Youth," Chesnutt acknowledges the existence of the barriers that so often separate the characters in his other works, but here he refuses to grant final authority to those barriers.

"The Wife of His Youth" examines how Mr. Ryder rediscovers himself only through coming to terms with his past voice, and then merging that voice into a union with that of his once and future wife. The story also suggests that to acknowledge, perhaps even to embrace, one's heritage can be both heroic and fortunate. Like "Her Virginia Mammy" and "Cicely's Dream," then, "The Wife of His Youth" has at its heart the exchange of narratives by two characters. But the transactions in the other works are ultimately interrupted or suspended, suggesting Chesnutt's acknowledgment that his linguistic model of family—while certainly a promising one for an author interested in erasing racial boundaries—could not ultimately overcome the pressures of American social history. It is only in "The Wife of His Youth," the sole story of its ilk populated exclusively by black characters, that the exchange results in a true and lasting family dialogue between long-separated voices.

But even this apparently optimistic message must be tempered, at least to some extent, by our awareness that Ryder seems ultimately to sacrifice a great deal. Although it is tempting to celebrate without reservation the reunion of this long-suffering woman with the husband of her youth, the conclusion of the story resonates with less happy implications. The seemingly inevitable remarriage interrupts, for example, the protagonist's upcoming union with the woman he *currently* loves, in a manner that strikingly recalls the depressing events in "Cicely's Dream." Perhaps even more troubling, though, is the extent to which a reunion with 'Liza Jane represents for Ryder a sort of reimmersion in slavery, or what early in the story the narrator terms a "servile origin" (103). Thus even the most "optimistic" of Chesnutt's fictional reimaginings of the American family has its barbs. Although the stories collected in The Wife of His Youth reflect his desire to explore the possibilities of a more inclusive notion of family,[17] one that seeks to erase or at least to moderate the barriers that separate men and women, blacks and whites, Chesnutt cannot finally bring himself to write a story that enacts those possibilities.

Notes

1. Eric J. Sundquist, *To Wake the Nations: Race in the Making of American Literature* (Cambridge: Harvard University Press, 1993), 394.

2. Ibid., 394–95.

3. Ibid., 395.

4. Chesnutt does not, of course, limit his consideration of these matters to *The Wife of His Youth* collection. See *The House behind the Cedars* (1900) and *The Marrow of Tradition* (1901) for equally blunt examinations of characters struggling to construct viable family identities within the constraints of the late-nineteenth-century American milieu. The recently published *Mandy Oxendine* hints provocatively that "passing" might be one way to bypass those constraints.

5. Kimberly W. Benston, " 'I yam what I am': the topos of (un)naming in Afro-American literature," in *Black Literature and Literary Theory,* ed. Henry Louis Gates Jr. (New York: Methuen, 1984), 152.

6. Although *The Conjure Woman* stories hint at Annie's superior reading skills, the works collected in *The Wife of His Youth,* along with a few of his other tales, most dramatically foreground the ways women interpret and shape the world in which they live. Each sustains Chesnutt's interest in remaking the family, but they add another, more gender-conscious layer to the theme. See also "A Limb of Satan," a work that comically explores the difficulties of single motherhood at the turn of the century; "Aunt Lucy's Search," on the other hand, melodramatically depicts the attempts of an ex-slave to locate her now grown children during

Reconstruction. "White Weeds" recounts how a white man's wedding-day receipt of an anonymous letter purporting to document his fiancée's black ancestry causes the marriage to fail miserably; the rest of the story focuses on the woman's measured response. And like "Cicely's Dream," "The March of Progress" features a white teacher whose decision to teach in black schools excludes her from social contacts in her adopted southern home. Taken together, these stories reveal Chesnutt's subtle handling of a variety of issues related to the way women construct identity.

7.   Charles W. Chesnutt, *Collected Stories of Charles W. Chesnutt,* ed. William L. Andrews (New York: Mentor, 1992), 115; hereafter cited in the text.

8.   Susan Fraiman, "Mother-Daughter Romance in Charles W. Chesnutt's 'Her Virginia Mammy,' " *Studies in Short Fiction* 22 (Fall 1985): 446.

9.   See Elaine K. Ginsberg, "Introduction: The Politics of Passing," in *Passing and the Fictions of Identity,* ed. Elaine K. Ginsberg (Durham, N.C.: Duke University Press, 1996), for a discussion of passing as a form of textual trespass.

10.   Although far different in temperament, Chesnutt anticipates such recent writers as Ishmael Reed and Charles Johnson in his willingness to make light of culturally sensitive topics.

11.   William L. Andrews, Introduction to *Collected Stories,* xv. See also J. Saunders Redding, *To Make a Poet Black* (Ithaca, N.Y.: Cornell University Press, 1988), 72, on the question of miscegenation in Chesnutt's fiction: "Whether written in the spirit of comedy or tragedy, all the stories in *The Wife of His Youth* deal with the entanglements resulting from miscegenation."

12.   Fraiman, 444.

13.   Ibid.

14.   See Gayl Jones, *Liberating Voices: Oral Tradition in African American Literature* (New York: Penguin, 1991), 131, for commentary on 'Liza Jane's "quaintness." Such a reading, however, discounts the rhetorical authority the wife of Ryder's youth demonstrates.

15.   In presenting 'Liza Jane as a figure of considerable rhetorical powers despite her heavy dialect and apparent lack of education, Chesnutt follows a pattern of inverting verbal hierarchies found elsewhere in his fiction. In *The Conjure Woman,* for example, Julius's rhetoric often seems to overwhelm John despite his "superior" education. And in "The March of Progress," the presumably untutored Abe, speaking in heavy dialect, converts his seemingly more "articulate" colleagues, and the reader, to his more compassionate way of thinking.

16.   "Lorne Fienberg, Charles W. Chesnutt's *The Wife of His Youth:* The Unveiling of the Black Storyteller," *American Transcendental Quarterly* 4 (September 1990): 225.

17.   See Sandra Molyneaux, "Expanding the Collective Memory: Charles W. Chesnutt's *The Conjure Woman* Tales," in *Memory, Narrative, and Identity: New Essays in Ethnic American Literatures,* ed. Amritjit Singh, Joseph T. Skerret Jr., and Robert E. Hogan (Boston: Northeastern University Press, 1994), 164. She credits Chesnutt with "broaden[ing] the cultural record by teaching Whites to read Negro 'texts.' " I would argue, though, that his real contribution to fiction is his ability to blur such distinctions as "white" and "black" texts.

Index

♦

The Author

♦

Joseph R. McElrath Jr., professor of English at Florida State University, is a specialist in post–Civil War United States literary study and the author or coauthor of six books on Chesnutt's contemporary Frank Norris. He coedited, with Robert C. Leitz III, *"To Be an Author": Letters of Charles W. Chesnutt, 1889–1905* (Princeton University Press, 1997). Together with Leitz and Jesse S. Crisler, he has also edited *Charles W. Chesnutt: Essays and Speeches* (Stanford University Press, 1999).

The General Editor

♦

Dr. James Nagel, J. O. Eidson Distinguished Professor of American Literature at the University of Georgia, founded the scholarly journal *Studies in American Fiction* and edited it for 20 years. He is the general editor of the Critical Essays on American Literature series, published by G. K. Hall/Macmillan, which now contains more than 130 volumes. He was one of the founders of the American Literature Association and serves as its executive coordinator. He is also a past president of the Ernest Hemingway Society. Among his 17 books are *Stephen Crane and Literary Impressionism; Critical Essays on "The Sun Also Rises"; Ernest Hemingway: The Writer in Context; Ernest Hemingway: The Oak Park Legacy;* and *Hemingway in Love and War,* which was selected by the *New York Times* as one of the outstanding books of 1989 and which has been made into a major motion picture. Dr. Nagel has published more than 50 articles in scholarly journals and has lectured on American literature in 15 countries. His current project is a book on the contemporary short story cycle.